FIGHTING WORDS

FIGHTING WORDS

CANADA'S BEST WAR REPORTING

MARK BOURRIE

DUNDURN
TORONTO

Editor: Jennifer McKnight
Design: Courtney Horner
Printer: Webcom

Library and Archives Canada Cataloguing in Publication

Bourrie, Mark, 1957-
        Fighting words : Canada's best war
reporting / Mark Bourrie.

  Issued also in electronic format.

ISBN 978-1-4597-0666-8

      1. War--Press coverage--Canada.

2. War correspondents--Canada. I. Title.

PN4784.W37B68 2012   070.4'333   C2012-903202-6

1   2   3   4   5   16   15   14   13   12

We acknowledge the support of the **Canada Council for the Arts** and the **Ontario Arts Council** for our publishing program. We also acknowledge the financial support of the **Government of Canada** through the **Canada Book Fund** and **Livres Canada Books**, and the **Government of Ontario** through the **Ontario Book Publishing Tax Credit** and the **Ontario Media Development Corporation**.

Care has been taken to trace the ownership of copyright material used in this book. The author and the publisher welcome any information enabling them to rectify any references or credits in subsequent editions.

J. Kirk Howard, President

Printed and bound in Canada.

Visit us at
Dundurn.com
Definingcanada.ca
@dundurnpress
Facebook.com/dundurnpress

Dundurn	Gazelle Book Services Limited	Dundurn
3 Church Street, Suite 500	White Cross Mills	2250 Military Road
Toronto, Ontario, Canada	High Town, Lancaster, England	Tonawanda, NY
M5E 1M2	LA1 4XS	U.S.A. 14150

For
Michelle Lang,
Kathleen Kenna,
and
Charles Dubois

.

TABLE OF CONTENTS

Acknowledgements . . . 9
Introduction . . . 11

First Contact . . . 19
The Conquest of Canada . . . 51
New Enemies: The Americans . . . 63
The Rebellions and Invasions of 1837–1838 . . . 89
The Fenian Raids . . . 110
The Northwest Resistance . . . 123
The Second Boer War . . . 130
The First World War . . . 140
The Second World War . . . 167
The Korean War . . . 306
Peacekeeping and Peacemaking . . . 315
The First Gulf War . . . 328
Afghanistan . . . 340

Image Credits . . . 365

ACKNOWLEDGEMENTS

THIS COLLECTION WAS AN OFFSHOOT OF MY DOCTORAL RESEARCH ON PRESS censorship, supervised by Professor Jeff Keshen, formerly at the University of Ottawa and now at Mount Royal University. I'd also like to thank Dr. James McKillip at the Department of National Defence Directorate of History and Heritage; Lieutenant-Colonel Rejean Duchesneau, formerly of the National Defence Public Affairs Learning Center; Tim Cook of the Canadian War Museum; Matt Symes at Wilfrid Laurier University; and Galen Perras and Nichole St-Onge of the University of Ottawa.

I would particularly like to thank my old friend Kathleen Kenna for her support and for providing me with one of the best pieces of writing in this book. Michael Petrou, formerly of the *Ottawa Citizen*, now at *Maclean's* magazine, was also extremely supportive and collegial.

David Halton, Michael Ignatieff, and Tom Clark were extremely generous with their time, their written material, and journalism owned by their family, respectively. Joanne MacDonald at the *Toronto Star*, Andrea Gordon at The Canadian Press, Cheryl Minnis at PostMedia, and Nicola Woods at the Royal Ontario Museum, along with the staffs of

Library and Archives Canada image department and the Brechin photo lab worked quickly and professionally to reproduce and clear copyright material. Thanks go to E. Kaye Fulton for lending me the November 1936 issue of *National Home Monthly* magazine, with its article on holidaying with Hitler. I owe a special debt to the Library of Parliament for giving me access to some of their rare books, especially those written by participants in the Rebellions of 1837.

I'd also like to thank Beth Bruder, Michael Carroll, Jennifer McKnight, and Shannon Whibbs at Dundurn. I've received a lot of personal support from my wife, Marion van de Wetering, and from friends and colleagues Sarah Brown, Fateema Sayani, Tom Korski, Steve Maher, Glen McGregor, and Noah Richler, among others.

This book simply would not exist without Library and Archives Canada. That institution is central to our national memory. We can't afford to lose it, and, at this time, it is in dire need of public and political support.

INTRODUCTION

PEOPLE SEEM TO HAVE A PATHOLOGICAL NEED FOR CONFLICT. THEY ALSO have a very strong urge to tell stories about it. And many of these stories are self-serving, biased, censored, and, at the same time, interesting. They're an important part of the historical record.

These articles are a selection of the country's best war journalism. I have cast a very wide net, since the first few stories were written before there were any news sheets, the first forms of newspapers. Still, like all of the stories in this book, they were meant to be read and to sway their readers towards a particular point of view. Those are the criteria I used in choosing these pieces, along with impact on public opinion, importance to the historical record, and quality of story-telling.

This collection shows that Canada is far from being a "peaceable kingdom." Violence has been an important factor in the creation of the country. Vikings fought, and were likely driven out by, First Nations people. The French intervened in a long-standing tribal war on the Great Lakes that involved genocide, "ethnic cleansing," and the use of starvation as a military strategy. The First Nations played their own roles in the struggle between France and Britain for control of what is now Canada. They also resisted incursions on their sovereignty. In the War of 1812, they played an important role that has finally been recognized by popular historians.

Canada was attacked in the nineteenth century by the Hunters' Lodges and the Fenians, two groups that seem ludicrous now but seemed to pose a real threat at the time. The stark fact is that the Fenians won the last battle fought on Ontario soil, and, if they had been better organized, could have caused much more damage in the province. As author Peter Vronsky argued in his recent book about the almost-forgotten Battle of Ridgeway, the Canadian defeat hastened the Confederation process.

While Britain engaged in its wars of imperialism against exotic cultures in Africa and Asia, Canada used force to subdue its Métis and First Nations on the Plains. Reportage from that conflict reflects the jingoism of the British press. This was the first war in which Canadian reporters were attached to the government's military forces, and they left us with one-sided accounts that galvanized public support in English Canada against the Métis and First Nations. The Métis and Cree had no reporters on their side of the lines. Perhaps if they had, Louis Riel might not have gone to the gallows.

Canadian journalists, especially in Montreal's English-language press and in Ontario, pushed hard for Canadian involvement in the Boer War and were eager to print copy sent back by war correspondents and soldiers. This was the heyday of war reporting, the time when Winston Churchill, who was both a soldier and a news writer, commanded the highest freelance rates in the world, and stars like Richard Harding Davis and George Warrington Steevens roamed the battlefield. The Boer War, which has long faded in public memory, taught the British tough lessons in censorship and propaganda. Stories written by French and German correspondents highlighted the brutality of the war, praised the Boers (ethnic Dutch settlers in South Africa who wanted an independent homeland) as heroes defending their farms and towns, and sharply criticized the British strategy of rounding up Boer civilians and holding them in "concentration camps." After the Boer War, western powers decided to leash correspondents by severely limiting their access to the battlefield and imposing tough compulsory censorship.

The Canadian Press felt the full weight of these restrictions during the First World War. Official versions of events were handed out by Max Aiken, working for the British under the pseudonym "Eyewitness." The British warned reporters that they would face a firing squad if they tried to reach the front lines without authorization. A few American reporters, like H.L. Mencken of the *Baltimore Sun*, were able to see the trenches from the German side, but the first Canadian newspaper correspondents did not arrive until 1917, and they missed important Canadian battles like Second Battle of Ypres, Amiens, and Vimy Ridge. Domestically, Canada had a very tough press censorship system that not only targeted newspapers, but vetted phonograph records, movies, and books. In Canada it was illegal to criticize the war effort and to blame anyone but Germany for starting the war. Censorship was steadily toughened through the war and stayed in place for a year after the Armistice as a tool for fighting Communists. Press censorship was "voluntary." Ernest Chambers, the chief censor, sent out rules to editors and publishers, who engaged in self-censorship. Except for the *Victoria Week*, the *Sault Ste. Marie Express*, *Le Bulletin* of Montreal, and Quebec City's *La Croix*, all of which were banned, editors of commercial newspapers toed the line rather than face jail and financial ruin under the War Measures Act. They did not, like the Sault Ste. Marie paper, question the reasons for sending more Canadian soldiers to the front. Even *Le Devoir*, the voice of Quebec nationalism and a leader in the fight against imposing a soldiers' draft, was whipped into line.

For the first three years of the war, papers relied on spoon-fed reports written by the British propaganda department and from U.S. wire service reports filtered through the domestic press censorship system. Much of the "journalism" came from eyewitness accounts published in propaganda books aimed at the then-neutral United States. Several excerpts are included in this collection to show the tone of the propaganda. The soldiers, as hungry for news as anyone, started their own trench newspapers. Published under stiff censorship, they still provide an interesting view of the soldiers' world.

Canada had a more sophisticated media strategy in the Second World War, and, from the beginning, Canadian correspondents were at the battlefront. Ross Munro saw more action than most Canadian soldiers, covering fighting at Spitzbergen, Dieppe, Sicily, Italy, and northwest Europe. He was joined by reporters like Ralph Allen of the *Globe and Mail* and William Boss of The Canadian Press, who pushed the boundaries of censorship and, in Allen's case, undermined it with a tough opinion piece published when Allen was back in Canada. After the war, Charles Lynch would describe their work to Philip Knightley as propaganda, but Lynch's opinion doesn't bear scrutiny. The Canadian reporters abroad did, for the most part, write articles that were not critical of the war effort. They also ignored the grievous lack of talent among the Canadian officer corps in France, Belgium, and Holland. They did believe in the moral righteousness of the struggle, a belief that was reinforced as they moved through Nazi-occupied territory and saw the misery of the civilians. Their disgust was evident when they wrote about the Nazi concentration camps that were liberated by Canadian soldiers. However, they sometimes did criticize what they saw as bungling: Ralph Allen's assessment of the British failure to clear the Scheldt estuary in 1944, allowing the Germans to regroup there and dig in at great cost in Canadian lives, was a solid piece of analysis. So was his attack on censorship, written in 1944. These journalists were as brave as the soldiers they covered, and their reporting, though stilted toward the Allies, captures the brutality of war, the struggles of the soldiers against both the Germans and the elements, the front-line men's frustrations, the plight of civilians, and the bone-weariness that quickly set in as Canadian troops slogged through Italy and northwest Europe. A comparison of First World War "reporting" and the correspondence filed by Canadian journalists overseas (and by the Halifax *Herald*'s reporters covering the Battle of the Atlantic and the sub attacks in the St. Lawrence) shows a remarkable change in just one generation.

Canadian correspondents were as "embedded" with the military during the Second World War as any reporter who went through boot camp and went overseas with military units in the Gulf and Afghan wars. They were given the courtesy rank of captain, and were provided with uniforms, Jeeps, and drivers. They lived with the troops, ate their food, and were subjected to military law. War correspondents usually depended on military transportation to get their stories out. Their work was subjected to censorship by Canadian officers and by British press censors at the information choke point of London. Rather than try to grasp the over-riding strategic situation, the correspondents tended to focus on front-line action. They did this job very well. When they did seek to write about more complex issues, their work tended to be weaker and more prone to inaccuracies. They ignored many important issues like friction between the Allies, the destruction of German towns and cities, the weakness of the Canadian officer corps and the unwillingness of some Canadian units to take prisoners.

Canada also had a home front during the Second World War. Halifax was a major convoy gathering place and a clearing station for casualties of the Battle of the Atlantic. Designated as a special censorship zone, the city was awash in submarine stories, but domestic censor H. Bruce Jefferson killed many of them. Eric Dennis' coverage of the sinking of the Nova-Scotia-to-Newfoundland ferry *Caribou* in the Halifax *Herald*, which was picked up by other Canadian newspapers, did give the country an idea of the U-boat threat in Canadian waters, but the public failed to grasp the menace. In 1942, the U-boats had driven shipping out of the St. Lawrence River.

In 1942 and 1943, Canadians along the Pacific Coast worried about a Japanese invasion. In the fall of 1944 and winter of 1945, the Japanese launched bomb-laden balloons against Canada that drifted deep into the Prairies. Censorship kept stories of those balloons out of the newspapers. And the surviving Japanese-Canadian newspaper, *The New Canadian*, was the most heavily-censored publication in Canada. Even contributions of poetry fell to the censors' scissors. One censored poem is published in this anthology.

Yet the censors believed material that was not valuable to the enemy should be published. That attitude comes across clearly in the memorandum on the Halifax Riot of 1945 written by Jefferson, the Halifax censor. Not only is it a riveting account of the trashing of downtown Halifax on VE-Day by thousands of soldiers, sailors, and civilians, it gives an insider's view of the motivation behind the news coverage of the riots. As I've said, I've cast a wide net. Jefferson's piece of war correspondence is published here for the first time.

Canadian newspapers and radio stations sent seasoned reporters to Korea. William Boss, who had already made his name in the Second

World War was there, along with a new breed of young men who were eager to show they were as good as the journalists who had covered the Second World War. Young Peter Worthington proved, with both writing skill and personal courage, that he was good enough to be a top-tier reporter. Soldier-authors also showed their worth in this war. The elegant account of the shelling on the Van Doos, written by Harry Pope, captures the helplessness of soldiers under an incessant barrage.

Canadian reporters went overseas to cover observation operations. Jack Cahill's delightful account of the torching of a Vietnamese brothel hotel was written while Canadian observers were deployed in their fruitless mission to maintain the truce between North and South Vietnam after the U.S. ended its combat mission. Canadian journalists also covered observation operations in Africa, Indochina, Cyprus, the Middle East, and the Balkans, where Canadians were caught in a vicious civil war where there was often little peace to keep.

The deployment of Canadian troops in the first Gulf War brought with it an influx of journalists to cover the biggest Canadian military operation since the Korean War. Faced with filing difficulties, severe limitations placed on travel, and the danger of travelling in an unforgiving landscape with a sometimes hostile population, Canadian reporters were reliant on the military both for protection and information. A similar situation existed during the Canadian deployment to Kandahar. In the first months of the Afghan War, Canadian journalists had some freedom of movement, although the attack on *Toronto Star* reporter Kathleen Kenna showed the degree of danger faced by Canadian correspondents. In the second phase of Canadian involvement, most Canadian reporters were sheltered in the Canadian fort at Kandahar air base, but they, like Canada's troops, were in great danger anytime they went off the base. Michelle Lang, 34, of the *Calgary Herald*, was killed by an improvised explosive device (IED) at the end of 2009. Four Canadian soldiers died with her. Lang had won a National Newspaper Award for beat reporting just a few months before. Mellissa Fung of CBC News was kidnapped by bandits in 2008 and held for nearly a month in miserable conditions. And in 2007, Radio-Canada journalist Charles Dubois suffered a severe leg injury and Patrice Roy was left in shock by an IED blast that killed two Canadian soldiers and an Afghan interpreter.

I hope this collection shows the talent and, sometimes, the brilliance of the people who have written about conflict in Canada or involving Canadians overseas. Many of these stories were written by people who courageously placed themselves in harm's way because they wanted to tell the stories. They made that decision for many reasons — faith, the desire for personal recognition, the desire for adventure, and, sometimes, the desire to whip up support for the war effort. Sometimes they wrote to try to clear their own names or to explain their own violence. Others were simply in the wrong place at the right time, or trying to make a living.

Whatever their reasons, they left us a legacy that, in these days when journalism and journalists are under constant political and often physical attack and their work denigrated both by academics and neo-conservative political operatives, should be exhibited, analyzed and celebrated. In many instances, their work stands the test of time. It also proves most journalists brought courage, integrity, honesty, and literary talent to a line of work that is dangerous, dirty, and thankless.

FIRST CONTACT

IN THE MILLENNIA BEFORE THE ARRIVAL OF EUROPEAN EXPLORERS, fishermen, and traders to what would become Canada's Atlantic coast, the Native people had lived in a constant state of migration and war. Over the course of centuries, First Nations people migrated from Siberia to a continent that was thickly populated with herds of big game that moved across the interior grasslands. Studies of Native languages provide evidence that bands split up, migrated hundreds of miles from each other, and entered the territories of earlier migrants — whether they were welcome or not.

War was relatively bloodless. The technology of mass killing didn't exist before the arrival of the Europeans. The Native people of the Great Lakes region had learned how to work copper at about the same time the people of Europe and the Mediterranean were discovering its uses, but there wasn't enough of it to replace flint and stone tools. They lacked the tin to make copper into bronze, that useful alloy that proved so lethal in the hands of the soldiers of the classical civilizations of Europe and Asia. The Romans and peoples of Western Europe mastered the working of bog iron, lumps of fairly pure metallic ore precipitated in springs along the marshlands of the

North Sea coast. A half-millennium after the fall of Rome, Vikings arrived on Canada's Atlantic coast, armed with metal tools made of iron and wearing the skins of domestic animals that were unknown on the west side of the Atlantic, but they didn't stay long enough to change Native warfare.

The first Viking explorers on the Canadian coast appear to have simply been looking for adventure and new lands. What they found was a country that could barely sustain them and, after a few years, they decamped from Newfoundland and headed back to the more welcoming climes of Iceland. Before they left, they managed to antagonize the local people, who seem, at first, to have been tolerant of these uninvited semi-permanent guests. The Greenland Saga gives an account of fighting between the Vikings and the Native people of Vinland. It was hardly a great victory for Norse arms.

Fishermen from the European coastal states arrived in these same waters about five hundred years later. Their world had evolved. New sailing technology made it easier for them to buck the prevailing winds and sail westward. Crowded European cities required protein and the Grand Banks teemed with fish. The Grand Banks were one corner of the world where English, French, Basque, Portuguese, and other Europeans exploited a natural resource with very little conflict. For several generations the fishermen got along with the First Nations people too, trading furs for European metal goods and cloth. The creation of colonies on the mainland upset that harmony and touched off three hundred years of struggle, first between the colonial powers, then between the United States and British-Canadians in the northern half of the continent.

The first French explorer to reach mainland Canada and systematically explore a part of it, Jacques Cartier, saw the Native people as something to exploit. He kidnapped about twenty-five of them, including the headman of the town of Stadacona, and took them to France against their will. Cartier's crime probably destroyed any chance the French could establish a permanent, safe foothold in the St. Lawrence Valley. It may be no coincidence that no other settlements were attempted until the Stadaconans and their rivals, the Hochelagans, had disappeared from the region, victims, it seems, of First Nations warfare and, possibly, germs left behind by Cartier and his men.

Freebooter Martin Frobisher, exploring the edges of the Canadian Arctic, was just as ham-fisted. The disappearance of five of his men was blamed on the Inuit, although there was no real evidence of their complicity and, in fact, Inuit people visited Frobisher's ship within a day or two of the incident and did not act as though they had any reason to expect retaliation from the English. A careful reading of the account of Frobisher's first voyage shows the Inuit were consistently wary of the English but were not aggressive. Perhaps some Inuit did kidnap Frobisher's men. It's also possible that they succumbed to an accident or, after months of misery and sickness aboard Frobisher's ship, simply deserted and cast their lot with the Inuit or struck out on their own. Sending a pirate to explore the Arctic and deal with its people was probably not the best idea of England's Elizabethan government, and Frobisher's violent method of dealing with strangers was fairly predictable.

Between the time that Jacques Cartier left the St. Lawrence Valley in 1543 and the arrival of Champlain sixty-five years later, something dreadful had happened. Cartier and his patron, the privateer Jean-François de La Rocque de Roberval, had stayed as unwelcome guests of the people of Stadacona, who lived near what is now Quebec City. Cartier sailed up the river and visited the town of Hochelaga, which lay near what is now the campus of Montreal's McGill University. Between these two towns, bands of Iroquoian people carved fields out of the forest along the St. Lawrence River. Their settlements extended up the St. Lawrence and Ottawa rivers above the island of Montreal. By the time Champlain arrived, these people were gone.

The fate of the St. Lawrence Iroquoians is still a mystery. Champlain asked about them and didn't get a clear answer from the Huron and Algonkian people who were using the St. Lawrence as a fishing trading ground. Archaeology shows that in the late 1500s thicker walls were built around the towns of the Huron country, on the southeast shore of Georgian Bay and near Lake Simcoe, perhaps to ward off whatever violence might have been taking place four hundred kilometres away. The Huron, however, also waged war against the people living along the Niagara Escarpment south of Georgian Bay and raided the country of the Iroquois Confederacy, which controlled the territory south of Lake Ontario.

Violence, though, may not be the answer. Plague may well have played a part. The French harboured diseases for which the Native peoples had no resistance. (Fortunately for the Iroquoians, Cartier had brought no poultry and livestock, which were carriers of yet more viruses such as measles and influenza. They would arrive a century after Cartier, to horrific and deadly effect.) Perhaps the St. Lawrence Iroquoians met a fate that was a combination of epidemic and conquest. At first, the Europeans stayed out of Native politics and avoided their settlements, which, south of the Canadian Shield, were towns of several hundred people living in longhouses and surrounded by cornfields that sometimes extended outwards for two kilometres or more. The early fur traders saw no need to spend time and money going inland when Natives would come to the Gulf of St. Lawrence to trade. That would change in the early years of the seventeenth century when Champlain tried to lock up the inland trade by building an official settlement at the natural fortress of Quebec. Then he began playing politics with the Natives. The Huron showed him the Great Lakes and gave Champlain some understanding of the vastness of the continent, but choosing sides would cost the French dearly as they were drawn deeper into intertribal warfare. To make things worse, they picked the losing side.

Champlain arrived to find the Native peoples of the Great Lakes and St. Lawrence region at constant war. The word "war" is somewhat misleading. The raids launched by both sides were usually incursions of a few dozen, maybe a few hundred, men who split into small groups and hunted for prisoners. This type of war kept the locals in a state of fear, terror, and anger. Periodically, one side challenged another to pitched battles, ritualized affairs with a fairly small amount of bloodshed, in which warriors publicly displayed their skill and cultivated fame among friends and foe. The Iroquoian world seems to have been very small: most of the best warriors knew each other, at least by reputation. Truces and short periods of real peace punctuated the violence, but slights, insults, and injury restarted it.

So instead of resisting the European invaders, the aboriginal peoples fought against each other. A Native resistance to the French would not have been a far-fetched thing: the Iroquois fielded an army of 1,200 men in the winter of 1648–49 and had reserves of several hundred more back home, and that was after epidemics had cut their population in half in the previous two decades. The Huron, who were about to be crushed by that force, probably still had nearly as many men. The Iroquoian tribes inland, along the Niagara Escarpment and Lake Erie, had hundreds more. But there would be no Tecumseh or Pontiac to unite them. The Iroquois made the second-best move: crush the Native allies of the French, incorporate and assimilate as many of them as possible, and keep the French pinned down in the St. Lawrence Valley. The strategy worked for more than half a century, even after regular French troops were sent by Louis XVI to scorch the earth of the Iroquois country, but as more French arrived and raised their sons to be militiamen and the Natives became more economically dependent on the Europeans, co-existence was the best deal the Iroquois could salvage.

But it was a close-run thing. From 1650, when the Huron were dispersed, to 1701, when peace was finally established, there were years when Quebec was starved of furs, its trade cut off by Iroquois dominance of the inland canoe routes. Hundreds of French settlers went into Iroquois captivity. A few lucky ones were assimilated to become loyal Iroquois, were ransomed, or, like Pierre Radisson, escaped. Most were killed. The story of the Iroquois War became the foundation of Quebec's political culture: survival in the face of overwhelming hostility, a beating of the odds against people determined to wipe out French society on the St. Lawrence. The Jesuit missionaries believed the fields of the Roman Catholic Church were watered with the blood of its martyrs. So, too, was the soul of the French Canadian nation.

The war began with Champlain's ill-advised attack on an Iroquois war party in the Mohawk country west of Lake Champlain. The Iroquois lost this fight to Champlain's musketry. They were, however, quick studies. When Champlain came back with an even larger war party a few years later, he was lucky to leave alive, and had to be carried, trussed up on the back of a strong Huron, across upstate New York and southern Ontario to the Huron country. The Huron and Iroquois raided each other for another three decades, but, armed by Dutch traders with a big shipment of war surplus guns, the Iroquois crushed the Huron in 1649 and, over the next few years, destroyed the other farming peoples along the southern Great Lakes, exterminated many of the hunting bands of the southern Canadian shield, and even drove the Sioux from the country around Lake Michigan onto the prairies. After a bloody and costly fight for the St. Lawrence Valley, the Iroquois made a permanent, if hostile, peace with the French in 1701 after long negotiations in Montreal. By the mid-1700s, the Iroquois were raiding the Pawnee and selling slaves to the French. Their fatal mistake came less than two decades after the fall of Quebec to Wolfe's army. Some would support the British in their fight against the American revolutionaries. Others would back the colonists or try to stay neutral. None of those choices, it would turn out, was the right one.

In these years, there was nothing resembling newspapers and the concept of a free press was, to those with power, both alien and subversive. The accuracy and credibility of accounts from the early years of settlement are often questionable. The Greenland Saga was written from oral traditions and its glowing description of Vinland, site of the main Viking settlement, bears little resemblance to the single confirmed Norse archaeological site at L'Anse aux Meadows, on the windswept northern coast of Newfoundland. Most of the writing of the post-Columbus period glorified the European explorers and was aimed at justifying the cost of their missions and at fundraising for their next voyage. The authors were the priests and explorers themselves or members of their expeditions, probably supplemented by ghost writers who torqued the achievements of their heroes to sell books and kept out anything that made them look bad. Objectivity was not one of the writers' goals, nor was fairness to the Native peoples. As well, these books and pamphlets were subjected to official censorship and licensing rules. At best, they're one-sided. At worst, they are propaganda geared to fundraising, pleas for government and public support, and justification of bad colonial policies.

Champlain's accounts of his fights with the Iroquois come from his published *Voyages*, one of a series of books and maps that Champlain and his backers issued to drum up financial and political support for his colonization scheme. The Jesuit *Relations*, a series of letters written by the senior members of the Jesuit mission in Canada, were published annually in Paris through the French regime. They appear to be fairly accurate reports of events, but with strong bias against Native people who resisted the Jesuits' attempts to convert them to Christianity. In them, the priests made frequent pleas for reader donations. The *Relations* were re-published in French in the mid-1850s and translated into English in the late nineteenth century by Reuben Gold Thwaites between 1896 and 1901. His work has been excerpted, repackaged, and republished through the twentieth century. Madeleine de Vercheres' account of her run-in with the Iroquois was written at the request of the governor of Quebec. She was a controversial woman throughout her life, and jealously guarded her reputation. In doing so, she carved herself a place in Quebec's historical tradition that fit very well with the Québécois' sense of self: innocent, besieged on the St. Lawrence, staring down a merciless enemy who wished to wipe her, and her country, from the face of the earth.

In the end, the authors failed to convince France to build a vibrant, viable colony in Canada. Only a few thousand settlers came to Canada during the French regime. Quebec was the local headquarters of a one-industry operation. While the British colonies to the south flourished into settlements that were fairly self-sufficient and usually very successful at defending themselves and expanding westward, Quebec was deliberately kept small and dependent. No amount of heroic writing and propaganda changed that. But the myths and stories of those early years lived on for generations as proof that the Catholic faith and the French nation in North America were gardens that had been watered with the blood of martyrs and defended by women and children in the face of the cruelest enemies.

CIRCA 950 A.D.: Viking Diplomacy Fails

In the tenth century, Viking settlers tried to develop a toehold in North America. Despite attempts by indigenous peoples to trade with the Europeans, relations quickly deteriorated to distrust, then violence. The Greenland Saga, an oral tradition written down long after the actual events, is unclear about the cause of the fighting, but gives some hints. The Native peoples do not seem to have shared the Viking's ideas about private space, and, when Natives entered the Viking hamlet, the settlers responded by fortifying the camp and challenging the "Skralings" to fight. The Vikings claim to have won the skirmish. They may have scored a tactical victory, but they abandoned their settlement soon afterwards. Presumably, the battle took place at L'Anse aux Meadows, in northeastern Newfoundland, but the Vikings were quite vague about the location.

THE GREENLAND SAGA

They [the Vikings] had with them all sorts of cattle, because they intended to settle in the country, if they were mighty to do that ... they had had with them one bull. After this first winter came summer, they became aware of Skralings, and came there out from the wood a great troop of men. There was near cattle of theirs, and the bull took to bellow and roar extremely, but this frightened the Skralings, and they ran away with their burdens, but those were greyfur and sable and all sorts of skin-wares; and they turned towards Karlsefne's abode and would there enter the houses; but Karlsefne made defend the doors. Neither understood the other's language. Then the Skralings took down their packs and loosened them, and offered them and desired weapons especially for them, but Karlsefne forbade them to sell weapons, and now he takes the counsel, that he bade the women carry out milk to them, and as soon as they saw the milk, then would they buy that and nothing else. Now was this the purchasing of the Skralings, that they carried their bargain away in their stomachs. But Karlsefne and his followers kept their packs and skinwares. Went they thus away. Now is this to be told, that Karlsefne let make a strong fence of poles round his abode and made all ready there. At this time Gudrid, Karlsefne's wife, brought forth a male child, and the boy was called Snorre. At the beginning of the next winter the Skralings came to meet with them, and were many more than before, and had the same wares as before. Then said Karlsefne to the women: now you shall carry out such meat, as was before most asked for, and nothing else. And when they saw it, they cast their packs in over the fence.

Gudrid sat within the door with the cradle of her son Snorre. Then fell a shadow through the door, and entered there a woman in a black narrow kirtle, rather low-built, and she had a ribbon round her head, and light brown hair, pale and large-eyed, so that nobody had seen so large eyes in any human skull. She went up there, where Gudrid sat and asked: what is thy name, says she. My name is Gudrid, but what is thy name? My name is Gudrid, says she. Then Gudrid the housewife stretched out her hand to her, that she should sit by her, but it happened in the same moment, that Gudrid heard a great crack, and was then the woman lost to sight, and at the same time one Skraling was killed by a house carle of Karlsefne's, because he would have taken their weapons. And went they now away as usual, and their clothes lay there behind, and their wares; no man had seen this woman, but Gudrid alone. Now we may be in need of counsel taking, says Karlsefne, for I think, that they may call at ours the third time with un-peace and with many men. [Karlsefne chose a place for battle and lured the Skralings to it.]

But there were such conditions, where their meeting was planned, that water was on one side but a wood on the other side. Now was this counsel taken, which Karlsefne proposed. Now the Skralings came to the place, which Karlsefne had fixed for the battle. Now was there battle, and were slain many of the Skralings host. One man was tall and fair in the Skralings host, and Karlsefne thought, he might be headman of them. Now one of them, the Skralings, had taken up an axe, and looked at for a while, and lifted it against his comrade and struck at him. He fell at once dead; then that tall man took the axe and looked at for a while, and hurled it after that into the sea as far as he could. But then they fled into the wood, every one as best he could, and ends now their encounter.

"*The Norse Discovery of America,*" *Sacred Texts.* www.sacred-texts.com/neu/nda/nda20.htm.

AUGUST 22, 1576:
Martin Frobisher and the Inuit Take Prisoners

Martin Frobisher was an Elizabethan seadog. Pirate, explorer, and commander during the great battle against the Spanish Armada, Frobisher set out to prove to his patron, Elizabeth I, that all parts of the planet were habitable and that a usable waterway to Asia existed in the Arctic. He explored the Russian coast before setting out for North America. This account comes from his first expedition. Later, an attempt to create a mining camp in the Arctic ended as a ludicrous failure: Frobisher brought back iron pyrite, more commonly known as fool's gold. Frobisher then went back to his more profitable career of privateering. He died in November 1594 from a wound inflicted at a siege in Brest, France. Sailor George Best was a member of Frobisher's crew and published his account in London soon after the expedition returned. Frobisher attacked the Inuit because he believed they had kidnapped five of his men. Whether Frobisher's men were actually kidnapped, killed by the Inuit, or deserted remains a mystery.

GEORGE BEST

[Frobisher] with courage [more than any man] presented, armed and prepared his ship with all things within necessary for defence; and also without he covered the [anchor] chain and shrouds and all other places where the enemy might take hold or place any ropes to clamber onto the ship with canvas nailed fast to the ship's sides. So as they could take no hold to enter into the ship being so low or near to the water. And in the waist of the ship he put a piece of ordinance minding to shoot to sink one of their great boats having men therein. And so with the ship under sail to recover some of them for prisoners, if otherwise he could not come by any of them to redeem his own men ... and thereupon we went to the contrary side of the ship from the ordinance, and stayed far off, only one boat with one man therein ... approached very near to the ship's side making signs of friendship and that we should go on land and take our rest. Whereat the captain made signs of friendship as though he would so do, and made signs of friendship, and placed himself at the waist of the ship, along the side along and having at his feet secretly his weapons and caused all his men to withdraw from him as though without any malice. And made offer of small things to give him at the ship's side, but the man a while stood in suspicion would not approach. Thereupon the captain cast into the sea a shirt and other things which the sea carried from the ship, and he took them up. And likewise made an offer of a bell in his hand, which he took with him hard at the ship's side.

Wherewith one of the mariners minded with a boathook to take hold of his boat, which so suddenly the man spied and put off his boat far from the ship, and in a long time would no more approach, which was no small grief to the captain and the rest. Yet at last with fair offers and enticements of gifts by the captain he approached with his boat to the ship's side.

[Frobisher pretended to try to pass the bell to the Inuit man but let it drop into the sea.]

Whereat the man seemed greatly sorry for the loss thereof and suddenly the captain called for another bell which he also reached out to him with a short arm, and in that reach he caught hold of the man's hand, and with his other hand he caught hold on his wrist, and by great force of strength plucked both the man and his light boat out of the sea and into the ship in a trice and so kept him without any show of enmity and made signs to him that if he would bring his men he should soon go again at liberty, but he did not seem to understand this meaning, and therefore he was still kept on the ship with sure guard.

This was done with all of the rest of his fellows being with arrow shot of the ship. Whereat they were all marvelously amazed and thereupon presently cast themselves into counsel and so departed with great haste toward the land with great hallowing and howling shouts after their manner; like the howling of wolves or other beasts in the woods. And the captain with his ship remained there all that day and anchored leagues from them all the night and the next day but could hear no news of his men or boat, nor perceived by the prisoner that they would come again.

[The next day, Frobisher and his officers decided to set sail for England, rather than risk being trapped in the Arctic for the winter. On a later voyage, Frobisher tried to find the five missing men but they were never seen again, nor does it appear that Frobisher's Inuit prisoner ever returned to the Arctic.]

George Best, A True Discourse of the Late Voyages of Discoverie: For Finding of a Passage to Cathaya *(London: Bynnyman, 1578).*

SUMMER 1609:
Champlain Outguns the Iroquois

Whether he felt pressured to, or simply because of bad judgment, Samuel de Champlain joined a Huron-Algonkian war expedition to the Mohawk country in the summer of 1609. There he and his allies took part in a pre-arranged battle that was fairly typical of Iroquoian warfare of the time. Champlain's introduction of firearms had the same effect on war in the North American forests that gunpowder warfare had on the battlefields of Europe: it ended chivalry. From now on, war in the Great Lakes country would be much more lethal and impersonal.

SAMUEL DE CHAMPLAIN

They [the Iroquois] said that as soon as the sun would rise, they would attack us, and to this our Indians agreed. Meanwhile, the whole night was spent in dances and songs on both sides, with many insults and other remarks, such as the lack of courage of our side, how little we could do or resist against them, and that when daylight came our people would learn all this to their ruin. Our side was not lacking in retort, telling the enemy they would see such deeds of arms as they had never seen, and a great deal of other talk, such is as usual at the siege of a city.

Having sung, danced and flung words at one another for some time, when daylight came, my companions and I were still hidden, lest the enemy should see us, getting our fire-arms ready as best we could, being however still separated, each in a canoe of the Montagnais Indians. After we were armed with light weapons, we took, each of us, an arquebus and went ashore. I saw the enemy come out of their barricade to the number two hundred, in appearance strong, robust men. They came ashore to meet us with a gravity and calm which I admired; and at their head were three chiefs.

Our Indians likewise advanced in similar order, and told me that those who had three big plumes were the chiefs, and that there were only those three, whom you could recognize by these plumes, which were larger than those of their companions; and I was to do what I could to kill them. I promised them to do all in my power, and told them that I was very sorry that they could not understand me, so that I might direct their method of attacking the enemy, all of whom we undoubtedly we should thus defeat; but they were no help for it, and that I was glad to show them, as soon as the engagement began, the courage and readiness that were in me.

As soon as we had landed, our Indians began to run some two hundred yards towards their enemies, who stood firm and had not yet noticed my white companions who went off into the woods with some Indians. Our Indians began to call to me with loud cries; and to make way for me they divided into two groups, and put me ahead some twenty yards, and I marched on until I was within some thirty yards of the enemy, who as soon as they caught sight of me halted and gazed at me and I at them. When I saw them make a move to draw their bows upon us, I took aim with my arquebus and shot straight at one of the three chiefs, and with this shot two fell to the ground and one of their companions was wounded who died thereof a little later. I had put four bullets into my arquebus.

As soon as our people saw this shot so favourable to them, they began to shout so loudly that one could not have heard thunder, and meanwhile the arrows flew thick on both sides. The Iroquois were astonished that two men could have been killed so quickly, although they were provided with shields made of cotton thread woven together and wood, which were proof against their arrows. This frightened them greatly. As I was reloading my arquebus, one of my companions fired a shot from within the woods, which astonished them again so much that, seeing their chiefs dead, they lost courage and took to flight, abandoning the field and their fort, and fleeing into the depths of the forest, whither I pursued them and laid low still more of them. Our Indians also killed several and took ten or twelve prisoners. The remainder fled with the wounded. Of our Indians fifteen or sixteen were wounded with arrows, but these were quickly healed.

Samuel de Champlain, Voyages *(Boston: Reprinted by the Prince Society, 1878).*

OCTOBER 10, 1615:
Champlain's Second Attack Fails

The Iroquois were quick studies. When Champlain attacked them a second time, the Iroquois did not flee. Instead, they defended themselves in a fortified village, which provided ample protection from Champlain's muskets. Champlain's attempt to import European siege tactics also failed. Champlain was wounded by an arrow in this siege and had to be nursed back to health in the Huron country. His allies were kind enough to carry him the 400 kilometres from the battle site to the village of Cahiague, near Lake Couchiching, where Champlain convalesced.

SAMUEL DE CHAMPLAIN

At three o'clock in the afternoon, we arrived before the fort of [the Huron and Algonkians' enemies], where the savages made some skirmishes with each other, although our design was not to disclose ourselves until the next day, which however the impatience of our savages would not permit, both on account of their desire to see fire opened upon their enemies, and also that they might rescue some of their own men who had become too closely engaged, and were hotly pressed. Then I approached the enemy, and although I had only a few men, yet we showed them what they had never seen nor heard before; for, as soon as they saw us and heard the arquebus shots and the balls whizzing in their ears, they withdrew speedily to their fort, carrying the dead and wounded in this charge. We also withdrew to our main body, with five or six wounded, one of whom died.

This done, we withdrew to the distance of cannon range, out of sight of the enemy, but contrary to my advice and to what they had promised me. This moved me to address them very rough and angry words in order to incite them to do their duty, foreseeing that if everything should go according to their whim and the guidance of their council, their utter ruin would be the result. Nevertheless I did not fail to send to them and propose means which they should use in order to get possession of their enemies.

These were, to make with certain kinds of wood a cavalier [an elevated, enclosed wooden platform] which would be higher than the palisades. Upon his were to be placed four or five of our arquebusiers, who should keep up a constant fire over their palisades and galleries, which were well provided with stones, and by this means dislodge the enemy who might attack us from their galleries.... This proposition they thought good and very reasonable, and immediately proceeded to carry them out as I directed.

[The next day] we approached to attack the village, our cavalier being armed by two hundred of the strongest men, who put it down before the village at a pike's length off. I ordered three arquebusiers to mount upon it, who were well protected from the arrows and stones that could be shot or hurled at them. Meanwhile the enemy did not fail to send a large number of arrows which did not miss, and a great many stones, which they hurled from their palisades. Nevertheless a hot fire of arquebusiers forced them to dislodge and abandon their galleries, in consequence of the cavalier which uncovered them, they not venturing to show themselves, but fighting under shelter. Now when the cavalier was carried forward, instead of bringing up the mantelets [large wooden shields] according to order, including ... one under cover of which we were to set [a] fire, they abandoned them and began to scream at their enemies, shooting arrows into the fort, which in my opinion did little harm to the enemy.

But we must excuse them, for they are not warriors, and besides will have no discipline or correction, and will do only what they please.

Samuel de Champlain, Voyages *(Boston: Reprinted by the Prince Society, 1878).*

JULY 4, 1648:
The Iroquois Take Teanaostaïaé

In the forty years following Champlain's first skirmish with the Mohawk, Iroquoian warfare had evolved from ritual fights between groups of warriors into campaigns of conquest and extermination. In those years, the Huron and Iroquois had lost half of their people to new diseases brought by Europeans and their livestock. At the same time, European technology and religious ideas were undermining Huron society. The balance between the two warring confederacies tipped toward the Iroquois once they were able to buy guns — surplus weapons from the Thirty Years' War — from Dutch traders in the Hudson Valley. In 1648, the Iroquois launched a two-year campaign to destroy the Huron, beginning with the town of Teanaostaïaé. This town, about 20 kilometres north of Lake Simcoe, was probably, at the time of its capture, the largest community in Canada, with somewhere around 2,500 people living in longhouses behind strong fortifications. Many of the people of the town were able to escape, but about 750 were taken prisoner. Most were adopted into the Iroquois confederacy and a few returned the next spring with Iroquois invaders to try to convince friends and relatives among the besieged Huron to voluntarily move to the Iroquois country. Some captives, however, were tortured to death, a common practice on all sides in Iroquoian warfare. Ritual torture of prisoners appears to have had religious significance to the Iroquoian people of the Great Lakes region.

The loss of this town marked the beginning of the end of the Huron Confederacy. Within two years, the Iroquois would have political and economic domination of the Great Lakes that would last for nearly a century and a half.

Ragueneau was the Superior of the Jesuit mission in Huronia, headquartered at the mission of Ste. Marie, about thirty kilometres north of Teanaostaïaé. He sheltered some of the refugees at Ste. Marie.

PAUL RAGUENEAU

Last Summer, in the past year, 1648, the Iroquois, enemies of the

Hurons, took from them two frontier villages, from which most of the defenders had gone forth — some for the chase, and others for purposes of war, in which they could meet no success. These two frontier places composed the Mission which we named for St. Joseph; the principal of these villages contained about 400 families, where the faith had long sustained itself with luster, and where the Christians were increasing in number, and still more in holiness, through the indefatigable labors of Father Antoine Daniel, one of the earliest Missionaries in these regions.

Hardly had the Father ended Mass, and the Christians — who, according to their custom, had filled the Church after the rising of the Sun — were still continuing their devotions there, when the cry arose, "To arms! and repel the enemy!" — who, having come expectedly, had made his approaches by night. Some hasten to the combat, others to flight; there is naught but alarm and terror everywhere. The Father, among the first to rush where he sees the danger greatest, encourages his people to a brave defense; and — as if he had seen Paradise open for the Christians, and Hell on the point of swallowing up all the Infidels — he speaks to them in a tone so animated with the spirit which was possessing him, that, having made a breach in hearts which till then had been most rebellious, he gave them a Christian heart.

The number of these proved to be so great that, unable to cope with it by baptizing them one after the other, he was constrained to dip his handkerchief in the water (which was all that necessity then offered him), in order to shed abroad as quickly as possible this grace on those poor Savages, who cried mercy to him — using the manner of baptism which is called "by aspersion."

Meanwhile, the enemy continued his attacks more furiously than ever; and, without doubt, it was a great blessing for the salvation of some that, at the moment of their death, Baptism had given them the life of the soul, and put them in possession of an immortal life.

When the Father saw that the Iroquois were becoming masters of the place, he — instead of taking flight with those who were inviting him to escape in their company — forgetting himself, remembered some old men and sick people, whom he had long ago prepared for Baptism. He goes through the cabins, and proceeds to fill them with his zeal — the

Infidels themselves presenting their children in crowds, in order to make Christians of them.

Meanwhile, the enemy, already victorious, had set everything on fire, and the blood of even the women and children irritated their fury. The Father, wishing to die in his Church, finds it full of Christians, and of Catechumens who ask him for Baptism. It was indeed at that time that their faith animated their prayers, and that their hearts could not belie their tongues. He baptizes some, gives absolution to others, and consoles them all with the sweetest hope of the Saints — having hardly other words on his lips than these: "My Brothers, today we shall be in Heaven."

The enemy was warned that the Christians had betaken themselves, in very great number, into the Church, and that it was the easiest and the richest prey that he could have hoped for; he hastens thither, with barbarous howls and stunning yells. At the noise of these approaches, "Flee, my Brothers," said the Father to his new Christians, "and bear with you your faith even to the last sigh. As for me," (he added) "I must face death here, as long as I shall see any soul to be gained for Heaven; and, dying here to save you, my life is no longer anything to me; we shall see one another again in Heaven." At the same time, he goes out in the direction whence come the enemy, who stop in astonishment to see one man alone come to meet them, and even recoil backward, as if he bore upon his face the terrible and frightful appearance of a whole company. Finally — having come to their senses a little, and being astonished at themselves — they incite one another; they surround him on all sides, and cover him with arrows, until, having inflicted upon him a mortal wound from an arquebus shot —which pierced him through and through, in the very middle of his breast — he fell. Pronouncing the name of Jesus, he blessedly yielded up his soul to God — truly as a good Pastor, who exposes both his soul and his life for the salvation of his flock.

It was then that those Barbarians rushed upon him with as much rage as if he alone had been the object of their hatred. They strip him naked, they exercise upon him a thousand indignities, and there was hardly anyone who did not try to assume the glory of having given him the final blow, even on seeing him dead.

The fire meanwhile was consuming the cabins; and when it had spread as far as the Church, the Father was cast into it, at the height of the flames, which soon made of him a whole burnt-offering. Be this as it may, he could not have been more gloriously consumed than in the fires and lights of a Chapelle ardent.

Paul Ragueneau to the Jesuit Superior, The Indians of North America: From the Jesuit Relations and Allied Documents, *Vol. II, Edna Kenton, ed. (New York: Harcourt, Brace & Co. 1927), 4.*

MARCH 16, 1649:
The Iroquois Crush the Huron Confederacy

In the fall of 1648, an army of 1,200 Five Nations (Iroquois) warriors, armed by Dutch traders with Thirty Years' War-surplus muskets, moved north from the Finger Lakes region of New York and attacked two villages of their traditional enemies, the Huron, who lived near the south shore of Georgian Bay. The late-winter attack was a shock to the Huron, who still managed to raise a force of warriors and came close to defeating the better-armed invaders. Jesuit missionaries Jean de Brébeuf and Gabriel Lalemant were captured on the first day of the campaign and were tortured to death that night. Within a few days of this battle, one of the largest fought in what is now Ontario, the Huron abandoned all of their towns.

Ragueneau watched the battle from the mission of Ste. Marie, on the outskirts of modern Midland, Ontario. The eight Jesuit martyrs killed in the Iroquois Wars, who Ragueneau had claimed were killed solely for their Catholic faith, were made saints of the Roman Catholic Church in 1930, and Pope John Paul II prayed over Brébeuf's battered and scratched skull during his visit to Ste. Marie in 1984.

PAUL RAGUENEAU

The 16th day of March in the present year, 1649, marked the beginning of our misfortunes — if, however, that be a misfortune which no doubt has been the salvation of many of God's elect.

The Iroquois, enemies of the Hurons, to the number of about a thousand men, well furnished with weapons — and mostly with firearms, which they obtain from the Dutch, their allies — arrived by night at the frontier of this country, without our having had any knowledge of their approach; although they had started from their country in the Autumn, hunting in the forests throughout the Winter, and had made over the snow nearly two hundred leagues of a very difficult road, in order to come and surprise us. They reconnoitered by night the condition of the first place upon which they had designs — which was Surrounded with a stockade of pine trees, from fifteen to sixteen feet in height, and with a deep ditch, wherewith nature had strongly fortified this place on three sides — there remaining only a little a space which was weaker than the others.

It was at that point that the enemy made a breach at daybreak, but so secretly and promptly that he was master of the place before people had put themselves on the defensive — all being then in a deep sleep, and not having leisure to re connoiter their situation. Thus this village was taken, almost without striking a blow, there having been only ten Iroquois killed. Part of the Hurons — men, women, and children — were massacred then and there; the others were made captives, and reserved for cruelties more terrible than death.

Three men alone escaped, almost naked, across the snows; they bore the alarm and terror to another and neighboring village, about a league distant. This first village was the one which we called Saint Ignace, which had been abandoned by most of its people at the beginning of the Winter — the most apprehensive and most clear-sighted having withdrawn from it, foreboding the danger; thus the loss of it was not so considerable, and amounted only to about four hundred souls.

The enemy does not stop there; he follows up his victory, and before Sunrise he appears in arms to attack the village of Saint Louys, which was fortified with a fairly good stockade. Most of the women, and the children, had just gone from it, upon hearing the news which had arrived regarding the approach of the Iroquois. The people of most courage, about eighty persons, being resolved to defend themselves well, repulse with courage the first and the second assault, having killed among the enemy some thirty of their most venturesome men, besides many wounded. But, finally, number has the advantage — the Iroquois having undermined with blows of their hatchets the palisade of stakes, and having made a passage for themselves through considerable breaches.

Toward nine o'clock in the morning, we perceived from our house at Sainte Marie the fire which was consuming the cabins of that village, where the enemy, having entered victoriously, had reduced everything to desolation — casting into the midst of the flames the old men, the sick, the children who had not been able to escape, and all those who, being too severely wounded, could not have followed them into captivity. At the sight of those flames, and by the color of the smoke which issued from them, we understood sufficiently what was happening — this village of Saint Louys not being farther distant from us than one league. Two Christians, who escaped from the fire, arrived almost at the same time, and gave us assurance of it....

On the evening of the same day, they sent scouts to reconnoiter the condition of our house at Sainte Marie; their report having been made in the Council of war, the decision was adopted to come and attack us the next morning — promising themselves a victory which would be more glorious to them than all the successes of their arms in the past....

All night our French were in arms, waiting to see at our gates this victorious enemy.... The whole day passed in a profound silence on both sides, — the country being in terror and in the expectation of some new misfortune. On the nineteenth, the day of the great Saint Joseph, a sudden panic fell upon the hostile camp — some withdrawing in disorder, and others thinking only of flight. Their Captains were constrained to yield to the terror which had seized them; they precipitated their retreat, driving forth in haste a part of their captives, who were burdened above their strength, like packhorses, with the spoils which the victorious were carrying off — their captors reserving for some other occasion the matter of their death.

Paul Ragueneau to the Jesuit Superior, The Indians of North America: From the Jesuit Relations and Allied Documents, *Vol. II, Edna Kenton, ed. (New York: Harcourt, Brace & Co. 1927), 6–10.*

MARCH 17, 1649:
Jean de Brébeuf and Gabriel Lalemant
are Killed at St. Ignace

Jean de Brébeuf was a mystic and a true Jesuit of his time who believed the tree of Christianity was watered with the blood of martyrs. He was the most dynamic of the Jesuit missionaries in Huronia. Brébeuf's missionary work caused a deep rift in Huron society. He also incurred their anger by courting alliances with other Great Lakes tribes. At one point, some Huron traders put a bounty on him, but Brébeuf survived, although he remained close to the fortified mission of Ste. Marie during his last years. Much of what we know of the Huron comes from Brébeuf's observations, and his dictionary of the Huron languages is invaluable to scholars. Lalemant was well-connected. One relative headed the entire North American mission. A frail, asthmatic man, Lalemant must have suffered grievously during his long ordeal. While Brébeuf suffered the full rage of his tormenters — most of whom were traditionalist Huron — Lalemant was killed much more slowly. Both men were buried at Ste. Marie. Their bones were taken back to Quebec in 1650. Their grave at Ste. Marie is a site of Roman Catholic pilgrimage, and was visited by Pope John Paul II in 1984. A note on the word "savage": the original French meaning lacks the negative nuance of the English word, and translates more closely to "wild people." The use of formal English words like "thou" is reflective of the original French of Regnaut's letter. The Huron and Iroquois had both formal and colloquial ways of speaking, and, during their tormenting of Brébeuf, mocked him with fake respect.

CHRISTOPHE REGNAULT

At Three Rivers,
September 21, 1649.

A veritable Account of the Martyrdom and Blessed death of Father Jean de Brébeuf and of Father Gabriel Lalemant, in New France, in the country of the Hurons, by the Iroquois, enemies of the Faith.

Having survived a similar torture session, Jesuit Francois-Joseph Bressani was able to accurately draw the killing of Jean de Brébeuf and Gabriel Lalemant eight years after the event.

This is what the [Huron refugees] told us of the taking of the Village of St. Ignace, and about Fathers Jean de Brébeuf and Gabriel Lalemant:

"The Iroquois came, to the number of twelve hundred men; took our village, and seized Father Brébeuf and his companion; and set fire to all the huts. They proceeded to vent their rage on those two Fathers; for they took them both and stripped them entirely naked, and fastened each to a post. They tied both of their hands together. They tore the nails from their fingers. They beat them with a shower of blows from cudgels, on the shoulders, the loins, the belly, the legs, and the face, — there being no part of their body which did not endure this torment." While the good Father was thus encouraging these good people, a wretched Huron renegade, — who had remained a captive with the Iroquois, and whom Father de Brébeuf had formerly instructed and baptized, — hearing him speak Paradise and Holy Baptism, was irritated, and said to him, "Echon," that is Father de Brébeuf's name in Huron, "thou sayest that Baptism and the sufferings of this life lead straight to Paradise; thou wilt go soon, for I am going to baptize thee, and to make thee suffer well, in order to go the sooner to thy Paradise."

The barbarian, having said that, took a kettle full of boiling water, which he poured over his body three different times, in derision of Holy baptism. And, each time that he baptized him in this manner, the barbarian said to him, with bitter sarcasm, "Go to Heaven, for thou art well baptized."

After that, they made him suffer several other torments. The first was to make hatchets red-hot, and to apply them to the loins and under the armpits. They made a collar of these red-hot hatchets, and put it on the neck of this good Father. This is the fashion in which I have seen the collar made for other prisoners: They make six hatchets red-hot, take a large withe of green wood, pass the six hatchets over the large end of the withe, take the two ends together, and then put it over the neck of the sufferer. I have seen no torment which more moved me to compassion than that. For you see a man, bound naked to a post, who, having this collar on his neck, cannot tell what posture to take. For, if he leans forward, those above his shoulders weigh the more on him; if he leans back, those on his stomach make him suffer the same torment; if he keeps erect, without leaning to one side or other, the burning hatchets, applied equally on both sides, give him a double torture.

After that they put on him a belt of bark, full of pitch and resin, and set fire to it, which roasted his whole body. During all these torments, Father de Brébeuf endured like a rock, insensible to fire and flames, which astonished all the bloodthirsty wretches who tormented him. His zeal was so great that he preached continually to these infidels, to try to convert them. His executioners were enraged against him for constantly speaking to them of God and of their conversion. To prevent him from speaking more, they cut off his tongue, and both his upper and lower lips. After that, they set themselves to strip the flesh from his legs, thighs, and arms, to the very bone; and then put it to roast before his eyes, in order to eat it.

While they tormented him in this manner, those wretches derided him, saying: "Thou seest plainly that we treat thee as a friend, since we shall be the cause of thy Eternal happiness; thank us, then, for these good offices which we render thee, — for, the more thou shalt suffer, the more will thy God reward thee."

Those butchers, seeing that the good Father began to grow weak, made him sit down on the ground; and, one of them, taking a knife, cut off the skin covering his skull. Another one of those barbarians, seeing that the good Father would soon die, made an opening in the upper part of his chest, and tore out his heart, which he roasted and ate. Others came to drink his blood, still warm, which they drank with both hands, — saying that Father de Brébeuf had been very courageous to endure so much pain as they had given him, and that, by drinking his blood, they would become courageous like him…

I saw and touched all parts of his body, which had received more than two hundred blows from a stick. I saw and touched the top of his scalped head; I saw and touched the opening which these barbarians had made to tear out his heart.

In fine, I saw and touched all the wounds of his body, as the savages had told and declared to us; we buried these precious Relics on Sunday, the 21st day of March, 1649, with much consolation.

Sir,
Your Very Humble and very obedient Servant
Christophe Regnault

Christophe Regnault, Jesuit Relations and Allied Documents, *Vol. 34, Reuben Gold Thwaites, ed. (Cleveland, OH: Burrows Brothers, 1901), 257.*

WINTER 1649–50:
Famine on Christian Island

Once the Iroquois left the Huron country, the Huron survivors fled to Christian Island in southern Georgian Bay, where hundreds, perhaps several thousand, starved to death the following winter. The Huron, reduced from about 15,000 in 1648 to a few thousand after the 1949 attacks, dispersed the following spring. Many joined the Iroquois. Some Christian Huron moved to the Quebec City area. The rest scattered throughout the Great Lakes basin, some eventually being forcibly re-settled in Oklahoma by the U.S. government.

Paul Ragueneau

I see a part of the miseries which war and famine have caused to poor desolate people. Their ordinary food is now nothing but acorns or a certain bitter root which they name otsa; and yet, fortunate is he who can have any of these. Those who have none, live partly on garlic baked under the ashes, or cooked in water, without other sauce; and partly on smoked fish, where-with they season the clear water which they drink, as they formerly did their sagamite [a sort of thick corn soup]. There are found still poorer ones than all that — who have neither corn, nor acorns, nor garlic, nor fish, and are poor sick people who cannot seek their living. Add to this poverty that they must work to clear new forests, make cabins, and erect palisades, in order to secure themselves in the coming year from famine and war; indeed, seeing them, you might conclude that these are poor corpses unearthed....

For, in truth, our Hurons are distressed not only by war, but by a deadly famine and a contagious plague; all are miserably perishing together. Everywhere, corpses have been dug out of the graves; and now carried away by hunger, the people have repeatedly offered, as food, those who were lately the dear pledges of love, — not only brothers to brothers, but even children to their mothers, and the parents to their own children. It is true, this is inhuman; but it is no less unusual among our savages than among the Europeans, who abhor eating flesh of their own kind.

Doubtless the teeth of the starving man make no distinction in food, and do not recognize in the dead body him who a little before was called, until he died, father, son, or brother. Nay, more, even the dung of man or beast is not spared. Fortunate are they who can eat the food of swine — bitter acorns, and husks — innocent food, and indeed not without relish, to which hunger adds a sauce; to these, the scarcity of this year has given a value far higher than, formerly, was usually placed upon Indian corn.

Paul Ragueneau to the Jesuit Superior, The Indians of North America: From the Jesuit Relations and Allied Documents, *Vol. II, Edna Kenton, ed. (New York: Harcourt, Brace & Co. 1927), 24–30.*

OCTOBER 1692:
Madeleine de Verchères fights off the Iroquois

Fourteen-year-old Madeleine was home alone at her fortified manor house near Montreal when the farm and its tenants were attacked by the Iroquois. Several tenant farmers were captured by the Iroquois, but Madeleine and a small group of defenders managed to hold the Verchères stockade for eight days until reinforcements arrived from Montreal. The Iroquois gave up their attack and left with their prisoners, but were intercepted by militia soldiers who freed the Verchères captives. Twenty-four years later, she recounted her adventure to the Marquis de Beauharnois, governor of Quebec. Her story of courage and survival in the face of overwhelming force, which recalled the story of Jeanne d'Arc, would become one of the great heroic tales of New France, and, later, Quebec. There is, however, some controversy about the danger Madeleine supposedly faced after the first Iroquois attack. Some critics claim the Iroquois may have lurked around the fort, but were not serious about a siege. In later life, Madeleine endured gossip about her femininity, and she went to court at least once to try to kill gossip that she had loose morals.

MADELEINE DE VERCHÈRES

I was five arpents away from the fort of Verchères, belonging to Sieur De Verchères, my father, who was then at Kebek by order of M. Le Chevalier De Callières, governor of Montreal, my mother being also in Montreal. I heard several shots without knowing at whom they were fired I soon saw that the Iroquois were firing at our settlers, who lived about a league and a-half from the fort. One of our servants called out to me:

"Fly, mademoiselle, fly! The Iroquois are upon us!"

I turned instantly and saw some forty-five Iroquois running towards me, and already within pistol shot. Determined to die rather than fall into their hands, I sought safety in flight. I ran towards the fort, commending myself to the Blessed Virgin, and saying to her from the bottom of my heart: "Holy Virgin, mother of my God, you know I have ever honoured and loved you as my dear mother; abandon me not in this hour of danger! I would rather a thousand times perish than fall into the hands of a race that know you not."

Meantime my pursuers, seeing that they were too far off to take me alive before I could enter the fort, and knowing they were near enough to shoot me, stood still in order to discharge their guns at me. I was under fire for quite a time, at any rate I found the time long enough! Forty-five bullets whistling past my ears made the time seem long and the distance from the fort interminable, though I was so near. When within hearing of the fort, I cried out: "To arms! To arms!"

I hoped that someone would come to help me, but it was a vain hope. There were but two soldiers in the fort and these were so overcome by fear that they had sought safety by concealing themselves in the redoubt. Having reached the gates at last, I found there two women lamenting for the loss of their husbands, who had just been killed. I made them enter the fort, and closed the gates myself. I then began to consider how I might save myself and the little party with me, from the hands of the savages. I examined the fort, and found that several of the stakes had fallen, leaving gaps through which it would be easy for the enemy to enter. I gave orders to have the stakes replaced, and heedless of my sex and tender age, I hesitated not to seize one end of the heavy stake and urge my companions to give a hand in raising it. I found by experience that, when God gives us strength, nothing is impossible.

The breaches having been repaired, I betook myself to the redoubt, which served as a guard-house and armory. I there found two soldiers, one of them lying down and the other holding a burning fuse. I said to the latter:

"What are you going to do with that fuse?"

"I want to set fire to the powder," said he, "and blow up the fort."

"You are a miserable wretch," I said, adding: "Be gone, I command you!"

I spoke so firmly that he obeyed forthwith. Thereupon putting aside my hood and donning a soldier's casque, I seized a musket and said to my little brothers: "Let us fight to the death for our country and for our holy religion. Remember what our father has so often told you, that gentlemen are born but to shed their blood for the service of God and the king!"

Stirred up by my words, my brothers and the two soldiers kept up a steady fire on the foe. I caused the cannon to be fired, not only to strike terror into the Iroquois and show them that we were well able to defend ourselves, since we had a cannon, but also to warn our own soldiers, who were away hunting, to take refuge in some other fort. But alas! what sufferings have to be endured in these awful extremities of distress! Despite the thunder of our guns, I heard unceasingly the cries and lamentations of some unfortunates who had just lost a husband, a brother, a child or a parent. I deemed it prudent, while the firing was still kept up, to represent to the grief-stricken women that their shrieks exposed us to danger, for they could not fail to be heard by the enemy, notwithstanding the noise of the guns and the cannon. I ordered them to be silent and thus avoid giving the impression that we were helpless and hopeless.

While I was speaking thus, I caught sight of a canoe on the river, opposite the fort. It was Sieur Pierre Fontaine with his family, who were about to land at the spot where I had just barely escaped from the Iroquois, the latter being still visible on every hand. The family must fall into the hands of the savages if not promptly succored.

I asked the two soldiers to go to the landing place, only five arpents away, and protect the family. But seeing by their silence, that they had but little heart for the work, I ordered our servant, Laviolette, to stand sentry at the gate of the fort and keep it open, while I would myself go to the bank of the river, carrying a musket in my hand and wearing my soldier's casque. I left orders on setting out, that if I was killed, they were to shut the gates and continue to defend the fort sturdily. I set out with the heaven-sent thought that the enemy, who were looking on, would imagine that it was a ruse on my part to induce them to approach the fort, in order that our people might make a sortie upon them.

This is precisely what happened, and thus was I enabled to save poor Pierre Fontaine, with his wife and children. When all were landed, I made them march before me as far as the fort, within sight of the enemy. By putting a bold face upon it, I made the Iroquois think there was more danger for them than for us.

They did not know that the whole garrison, and only inhabitants of the fort of Verchères, was my two brothers aged 12 years, our servant, two soldiers, an old man of eighty, and some women and children....

I can truthfully say that I was on two occasions, for twenty-four hours without rest or food. I did not once enter my father's house. I took up my station on the bastion, and from time to time looked after things on the redoubt. I always wore a smiling and joyful face, and cheered up my little troop with the prospect of speedy assistance.

On the eighth day (for we were eight days in continual alarms, under the eyes of our enemies and exposed to their fury and savage attacks), on the eighth day, I say, M. De La Monnerie, a lieutenant detached from the force under M. De Callières, reached the fort during the night with forty men. Not knowing but the fort had fallen, he made his approach in perfect silence. One of our sentries hearing a noise, cried out: "Qui vive?"

I was dozing at the moment, with my head resting on a table and my musket across my arms.

The sentry told me he heard voices on the water. I forthwith mounted the bastion in order to find out by the tone of the voice whether the party were savages or French. I called out to them:

"Who are you?"

They answered: "French! It is La Monnerie come to your assistance."

I caused the door of the fort to be opened and put a sentry to guard it, and went down to the bank of the river to receive the party. So soon as I saw the officer in command I saluted him, saying:

"Sir, you are welcome, I surrender my arms to you."

"Mademoiselle," he answered, with a courtly air, "they are in good hands."

"Better than you think," I replied.

Madeleine de Verchères, Narrative of the Heroic Deeds of Madeleine de Verchères, Aged 14 Years, Against the Iroquois October 22–30, 1692. Supplement to the Report of the Public Archives of Canada for 1899 (Ottawa: King's Printer, 1899).

JULY 17, 1771:
Massacre on the Coppermine River

The work of explorers like Hearne allowed Britain and, later, Canada, to exert a strong claim over the Arctic. Hearne's account, which was probably embellished by an editor or ghost writer named William Wales, was part of a spellbinding description of his travels through the flat, almost treeless, expanse of southwestern Nunavut and the eastern

Northwest Territories. While the Coppermine River never yielded the mineral riches that Hearne had hoped for, his travels did cement the authority of the Hudson's Bay Company, and, later, Canada, to the northern edge of the continent. Hearne was twenty-six years old when he made this journey. He died in 1792 at the age of seventy-four, and this account, in *A Journey from Prince of Wales's Fort in Hudson's Bay to the Northern Ocean*, was published three years later. Recent scholarship suggests this incident was probably an attack on a small group of Inuit who had strayed from a larger temporary settlement on the other side of the river. Explorers like Hearne legitimized Charles II's grant of the huge watershed of Hudson Bay and stake out Britain's sovereignty over what is now the Canadian North.

SAMUEL HEARNE

[W]e began to advance toward the Esquimaux tents; but were very careful to avoid crossing any hills, or talking loud, for fear of being seen or overheard by the inhabitants; by which means the distance was not only much greater than it otherwise would have been, but for the sake of keeping in the lowest grounds, we were obliged to walk through entire swamps of stiff marly clay, sometimes up to the knees.... The land was so situated that we walked under cover of the rocks and hills till we were within two hundred yards of the tents. There we lay in ambush for some time, watching the motions of the Esquimaux; and here the Indians would have advised me to stay till the fight was over, but to this I could by no means consent; for I considered that when the Esquimaux were surprised, that they would try every way to escape, and if they found me alone, not knowing me from an enemy, they would probably proceed to violence against me when no person was near to assist. For this reason, I determined to accompany them, telling them at the same time that I would not have any hand in the murder they were about to commit unless I found it necessary for my own safety. The Indians were not displeased at this proposal; one of them immediately fixed me a spear, and another lent me a broad bayonet for my protection, but at that time I could not be provided with a target; nor did I want to be encumbered with such an unnecessary piece of lumber.

While we lay in ambush, the Indians performed the last ceremonies which were thought necessary before the engagement. These chiefly consisted in painting their faces; some all black, some all red, and others with a mixture of the two; and to prevent their hair from blowing into their eyes, it was either tied before and behind, and on both sides, or else cut short all round. The next thing they considered was to make themselves as light as possible for running; which they did, by pulling off their stockings, and either cutting off the sleeves of their jackets, or rolling them up close to their armpits; and though the muskettoes [mosquitoes] at the time were so numerous as to surpass all credibility, yet some of the Indians actually pulled off their jackets and entered the lists quite naked, except their breach-cloths and shoes. Fearing I might have occasion to run with the rest, I thought it also advisable to pull off my stockings and cap, and to tie my hair up as close as possible.

By the time the Indians had made themselves completely frightful, it was near one o'clock in the morning of the seventeenth; when finding all the Esquimaux quite in their tents, they rushed forth from their ambuscade and fell on the poor unsuspecting creature, unperceived till close at the very eves of their tents, when they soon began the blood massacre, while I stood neuter in the rear.

In a few seconds, the horrible scene commenced; it was shocking beyond description; the poor unhappy victims were surprised in the midst of their sleep, and had neither time nor power to make any resistance; men, women, children in all upward of twenty, ran out of their tents stark naked, and endeavoured to make their escape; but the Indians having possession of all the landside, to no place could they fly for shelter. One alternative only remained, that of jumping into the river; but, as none of them attempted it, they all fell sacrifice to Indian barbarity!

The shrieks and groans of the poor expiring wretches were truly dreadful; and my horror was much increased at seeing a young girl, seemingly about eighteen years of age, killed so near me, that when the first spear was stuck in her side, she fell down at my feet and twisted herself around my legs, so that it was with difficulty that I could disengage myself from her dying grasps. As two Indian men pursued this unfortunate victim, I solicited for her life; but the murderers made no reply until they had stuck both their spears into her body, and transfixed her to the ground. They then looked me sternly in the face, and began to ridicule me by asking if I wanted an Esquimaux wife; and paid not the smallest regard to the shrieks and agony of the poor wretch, who was twisting around their spears like an eel! Indeed, after receiving much abusive language from them on the occasion, I was at length obliged to desire that they would be more expeditious in dispatching their victim out of her misery, otherwise I should be obliged, out of pity, to assist in the friendly office of putting an end to the existence of a fellow-creature who was so cruelly wounded. On this request being made, one of the Indians hastily drew his spear from the place where it was first lodged, and pierced it through her breast near the heart. The love of life, however, even in this most miserable state, was so predominant, that though this might justly be called the most merciful act that could be done for the poor creature, it seemed to be unwelcome, for though much exhausted by pain and loss of blood, she made several efforts to ward off the friendly blow. My situation and the terror of my mind at beholding this butchery, cannot easily be conceived, much less described; though I summed up all the fortitude I was master of on the occasion, it was with difficulty that I could refrain from tears; and I am confident that my features must have feelingly how sincerely I was affected at the barbarous scene I then witnessed; even at this hour I cannot reflect on the transactions of that horrid day without shedding tears.

Samuel Hearne, A Journey from Prince of Wales's Fort in Hudson's Bay to the Northern Ocean, 1795 (Toronto: Reprinted by the Champlain Society, 1911).

THE CONQUEST OF CANADA

THE CONQUEST OF CANADA WAS NOT ONE OF BRITAIN'S MAIN MILITARY or political goals. In fact, the British would rue the day they took control of Quebec because the removal of the French threat allowed the British colonies along the Atlantic coast to seriously consider independence. The colony of New France was never lucrative for the French government, and its loss reduced the need for French naval squadrons in the northwest Atlantic. France chose the far more lucrative sugar-growing island of Guadeloupe when given a choice at the Paris peace conference in 1763, and Napoleon wisely turned down a British offer of the return of Quebec during the negotiations of the Treaty of Amiens in 1802.

Still, the capture of Quebec thrilled the British public. It had all the great plotlines: revenge for the massacre of British troops who had surrendered at Fort William Henry in 1757 (an incident later made famous in James Fennimore Cooper's *The Last of the Mohicans*); the sickly General Wolfe using guile to get his soldiers onto the Plains of Abraham and drawing the aristocratic Marquis de Montcalm onto the battlefield; the heroic death of Wolfe, immortalized in the great painting by Benjamin West that mimics the Renaissance "pieta" imagery of Christ taken down from the cross; and Montcalm's own death, the gallant general laying down his life for his lost cause.

There were no journalists at these battles. The modern newspaper was taking shape, but it would be another fifty years before a very few of them started sending their own reporters into the field. Instead, they relied on the letters of soldiers, men who were often very skilled observers, but who had their own fairly transparent limitations and biases. What have come down to us are the stories of battlefield action, but much has been lost. It is, for example, difficult to find a description of life in the city of Quebec in the summer of 1759, when most of the houses and public buildings were knocked down by British artillery fire. While most people fled the city, a large number stayed behind to support the French army and tend to the wounded. Many of these people were women, including the nuns who ran the city's main hospital and buried its dead in the craters left by British cannon fire.

Those people who fled to the country were not out of danger. British raiding parties pillaged and burned farms on both sides of the river and on the Île d'Orléans. People everywhere were exploited by corrupt French officials and their friends who profited from their monopoly on food.

Two battles were fought at Quebec: The Plains of Abraham, won by the British in September of 1759, and the Battle of St. Foy, a bloodier affair fought on the same ground the following spring and won by the French. The arrival of the British fleet a few days after the Battle of Ste-Foy ended the Canadian campaign. The decision on the fight for Quebec had been made at the naval Battle of Quiberon Bay, where the French Atlantic fleet was defeated by Sir Edward Hawke. There would be no French reinforcements of Canada. Montreal surrendered later that summer, the French forces in Newfoundland were subdued at the Battle of Signal Hill, and people in New France, along with their occupiers, waited for the treaty that would determine the colony's fate. In the end, Canada became British territory.

France's Native allies were not part of the peace process and were not happy with the outcome. They believed the Treaty of Paris and the end of the French check on the Thirteen Colonies would open a flood of English settlers into the Ohio Valley and the Great Lakes country. Under Pontiac, they fought back, vainly hoping for help from the French king. In the end, the British guaranteed, at least for the time being, Native control of the lands west of the Appalachian Mountains. In the Thirteen Colonies, this decision was added to the list of grievances of the merchants, planters, and land speculators who engineered the American Revolution.

SEPTEMBER 13, 1759:
Scaling the Heights of Abraham

Wolfe's attack was a bold and desperate move. His other lunges had been rebuffed and the people of Quebec had resisted a summer-long siege, living in cellars to hide from the non-stop bombardment from British artillery firing from Point Lévis and ships in the river. With winter and the end of the 1759 campaign season closing in, Wolfe decided to try to lure the French out of the fortress of Quebec to fight on open ground. Rashly, the Marquis de Montcalm took the bait without waiting for French reinforcements that could have arrived at Quebec within hours. The anonymous junior officer does not gloss over the misgivings that Wolfe's staff officers had for his plan and the inter-service antagonisms among the British.

In a desperate move, the besieged French tried to use fire ships to drive the British fleet from its moorings east of the city.

A contemporary painting of British soldiers rowing towards the St. Lawrence River's north shore the night before the Battle of the Plains of Abraham.

BY A JUNIOR OFFICER ON WOLFE'S STAFF

The Ships mov'd up the River as well to receive them as to draw the enemies attention up upwards. The General gave orders that the Troops for the first attack shou'd get into the Boats during the latter Part of the Tide of Flood, as the violence of The Ebb would make it more difficult, the Ebb uniting to its own force, the Natural Rapidity of The River: Mr. Wolfe was desirous that the Boats shou'd arrive at the Foulon as the Day dawn'd, to answer which They fell down about half hour after three, and arriv'd at the Foulon half after four without striking with the oars, merely by the Force of the Tide which was 9 mile. The Boats were not Discover'd by any of the Enemy's Centinels untill [*sic*] we came opposite to the Battery of St. Augustine, to the Centinel's Challenge there, Captn. Fraser answer'd according to the French manner, told them we were loaded with Provisions for the Town, and desir'd them to be silent as there was an English ship of War not far off. [The Enemy expected at this time a Convoy of Provision from their ships, which lay at Batiscan.] They did not begin to fire on the Boats untill [*sic*] They drew in towards the Foulon. The ships with the Remainder of the Troops fell down some Distance of time after the Flat Boats, so as not to give the Alarm.

Col. Howe with The Light Infantry gain'd the Heights with little loss, the Enemy had an hundred men to Guard the Foulon which were soon dispers'd: Mr. Wolfe was Highly Pleased with the measures Col. Howe had taken to gain the Heights, wish'd that Mr. Howe might outlive the Day that He might have an opportunity of stamping his merit to the Government.

The General stop'd a further Debarkation of the Troops untill the first were well establish'd above, saying if the Post was to be carry'd there were enough ashore for that Purpose, if They were repuls'd a greater number wou'd breed more confusion: The boats were kept empty to be ready to bring off the 1st debarkation in case of Repulse. — As soon as the Heights were carry'd the whole landed with all possible expedition.

"Officer on Wolfe's Staff," letter, Library and Archives Canada, Dobbs Collection, Microfilm A562.

SEPTEMBER 13, 1759:
The Death of Wolfe

Wolfe's death, leading his troops in their moment of glory, turned a short battle into a real tragedy. The previously unknown general quickly became famous in England, and what had been a short and fairly sloppy battle is now more famous than the war in which it was fought. The people who fought at Quebec were unsure whether their courage would mean anything. The official capitulation, letters, and journals of the time suggest most people involved thought France would likely get New France back in treaty negotiations. Americans involved in the conquest hoped France was out of North America for good. The descriptions of Wolfe's death were the foundations of the heroic myths about a man who had previously been so obscure that very few images were made of him in his lifetime.

John A. Knox

After our late worthy general, of renowned memory, was carried off wounded, to the rear of the front line, he desired those who were about him to lay him down; being asked if he would have a Surgeon, he replied, "It is needless; it is all over with me." One of them cried out, "They run, see how they run." "Who runs?" demanded our hero, with great earnestness, like a person roused from sleep. The Officer answered, "The enemy. Egad they give way everywhere." Thereupon the General rejoined, "Go one of you, my lads, to Colonel Burton; tell him to march Webb's regiment with all speed down to Charles's river to cut off the retreat of the fugitives from the bridge." Then, raised on his side, he added, "Now God be praised, I will die in peace," and thus expired.

John A. Knox, Historical Journals of the Campaigns in North America 1757–1760 by Capt. John Knox, A.G. Doughty, ed. (Toronto: The Champlain Society, 1906).

SEPTEMBER 13, 1759:
Quebec's Last French Governor Blames Montcalm

Canadian-born governor Vaudreuil's self-serving account, published as a defence for the loss of Quebec, leaves out the crippling effects that Vaudreuil and his henchmen's corruption and arrogance had on morale in the besieged city and among the French regular troops. Later, Vaudreuil would negotiate the terms of surrender of Montreal with General Jeffrey Amherst. The concessions wrung from the British by Vaudreuil became the framework for the religious and legal rights that were guaranteed to the French in the Royal Proclamation of 1763. Blaming Montcalm for the loss of Quebec did not save Vaudreuil from the loss of his career and a short stint in the Bastille. Vaudreuil sold his Canadian holdings after the Treaty of Paris confirmed the loss of New France and he died broke in Paris in 1778. He's still commemorated in the names of two Montreal suburbs.

PIERRE DE RIGAUD DE VAUDREUIL

I notified M. de Montcalm that the advantage the English had obtained by forcing our sentry posts must be the cause of their defeat but that it was in our interests not to act prematurely, that the English must be attacked simultaneously by our army, 1,500 men who could easily be ordered out of the city, and by the corps of M. de Bougainville. In this manner, the English would be completely surrounded with only their left as an avenue of retreat, where their defeat would also be certain.

This letter was delivered by an orderly, and then I left to join M. le Marquis de Montcalm, followed by my aides de camp. The small army which he (Montcalm) had assembled numbered 3,000 men at the most and was already in battle order. Part of the Quebec and Montreal militias were on the right, the Trois Rivieres militia and some from Montreal on the left. The French regulars were at the center. Several squadrons of colonial regulars, militia and Indians had been placed between the two armies on the right and the left and had been firing successfully for some time.

Such was the state of affairs when M. le Marquis de Montcalm received my letter, but hastiness was his sole counsel. He marched against the enemy, unmindful of the fact that he was giving up the heights which his army occupied, putting his soldiers out of breath, and yielding the advantage of terrain to the enemy all at once. Disorder was the inevitable consequence of the hastiness of the march. Our troops fired a general volley, not saving a single shot, and fell back in great confusion. The enemy troops, who were in good order, pursued them as far as the Faubourg St. Louis. It was at this moment that I arrived on the Quebec heights. At first I thought I might rally our troops, but there was nothing that could check their flight or overcome their discouragement. The Canadians were more responsive to my voice. I assembled 1,000 to 1,200 of them, who came back to the heights, where they continued to fight for a long time. This facilitated the retreat of our right commanded by M. Dumas, which was still engaged with the enemy's left, which they had thrown back no less than three times. I was momentarily expecting the arrival of the militias I had left behind, but they had been stopped at the bridge (over the St. Charles River) by the order of the major general (of Quebec) on the pretext that forty boats had been seen before Quebec, as if that mattered! I was therefore obliged to follow our army across the St. Charles River and return to our camp at Beauport.

Pierre de Rigaud de Vaudreuil, letter to the Minister of Marine, Center Archives Overseas (CAMO), Aix-en-Provence (France), Archives of colonies, General Correspondence. Canada, (1-MG Series C11A).

JUNE 4, 1763:
Massacre at Michilimackinac

The transfer of New France from French to British control incited fear and fury among France's Native allies in the Great Lakes region. In May 1763, Odowa war chief Pontiac, or Obwandiyag, tried to take Detroit, but failed. The "rebellion" spread though the Great Lakes region. New Jersey-born Alexander Henry, who worked for a syndicate of Montreal-based fur traders, had been at the former French post of Michilimackinac since 1761. In the days before, about 400 of Pontiac's warriors attacked this key Upper Lakes fort; twenty-four-year-old Henry and some of the British officers who commanded the seventy troops at the post had received hints that trouble was brewing. Henry was fortunate to have made a friend of the forty-five-year-old Ojibwe headman, Wawatam, who was drawn to the young British trader by a dream. After he was found hiding in the fort, an Ojibwe leader saved Henry's life, although, in the days after the battle, several warriors tried to kill him and the twenty other British survivors. Eventually, Wawatam let Henry join his extended family.

Years later, most of the tribes that had joined Pontiac's rebellion would fight on the side of the British against the Americans. Many of the descendants of the French-Canadians at the post eventually settled in Penetanguishene, Ontario, after Michilimackinac was ceded to the United States. Henry became a prominent fur trader, working in the Great Lakes country until 1796. That year, he settled in Montreal, where he became a wealthy merchant, and died there in 1824.

Pontiac's war fizzled out and officially ended after negotiations at Oswego, New York, in 1766. Less than three years later, Pontiac was murdered by a member of the Peoria tribe in what is now St. Louis, Missouri.

Alexander Henry

The game of bag'gat'iway, which the Indians played upon that memorable occasion, was the most exciting sport in which the red man could engage. It was played with bat and ball. The bat, so called, was about four foot in length, and an inch in diameter. It was made of the toughest material that could be found. At one end it was curved, and terminated in a sort of racket, or perhaps more properly a ring, in which a network of cord was loosely woven. The players were not allowed to touch the ball with the hand, but caught it in this network at the end of the bat. At either end of the ground a tall post was planted. These posts marked the stations of the rival parties, and were sometimes a mile apart. The object of each party was to defend its own post and carry the ball to that of the adversary....

In the heat of the contest, when all are running at their greatest speed, if one stumbles and falls, fifty or a hundred, who are in close pursuit and unable to stop, pile over him forming a mound of human bodies; and frequently players are so bruised as to be unable to proceed in the game. This game, with its attendant noise and violence, was well calculated to divert the attention of officers and men, and thus permit the Indians to take possession of the fort.

To make their success more certain, they prevailed upon as many as they could to come out of the fort, while at the same time their squaws wrapped in blankets, beneath which they concealed the murderous weapons, were placed inside the enclosure. The plot was so ingeniously laid that no one suspected danger. The discipline of the garrison was relaxed, and the soldiers permitted to stroll about and view the sport, without weapons of defense. And even when the ball, as if by chance, was lifted high in the air, to descend inside the pickets, and was followed by four hundred savages, all eager, all struggling, all shouting in the unrestrained pursuit of a rude, athletic exercise, no alarm was felt until the shrill war-whoop told the startled garrison that the slaughter had actually begun.

I did not go myself to see the match which was now to be played without the fort, because, there being a canoe prepared to depart on the following day, for Montreal, I employed myself in writing letters to my friends; and even when a fellow-trader, Mr. Tracy, happened to call upon me, saving that another canoe had just arrived from Detroit, and proposing that I should go with him to the beach, to inquire the news, it so happened that I still remained, to finish my letters, promising to follow Mr. Tracy in the course of a few minutes. Mr. Tracy had not gone more than twenty paces from my door, when I heard an Indian war-cry, and a noise of general confusion. Going instantly to my window, I saw a crowd of Indians, within the fort, furiously cutting down and scalping every Englishman they found. In particular I witnessed the fate of Lieutenant Jemette.

I had, in the room in which I was, a fowling-piece, loaded with swan-shot. This I immediately seized, and held it for a few minutes, waiting to hear the drum beat to arms. In this dreadful interval I saw several of my countrymen fall, and more than one struggling between the knees of an Indian, who, holding him in this manner, scalped him while yet living.

At length, disappointed in the hope of seeing resistance made to the enemy, and sensible of course, that no effort of my own unassisted arm could avail against four hundred Indians, I thought only of seeking shelter. Amid the slaughter which was raging, I observed many of the Canadian inhabitants of the fort calmly looking on, neither opposing the Indians nor suffering injury; and, from this circumstance, I conceived a hope of finding security in their houses.

Between the yard-door of my own house and of M. Langlade, my next neighbor, there was only a low fence, over which I easily climbed. At my entrance I found the whole family at the windows, gazing at the scene of blood before them. I addressed myself immediately to M. Langlade; begging that he would put me into some place of safety until the heat of the affair should be over, an act of charity by which he might perhaps preserve me from the general massacre; but, while I uttered my petition, M. Langlade, who had looked for a moment at me, turned again to the window, shrugging his shoulders, and intimating that he could do nothing for me….

This was a moment for despair; but the next, a Pani [Pawnee] woman, a slave of M. Langlade, beckoned me to follow her. She brought me to a door, which she opened, desiring me to enter, and telling me that it led to the garret, where I must go and conceal myself. I joyfully obeyed her directions; and she, having followed me up to the garret door, locked it after me, and with great presence of mind took away the key.

This shelter obtained, if shelter I could hope to find it, I was naturally anxious to know what might still be passing without. Through an aperture, which afforded me a view of the area of the fort, I beheld, in shapes the foulest and most terrible, the ferocious triumphs of barbarian conquerors. The dead were scalped and mangled; the dying were writhing and shrieking under the unsatiated knife and tomahawk; and from the bodies of some, ripped open, their butchers were drinking the blood, scooped up in the hollow of joined hands, and quaffed amid shouts of rage and victory. I was shaken, not only with horror, but with fear. The sufferings which I witnessed, I seemed on the point of experiencing.

No long time elapsed before, everyone being destroyed who could be found, there was a general cry of "All is finished!" At the same instant I heard some of the Indians enter the house in which I was. The garret was separated from the room below only by a layer of single boards, at once the flooring of the one and the ceiling of the other. I could therefore hear everything that passed: and the Indians no sooner came in than they inquired whether or not any Englishmen were in the house. M. Langlade replied that "he could not say"; he "did not know of any" — answers in which he did not exceed the truth, for the Pani woman had not only hidden me by stealth, but kept my secret, and her own. M. Langlade was therefore, as I presume, as far from a wish to destroy me as he was careless about saving me, when he added to these answers, that they might examine for themselves, and would soon be satisfied as to the object of their question.

Saying this, he brought them to the garret door.

The state of my mind will be imagined. Arrived at the door, some delay was occasioned by the absence of the key, and a few moments were thus allowed me in which to look around me for a hiding place. In one corner of the garret was a heap of those vessels of birch bark used in maple-sugar making, as I have recently described.

The door was unlocked, and opening, and the Indians ascending the stairs, before I had completely crept into a small opening which presented itself at one end of the heap. An instant later four Indians entered the room, all armed with tomahawks, and all besmeared with blood upon every part of their bodies.

The die appeared to be cast. I could scarcely breathe, but I thought that the throbbing of my heart occasioned a noise loud enough to betray me. The Indians walked in every direction about the garret, and one of them approached me so closely that at a particular moment, had he put forth his hand he must have touched me. Still I remained undiscovered, a circumstance to which the dark color of my clothes, and the want of light in a room which had no window, and in the corner in which I was, must have contributed.

In a word, after taking several turns in the room, during which they told M. Langlade how many they had killed, and how many scalps they had taken, they returned down stairs, and I, with sensations not to be expressed, heard the door, which was the barrier between me and my fate, locked for the second time.

There was a feather-bed on the floor, and on this, exhausted as I was by the agitation of my mind, I threw myself down and fell asleep. In this state I remained till the dark of the evening, when I was awakened by a second opening of the door. The person that now entered was M. Langlade's wife, who was much surprised at finding me, but advised me not to be uneasy, observing that the Indians had killed most of the English, but that she hoped I might myself escape. A shower of rain having begun to fall, she had come to stop a hole in the roof. On her going away, I begged her to send me a little water to drink, which she did.

As night was now advancing, I continued to lie on the bed, ruminating on my condition, but unable to discover a source from which I could hope for life. A flight to Detroit had no probable chance of success. The distance from Michilimackinac was four hundred miles; I was without provisions; and the whole length of the road lay through Indian countries, countries of an enemy in arms, where the first man whom I should meet would kill me. To stay where I was, threatened nearly the same issue. As before, fatigue of mind, and not tranquility, suspended my cares, and procured me further sleep.

Alexander Henry, Travels and Adventures in Canada and the Indian Territories Between the Years 1760 and 1776 (New York: I. Riley, 1809).

NEW ENEMIES: THE AMERICANS

THE END OF THE FRENCH REGIME DRAMATICALLY ALTERED THE relationship between the American colonists and the British. No longer faced with an enemy to the north, the Thirteen Colonies felt free to shake off the authority and the protection London. Very early in the Revolution two rebel armies struck northward. One, led by British-born Richard Montgomery, took the line of forts along the Richelieu River, then captured the town of Montreal. Leaving behind a small garrison, Montgomery led his troops to Quebec, where they joined a second army led by Benedict Arnold that had moved north over the Appalachians and down the Chaudiere River. The Americans laid siege to Quebec, expecting the local people to support their cause and surrender the city. Instead, their resistance proved a disaster to Montgomery.

Quebec became the launching ground for the disastrous Bourgoyne invasion, which the Americans crushed at Saratoga. Various acts of aggression were launched into New York State with the help of Iroquois allies, but the centre of gravity of the Revolution had shifted south of New York City by 1777.

Masses of English, German, and Native loyalist refugees moved into Canada after the Revolution. The anti-American attitudes of these loyalists, who abhorred everything to do with the Revolution and considered republican democracy a suspect and alien idea, dominated the politics of Canada for more than a century. Meanwhile, a strong lobby in the United States Congress argued that British North America was a loose end to be tied up.

The Americans took advantage of the British preoccupation with Napoleon to declare war. Unfortunately for them, their timing was off. By 1813, the Grand Armee had perished on the Russian steppes and Wellington had driven the French from Spain. The Americans quickly made peace when the British began large troop transfers to America. The War of 1812 had never caught on with the American public. What had seemed to have been an easy adventure collapsed in the face of British, Canadian, and Native resistance. The American land forces were usually defeated. American sailors were surprising successful, taking individual British warships in the Atlantic and an entire Royal Navy squadron on Lake Erie. By 1814, the arms race on the Great Lakes was being won by the British, who were building full-sized ships of the line at Kingston by the time the war ended.

The Treaty of Ghent brought an uneasy and suspicious peace. While American settlers continued to trickle into southern Ontario after the war, the ruling elite despised anything resembling the American system of government. By 1835, they could look warily at Texas, where American settlers had yanked a state out of the hands of the Mexicans and declared it an independent, democratic republic. The settlers of Upper and Lower Canada knew many people on the American side of the border saw the Canadian provinces with the same hunger.

Good journalism from the early part of this period is scarce. During the War of 1812, there were only a few papers in all of the colonies and they were small, family-run operations that could not afford to send reporters into the field, even if their owners had wanted to. All of them relied on government advertising to survive. As well, the British had control of paper supplies. And if that didn't keep them in line, peacetime seditious libel laws, coupled with martial law beginning in 1812 and full suspension of civil liberties in 1814, made any real analysis of the war impossible. During the rebellions and invasions of 1837–1838, editors not only faced the anger of authorities, but also risked being attacked by their neighbours. During this period, William Lyon Mackenzie's press was trashed in Toronto. Within a ten-year span during the rise of responsible government in Ontario, newspaper offices were wrecked in Brockville, Kingston, Belleville, and London, Ontario. To hear the rebels' side of the story of the Rebellion of 1837, people relied on newspapers smuggled into the United States and, after the return of some of the prisoners sent to Australia and Tasmania, from the magazine-like autobiographies that were issued in the 1840s.

JANUARY 1, 1775:
The Americans are Turned Back at Quebec

The brilliant thirty-eight-year-old American general Richard Montgomery attacked Quebec in the fall of 1775, almost a year before the signing of the Declaration of Independence. Montgomery gathered his forces in the late summer of 1775, moved through the Lake Champlain and Richelieu River valleys, captured several Canadian forts, and took Montreal without a fight. Montgomery hoped to score strategic and propaganda coups by seizing Quebec's 1,500 houses, which had fallen to Wolfe's forces just eighteen years before. On December 3, Montgomery was joined by Colonel Benedict Arnold's force of 700 men. They set up a camp outside the walls of Quebec, but they lacked the artillery and men to conduct a strong siege. As winter closed in, Montgomery gambled everything in a nighttime attack on New Year's Eve. The British, supported by Canadian militia, were ready. He lost his life, the battle, and the campaign. The retreat of Arnold's forces in the spring of 1776 was a major defeat of the Continental army. The writer was a member of the American forces.

JOHN J. HENRY

General Montgomery had marched at the precise time stipulated, and had arrived at his destined place of attack, nearly about the time we attacked the first barrier, he was not one that would loiter. Colonel Campbell, of the New York Troops, a large, good-looking man, who was second in command of that party, and was deemed a veteran, accompanied the army to the assault, his station was rearward, General Montgomery with his aides, were at the point of the column ... within Cape Diamond, and probably at a distance of fifty yards, there stood a block-house, which seemed to take up the space between the foot of the hill and the precipitous bank of the river, leaving a cartway or passage on each side of it....

A block-house, if well-constructed, is an admirable method of defense, which in the process of the war, to our cost, was fully experienced. In the instance now before us, it was a formidable object. It was square of perhaps forty or fifty feet. The large logs, neatly squared, were tightly bound together by dove-tail work. If not much mistaken, the lower story contained loop-holes for musketry, so narrow that those within could not be harmed from without. The upper story had four or more portholes, for cannon of a large calibre. These guns were charged with grape or canister shot, and were pointed with exactness towards the avenue at Cape Diamond.

The hero Montgomery came. The drowsy or drunken guard did not hear the sawing of the posts of the first palisade. Here, if not very erroneous, four posts were sawed and thrown aside so as to admit four men abreast. The column entered with a manly fortitude. Montgomery accompanied by his aides, McPherson and Cheeseman, advanced in front. Arriving at the second palisade, the General, with his own hands, sawed down two of the pickets, in such a manner as to admit two men abreast. These sawed pickets were close under the hill, and bit a few yards from the very point of the rock, out of view and fire of the enemy from the Blockhouse. Until our troops advanced to that point, no harm could ensue but by stones thrown from above. Even now there had been but an imperfect discovery of the advancing of an enemy, and that only by the intoxicated guard. The guard fled; the General advanced a few paces. A drunken sailor returned to his gun swearing he would not forsake it while undischarged. This fact is related from testimony of the guard on the morning of our capture, some of those sailors being our guard. Applying the match, this single discharge deprived us of our excellent commander. Colonel Campbell, appalled by the death of our

General, retreated a little way from Cape Diamond, out of the reach of the cannon of the block-house, and called a council of officers, who it was said, justified his receding from the attack.

John H. Henry, Account of Arnold's Campaign Against Quebec, and of the Hardships and Sufferings of that Band of Heroes Who Traversed the Wilderness of Maine from Cambridge to the St. Lawrence, in the Autumn of 1775 *(Albany: Joel Munsell, 1877).*

JULY 1812:
The War of 1812 Breaks Out

Congress's declaration of war reached British North America before militia leaders in upstate New York learned of it. An agent of fur trader John Jacob Astor hurried to Canada with the news, hoping to protect Astor's business interests on the north side of the border. Mackinac was a strategically-important, strong stone fort on an island in Lake Michigan, near that lake's junction with Lake Huron. General Isaac Brock sent a strong force of British troops and Native warriors to seize it from the Americans, who surrendered to Captain Robert's much stronger forces. The Americans were never able to take the fort back, despite making a serious effort in 1814. The Metis community at Mackinac later moved with the British garrison to Drummond Island, then to Penetanguishene.

THE MONTREAL HERALD

COMMENCEMENT OF HOSTILITIES.

The following are copies of Letters received from Upper Canada, containing the account of the Capture of Fort Michilimackinac

MAKINAC, 18th July, 1812.
Dear Sir — I am happy to have it in my power to announce to you, that Fort Mackana capitulated to us on the 17th inst. at 11 o'clock, A. M. — Captain Roberts at our head, with part of the 10th R. V. Battalion — Mr. Crawford had the command of the Canadians, which consisted of about

200 men; Mr. Dickson 113 Scoux Forlavoins and Winebegoes, myself about 280 men Attawas and Chippwas, part of Attawas of L'arbre Croche, had not arrived. It was a fortunate circumstance that the Fort capitulated without firing a single gun, for had they done so, I firmly believe not a soul of them would have been saved.

The Montreal Herald, *July 21, 1812.*

JULY 28, 1812:
Sir Isaac Brock Pleads for the Suspension of Civil Rights

Many of the civil rights of the people of Upper Canada were quickly swept away by the British, who used martial law to appropriate war supplies and draft local people into militia units. Still, the legislature of Upper Canada did not suspend all civil rights until 1814. In May of that year, a special court session was held in a hotel in Ancaster to try men accused of treason for aiding the Americans. One man, who was dying, pled guilty and fourteen more were convicted and condemned. Eight men were hanged afterwards. They were forced to stand on farm carts under a makeshift gallows. When the horses where led off, the carts were pulled out from under the men, who slowly strangled. To complete the ancient English penalty for treason, the corpses of the men were gutted, their entrails were burned, their remains were hacked into quarters, and their heads were chopped off and placed on display. The lands of suspected traitors and people who had fled the province were seized by the government. Terror, as well as loyalty, was used to keep the settlers of the Great Lakes country in line.

THE YORK GAZETTE

Yesterday at an early hour, His Honour ISAAC BROCK, Esquire, President, administering the Government of Upper Canada, and Major General Commanding His Majesty's Forces therein, arrived at this place from Fort George; and accompanied by a numerous suite, proceeded to the Government Buildings at 4 P. M. when he opened the present extra Session of the Legislature, and delivered the following Speech to both Houses: —

Hon. Gentlemen of the Legislative Council, and Gentlemen of the House of Assembly.

The urgency of the present crisis is the only consideration which could have induced me to call you together at a time when public as well as private duties elsewhere, demand your care and attention....

From the history and experience of our Mother Country, we learn that in times of actual invasion or internal commotion, the ordinary course of Criminal Law has been found inadequate to secure his Majesty's Government from private treachery as well as from open disaffection, and that at such times its Legislature has found it expedient to enact Laws restraining for a limited period the liberty of individuals, in many cases where it would be dangerous to expose the particulars of the charge, and although the actual invasion of the Province might justify me in the exercise of the full powers reposed in me on such an emergency, yet it will be more agreeable to me to receive the sanction of the two Houses.

A Few traitors have already joined the Enemy, have been suffered to come into the Country with impunity, and have been harboured and concealed in the interior; yet the general spirit of Loyalty which appears to pervade the Inhabitants of this Province, is such as to authorize a just expectation, that their efforts to mislead and deceive, will be unavailing. — The disaffected I am convinced, are few — to protect and defend the Loyal Inhabitants from their machinations, is an object worthy of your most serious deliberation.

The York Gazette, *July 28, 1812*

JUNE 22, 1813:
Tribute to General Brock

The British were fortunate to have a general of Isaac Brock's calibre. His surprise attack on Mackinac and brilliant psychological warfare against American General William Hull that resulted in the capture of Detroit in August 1812 were masterstrokes that crippled the American plan for the invasion of Upper Canada. It's no wonder Brock's death at the Battle of Queenston Heights left the British demoralized and depressed.

THE *QUEBEC MERCURY*

HEAD QUARTERS, KINGSTON.
Adjutant General's Office, 8th June, 1813.

Major-General Sir Isaac Brock was deprived of his valuable life at the early age of 42. He was born in Guernsey, in the month of October, 1769; was only 16 when he entered the army; and was Lieut. Col. of the 49th Regt. from the year 1797 to the period of his death. During the campaign in Holland, in 1799, he acquired considerable distinction at the head of his regiment; and was second in command of the land forces in the memorable battle of Copenhagen, under Lord Nelson. He was of tall stature, athletic, and well proportioned, and in his manners elegant and engaging.

Of this distinguished officer, the writer of this article was, from his earliest year, the bosom friend. No man can delineate his character with a more faithful hand. His portrait should be drawn by a master. Though incompetent to the task, he is yet animated by the memory of their mutual Friendship; and the tears which flow, while with a trembling pen, he strives to render justice to the departed hero, are a worthier tribute of affection to his blessed spirit, than any eulogism composed with more art, but dictated with less sincerity.

General Brock was indeed a hero — a hero, in the only true and in the most extensive sense, resembling what history or fable has represented, rather as the offspring of the imagination, than as a personage that could have real existence; so entirely was every great quality comprehended in his character; brave and undaunted, yet prudent and calculating; devoted to his Sovereign, and loving his country with romantic fondness, but gentle and persuasive to those who were impressed with less ardent feelings. Elevated to the government of Upper Canada, he reclaimed the disaffected by mildness, and fixed the wavering by argument; all hearts were conciliated; and, in the awful and trying period of invasion, the whole province displayed a spirit of zealous and even enthusiastic loyalty, that astonished those most, who had believed they knew the Canadians best.

The Quebec Mercury, *June 22, 1813.*

APRIL 27–28, 1813:
The Burning of York

These articles were published in August 1814, as British forces menaced Washington, to justify the destruction of the newly built government buildings in the American capital. The British retaliated for the burning of York by destroying public buildings like the Capitol, the presidential mansion, and other public buildings. They also dismantled the building of the city's most vocal pro-war newspaper. The raid had little effect on the outcome of treaty negotiations under way in Ghent, Belgium. The British, like the Americans at York, had no serious plans to try to hold the capital. Like most actions in the War of 1812, the attacks on both York and Washington had more propaganda value than real military consequences.

The *Kingston Gazette*

August 10, 1814

We are not surprised at the 'anxiety, bustle and alarm', created by this approach to the Capital of the United States, when the barbarian conduct of the Americans is recollected in the burning of the Houses of Legislature, Courts and Public Records, in their late occupation of York; and a private dwelling was sacrificed in the same manner, because it had once been a Government House.

August 17, 1814

They [the Americans who had captured York], it is true, entered into a formal stipulation not only that private property should be respected, but that the papers belonging to the Civil Departments of the Government should not be removed or destroyed. Yet the first object they selected for their depredations was the Printing Office. They broke and otherwise destroyed the Press; carried off or rendered useless the Types; and burned a large number of Copies of the Provincial Statutes that had been recently printed for general distribution. They then pillaged the Public Subscription Library kept at Elmsley House [the former Government House], carried away a great part of the Books, and did great injury to the house itself. And, to crown all, before they reembarked they set fire to the two houses erected for the accommodation of our Provincial Legislature and Courts of Justice … which were neat and substantial buildings, and had been erected and fitted up at an expense of several thousand pounds. These with the Offices containing all the Journals, a large collection of Books, and other appendages connected with such an establishment, were all consumed by the flames; and the bare walls remain, a monument of the Gothic ferocity and worse than the Punic faith of our enemies.

Of these exploits, no notice has been taken in the States. They are not attended to in the dispatches of General Dearborn or Commodore Chauncey; though in the latter, in order perhaps to vindicate what he is yet ashamed to avow, condescends to state in his dispatch that 'in the House of Assembly a scalp has been found appended to the Mace', a most palpable falsehood, calculated for the prejudices of the most violent and ignorant only; and which it is impossible that he or any other man of common sense could believe.

The Kingston Gazette, *August 10 and August 17, 1814.*

JUNE 21–22, 1813:
Laura Secord Warns the British at Beaver Dams

Laura Ingersoll moved with her family to Upper Canada from Massachusetts after the Revolution. There she married James Secord, a farmer and shop owner in Queenston. James Secord is conspicuously absent from history. Wounded at Queenston Heights, Secord was left on the battlefield, where Laura found him and tried to treat his injuries. When three American soldiers tried to dispatch Secord, Captain John Wool stepped in to rescue him. James Secord and John Wool became lifetime friends. Wool rose through the ranks and was a major general at the outbreak of the Civil War.

Laura Secord was vague about how she heard of the American plan to attack British forces in the interior of the Niagara Peninsula. In one account, the British commander, James FitzGibbon, says James Secord had learned of the march from an American officer. The historical record is clear that Laura Secord made her famous walk to warn the British, although some details, such as her walking with a cow, were added through the years. Secord is one of the few civilian actors in the War of 1812 who is still remembered and celebrated. Although there's some dispute on whether Secord brought the British any information of value, her story was put forward by the British commander as an example of pioneer loyalty and courage. Interestingly, the tale of Laura Secord's heroism and loyalty surfaced years after the actual event. Both gained fame in the mid-century, at a time when the province was recovering from the Rebellion of Upper Canada and nationalism was starting to stir in Canada. Since then, Secord's story has been embraced by feminists, Canadian nationalists, and people looking for Canadians to honour as heroes.

After the war, the Secords lived in poverty, and Laura's account comes from her petition for a pension. She was not recognized for her courage until 1860. FitzGibbon became the military leader of the colony and led government forces in the Toronto region during the Rebellion of Upper Canada.

LAURA SECORD

I shall commence at the battle of Queenston, where I was at the time the cannon balls were flying around me in every direction. I left the place during the engagement. After the battle I returned to Queenston, and then found that my husband had been wounded; my house plundered and property destroyed.

It was while the Americans had possession of the frontier, that I learned the plans of the American commander, and determined to put the British troops under FitzGibbon in possession of them, and, if possible, to save the British troops from capture, or, perhaps, total destruction. In doing so, I found I should have great difficulty in getting through the American guards, which were out ten miles in the country. Determined to persevere, however, I left early in the morning, walked nineteen miles in the month of June, over a rough and difficult part of the country, when I came to a field belonging to a Mr. Decamp, in the neighbourhood of the Beaver Dam.

By this time daylight had left me. Here I found all the Indians encamped; by moonlight the scene was terrifying, and to those accustomed to such scenes, might be considered grand. Upon advancing to the Indians they all rose, and, with some yells, said "Woman," which made me tremble. I cannot express the awful feeling it gave me; but I did not lose my presence of mind. I was determined to persevere.

I went up to one of the chiefs, made him understand that I had great news for Capt. FitzGibbon, and that he must let me pass to his camp, or that he and his party would all be taken. The chief at first objected to let me pass, but finally consented, after some hesitation, to go with me and accompany me to FitzGibbon's station, which was at the Beaver Dam, where I had an interview with him. I then told him what I had come for, and what I had heard — that the Americans intended to make an attack upon the troops under his command, and would, from their superior numbers, capture them all. Benefiting by this information, Capt. FitzGibbon formed his plans accordingly, and captured about five hundred American infantry, about fifty mounted dragoons, and a field-piece or two was taken from the enemy.

I returned home next day, exhausted and fatigued. I am now advanced in years, and when I look back I wonder how I could have gone through so much fatigue, with the fortitude to accomplish it.

Laura Secord, The Anglo-American Magazine, *November 1859.*

JUNE 30, 1813:
Botched Raid on Sackett's Harbor

Sackett's Harbor (now known as Sackets Harbor), on Lake Ontario just south of the border, was the main American naval base on the lake. It was just a few kilometres across the lake from the important British docks and shipyard at Kingston. James Yeo, commander of the British forces, and Isaac Chauncey, the commander of the American squadron, fought a cat-and-mouse game through the war but never had the decisive fight that both men wanted. It was nothing personal: at the end of the war Yeo went back to England through New York, and, on the way, stopped at Sackett's Harbor to have a drink with Chauncey.

THE KINGSTON GAZETTE

A daring and well-planned enterprise under the command of Commodore Sir James Yeo, for surprising the American squadron under their batteries at Sackett's Harbor, was undertaken on Wednesday last but given up in consequence of discovering that a desertion had taken place from the party to the enemy.

Our brave tars, with a small detachment of the Royal Scots and 100th regiment lay concealed in the woods within ten miles of the enemy's squadron the whole of Thursday, and the attack was to have taken place on that night.

While the party was retiring the next morning, Commodore Chauncey with his whole party got under way and stood out of Sackett's Harbor, but our brave fellows, notwithstanding that they had a distance of nearly 30 miles to row, effected their return to Kingston without difficulty or loss.

The Kingston Gazette, *July 7, 1813.*

SEPTEMBER 12, 1813:
The British are Defeated on Lake Erie

Robert Barclay was one of the great, forgotten tragic figures in Canadian history. He was just twenty-seven when he lost the Battle of Lake Erie to Oliver Hazard Perry. Through his career, Barclay proved his bravery and skill but seemed saddled with terrible luck. Barclay had seen action in minor fights through the Napoleonic Wars and served at Trafalgar. He lost an arm while leading a boarding party against a French transport in the English Channel. Sent to North America, Barclay was expected to defend the upper Great Lakes with a thrown-together collection of provincial troops, local sailors, and a handful of British tars. Barclay, knowing the Americans were gathering strength at the west end of Lake Erie, launched a pre-emptive strike. He very nearly won at Put-in-Bay, but had his victory snatched from him late in the action when the wind changed and his larger ships succumbed to superior American cannon fire. Barclay's good arm was crippled in the action. He was exonerated by a court martial but never held another command.

This drawing of the battered British and American warships that fought at Put-in-Bay shows the violence of the battle. Because these ships were built quickly of green wood, they provided very poor protection against cannon fire.

ROBERT HERIOT BARCLAY

His Majesty's late Ship Detroit
Put-in-Bay Lake Erie 12th. Septr. 1813

Sir,
The line was formed according to a given plan so that each Ship might be supported against the Superior force of the two Brigs opposed to them. About ten the Enemy had cleared the Islands, and immediately bore up under easy sail in a line abreast, each Brig being also supported by the small Vessels. At a quarter before twelve I commenced the Action by firing a few long guns. About a quarter past the American Commodore also supported by two Schooners one carrying four long twelve Pounders, the other a long thirty two and twenty four Pounder came to close Action with the Detroit, the other Brig of the Enemy apparently destined to Engage the Queen Charlotte supported in like manner by two Schooners. Kept so far to Windward as to render the Queen Charlottes 24 Pounders useless while she was with the Lady Prevost exposed to the heavy and destructive fire of the Caledonia, and four other Schooners Armed with long and heavy

Guns like those I have already described; — so soon alas was I deprived of the Services of the Noble and intrepid Captain Finnis, who soon after the commencement of the Action fell and with him fell my greatest support. — soon after Lieutenant Stokoe of the Queen Charlotte was struck senseless by a Splinter which deprived the Country of his Services at this very critical period. As I perceived the Detroit had enough to contend with without the prospect of a fresh Brig. Provincial Lieutenant Irvine, who then had charge of the Queen Charlotte behaved with great courage but his experience was much too limited to supply the place of such an Officer as Captain Finnis hence she proved of far less assistance than I expected.

The Action continued with great fury until half past two when I perceived my opponent drop astern and a Boat passing from him to the Niagara (which Vessel was at this time perfectly fresh) the American Commodore seeing that as yet the day was against him (his Vessel having struck soon after he left her) and also the very defenseless state of the Detroit which Ship was now a perfect Wreck principally from the Raking fire of the Gun Boats, and also that the Queen Charlotte was in such a situations that I could receive very little assistance from her and the Lady Prevost being at this time too far to leeward from her Rudder being injured, made a noble and alas too successful an effort to regain it, for he bore up and supported by his small Vessels passed within Pistol Shot and took a Raking position on our Bow — nor could I prevent it as the unfortunate situation of the Queen Charlotte prevented us from weaving in attempting it, we fell on board her My Gallant first Lieutenant Garland was now mortally wounded and myself so severely, that I was obliged to quit the Deck, — Manned as the Squadron was with not more than fifty British Sea-men, the rest a mixed Crew of Canadians and Soldiers, and who were totally unacquainted with such Service, rendered the loss of Officers more sensibly felt — and never in any Action was the loss more severe every Officer commanding Vessels and their seconds was either Killed or Wounded as severely as to be unable to Keep the Deck....

(Signed) R. H. Barclay
Commander & late Senr. Officer

Robert Heriot Barclay, RN, Select British Documents of the Canadian War of 1812, *William Wood ed.* (Toronto: The Champlain Society, 1920), 274–77.

SEPTEMBER 1813:
Dr. Usher Parsons Nurses the Casualties at Put-In-Bay

Dr. Usher Parsons was one of the very few physicians in Perry's fleet. After the battle, he found himself in the midst of a medical disaster. More than 150 men were wounded by bullets and cannon fire that left grotesque injuries that often required surgery. Parsons' account of the battle and its aftermath was published in October 1818.

Dr. Usher Parsons

The action terminated shortly after three o'clock and, of about one hundred men reported fit for duty in the morning, twenty-one were found dead, and sixty-three wounded. The wounded arteries occupied my first attention, all which, except where amputation was required, were rendered secure before dark. Having no assistant (the surgeon on board with me being very sick) I deemed it safer to defer amputating till morning, and in the meantime suffered the tourniquets to remain on the limbs. Nothing more was done through the night than to administer opiates and preserve shattered limbs in a uniform position. At daylight a subject was on the table for amputation of the thigh, and at eleven o'clock all amputations were finished. The impatience of this class of the wounded, to meet the operation, rendered it necessary to tale them in the same succession in which they fell. The compound and simple fractures were next attended to, then luxations, lacerations, and contusions, all which occupied my time till twelve o'clock at night.

The day following I visited the wounded of the Niagara, who had lain till that time with their wounds undressed. I found the surgeon sick in bed with hands too feeble to execute the dictates of a feeling heart. Twenty one wounded were mustered, most of whom were taken on board the Lawrence and dressed, and afterwards such as were lying in like manner on board the small vessels. In the course of the evening the sick were prescribed for, which was the first attention I had been able to render them since the action.

The whole number of wounded in the squadron was ninety-six. Of these, twenty-five were cases of compound fracture: viz: of the arm six; of the thigh, four; of the leg, eight; of the shoulder, three; of the ribs, three; and skull, one. Of simple fracture, there were four cases: viz. of the thigh, leg, arm and ribs. Grapeshot wounds, large and small were thirty-seven. There were two cases of concussion of the brain; three of the chest, and two of the pelvis. The contusions, large and small, were ten, and sprains, six.

Of the whole number, three died; viz: midshipman Claxton with compound fractures of the shoulder, in which a part of the clavicle, scapula, and humerus was carried away; a seaman with a mortification of the lower extremity, in which there had been a compound fracture, and another with a fracture of the skull, where a part of the cerebral substance was destroyed.

The compound fractures of the extremities were much retarded in their cure, by the frequent displacement of the bones, by the motion of the ship in rough weather, or by some other unlucky disturbance of the limb. In this way the bones in one case did not unite, until after forty days had elapsed, and in two or three other cases, not till after twenty-five days. The delay of amputations already mentioned had no effect on the success of the operations. Every case did well.

There were not more than two very singular wounds, or such as would be unlikely to occur in any sea engagement. In one of these cases a grapeshot four times as large as a musket ball, passed under the pyramidal muscle, without injuring the peritoneum. In the other, a canister shot twice the size of a musket ball entered the eye, and on the fifth or sixth day was detected at the inside angle of the lower jaw and cut out. In its passage it must have fractured the orbitar sphenoid bone, and passing under the temporal arch, inside the coronal process of the lower jaw, must have done great injury to the temporal muscle, and other soft parts, lying in its way.

The recovery of so great a proportion of the wounded may in a great measure be attributed to the following causes: First to the purity of the air. The patients were ranged along the upper deck, with no other shelter from the weather than a high awning to shade them. They continued in this situation for a fortnight, and when taken on shore, were placed in very spacious apartments, well ventilated. Secondly, to the supply of food best adapted to their cases, as fowls, fresh meat, milk, eggs and vegetables in abundance. The second day after the action, the farmers on the Ohio shore brought alongside every article of the above description, that could be desired. Thirdly, to the happy state of mind which victory occasioned.

Usher Parsons, The New England Journal of Medicine, October 1818.

OCTOBER 9, 1813:
Kingston Braces for Attack

The town of Kingston was a natural target for the Americans, but they never launched a serious effort to take it. Alarms were common through the war, and even after peace was made, there were fears of another American attack. The fear and rage lasted more than a generation. When the next invasion finally happened, at Prescott in 1838, the people of Kingston reacted with violence against the hapless members of the Hunters' Lodges that were brought to Fort Henry as prisoners. Lingering tension in the region accounts for Kingston's failure to be named capital of the country. It was passed over for Ottawa, 195 kilometres inland.

THE *KINGSTON GAZETTE*

By all accounts we understand that the Americans are on the eve of attacking this place. It is our province to observe that their intentions have been completely anticipated and every necessary preparation has been made to give them a warm reception.

We are happy to announce the arrival of Lt. Col. Drummond with the first detachment of the 104th Regiment from Burlington Heights. This Regiment with the 49th and the corps of Voltigeurs may be expected here in the course of to-day or to-morrow. These three gallant Regiments together with our brave Militia who have already assembled in considerable numbers will be a sufficient reinforcement and with our present respectable garrison will be able to repel any force which the enemy may be able to bring against us.

We are glad to observe that every piece of artillery is most advantageously posted and we must really congratulate our fellow citizens on the formidable appearance of every defensible position in the vicinity of this town.

The Kingston Gazette, *October 9, 1813.*

OCTOBER 26, 1813:
Canadian Militia Repulses the Americans at Châteauguay

The young Charles de Salaberry, scion of Quebec's old nobility, led about 200 Canadian volunteer troops against an American invasion force that was about eight times as strong. The Canadians used a clever mixture of skill and trickery against U.S. General Wade Hampton and his men, who were marching along the Châteauguay River toward La Prairie, Quebec, on the south shore of the St. Lawrence River. The Canadians felled trees to block the Americans' path (a tactic used by the Continental army against John Bourgoyne's British army in the lead-up to the Battle of Saratoga in 1777), and de Salaberry posted buglers through the dense forest. Their calls convinced the Americans that the Canadian force was far larger than its true size. The ensuing battle was relatively bloodless, with just five Canadians and twenty-three Americans confirmed killed. The low casualties mask the battle's strategic importance. At Châteauguay, de Salaberry's loggers and buglers saved Montreal. The second prong of the American invasion was blunted at Crysler's Farm on November 11, with more loss of life. The Americans' fall 1813 campaign, ineptly led and badly supplied, collapsed. Better U.S. commanders could easily have overcome the setbacks.

CHARLES-MICHEL DE SALABERRY

My dear Father,

The 26th has been a glorious day for me and those of my troops engaged. The American army commanded by Gen'l Hampton and another general has been repulsed by a little band — all Canadians — and yesterday that army commenced its retreat, or will endeavor to get into this country through some other road. The enemy's force consisted of all his troops, about 7,000 men and 5 pieces of cannon, 300 cavalry. The action lasted four hours, and it ended in the enemy being obliged to return to his former position five miles back, leaving many of his dead and wounded behind and a great number of his men scattered in the woods, also many drums, 150 firelocks and baggage.

The number of my men engaged did not exceed three hundred. The rest were in reserve in the lines I had constructed. Our killed and wounded were only 24 including officers, there were none but Canadians amongst us. I was in the first line during the whole of the action and afterwards, with a small reserve, beat off a large body of Americans and saved Capt. Daily and his company. I chose my own ground and after the action pushed in my pickets two miles in advance of where they were before. Without arrogating to myself too much credit, I am proud to think that this defence, on our part, has at least prevented the American army from penetrating to La Prairie. We are here situated about 35 miles from Montreal. This is certainly a most extraordinary affair. Chevalier and all officers in this action conducted themselves with great bravery. The prisoners have been about 25. We are all very much harassed and I am not well.

I remain in haste, my dear Father, Yours faithfully,
Ch. de Salaberry

Charles-Michel de Salaberry, "Letter from Charles-Michel de Salaberry to his Father a Few Days After the Battle," Parks Canada, www.pc.gc.ca/lhn-nhs/qc/chateauguay/natcul/natcul1/natcul1e.aspx.

NOVEMBER 11, 1813:
News from Crysler's Farm

The British expected an attack on Kingston, not a march on southern Quebec, so the Americans had the element of surprise when troops based at Sackett's Harbor set out for Montreal near the end of the campaign season of 1813. American troops crossed the St. Lawrence River near the modern Ogdensburg-Prescott bridge and headed downriver toward Montreal, harassed by militia. At Crysler's Farm, near Morrisburg, British troops mauled the Americans. The U.S. forces were led by James Wilkinson, one of the most overrated and inept American generals. Both Wilkinson and his second-in-command, Morgan Lewis, were "indisposed" during the battle, leaving command to Brigadier-General John Parker Boyd.

Despite losing at Crysler's Farm, American troops chased off the Glengarry militia and Wilkinson's force reassembled, relatively intact, on the American side of the river. The Americans continued down the river toward Montreal, but Wilkinson used the excuse of a shortage of supplies to call off the campaign. Another American force, heading to Montreal from the south, was defeated at Châteauguay. It took the *Kingston Gazette* several days to get a definitive account of the Battle of Crysler's Farm. Although the battle happened fairly close to Kingston, no journalists were travelling with the British forces.

THE *KINGSTON GAZETTE*

We are assured on good authority that the loss of the enemy in the late action at Williamsburg exceeded 1000 in killed, wounded, prisoners and deserters. Their flight was precipitate during the remainder of the day and night after the action; on the morning of the 12th they regained their own shore in the greatest confusion and in momentary expectation of being attacked. Several officers of distinction were killed or wounded, Major-General Covender [actually Brigadier-General Leonard Covington] was dangerously wounded and is since dead; Lt.-Col. Preston, noted for his ridiculous and insulting proclamation at Fort Erie inviting the inhabitants of Upper Canada to place themselves under his protection, was dangerously wounded. One six-pounder field piece was taken on the charge and about 120 prisoners — 350 or 400 stand of arms were collected on or near the field of action.

The militia of Cornwall and the neighbouring townships have come forward in the most spirited and loyal manner and are daily joining the troops, showing a spirit worthy of their ancestors and setting a noble example for their countrymen. We sincerely hope it will be followed and if the inhabitants of Upper Canada are true to themselves they can have no reason to fear all the efforts of the enemy.

The Kingston Gazette, *November 13, 1813*

JULY 25, 1814:
The Battle of Lundy's Lane

The Battle of Lundy's Lane was a bloody engagement of little strategic value, other than to demonstrate the professional calibre of the American army. The battle, fought near Niagara Falls, raged through the day and into the night, with some artillery pieces being the focus of attacks and counter attacks. The battle was one of the bloodiest fought on Canadian soil, with eighty-four British dead and about 550 wounded. American losses were 174 dead and nearly 600 wounded. American troops were back across the Niagara River by the end of the summer. When news of peace arrived the following spring, British and American forces were back where they started in the summer of 1812.

THE MONTREAL HERALD

The enemy on the 27th had retired across the Chippewa towards Fort Erie, pursued by the Militia and Indians, having previously burnt Street's Mills, and destroyed the bridge over that river.

Reinforcements were rapidly advancing on the Right Division: and the left wing of De Watteville's Regiment would join it about the 28th.

Extract of a letter from a gentleman of respectability, dated Kingston, July 30, 1814:

Intelligence has just arrived of another action on the Niagara Frontier … Gen. Drummond, immediately on the arrival of the 89th, attacked the Americans in two Divisions, at Lundy's Lane, about 3 miles below Chippaway … the attack from the Fort George side completely succeeded; and capturing every article of camp equipage that that part of the American army possessed. The attack from the Chippawa side was only partially successful, as the enemy succeeded in cutting their way through. They captured 3 of our field-pieces, which were however retaken, and two of theirs. They retreated to Fort Erie; and as every one of their boats are taken, unless their Erie fleet should come to assist them, they cannot escape. Gen. Drummond sent the four vessels immediately to York for reinforcements; where, fortunately, 600 of De Wattevilles had just arrived and were instantly embarked ... On their joining, it is intended to attack the enemy again.

Our loss was very severe, but I hope much exaggerated. Gen. Drummond slightly wounded in the neck; Gen. Riall lost an arm and prisoner; colonels Morrison and Robertson wounded; and I was told Lieut. Moorsom of the 104th killed; the 89th dreadfully cut up; the Light Company 41st annihilated.

The Montreal Herald, *August 7, 1814.*

JULY 25, 1814:
Surgeon William Dunlop Tends to the Wounded at Lundy's Lane

William "Tiger" Dunlop was a twenty-one-year-old assistant surgeon with the 89th British Foot. After the battle of Lundy's Lane, Dunlop was the only doctor available to help the hundreds of wounded. Like Dr. Usher Parsons at Put-in-Bay, Dunlop had to deal with a medical catastrophe: men suffering massive gunshot and artillery wounds, crushed skulls, broken bones, puncture wounds to the chest and gut, and deep lacerations. Dunlop later went on to survey the Penetanguishene Road to link York to Georgian Bay, and returned to Canada a few years after the war to become an important member of the provincial parliament. Dunlop's work at Lundy's Lane disabused him of any romantic ideas about the glories of war:

WILLIAM "TIGER" DUNLOP

There is hardly on the face of the earth a less enviable situation that that of an Army Surgeon after a battle — worn out and fatigued in body and mind, surrounded by suffering, pain and misery, much of which he knows it is not in his power to heal or even to assuage. While the battle lasts these all pass unnoticed, but they come before the medical man afterwards in all their sorrow and horror, stripped of all the excitement of the 'heady fight.'

It would be a useful lesson to cold-blooded politicians, who calculate on a war costing so many lives and so many limbs as they would calculate on a horse costing so many pounds — or to the thoughtless at home, whom the excitement of a gazette, or the glare of an illumination, more than reconciles to the expense of a war — to witness such a scene, if only for one hour.

This simple and obvious truth was suggested to my mind by the exclamation of a poor woman. I had two hundred and twenty wounded turned in upon me that morning, and among others an American farmer, who had been on the field either as a militia man or a camp follower. He was nearly sixty years of age, but of a most Herculean frame. One ball had shattered his thigh bone, and another lodged in his body, the last obviously mortal. His wife, a respectable elderly looking woman, came over under a flag of truce, and immediately repaired to the hospital, where she found her husband lying on a truss of straw, writhing in agony, for his sufferings were dreadful.

Such an accumulation of misery seemed to have stunned her, for she ceased wailing, sat down on the ground, and taking her husband's head on her lap, continued long, moaning and sobbing, while the tears flowed fast down her face; she seemed for a considerable time in a state of stupor, till awakened by a groan from her unfortunate husband, she clasped her hands, and looking wildly around, exclaimed, "O that the King and the President were both here this moment to see the misery their quarrels lead to — they surely would never go to war without a cause that they could give as a reason to God at the last day, for thus destroying the creatures that He hath made in his own image."

In half an hour the poor fellow ceased to suffer.

William "Tiger" Dunlop, Recollections of the American War, 1812–14 *(Toronto: Historical Publishing Company, 1905).*

SEPTEMBER 11, 1814:
The Battle of Plattsburg

In the late summer of 1814, British troops marched southward through the Richelieu River Valley to Lake Champlain. British naval

The Battle of Plattsburgh was a major failure for the British, who outnumbered American defenders of the Lake Champlain border region.

and military forces converged at the north end of the lake. The British had 10,000 regular troops — a huge army by War of 1812 standards — against a force of about 3,500 American regulars and militia. The British commander, George Prevost, was timid and inept. Rather than coordinate his marine and land forces, Prevost fought two separate battles, both of which he lost. On land, Prevost's troops suffered 104 killed and about 140 wounded. A force his size should have easily absorbed these losses. Prevost, however, was demoralized by the decisive simultaneous American naval victory and withdrew his forces back to the safety of Montreal. Prevost's blundering campaign and abject failure ensured the Americans would retain control of Lake Champlain in the Treaty of Ghent. The *Montreal Herald* tried to downplay the British naval loss, but could not hide its distress and dismay at the failure of the land assault. Prevost received criticism from the press, but it was the shock and disgust of his military colleagues that ended his career.

THE MONTREAL HERALD

Shortly after the action commenced, our batteries were opened upon the enemy's forts and works, and our troops were preparing to assault them, when in consequence of the disastrous result of the naval contest, it was deemed expedient to recall the storming parting then advancing.

The object of the expedition having been completely frustrated by the loss of the fleet, the possession of the enemy's forts and works, were not considered of sufficient importance to compensate for the valuable lives of the many brave men which must have been sacrificed to obtain them, particularly as the position could not have been maintained even if we had gained possession of it. Our fleet was not fired upon during any part of the action from the enemy's batteries. The only one from where it was supposed the squadron could have been annoyed, was a battery constructed by the enemy upon the beach, from which they were driven without a shot having been fired from it, immediately after the fire of our batteries had opened.

Our whole loss in the action is estimated at about 170 in killed and wounded; that of the enemy is nearly as great. — The enemy's ship was much damaged both in her hull and rigging, and her side first opposed to the *Confiance* nearly disabled. Our army retired from Plattsburgh on the 12th to Champlain, where part of it is now posted and the remainder immediately upon our own frontier.

The brave and lamented Captain Downie, in the *Confiance*, led our small flotilla into battle in a gallant style, and as far as talents, the valor of British tars, and enthusiastic devotion to their country, could command victory, the most successful event one reasonably expected. That noble officer fell in his country's cause, the second shot, but his place was ably filled by his Lieutenant, who continued the engagement with unabated vigor, and was in the act of laying alongside the largest ship of the enemy, when the leader of the *Confiance* was unshipped by a shot from the enemy. The *Linnet*, a small brig, which with the *Confiance* was the only vessel of any size in our flotilla, went ashore; in this state laying like a log on the water, the *Confiance* maintained the unequal contest with the whole flotilla of the enemy, in which were four vessels of large size.

The Montreal Herald, *September 17, 1814.*

THE REBELLIONS AND INVASIONS OF 1837–1838

THE ORIGINS OF THIS REBELLION ARE VERY COMPLICATED. BY 1837, MANY of the settlers of Upper Canada were American-born or second-generation Canadians. While many of them had opposed the American Revolution, they still expected a fair amount of self-rule. The colony was controlled by an English elite that kept a tight grip on patronage and land sales. There was blatant discrimination against Scottish and Irish newcomers who were not members of the Church of England. Several of the colonial administrators sent from London shared the reactionary views of the Toronto-based elite.

Some politicians, including Dr. Robert Baldwin, worked to reform the situation from within. Others, especially William Lyon Mackenzie, used disruptive political tactics, nasty press attacks, and, eventually, armed resistance to bring the government down. Farmers living north of Toronto and in the Brantford area supplied the manpower for the rebel forces in the first months of the campaign, but by 1837 the rebellion entered a second, more bloody phase.

American speculators and agitators in border cities organized "Hunters' Lodges" — semi-secret societies organized on military lines. With the recent grab of Texas by U.S. settlers in Mexico as their inspiration, they sought to invade Canada, defeat the British, establish a democratic, republican government, and divide the farmland of the colony among themselves. Their officers expected to be rewarded with huge tracts of land.

The first part of the rebellion is fairly well-known to Canadian history students. Mackenzie marched his men down Yonge Street in December 1837. Near Yonge and Bloor Streets, Mackenzie's men broke and fled after a very short exchange of fire with the loyal local militia. Mackenzie fled to the United States and a few of his senior commanders were hanged or sent to penal colonies overseas.

Then the rebellion entered its second phase. Hunters' Lodge fighters teamed up with local malcontents to fight a short campaign in the Niagara Peninsula in 1838. At the same time, government forces set out to destroy Mackenzie's little republic on Navy Island in the Niagara River. Farther east, Hunters' Lodge members teamed up with Bill Johnson, the pirate of the Thousand Islands, and launched attacks along the St. Lawrence River, culminating in the Battle of the Windmill, a sort of mini-Alamo near Prescott, Ontario. Then, at the end of 1838, more Hunters' Lodge fighters tried to invade across the Detroit River and Lake Erie, fighting battles on Pelee Island and near Wallaceburg. This phase of the rebellion was far bloodier than the domestic insurrection. Hunters' Lodge leaders were hanged at Niagara and Fort Henry and many of their subordinates were deported to the brutal penal colonies in Australia and Tasmania.

In Lower Canada (modern Quebec), the divisions were mainly on religious and linguistic lines. French-speaking dissidents joined with Roman Catholics and "nonconformist" Protestant Anglophones to fight the British colonial regime in a series of bloody confrontations along the St. Lawrence, Richelieu, and Ottawa Rivers in the Montreal area. The British authorities used scorched earth tactics on the local population, burning farms, churches, and entire villages and plundering livestock. The rebels were badly defeated at the Battle of St. Eustache at the end of 1837, but violence flared up again the following autumn.

The newspapers of the time made no secret of their bias. The pro-rebel press in the Canadian colonies was shut down and sometimes looted as soon as the rebels took to the battlefield, so most of the coverage of their side of the fighting was published in American newspapers and in books printed in the United States in the months and years after the fighting. The Canadian newspapers carried accounts of the fighting that were, essentially, handouts from the British political and military authorities. During the rebellions and invasions of 1837–1838, editors not only faced the anger of authorities, but also risked being attacked by their neighbours. Before the rebellion, William Lyon Mackenzie's press was trashed in Toronto. Within a ten-year span during the rise of responsible government in Ontario, newspaper offices were wrecked in Brockville, Kingston, Belleville, and London, Ontario. To learn the rebels' side of the story of the Rebellion of 1837, people relied on newspapers smuggled into the United States and, after the return of some of the prisoners sent to Australia and Tasmania, from the magazine-like autobiographies that were issued in the 1840s.

Within a decade of the end of the fighting, Canada — the now united provinces of Upper and Lower Canada — had an elected government that instituted many of the reforms demanded by the Canadian rebels of 1837. The leaders of the rebellion were pardoned and allowed to return to the colony, although none of them held important posts in the new parliamentary regime.

DECEMBER 1837:
William Lyon Mackenzie Fails to Take Toronto

Mackenzie was a political gadfly who garnered political support from "late loyalist" immigrants from the United States, fellow Scots, newly arrived Irish settlers, and other people who felt alienated from the English-Anglican ruling class of Upper Canada. The people of the colony were not happy with the political administration and the oligarchy that controlled patronage and land sales. Sir Francis Bond Head, the governor, was a successful author of travel books but was a poor administrator who had managed to annoy and alienate many of the people of Upper Canada. Most, however, did not believe Mackenzie was the man to lead them to democracy and independence. Many feared Canada would become another Texas: independent for a short time, then swallowed by the United States.

William Lyon Mackenzie

The presses under my control sent forth nearly 3000 copies of a periodical filled with reasons for revolt, and about the third week in November it was determined that on Thursday the 7th of December, our forces should secretly assemble at Montgomery's Hotel, three miles back of Toronto, between six and ten at night, and proceed from thence to the city, join our friends there, seize 4000 stand of arms, which had been placed by Sir Francis [Bond Head, the colony's governor] in the city-hall, take him into custody, with his chief advisers, place the garrison in the hands of the liberals, declare the Province free, call a convention together to frame a suitable constitution, and meantime appoint our friend Dr. Rolph, provincial administrator of the government. We expected to do all this without shedding blood, well knowing that the vice regal government was too unpopular to have many real adherents....

Next day (Tuesday) we increased in number to 800, of whom very many had no arms, others had rifles, old fowling pieces, Indian guns, pikes, &c. Vast numbers came and went off again, when they found we had neither musquets or bayonets. Had they possessed my feelings in favour of freedom, they would have stood by us even if armed but with pitch forks and broom handles.

About noon we obtained correct intelligence that with all his exertions, and including the college boys, Sir Francis could hardly raise 150 supporters in town and country; and by 1 p.m. a flag of truce reached our camp near the city, the Messengers being the Honorables Messrs. Rolph and Baldwin, deputed by Sir Francis to ask what would satisfy us. I replied, "Independence;" but sent a verbal message that we had no confidence in Sir F's word, he would have to send his messages in writing, and within one hour. I then turned round to Colonel Lount and advised him to march the men under his command at once into the city, and take a position near the Lawyer's Hall, and rode westward to Col. Baldwin's where the bulk of the rebels were, and advised an instant march to Toronto. We had advanced as far as the College Avenue, when another flag of truce arrived, by the same messengers, with a message from Sir F. declining to comply with our previous request. We were proceeding to town, when orders from the executive arrived that we should not then go to Toronto, but wait till 6 o'clock in the evening and then take the city.

True to the principle on which the compact was made for our rising, the order was obeyed, and at a quarter to six the whole of our forces were near the toll bar, on Yonge-street, on our way to the city. I told them that I was certain there could be no difficulty in taking Toronto; that both in town and country the people had stood aloof from Sir Francis; that not 150 men and boys could be got to defend him; that he was alarmed, and had got his family on board a steamer, that 600 reformers were ready waiting to join us in the city, and that all we had to do was to be firm, and with the city would at once go down every vestige of foreign government in U[pper] C[anada].

It was dark, and there might be an ambush of some sort, I therefore told six rifle men to go ahead of us a quarter of a mile on the one side of the street, inside the fences, and as many more on the other side, and to fire in the direction in which they might see any of our opponents stationed. When, within half a mile of the town, we took prisoners the Captain of their Artillery, a Lawyer and the Sheriff's horse. Our riflemen ahead saw some 20 or 30 of the enemy in the road and fired at them, the 20 or 30, or some of them, fired at us, and instantly took to their heels and ran towards the town. — Our riflemen were in front, after them the pikemen, then those who had old guns of various kinds, and lastly those who carried only clubs and walking sticks. Colonel Lount was at the head of the riflemen, and he and those in the front rank fired, and instead of stepping to one side to make room for those behind to fire, fell flat on their faces, the next rank fired and did the same thing. I was rather in front when the firing begun, and stood in more danger from the rifles of my friends than the musquets of my enemies. I stepped to the side of the road and bade them stop firing, and it appeared to me that one of our people who was killed was shot in this way by our own men. Certainly it was not by the enemy.

William Lyon Mackenzie, The Jeffersonian Newspaper *(Watertown, NY). Reprinted in John Mercier McMullen,* The History of Canada: From its First Discovery to the Present Time *(Brockville, Canada West: J. M'Mullen Publisher, 1855).*

DECEMBER 14, 1837:
The Rebellion of Lower Canada is Crushed at St. Eustache

This account is a fairly accurate description of the Battle of St. Eustache. The destruction of the town left dozens of innocent people homeless at the beginning of a tough winter. It is doubtful that the rebel commander, Dr. Jean-Olivier Chenier, was deliberately "quartered" — hacked into four pieces — by the British. His mutilated body was, however, placed on display for several days. Years later, the Front de libération du Québec (FLQ) would name their Chenier Cell after the Patriote commander. *The Caroline Almanac and Freeman's Chronicle* was a rebel magazine published in the United States. Its writers advocated the annexation of Upper Canada by the United States.

THE CAROLINE ALMANAC AND FREEMAN'S CHRONICLE

This beautiful village is 21 miles north of Montreal, on an arm of the Ottawa, on the high banks of the river. It was attacked by Sir John Colborne this day at noon, with 200 cavalry, a large train of artillery, several regiments of European soldiers and Canadian soldiers and a portable gallows to hang the leaders who might be taken in arms. Sir John's army was 2,250 strong, and St. Eustache was single out for vengeance because its people had protected from arrest some of the honest members of the Assembly whom the government wished to destroy. The Canadians, as at St. Dennis, were some 300 persons, badly armed and so scarce of balls that some of them fired off marbles.

They were manly, and took possession of several buildings for defence. Dr. Chenier and 60 more threw themselves into the church, a very massive building, in a very commanding situation, and flanked by two long stone houses. The enemy surrounded the village and cut off all retreat.

The clergyman's house was first burnt, having been fired with Congreve rockets, and the people who retreated to the cellars of the convent were either burnt or stifled to death — the soldiers next surrounded the church, under the cover of the smoke, and two of the officers of the royals set fire to it, leaving the wounded to perish in the flames; others leaped from the windows and were met with volleys of musketry.

Dr. Chenier and a few men leapt through a window into the graveyard, where they fought with all the desperation of a forlorn hope. A ball soon brought their leader down, but he rallied his sinking strength, rose and discharged his gun at the enemy — twice again he was brought to the ground, and twice again he rose to the attack. The fourth time HE FELL TO RISE NO MORE.

Chenier's fall was the signal for the indiscriminate slaughter of the remainder of his brave band. "NO QUARTER" was the cry, and with few exceptions all were massacred. Some few made for the ice, in the hope of gaining the opposite woods. One by one they were picked off by the marksmen posted at certain distances, and the stragglers fell and perished midst the bleak wintry snows of Canada.

After four and a half hours' fighting, Sir John obtained possession of the village — many lay dead and wounded; the stench from the burning bodies was very offensive; the village was given over to be pillaged, property was plundered, women were violated and seventy of the best houses in town and country were burned to the ground. The gallant Dr. Chenier's mutilated body was exposed — his clothing stripped from his yet warm limbs — the body was cut into four quarters, and his heart was torn from his body and exposed to the gaze of the barbarous soldiers. His property was destroyed; even his beautiful and accomplished wife had to fly for her life. Night closed upon England's sacking of St. Eustache, and the whole country round seemed one sheet of flame, in the midst of the horrors of a Canadian winter.

The Caroline Almanac and Freeman's Chronicle, 1840 (Rochester, NY: Mackenzie's Gazette Press, 1840).

DECEMBER 17, 1837:
The British Accused of Paying for Rebel Scalps

Those Native people who took sides in the Canadian rebellions invariably allied themselves with the British authorities. They took an active part in the fighting on the south shore of the St. Lawrence River near their settlement at Caugnawaga. Having seen the American treatment of Native people, the Iroquois, Ojibwe, and Mississauga people living along the lower Great

Lakes and St. Lawrence River felt they had a better future under British rule. This report of Native atrocities and British use of aboriginal scalp hunters in the suppression of Dunscombe's Rebellion in the Brantford area in Upper Canada is unique and may have been crafted for an American audience. War of 1812 hero Colonel Allan McNab did march a large force along the northeast shore of Lake Erie, trying to find Dr. Dunscombe and his supporters, but by the time he arrived in Haldimand and Norfolk counties Dunscombe's forces had melted away. McNab, frustrated by the lack of action, had to satisfy himself with collecting stragglers and burning some buildings owned by rebels. McNab later went on to be an important political leader in Ontario and his children married into the English gentry. He is an ancestor of Camilla, Duchess of Cornwall.

THE ROCHESTER DEMOCRAT

To the eternal disgrace of British chivalry be it spoken, the Indians were sent out at Scotland [Ontario], against the unresisting radicals, like blood-hounds, to hunt them from the forests — murdering and scalping unarmed men. On my return to that place, two men were found in the same wood through which I had passed, with withes about their necks, hanging to small saplings, which had evidently had been bent down for that purpose and sprung with them into the air. This circumstance I related to a retired navy officer who was amongst them, and who spoke exultantly of the event, and boasted that he had offered one of the chiefs a dollar apiece for the scalp of every damned rebel he would bring in.

Colin Read and Ronald J. Stagg, The Rebellion of 1837 in Upper Canada: A Collection of Documents *(Toronto: Champlain Society, 1985).*

DECEMBER 26, 1837:
Dundas Is a Nest of Traitors

Hamilton and the communities around it have always had a measure of rivalry. The *Hamilton Gazette* probably did not win any subscribers in Dundas with its attack on the patriotism of its citizens. In 1837 Upper

Canada was more divided on ethnic and class lines than geographic ones. There were, however, rebel hotspots: the farm country outside Toronto (from what is now Bloor Street north to Holland Landing); southern Simcoe County; the Brantford area; and in extreme southwestern Ontario. Government strength lay in Toronto and in old Loyalist communities along Lake Ontario, the Niagara Peninsula, and the St. Lawrence River. In those parts of the country, the War of 1812 was still strong in public memory and there was little trust in the Americans living across the water. Fears the Americans would use the unstable political situation for their own profit turned out to be well-founded.

THE ROCHESTER DEMOCRAT

The whole population of Hamilton were under arms — Ancaster, with a population somewhat less than 500, turned out 170 men! Whilst Dundas, with a population exceeding 1,000, turned out but NINE!!!

… In fine, this pestilent swamp, true index of the character of its population, is a foul blot on the fair fame of Upper Canada. Many of its merchants, brewers, wharfingers, canal-men, upholsterers, masons and *others* are steeped to their very chins in sedition.

Colin Read and Ronald J. Stagg, The Rebellion of 1837 in Upper Canada: A Collection of Documents *(Toronto: Champlain Society, 1985).*

DECEMBER 27, 1837:
The Burning of the *Caroline*

The *Caroline* was an American-flagged steamboat that supplied Mackenzie's little republic on Navy Island, on the Canadian side of the border in the Niagara River. Just after Christmas 1837, Canadian loyalists crossed into the United States, attacked the ship, and burned it. The destruction of the *Caroline* caused friction between American and colonial authorities and was used by Mackenzie and the Hunters' Lodges in anti-British propaganda.

THE CAROLINE ALMANAC AND FREEMAN'S CHRONICLE

At 5 in the evening the *Caroline* was moored at the wharf — the tavern being very full, a number of the gentlemen took beds in the boat — in all, about 33 people slept there. A watch was placed on the deck at 8, the watchman unarmed — there was only one pocket pistol on board, and no powder; at midnight, the *Caroline* was attacked by five boats full of armed men from the English army at Chippewa, who killed (as themselves say) six men, or as the American account has it, eleven. A number were severely wounded, as the people in the American port could make no resistance.

To kill them was therefore a wanton assassination. The cry of the assailants was "G-d d — n them — no quarter — fire, fire!" Amos Durfee of Buffalo was found dead upon the dock, a musket ball having passed through his head. The *Caroline* sailed under the American flag, which the assailants took to Toronto and displayed at annual festivals in honor of this outrage. She was set ablaze, cut adrift and sent over the falls of Niagara.

We witnessed the dreadful scene from Navy Island. The thrilling cry went around that there were living souls on board; and as the vessel, wrapped in vivid flames, which disclosed her doom as it shone brightly on the water, was hurrying down the resistless rapids to the tremendous Cataract, the thunder of which, most awfully distinct in the midnight stillness, horrified every mind with the presence of their inevitable fate; numbers caught, in fancy, the wails of dying wretches, hopelessly perishing by the double horrors of a fate which nothing could avert; and watched with agonizing attention the flaming mass, till it was hurried over the falls to be crushed in everlasting darkness in the unfathomed waters below.

Several Canadians who left the island in the *Caroline* that evening, to return the next day, have not since been heard of, and doubtless were among the murdered or hid on board and perished with the ill-fated vessel.

Why did the English pass Navy Island, in Canada, where the Patriots had hoisted their flag, and waited for them and attack an unarmed boat in N.Y. State and in the dead of night, butcher them in cold blood? Sir Francis Head planned, ordered and sanctioned the whole massacre, the Queen of England and her government approved it, and rewarded the villains.

The Caroline Almanac and Freeman's Chronicle, 1840 *(Rochester, NY: Mackenzie's Gazette Press, 1840).*

APRIL 12, 1838:
Rebel Commanders Lount and Matthews Hang at Toronto

Lount and Matthews, two of Mackenzie's closest lieutenants, were hanged as a lesson to anyone who took up arms against the colonial regime. The executions, however, made the men martyrs and spurred more violence along the border. The day before the executions, Upper Canada Chief Justice John Beverley Robinson sentenced rebels John Anderson, Ralph Morden, Dr. Theller, and John Montgomery to be hanged, drawn, and quartered. Weeks later, all four men "escaped," three from Fort Henry in Kingston and one from jail in Quebec. The government preferred to let the condemned men flee to the United States than to enrage the population with wholesale executions that might generate support for the rebel cause.

THE CAROLINE ALMANAC AND FREEMAN'S CHRONICLE

The spectacle of LOUNT after the execution was the most shocking sight that can be imagined. He was covered over with his blood; the head being nearly severed from his body owing to the depth of the fall. More horrible to relate, when he was cut down, two ruffians seized the end of the mangled rope and dragged the corpse along the ground into the jail yard, someone exclaiming, "this is the way every d—d rebel deserves to be used."

Their families are impoverished. Mrs. Lount is in Michigan …

Mrs. Lount was, for two months, prevented from even seeing her husband, by the monster Head. When she was allowed to enter his dungeon (his son writes that) "his eyes were settled in their sockets, his face was pale as paper, he was worn down to the form of a living skeleton, and bound in heavy chains. My poor father had travelled hundreds of miles through forests, rivers, swamps and desolate places, by night and by day, and at last while attempting to cross Lake Erie, and once more in sight of his native shore, where freedom loves to dwell, he was driven back upon the Canada inhospitable coast, surrounded by a horde of negroes and Queen's volunteers, carried before their magistrates, and about to be examined as a salt smuggler, when he would have got clear off. But Sam Jarvis [the Toronto sheriff] came in, cried out that it was the rebel LOUNT, and ordered his close detention."

Mr. Charles Durand, then under sentence of death, gives the following account of the last days of these glorious martyrs: — "Matthews always bore up in spirits well. He was, until death, firm in his opinion of the justice of the cause he had espoused. He never recanted. He was ironed and kept in the darkest cell in the prison like a murderer. He slept sometimes in blankets that were wet and frozen. He had nothing to cheer him but the approbation of his companions and his conscience. Lount was ironed, tho' kept in a better room. He was in good spirits. He used to tell us often, in writing, not to be downcast, that he believed 'Canada would yet be free,' that we were 'contending in a good cause.' He said he was not sorry for what he had done, and that 'he would do so again.' This was his mind until death.

Lount was a social and excellent companion, and a well-informed man. He sometimes spoke to us under the sill of the door. He did so on the morning of his execution! He bid us 'farewell! that he was on his way to another world.' He was calm. He and Matthews came out to the gallows that was just before our window grates. We could see all plainly. They ascended the platform with unfaltering steps like men. Lount turned his head at his friends who were looking through the iron-girt windows, as if to say a 'long farewell!' He and Matthews knelt and prayed, and were launched into eternity without almost a single struggle. Oh! The horror of our feelings, who can describe them!"

The Caroline Almanac and Freeman's Chronicle, 1840 (Rochester, NY: Mackenzie's Gazette Press, 1840).

JUNE 23, 1838:
Preventing a War Crime on the Niagara Frontier

The Short Hills is a region of rolling country at the top of the Niagara Escarpment about ten kilometres inland from St. Catharines. It was the scene of an abortive and somewhat ridiculous invasion of Canada by Canadian rebels and members of the American Hunters' Lodges in the summer of 1838, while William Lyon Mackenzie was still ruling Navy Island in the Niagara River. The Hunters' Lodges were a secret society of Americans who hoped to seize Upper Canada in league with local democrats, generously reward themselves with farmland, then petition for admission to the Union. Miller, an American in his early twenties, had a remarkable career. After he joined the Hunters' Lodges, he hooked up with the followers of Thousand Island pirate Bill Johnson, crossed into Canada, and hoped to be one of the fighters for liberty who would be well rewarded for their revolutionary zeal.

The rage of Miller's colleague Jacob "The Traitor" Beemer's at the British was generated by the hanging of Lount and Matthews, two of Mackenzie's men, in Toronto a few weeks before. After the failure of the Short Hills raid, Beemer made a deal with the British, turning Crown evidence in the trial that resulted in a death sentence for the leaders of the rebels. Miller's adventures in Niagara ended with him being cornered in a swamp by British cavalry. He was tried at Niagara and pleaded insanity, but was sentenced to be hanged and quartered — the messy "drawing" part being omitted from the sentence. The lancers whose near-death experience is recounted below wrote a letter to the colonial governor asking for a reprieve, as did prominent New York politician William Seward. The appeals worked. Miller was shipped out to Tasmania, where he spent five years dragging rocks in a stone quarry. He was pardoned by the British and made his way back to upstate New York. He published an account of his adventures, which he dedicated to Seward. By then, he had taken up the cause of American slaves, noting on the title page of his autobiography that "slaves can breathe in England."

LINUS MILLER

The second division left two hours afterwards, to attack a party of volunteers, who were stationed in the vicinity; and the third, soon after, took up their line of march for the little village of St. Johns, where was a party of Her Majesty's lancers, and was joined by Beemer on the road. Morrow and myself accompanied the third division as volunteers wishing to share in the fight, and prevent what mischief we could. About 2 o'clock in the morning, we arrived at St. Johns. The sentry gave the alarm by firing his carbine at us, and fled. After half an hour's fighting, during which two of our men and two of the enemy were wounded, the lancers surrendered, but not until our men had become greatly incensed, and the fearful cry, "Give them no quarter! Accept no surrender!" rang in their ears; when the counter one of "quarter! quarter! for God's sake quarter!" was soon heard. They occupied a hall in the second story of the village hotel.

Beemer [a Hunter's Lodge officer] ordered them to be pinioned, and then commenced his work of plunder. At 6 o'clock, a.m., he ordered ropes to be prepared to hang seven of the lancers, whom he selected for that purpose, telling them to prepare to die; "for," said he, "as sure as there is a God in heaven, I will hang you on the trees of yonder forest, to avenge the death of Lount and Matthews." The poor fellows begged him to consider that they had nothing to do with the execution of those men; that they had wives and children, who were innocent and helpless; and that he had accepted their surrender as prisoners of war, imploring him with tears, to spare their lives; but he replied, that he had only accepted their surrender for the purpose of hanging them; that he was not to be turned from this purpose; and again bade them make their peace with their Maker, as their time was short.

By this time, the other division had joined us, and our prisoners numbered about seventy. These, with the exception of the wounded, who were discharged, were all marched in procession, the doomed men in front, to witness the intended hanging match. When, however, within about 200 yards of the bush, fearing that longer delay would be fatal, and having consulted Colonel Morrow, who approved of my intention, I gave the word of command to halt! The whole party obeyed, and all eyes were instantly turned upon me. Beemer turned round, and was met by my trusty pistols staring him in the face, and I noticed that the coward quailed before them: the man who was about send seven men, unprepared, into eternity, could not look, without the greatest trepidation, into the muzzle of a cocked pistol!

"Jacob Beemer, by virtue of the commission I hold in the Patriot service, which entitles me to command here, and, in the name of the provisional government of Canada, whose orders you have disobeyed, I now place you under arrest." Calling two men from the ranks, I ordered them to take him in charge. They at first hesitated, but the sight of my pistols brought them to their senses. Inquiring of the other leaders, if they disputed my right to command the party, Major Wait answered promptly, "No, I wish you to do so, and put an end to these horrid proceedings." After promising to send a ball through the first man who should hesitate to obey my orders, I continued, "Your conduct, Beemer, has been most disgraceful. Disregarding the common usages of war, you have been guilty of the most shameful excesses; setting at defiance the authority of the provisional government, you have, under the guise of patriotism, committed the crime of midnight robbery; you have plundered your prisoners in open day, in the presence of the people of Canada, in whose behalf, you profess to have made this movement; and, what is still worse, having accepted the surrender of these men as prisoners of war, you were now about to add to the black catalogue the horrid crime of hanging seven of their number upon the trees of yonder forest. There lie the ropes, prepared by your orders, for the consummation of the cold-blooded murder. Your conduct, should you and I have the good fortune to reach the American shore, will be investigated by the proper authorities. But I am unwilling to believe, notwithstanding these ominous preparations for bloodshed, that you really intended to carry out the measures you have avowed; and I now give you an opportunity to retract. In the presence of these witnesses, I implore you, for your own sake, if you are aught but a demon in heart, to disown the intention of murder."

Without hesitation he replied, with an oath, that such was his determination, and, but for my interference, he would have hung them all, to avenge the blood of Lount and Matthews.

"I thank Heaven," I replied, "that I am here to thwart you. Now; sir, empty your pockets of the booty you have collected this morning." With great reluctance, and quivering with rage, he allowed one of his guards to search him; and, from his coat, waistcoat, and breeches pockets, watches, purses of money, and valuable trinkets were drawn forth and laid in a heap before him.

"Now, sir, whose coat and waistcoat have you purchased this morning?"

"They are nine," answered one of the prisoners, "he compelled me to exchange for his old ones, after our surrender."

"Strip, scoundrel, let us see you in your own regimentals again."

A loud laugh arose from all hands while the re-exchange took place. Ordering the prisoners to be untied, I directed them to come forward and select their property from the heap which Beemer's pockets had yielded; which being done, I said to them, "I am about to discharge you, provided you are willing to swear upon the Bible I hold in my hand, that you will immediately retire from the British service, and never again take up arms against the Patriot forces." I then administered a solemn oath to each to that effect, and concluded by saying, "You are now discharged from custody. Return to your homes; and when you see the standard of liberty unfurled by your county, I hope to see some, if not all of you foremost in our ranks. But carry with you, wherever you go, the conviction that the Patriots of Canada are neither robbers or murderers, but actuated by more noble purposes than have been evinced by the commander of this party; and rest assured that he will receive that punishment at their hands which his disgraceful conduct deserves. And, inasmuch as mercy has been extended to you on this occasion, and some of your number have been saved from a fearful death, should any of this party, who have been your captors, and are not accountable for the acts of Beemer, unhappily fall into the power of the authorities you have served, (which may Heaven forbid,) let the remembrance of this day's deliverance warm your hearts towards them, and lead you to exertions in their behalf.

"For the part which I have acted on this occasion, I ask not your thanks nor your gratitude. I have only done my duty to the cause I serve; and now, farewell." Warmly did they shake my hand, and many a "God bless you" escaped from their lips. Those whose danger had been most imminent wept freely during the occurrence of the foregoing scene. Every man in our party, except Beemer, appeared to rejoice at their liberation. One of the released lancers asked to have his arms restored to him, but I told him they were ours by the usages of war, and he must content himself to walk home without them, where they could be of no service, if he intended to keep the oath he had just taken. The officer in command of the lancers also requested to have the colors of his company returned, but was informed that trophies of that kind were very valuable in the United States.

Linus Miller, Notes of an Exile to Van Dieman's Land: Comprising Incidents of the Canadian Rebellion of 1838, Trial of the Author in Canada … and Transportation to Van Diemen's Land *(Fredonia, NY: W. McKinstry, 1846).*

NOVEMBER 9, 1838:
Cold, Fear, and Bad News Defeat the Rebels at Beauharnois

Francois Xavier Prieur's account is evidence of the accuracy of Carl von Clausewitz's claim that wars are won or lost as much in the mind as on the battlefield. The Lower Canada rebels won a skirmish at Beauharnois, upriver from Montreal, early in the morning of November 9, 1938. Then they spent a cold, dreary November day and night sitting in a field, waiting for orders and listening to bad news that arrived from other rebel groups in the Montreal area. By the next day, dampness, cold, gloom, and post-battle fatigue and depression snatched the victory away from the rebels, who drifted off to their homes. Prieur, a rebel soldier, eventually ended up in an Australian penal colony but was pardoned and returned to Quebec in the early 1840s.

FRANÇOIS XAVIER PRIEUR

On the 9th of November, about nine o'clock in the morning, some men on picket duty came and warned us that the enemy was advancing. Shouts of joy within our ranks welcomed this news, and the order was immediately given for us to draw up in battle array to await the coming of the enemy … We rushed upon the enemy, enfilading him and discharged a round which could not have had any great effect being fired from too great a distance; but of which the noise added to the yells that our companies uttered, as soon as they appeared, and of those numbers the enemy was wholly unaware, and that undoubtedly they exaggerated, had the effect of creating a certain amount of panic and of which we took advantage to reload our weapons without relaxing our cries, and scarcely retarding our course. A general but ill-directed volley caused a shower of bullets to whistle above our heads, of which not a single one struck us. No more than did any of the succeeding volleys. During this time we continued to advance across ploughed fields, ditches and fenced paddocks, firing at will, but with a certain amount of effect, as we discovered a little later.

Finally, we were about to come to close quarters with the enemy, accompanied by redoubled shouts, succeeded in demoralizing them, and we saw them take to flight, carrying off two dead and several wounded, according to what we ourselves noticed, and the information which we received later from the folk in the vicinity. Our forces were already along the road in pursuit, when Dr. Perrigo, who had rejoined us at the sound of the first volley, advanced to the front rank and gave the order to stop....

This particular day was a cold one, with a little snow. The dreariness of the atmosphere harmonized with our dissatisfaction at not having derived any profit from our victory, gained without any sacrifice on our part, and which would have been able, in our opinion, to provide us with arms and ammunition in abundance.

Just as evening approached, a messenger came and brought us the unpleasant news of the defeat of our friends from Lacolle and the Cotes; he added that many had been taking prisoner, and that the news everywhere was bad.

It was evident that our position was becoming untenable, and that to remain longer assembled in this place meant merely to attract disaster to the spot, without any possible good result for the cause that we were defending. The whole of the night from the 9th to the 10th was spent in discussion; we agreed then that the day following the victory might be a very unhappy one for us....

The weather was cold; night was already beginning to fall. There we were on our knees on the frozen soil, guns on hips, telling our beads [saying the rosary], after having repeated the litanies together. Already could be heard the noise of the heavy vehicles and of the cavalry which were advancing slowly and heavily upon the hard road, when Captain Roy came to me, and, addressing himself to us all, told us it was madness to wish to make any sort of attempt with this handful of ill-armed men, that to begin an impossible resistance was merely to spill blood uselessly, and to bring down on our parishes the vengeance of a powerful and implacable enemy; he proposed that we should abandon all idea of attacking the troops.

I could not refuse to admit the justice of his argument, and he gave the order to disarm. Each one then reconciling himself to the inevitable, made his way across the fields to his own residence.

François Xavier Prieur, Notes of a Convict of 1838, translated from the original, with an introduction and notes by George Mackaness *(Dubbo, Australia: Review Publications, 1976).*

DECEMBER 4, 1838:
Rebel Prisoners Are Murdered on Windsor's Main Street

As the Upper Canada Rebellion of 1837–38 dragged on, it became progressively more violent. The farce of Mackenzie's abortive march on Toronto in December 1837, and the establishment of his comical little fiefdom on Navy Island in the Niagara River, should have shown the opponents of British rule that their fight had little chance of success. The arrival of the members of the Hunters' Lodges changed the nature of the rebellion. The Battle of the Windmill near Prescott and the attacks at Windsor and Pelee Island were ugly fights with serious casualties, especially along the St. Lawrence. On the Detroit River frontier, U.S. Army officers made it clear they were willing to engage in a shooting war if the British launched a strike against Michigan to stop "Patriots" and their American supporters who scuttled back and forth across the Detroit River, burning ships and destroying property.

After a short fight, the rebels, lacking rifles and artillery, finally returned to Michigan, leaving behind a handful of men in British jails. Most were sent to London, Ontario, for trial, but at least four were gunned down on the spot. The killings, including militia Colonel Prince's planned execution of seven Patriot prisoners at the Windsor barracks, were finally stopped by the enraged public in Windsor and the nearby town of Sandwich. Soon afterwards, handbills circulated in the towns denouncing Prince as a murderer and the colonel had to resort to fighting a duel to try to reclaim his honor. Prince's murderous actions were raised in the British Parliament, where the Duke of Wellington managed to defuse the issue. Fighting at Windsor and nearby Pelee Island marked the end of the violence. The Canadian rebels and their American supporters sulked along the American side of the border in the early winter of 1838–39, but there would be no spring campaign. Some of the Canadians settled in the United States. Others, like Mackenzie, returned years later when the British and colonial governments offered an amnesty. This article in Mackenzie's almanac is confusing, claiming five prisoners were shot. It's likely that the last victim was the same man as one of the prisoners whose story was told earlier in the narrative.

THE CAROLINE ALMANAC AND FREEMAN'S CHRONICLE

The refugees and their friends, 164 strong, with arms for themselves only, borrow a steamboat and cross from Detroit to Windsor, Upper Canada — their watchword "Remember Prescott!" — they attack the barracks and carry and burn them — *burn* a British steamboat — take 25 prisoners, touch no private property — are attacked by Colonel Prince, the militia and a party of regulars from Sandwich — a division only of their party only engaged in the defence and fight nobly — Colonel Putnam, a Canadian relative of the celebrated General Putnam of the American revolution, is killed, also Major Harvell, a gallant Kentuckyan, and Capt. Lewis — the Patriots retreat — some of them taken by Prince, an English Attorney from Cheltenham — he murders four of his prisoners without trial, several hours after the engagement. His letter to Airey said that "of the Brigands and Pirates 21 were killed, *besides four which were brought in just after the close and immediately after the engagement, all of whom I ordered to be shot upon the spot, which was done accordingly.*" Putnam was American born, 45 years of age, and left a widow and eight children in Canada. His wife is the niece of General Herkimer [an American commander killed in upstate New York in the Revolutionary War]. He wrapped the tri-color flag round his mangled body, laid down, and expired.

Before leaving the field, Adjutant Cheeseman of the 2nd Essex brought up a prisoner whom he had taken. He surrendered him to Colonel Prince, who ordered him to be immediately shot on the spot, and it was done. The man was first shot in the shoulder and severely but not mortally wounded — a second shot carried away part of his cheek — a third wounded him in the neck, after which he was bayoneted to death! The 2nd prisoner (who was wounded) was brought into the town of Sandwich at *least two hours after the engagement*, and was ordered to be shot on the spot. It was proposed to give him *"a run for his life."* This barbarous proposition was acceded to and in a moment a dozen muskets were leveled for his execution. At this moment, Col, Wm. Elliott exclaimed *"D—n you, are you going to murder your prisoner!"* This exclamation for one minute retarded the fire of the party, but in the next the prisoner was brought to the ground, he sprang to his feet and ran round the corner of the fence where he was met and shot through the head. His name was BENNETT, late a resident in the London District. *His death took place in our most public street, and in the presence of several ladies and children.*

Another prisoner named DENNISON, also wounded and unarmed, taken after the action, was brought in during the morning. Charles Elliott Esq. who was present when Col. Prince ordered this man to be shot, entreated that he might be reserved to be *dealt with according to the laws of the country,* but Col. Prince's reply was '*Damn the rascal, shoot him!*' and it was done!!

When Col. Prince reached Windsor he was informed that Stephen Miller, one of the Patriots, was lying wounded at the house of Mr. William Johnson. The man, whose leg had been shattered by a musket ball, had been found by Francois Baby, Esq. Col. Prince gave the order for his execution and *he was dragged out of the house and shot.* The wounded man said he was 35 years old, owned a farm in the town of Florence, Huron County, State of Ohio, and he had a wife and boy about 12 years old; he talked about his wife and son, and wished that his wife might be written to. Soon after this, a party of militiamen dragged him out of the house and shot him. Miller was wounded between 7 and 8 in the morning and shot at noon; the action was over about eight o'clock. *Miller lay unburied all night in the street and was completely disemboweled, and other parts of him eaten by the hogs!*

Capt. Broderick of the Regulars left a prisoner in charge of a dragoon. Prince fell in with this prisoner, *ordered him to be taken from his guard and shot, which was done!!*

A party of Indians who were sent into the woods took 7 prisoners. When they brought them out a cry was raised *"bayonet them!"* but Martin, one of the Indian braves, replied, *"No, we are Christians! We will not murder them!"* — But when these men were delivered to Col. Prince, he had them placed in a wagon, and when it reached an open spot outside the barracks, he commanded them to be taken out and shot. On this Mr. James cried, "For God's sake, do not let a white man murder those whom an Indian has spared!"

The Caroline Almanac and Freeman's Chronicle 1840 *(Rochester, NY: Mackenzie's Gazette Press, 1840).*

THE FENIAN RAIDS

SINCE HENRY II'S INVASION OF IRELAND IN 1171, THE IRISH HAD RESISTED English rule. For nearly 500 years, the tide of independence moved in and out. Sometimes the English held most of the island, at other times they were confined to a small "pale" surrounding Dublin.

Irish fortunes collapsed during the English Civil War and in the invasion by Cromwell's forces that followed. Cromwell's army had been toughened by years of fighting Royalists. Its soldiers had few qualms about destroying Irish towns and laying waste to vast swaths of the countryside. Places like Drogheda, where Royalist Catholics resisted, were destroyed and their garrisons massacred or sold into slavery to sugar planters. Jamaica's accent owes much to the Cromwellian campaigns. A generation later, the Battle of the Boyne, fought between the Protestant forces of William of Orange and the predominantly Catholic army of James II, marked the final collapse of Catholic Ireland. In the north, "plantations" of Calvanist Scots were established in Ulster. A series of discriminatory laws made it almost impossible for Catholics to inherit land, barred them from universities and professions, and transferred large tracts of land to absentee landlords living in England.

In the late 1700s, the peasants of Ireland seemed to have one bit of luck. Selective breeding had developed the potato from a walnut-sized tuber to a mass of starch the size of a man's fist. Potatoes grew well in Ireland, and the small holdings of a peasant could feed a family. Ireland's population doubled.

It was the cruelest of bubbles. In the middle of the 1800s, mould swept through the potato crops, destroying them. Ireland continued to export grain and dairy products from the estates of the absentee landlords, but the peasants were left to starve. Disease swept through towns and countryside where people were already weakened by hunger. Hundreds of thousands starved, more than a million emigrated in horrific and disgusting conditions. When they arrived in America, the displaced Irish came with a burning hatred for England.

Their numbers swelled during the American Civil War, when the Union offered work and U.S. citizenship to Irish who joined Lincoln's armies. When the Civil War ended, tens of thousands of Irish veterans, trained in the latest military tactics and toughened by war, wondered how they could use their new skills.

In 1858, Irish-Americans founded the Fenian Brotherhood as a fraternal and political society. Its leadership came up with a plan that sounds ludicrous today but was frightening at the time: Fenian fighters would take Canada and either trade it for Irish independence or exploit it to finance a full-scale war back home. American authorities had a mixed view of the Fenian plan: senior members of Andrew Johnson's administration thought the Fenian plan was ludicrous, but some top army officers were willing to let the Fenians take their chance. The Fenian plan was illegal under American neutrality laws, but very little was done to stop Fenians — veterans of both the Union and Confederate armies — from assembling in towns along the U.S.-Canada border. In the summer of 1866, General Ulysses S. Grant set up a headquarters in Buffalo, New York, and did very little to prevent the Fenians from assembling and crossing the Niagara River to invade Canada West.

The invasion caused terror in Canada. The government had infiltrated the Fenians, but it could not trust its own people. Fenian members and sympathizers lived in the countryside and in cities like Toronto, Montreal, and Ottawa. To ensure those Fenians did not rise up, the government of Sir John A. Macdonald suspended most civil rights.

The Fenians won the Battle of Ridgeway near Fort Erie, the last battle fought in Ontario, but could not exploit their victory. They had planned a much larger invasion that called for the cutting of the Welland Canal and the railway line from Toronto to Windsor. The Fenians, with enough men and a better supply system, could have pulled off their plan, but it's doubtful they could have held their gains against reinforcements from Britain. Smaller raids occurred in the eastern townships of Quebec, in New Brunswick, and, finally, in an aborted Fenian attempt to horn in on Louis Riel's attempt to create a republic in Manitoba in 1870.

For the first time, Canadian journalists had telegraph systems to file their war stories and daily newspapers to publish them. The coverage was invariably negative. Journalists who might sympathize with Fenian goals could hardly explain away the invasion of their country and the gunning down of militia soldiers, most of them University of Toronto students. Ireland's political and social problems would have to be solved in the United Kingdom, not in the fields of Canada.

JUNE 3, 1866:
Ridgeway: The Opening Moves

This is a classic case of getting a story half right and half very, very wrong. Almost all of the troop movements are described accurately, although it's likely that Booker sought out the Fenians rather than move toward Stevensville, where he was supposed to link up with a larger British regular force. The account completely breaks down at the point where the Fenian skirmishers retreat to their own lines. They didn't do it in a panic. The Fenian commander, O'Neill, was not shot from his horse. And the Fenians did not flee the battlefield. Instead, they crossed it, chased Booker's militiamen for three miles, gathered their wounded, and fell back on Fort Erie. Whatever was left behind was abandoned mainly because the Fenians, unlike the Canadians, had far more rifles and ammunition than they needed. By the time this piece was printed on the front page of the *Globe*, beneath a stirring call to arms by Thomas D'Arcy McGee, most people knew that the battle had been lost, and rumours of Booker's tactical blunders were already well-known.

THE *HAMILTON SPECTATOR*

Thus placed, the advance was sounded, and the column marched forward towards Stevensville, a distance of some six or seven miles, and which they would thus reach at the exact time as agreed upon with Colonel Peacock, from nine to half-past nine o'clock. After they had proceeded about three miles the leading men of the advanced guard were fired upon from the edge of the woods fringing the open ground on each side of the road.

The moment the attack was made, supports of the Queen's Own were thrown out on each side of the road, with instructions to clear the wood on either flank. In this force the column steadily advanced some distance when a rattling rifle fire from the Fenian skirmishers

A Fenian officer seized the rifle of a Canadian militiaman, saying the gun would never cause harm to an Irishman again, and slammed it on a rock. Turned out, he was wrong.

was opened upon the Volunteers, who replied, gradually forcing the Fenians back. This, which may be said to be the first of the actual battle, commenced at about eight o'clock and at three to three and a half miles from Stevensville. The movement of throwing out supports and advanced firing was performed by the Queen's Own with all the steadiness of well-trained regulars.

They pressed forward still, when Major Gillmor, in command of the Queen's Own, reported his men were running out of ammunition, and the right wing of the Thirteenth Battalion and the York Rifles relieved them. The movement of changing front was well executed, and the appearance very fine. The Queen's Own being in green uniform, and the 13th in red, the change of green for a red front had a picturesque effect. Whether the appearance of the red coats caused the Fenians to fear that they were regulars, or that the general steadiness of the whole column evidently impressed them with the idea that the entire column were veteran troops, certain it is that at this point they made a rapid movement to the rear, making for the woods, and, as it turned out afterwards, on their reserves. They were closely pressed, and had been driven about a mile, and during their advance, the commanding officer of the Fenians, who rode a light bay or cream-coloured horse, was shot, and the Fenians threw away their arms, camp kettles, papers &c., many of which have been picked up by farmers and others as trophies of the Fenian invasion.

"The Battle of Lime Ridge," Hamilton Spectator, June 4, 1866. Reprinted in the Globe (Toronto), June 5, 1866.

JUNE 2, 1868:
The IRA Defeats U of T at Ridgeway

On Friday, June 1, a force of Irish republicans under former Union cavalry officer John O'Neill crossed the Niagara River from Buffalo. They easily took the town of Fort Erie, then moved inland to attack Port Colborne and seize the Welland Canal. The invasion was part of a grand, if bizarre, plan to capture Canada and somehow trade it to

Britain for Irish independence. While U.S. law prohibited the Fenians from using American soil for organizing their raids, politicians and generals in New York State and Vermont turned a blind eye to Fenian activities until the end of that summer, when it was clear the Fenian plan was a failure. The Fenians were opposed by Canadian militia under Lieutenant-Colonel Albert Booker. Both sides had about 800 men under arms, all of them infantry. The bulk of the Canadian soldiers who fought at the Battle of Ridgeway were University of Toronto students and farmers from the Hamilton area. The Canadian volunteers were poorly led by militia officers who had never seen action and relied on Napoleonic War tactics. Booker was incompetent. He sent his men went into battle exhausted, hungry, and thirsty. Although they fought bravely, the militiamen panicked after becoming confused by contradictory bugle calls. Thinking they were about to be attacked by cavalry, some of the Canadians formed a square, a tactic that worked at Waterloo but was worse than useless against infantry with rifles. They were very lucky not to have been slaughtered en masse.

Many of the Irish nationalists were veterans of the American Civil War, armed with war surplus rifles and trained in the newest tactics. The Canadians were routed north of Ridgeway village with a loss of nine dead. The Fenians, who lost five men, failed to exploit their victory and, a day after the battle, fled back across the border. Toronto went into deep mourning when the bodies of the Canadian casualties were brought to the city. Fenian prisoners taken on the Niagara Frontier were sentenced to hang, but were eventually released. An anonymous *Toronto Leader* reporter was near the battlefield and saw the immediate aftermath. He went to work on the field helping and comforting the wounded on both sides. Alexander von Erickson, a war artist who had made his reputation drawing battles in the American Civil War, accompanied the Fenians. Several of his watercolours from Ridgeway are known to have survived and are now owned by the Fort Erie Historical Museum.

The Fenian Raids showed the need for some sort of coordinated British North American defense and gave impetus to negotiations that resulted in Confederation just thirteen months after the Battle of Ridgeway.

Civil War artist Alexander von Erichsen, a Fenian sympathizer, accompanied soldiers to the Battle of Ridgeway and painted eighteen images, including this bird's-eye view of the battle.

SPECIAL CORRESPONDENT OF THE GLOBE

First Dispatch

Port Colborne, June 2, 1866

Last night the forces at Port Colborne were augmented by the arrival of the Toronto University Company.

Early this morning the troops took train to Ridgeway, under command of Colonel Booker, Col. Dennis having gone on an expedition down the river.

At three miles from Ridgeway Station the Fenians were found encamped in the bush. The column at once attacked them, the "Queen's Own" firing the first shot. The fight is now general. The Volunteers are now driving the Fenians. Several are killed on both sides. Col. Peacock, with the artillery, has sent dispatches that they cannot be here at once. It is thought the volunteers will, at last, hold their own until the arrival of the regulars.

The Volunteers behaved splendidly, pushing upon the retreating Fenians with the greatest gallantry.

<u>Second Dispatch</u>
Port Colborne, June 2, 1866
The Fenians, after having been driven back half a mile, have rallied and have succeeded in driving back the Volunteers, who are now retiring with 15 killed and upwards of 50 wounded. It is thought the Fenians will not be able to carry on the pursuit far. Volunteers hope for the arrival of the Regulars. In the meantime, they have retired on Port Colborne at 12 a.m., where they have arrived. The fight commenced two miles from Ridgeway at 7 a.m. The Fenians were secreted in the bush. The volunteer columns, under the command of Col. Booker, left Port Colborne this morning at 5 o'clock and on arrival at Ridgeway attacked the Fenian position. No. 5 Company, The Queen's Own, opened the fight — attacking the Fenian defenders, whom they found behind a snake fence [a fence of stacked cedar rails]. The main body being in the bush, the fight soon became general. At first the Fenian skirmishers were driven back, the Volunteers soon found themselves outnumbered, and forced to retreat when the whole body of Fenians advanced upon them.

Some confusion then spread in the volunteers' ranks and the officers had difficulty keeping the men in their ranks. On arrival at the Railway [at Ridgeway village] station the volunteers were got into some order and the Column is now in Port Colborne in full retreat.

"Dispatches from Ridgeway," Globe *(Toronto), June 4, 1866.*

JUNE 3, 1866:
A Journalist Is Caught in the Fenian Advance at Ridgeway

The Canadian volunteers at Ridgeway were lucky more of them were not killed. The battlefield was a potential slaughterhouse. A wooded ridge along its right side was used by the Fenians to set up an enfilade, with men hiding in the trees to fire into the right side of the Canadian ranks as they moved north toward the main body of the Fenians. The open ground below the ridge was crisscrossed by cedar rail fences that the Canadians had to climb over or tear down as they moved forward. The day was extremely hot, the Canadians had no canteens and had not eaten anything but bread in the previous night and day, and they were short of ammunition. Many of the volunteers had never fired a gun. Booker, rather than avoid the Fenians and hook up with a strong British force, chose to attack.

A Hamilton auctioneer who had never seen a shot fired in anger, Booker had a weak grasp of modern tactics. In the confusion of the battle, Booker ordered his men to form a defensive square after rumors went through their lines that the Fenians were going to mount a cavalry charge. Squares had worked well for Wellington at Waterloo, but they were the wrong tactic in a battle against soldiers armed with new high-powered rifles. Soon after, the Canadians realized their mistake, broke, and fled, chased by the Fenians, who mounted a bayonet charge. The Fenians seem to have shown considerable restraint, as they had the firepower to slaughter the Canadian militiamen, and the Battle of Ridgeway tests modern theories about the compulsion of soldiers to kill. Accounts of the battle speak of the Fenians shooting high, and several of the Canadian casualties were men hit as they climbed over the top of

Alexander von Erichsen painted this picture of Canadian militiamen fighting at Ridgeway. It's not clear if von Erichsen had freedom of movement on the battlefield or based this image on conjecture.

rail fences. The field was left to the Fenians, who, along with the local farmers, tended to the wounded. The Fenians later withdrew, taking very little property with them and leaving the local people relatively unmolested. Booker had a breakdown after the battle and, despite Sir John A. Macdonald's government's efforts to cover up the debacle by holding a whitewash inquiry, endured pubic disgrace until his death — possibly by suicide — in 1871 at the age of forty-seven.

O'Neill, the Fenian commander, led a botched raid in the Eastern Townships of Quebec in 1870 and was beaten at the Battle of Eccles Hill. Also that year, he tried to forge an alliance with Louis Riel and his Metis supporters. He went on to found an Irish community in Nebraska, where the town of O'Neill claims to have the world's biggest shamrock, made of green cement, embedded in the pavement of the town's main intersection. He died in 1878 at the age of forty-four and was given a hero's funeral. A Toronto *Leader* reporter was in a nearby tavern looking after a wounded Canadian when Fenians burst in.

Toronto *Leader*

They presented such an appearance as I certainly shall not soon forget. They were the most cut-throat-looking set of ruffians that could well be imagined. Supposing me to be the landlord, they immediately demanded liquor. In vain I urged that I was as much a stranger as themselves. Their leader presented a revolver at me, and ordered me behind the bar; every decanter was empty. They insisted that I had hid everything away. I examined every jar, without success. Fortunately I discovered a small keg, which on examination I found to contain about a gallon of old rye whiskey. This I distributed among them and think I must have treated about fifty. This mollified them in some degree, and after slaking their thirst at the well, that party proceeded on its way without molesting me further. I then, assisted by the young volunteer whose comrade we had brought in, proceeded to render what assistance we could to the wounded men, one of whom was Private Lugsden of the Queen's Own, badly wounded in the chest, when we were interrupted by the arrival of another detachment under the command of a Capt. Lacken, who marched my assistant off a prisoner.

I remonstrated with him upon the cruelty of leaving me alone with all the wounded, when he detailed one of his own men to assist me and went his way. About one hundred yards from the tavern, on the west side of the road, I found a poor fellow of the Queen's Own lying on his face near the fence. I knelt down beside him and found that he was sensible. He told me his name was Mark Defries, and that he was shot through the back. He knew that he was dying. He requested me to take a ring from his finger and send it with a message to a young lady in Toronto. He also requested me to take his watch and send it to his father, whose address he gave me. This I attempted to do, but he could not endure to be touched. He told me it would do to take it after he was dead. I conversed with him for some time, when I left him to try to obtain some assistance to have him removed into the house.

I was then placed under arrest by a Fenian, by order of his commanding officer, and conveyed to a farm house, where I found two of our wounded men, young Van der Smissen, of the University Rifles, badly wounded in the thigh, and Corporal Lakey, shot through the mouth. With the assistance of the Fenian sentry I had them both put to bed and rendered them all the assistance in my power; for, be it noticed, that we could not find man, woman nor child in a circuit of miles, all fled in terror. When I could not do any more in that house, I requested the sentry to march me to the commanding officer, who was then at the tavern. He rode a sorrel horse, which was then at the door, and about half a mile from where we then were. I found him to be a very mild-looking young man, civil and courteous, evidently well educated. I stated my business at once, which was that I might obtain from him a written authority to go through their lines and visit the wounded on both sides without molestation....

I found there were more of our wounded men in another frame house about a mile further, on the Fort Erie road. I proceeded there and found the place guarded with Fenian sentries, but my protection was all potent. They, supposing me to be a surgeon, gave me every facility. I found, among others whose names I failed to ascertain, young Kingsford, of the University Rifles, lying on a lounge, badly wounded in the leg, but remarkably cheerful. I also found a young man named Hamilton, of the 13th Battalion, with a very bad wound

Officials of the Welland Railway pose with the engine that carried Canadian volunteers from St. Catharines to fight the Fenians near Fort Erie, July 1, 1866.

in the right side. He had been attended to by a Fenian surgeon; he was lying on his face and suffering much. At his request I examined his wound and placed a bandage around it to stop the bleeding. There was also another young man of the Queen's Own lying on the floor in strong convulsions, evidently in a dying state, singular to say, without a wound upon his body. In another room in the same house I found another young man badly wounded.

At this time a Fenian was brought in on a stretcher in a dying state. I ordered his comrades to cut his shirt open, when I found an ugly wound just under his left arm, which I have no doubt penetrated a vital part. I got water and washed the wound; he was sensible and able to tell me that his name was James Gerrahty, from Cincinnati, and that one of his own comrades had shot him by mistake, and that he freely forgave him. He died in about thirteen minutes, one of his comrades holding a crucifix before him as long as he could see it. We buried him in an orchard adjoining, the same evening.

Another Fenian was now brought in with a very bad wound in the neck. He was a very rough-looking fellow. I washed his wound also. He was afterwards removed to the hospital at St. Catharines. On leaving the house my attention was called to the dead body of one of the Queen's Own lying across the road, a very powerful man. He was shot through the head and presented a horrid spectacle. A little further on I found a group of three armed Fenians, who were watching over a wounded comrade. I was called upon to assist him. His comrades stripped him, and I found a gunshot wound in the hip, having passed right through, leaving two very ugly wounds. I washed him also and left him.

The Toronto Leader, *June 7, 1866.*

THE NORTHWEST RESISTANCE

THIS SMALL WAR HAS A NUMBER OF NAMES. THERE'S BEEN QUIBBLING for years over whether it was a "rebellion" or a "resistance." Rebellions can only be waged by people who are citizens or subjects of the country they're rebelling against. Most of the First Nations of the Plains had never surrendered their sovereignty to the Crown or placed themselves under its protection. (Sitting Bull, fleeing the Americans after the Battle of the Little Bighorn in 1876, was an interesting exception.) The Metis had made a deal with Ottawa that resulted in the creation of the province of Manitoba, but they had moved into old Hudson's Bay Company lands in what is now Saskatchewan and Alberta. So, for my purposes, I'll give the supporters of Louis Riel, Big Bear, and Poundmaker the benefit of the doubt and call this fight the Northwest Resistance.

That's not how it was viewed in 1885 by the newspapers of the English-speaking regions of Canada. Riel and his allies were seen as traitors to Canada and the British Empire. They threatened the creation of a nation stretching from sea to sea, endangered the new transcontinental railway and blocked the settlement of the West. The Americans had been fighting and slaughtering their Plains and Southwest tribes since the decade before the Civil War. The buffalo had been hunted to near-extinction, but the warfare hadn't stopped. It would culminate five years after Riel's hanging with the massacre at Wounded Knee, and sporadic violence would continue until the early years of the twentieth century.

Having been humiliated by Riel in 1870, the government decided to use overwhelming force to subjugate him and his allies in the Plains tribes and stamp out any further resistance. Journalists and war artists accompanied the army, and some officers had made deals with newspapers back home to send them dispatches. Considering the jingoism and imperialism of the time, the war reporting seems rather fair to Riel's fighters. This is especially true in eyewitness accounts. Stories that were filed on events that reporters did not actually see contain more extreme wording. "Massacre" stories always came from second or third-hand information.

There was no active censorship of reporters' copy, although there were bounds that reporters kept within. They reported on few of the problems that plagued government forces. After Riel's capture, the tenor of the reporting changed. Articles sent from the West, along with opinion pieces written in newsrooms in Toronto and small-town Ontario, goaded Sir John A. Macdonald to send Louis Riel and eight Native leaders to the gallows. In the end, the government did agree to examine the Metis' complaints and held elections in the territory, but bad feelings over the execution of Riel widened the gulf between French and English Canada and linger to this day.

APRIL 28, 1885:
Fish Creek

Much of the coverage of the Northwest Resistance — then called the North-West Rebellion, the Saskatchewan Uprising or the Second Riel Rebellion — consisted of letters sent to newspapers by soldiers or their families. Thomas McMullen puts the best face on what was a complete defeat for the Canadian forces. Outnumbered four to one, Metis leader Gabriel Dumont brilliantly exploited General Frederick Middleton's blunder of splitting his forces. Middleton did, however, hold off a Cree

Burying the Metis dead after the Battle of Fish Creek, Northwest Campaign, 1885.

force that tried to link up with Dumont. Had he not done so, Middleton's 200 men might have been massacred. Dumont's men, who were hungry, exhausted, and low on ammunition, could not follow up their victory.

Thomas McMullen

The bluff is sloping on all sides and the Indians were all hidden in formidable rifle pits which were swimming in blood, telling us that many a Halfbreed or Indian had fallen. The pits rose upon one another and were very neatly contrived, the Indians showing much ingenuity in their construction. We are lying encamped at Fish Creek and will remain here probably for some time. I suppose they are greatly excited in Toronto over the news of the fight, but don't mind the papers if they say any of our men were hurt, as with the exception of Jim Cane, no one was hurt among us. I am glad to hear that you are all well, and am happy to say that I could not be in better health, and may say that about the rest of the boys. We are greatly inconvenienced by not having our tents on this side of the river, but had to do our best until Monday, when we pitched our own alongside of the 90th. I received letters from Pvt. Honey who we left at Qu'Appelle, and he is getting along fine. The 12th and 35th are staying there and are all well. When you write send me that all the paper and envelopes you can, as it is impossible to write any more without them. Tell my enquiring friends to write me, as we like to get news from home. It is so long before we get them, so we like to have as many as possible at once.

Thomas McMullen, the Globe *(Toronto), May 1, 1885.*

APRIL 1885:
Army Doctors Turn Down Requests for Medicinal Liquor

The Canadian volunteers who fought the Metis had cause to wonder whether their own army really cared about their physical and mental well-being.

A CANADIAN GRENADIER

The wounded are in charge of the 90th and the Battery doctors, and they get treated well, but I pity them if they had to depend on our doctor and ambulance corps. After the fight on Friday it rained very hard and we got soaked, and some of us had to lie in water six inches deep from six until 12. Our clothes were soaked for a day after, and one of the boys who got a slight touch of rheumatism went to the doctor's tent and asked him for something to brace him up again, but he was told to come around again in half an hour. He said he wanted it right away, and the sergeant said he was not so d— bad but that he could wait for a short time. Another of the boys named — got his toe frozen at Calamity camp, and part of it fell off. Every time he goes to get it dressed they tell him he is a d—d nuisance. If it were not for the 90th doctors he would have to suffer a great deal.

A Canadian Grenadier, the Globe *(Toronto), May 8, 1885.*

MAY 9, 1885:
The Battle of Batoche

Riel's forces collapsed after the Battle of Batoche. The Canadian forces pounded Riel's forces with artillery for several days, then stormed the position of the Metis, who were short of ammunition. After the Canadians took the Metis capital, the surviving Metis fighters surrendered or fled. Riel was hanged the following autumn. Gabriel Dumont, the best Metis strategist, rode to the United States. Eight years later, he was pardoned and allowed to return to Batoche, where he is buried. The town is a National Historic Site.

THE GLOBE

ON BOARD THE STEAMER *NORTHCOTE*, four miles below Batoche, May 9, 1885, via HUMBOLT, NWT, May 13 — Another engagement with the rebels took place this morning, with what result is unknown at this writing. According to Gen. Middleton's pre-concerted plan, the steamer *Northcote*, with two heavily-laden barges, left Gabriel's at 6 a.m. and after anchoring a short time so as not to anticipate the arranged time of arrival at Riel's headquarters, reached within one and one-half miles of her destination where she was to remain until the bombardment of the rebels' stronghold by Middleton was heard, he started at daybreak from the camping ground reached the previous day, nine miles east of the place. The rebels, however, materially interfered with the carrying out of the plans by opening fire on the steamer at ten minutes past eight, just after she had just gotten under headway, the first bullet passing through the pilot house. The rebel spies had watched the steamer the previous night on the opposite bank from Gabriel's and the sentry could hear them talking, one boastfully shouting as he departed, "Now come on, you b— s—."

This first shot was evidently a signal to the rebels of the boat's approach, and as she rounded the bend a moment later she was raked fore and aft with a storm of bullets coming from either bank. From almost every bush rose puffs of smoke and from every house and tree top on the banks came bullets. The fire was steadily returned by the troops on board,

"C" School of Infantry, and notwithstanding the rebels being protected by bush and timber, evidently some injury was inflicted upon them. Volley after volley was fired, and several of the lurking enemy were heard to drop headlong down the sloping banks. So the fight went on fierce and hot. As we approached Batoche, the pretty little church of St. Antoine de Padua lifted its cross-covered steeple above the other buildings on the eastern bank, and stood in its holy mission of peace in terrible contrast to the horrible spectacle that met the gaze on the opposite bank.

A man, presumably one of the prisoners, was dangling by the neck from a branch of an almost limbless tree, the victim of rebel rage and vindictiveness. Near at hand were the rebels, who also lined both banks for a couple of miles, or running swiftly, they kept pace with our progress and were concentrated in strong force. Several mounted men, evidently leaders, were directing their movements. A few volleys quickly dispersed them to their hiding places, where they fought in the traditional bush fight manner. They completely riddled the steamer with bullets, but it being strongly bulwarked on the boiler deck, where the soldiers were standing, our casualties were consequently very light. Just above Batoche the rapids commence, and a boulder covered by a sand bar juts out into the stream, leaving a narrow channel immediately upon the western side, the head of which is at a sharp bend, to round which the boat had to run her nozzle almost on the bank. It was here that the fire became terrifically hot from a favourably-located ravine directly in front of which the rebels were hidden.

The rapids were passed safely, notwithstanding the pilot was totally unacquainted with the river, and the heavily-laden barges handicapped him in the handling of the steamer. Fortunately, there was no wind to render the duties of the crew still more arduous in controlling the boat's movement. In a few moments the crossing was reached, and passing it, the ferry cable caught the smoke-stack, which came crashing down on the hurricane deck, tearing with it spars and mast. Our misfortune elicited loud cheers from the Metis, mingled with the fiendish war whoops of the Indians. The cable, which is strung from the upper banks, was lowered just as we approached it, the intention of the rebels being to corral the steamer and in the confusion naturally expected to capture the boat and massacre the human freight. Very fortunately this scheme failed, but only by the nearest chance, for had the cable caught in the pilot house, which it barely missed, the wheelsman exposed to the enemy's fire would have been shot down and the steamer rendered utterly helpless. It was successful, however, in cutting our communication with Gen. Middleton by the code of whistling signals previously arranged, the whistle being carried away with the pipes.

Just then the steamer, to avoid two large boulders directly in its course, was allowed to turn around and floated downstream stern forward for a while. One barge barely grazed the bank, and the boat could have been boarded by the rebels, were it not for the steady volley of our men poured at them. A withering fire was still maintained from the rifle pits which the enemy had dug at different places, and this was formally and continuously returned until nine o'clock, when the rebels' firing was silenced, save a stray shot or two. We had run the gauntlet of their fire for five miles. Many of the enemy's bullets fell short of their mark when we were in mid-stream, shotguns with common ball being mainly their weapons, although they were not without Winchester and Snider Enfields. So fast and furious the lead hail poured in that it was evident that the whole rebel force had gathered here to make a determined stand. As some of the red coats were coming up in skirmishing order in the distance, our small force gave three lusty cheers.

The Globe (Toronto), May 15, 1885.

THE SECOND BOER WAR

THE SECOND BOER WAR (1899–1902) CAUSED AN EVEN GREATER SPLIT
between English and French Canada. The *Montreal Star*, which was at
the time the most important newspaper in the country, pushed hard for
Canadian soldiers to join British troops fighting ethnic Dutch farmers
for control of South Africa and its resources. *La Presse* and other French-
language papers opposed the war. The papers' views represented those of
politicians and citizens. French Québécois leaders like Henri Bourassa
wanted no part in the war. The plight of the Boers — stranded European
farmers fighting against the British for control of their adopted homeland
— had a certain resonance in Quebec. The Imperialist English press tried
to make the Boer War a test of patriotism. In Montreal, fighting broke
out between French and English-speaking university students. In cities
throughout English Canada, any reservations against fighting the Boers
were drowned out by press and political jingoism.

Prime Minister Wilfrid Laurier came up with a solution. Canadian
soldiers could go to South Africa as "volunteers." They would serve in a
Canadian Regiment. They would hold the same ranks as they did back in

Canada. It looked a lot like a Canadian commitment, and it satisfied very few critics of the war.

Seven journalists — R.E. Finn and S.C. Simonski of the *Montreal Herald*, W.R. Smith, Richmond Smith and W.H. White of the *Montreal Star*, C.F. Hamilton and J.A. Ewan of the Toronto *Globe*, and S.M. Brown of the Toronto *Mail and Empire* — travelled with the Canadian troops and covered the war, mainly from headquarters but with some trips into the field.

Most of their work reflected the jingoism of their editorial pages and often crossed the line into propaganda. Richmond Smith wrote that soldiers of Lord Strathcona's Horse had "covered themselves with Glory" and done "a great deed that will live in history" by blowing up the Komati Poort railway bridge, cutting off the Boer supply lines to the sea. It was a fabrication, possibly written and filed before the actual attack was supposed to begin. British commanders had called off the assault when they learned the Boers had caught wind of the secret mission. By September 1900, as the war went into its final, most brutal phase and the British began rounding up Boer civilians to break the morale of the Dutch guerillas, the Canadian reporters had come home. By 1902, when the war ended, Canadians were tired of stories from South Africa. German, French, and other European journalists had provided much different, more aggressive coverage, one that cast the British in a very bad light and inspired them to develop much more effective methods of media control and propaganda.

JANUARY 1900:
A Loyal Dog and an Officer's Order Prevent the Looting of a Boer Farm

Samuel Brown travelled with the Royal Canadian Regiment as it marched toward Paardeberg and its first major fight in the Boer War. Here, Brown writes about a rest stop at a farm owned by a suspected Boer farmer who had already been arrested by the British. The Boer War was an ugly affair that saw atrocities on both sides, including the rounding up of civilians and their internment in "concentration camps." In this instance,

Canadian troops behaved with great civility toward the wife and children of the detained Boer farmer.

SAMUEL MCKEOWN BROWN

The Dutch farmer's place proved to be a veritable oasis in the desert, for here from the pump of a windmill and a deep stone well, the men drank of the clear sparkling water, till the regimental police had to be put on guard, to keep the men from overtaxing themselves.

Of course, orders were issued that the farmer's garden of vegetables was to be left alone — though longing eyes were cast at the little patches of green groceries Herr Van Wyck had in a certain state of cultivation. A vicious big watch-dog, which did duty at the front door of the three-roomed house, added force to these orders, and disinclined the too venturesome from coming within a shorter distance than twenty yards of the domicile. The garden was so thoroughly protected, the men at once turned their attention to a deep unused well at the side of the windmill, where they "fished with all nets" — principally string, a bent pin, and locusts for bait — for the lazy frogs which disported themselves in the stagnant waters of the shady pool. Some of the best disciples of Isaac Walton [author of *The Compleat Angler*] were able to secure enough of this long-legged game to have a side-dish for supper, but, for the most part, the efforts of the soldiers were not attended with success.

Samuel McKeown Brown, With the Royal Canadians *(Toronto: Publishers' Syndicate, 1900).*

FEBRUARY 23, 1900:
Cronje Is Now In a Death Trap

J.A. Ewan was one of the group of reporters sent overseas with the Canadian volunteer unit that fought in the Boer War. Piet Cronje, one of the better Boer generals, earned the respect of the British and Canadians by his brilliant tactics and his daring strategy. When finally cornered at the central South African town of Paardeberg, Cronje made his enemies pay in blood for his surrender.

J.A. EWAN

Paardeberg Drift, Orange Free State — Gen. Cronje's magnificent night march from Magersfontein now appears likely to end in disaster. The main body of the Boers is enclosed in a terrible death trap. The enemy is hiding in the bed of the Modder [River], commanded by the British artillery, and enclosed in the east and west by British infantry.

Sunday witnessed a gallant stand on the part of the retreating foe. Though tired and harassed, they continue to maintain a bold front.

It is somewhat difficult to explain the Sunday action, in which all the British force was engaged, and in which Gen. Cronje, under difficult conditions, managed to hold his own. On Saturday night the British mounted infantry came into touch with Cronje's rear guard, driving them back upon the main body. On Sunday morning the action was renewed, but the Boers, who had entrenched the river bed during the night, prevented a further advance of the mounted infantry in this direction.

Meanwhile the Highland brigade consisting of the Seaforths, the Black Watch, and the Argyles, advanced from the south bank, and the Essex, Welsh and Yorkshires formed a long line on the left which rested on the river, the extreme right being the Welsh. The whole line was ordered to envelop the Boers, who lined both sides of the river.

J.A. Ewen, the Globe *(Toronto), February 23, 1900.*

FEBRUARY 1900:
Hiding Behind Ant Hills at Paardeberg

Sam Brown was one of the handful of Canadian war correspondents who went with the Canadian contingent to South Africa. British censors stopped Brown from seeing much of the fighting, but he was able to get close to the action at the Canadian fight at Paardeberg. Brown's report shows how the Boer's use of smokeless gunpowder made the guerilla fighters nearly invisible, and the desperation of Canadian soldiers fighting in the open under artillery and small arms fire. Brown's paper, owned by a consortium of Conservatives and founded by John A. Macdonald, was a big booster of Canadian participation in the war. His description of the fighting begins when Canadian soldiers were deployed on the morning of February 23, 1900. Boer commander Piet Cronje, outnumbered and surrounded, surrendered the following morning in a dignified ceremony.

Samuel McKeown Brown

The clump of trees where the men lay down was a haven which granted them a resting place but for a short time, and the relaxation from fatigue, which had been following like a pot of gold at the rainbow's end, was still further from their grasp than ever.

A ripple of rifle fire could be heard ahead as some of the men managed to get from the cooks a biscuit and a little coffee, but when the sound of big guns shook it, there came with it an order to move. Not all the men by any means were given the opportunity of getting hard tack and coffee, but there was time enough to fortify the soldiers with a ration of rum, which was a welcome stimulant.

At first the Canadians took position on a low ridge near the river's bank and then it was decided to send them through the river, on the farther side of which the fighting of the day was to be done.

Deep dongas [stream cuts in the plain], caused by the washing away of the earth in rain time, were spread far and wide on the river sides, and farther north supplied the Boers with the best of trenches flush with the ground. The muddy Modder, swollen as it was by recent rains, gurgled over the huge, rough stones which abounded at the bottom of it, and flowed at a rapid rate, fast enough in the swifter currents to take a man off his feet. Ropes had, in places, been stretched from one bank to the other, by means of which the crossing of the treacherous stream was more easily effected by the soldiers. With their rifles held high, and valuables in their helmets above the water, the Canadians plunged into the fast-flowing coffee-colored water, and gained the far shore with water up to their chins and necks.

Drenched to the skin, they started top ascend the sloping banks of the river and, once they had gained the level, they could see to the right of them the open plain which was so soon to form the historic battlefield of Paardeberg.

In front of the regiment there was an undulating bare plateau, with a few trees in places reaching out from the small grove fringes on the river banks, and here and there a bush dotted in the sand. Close to the place where our men crossed the river, and on the plain they were entering, stood a small circular kopje [granite knoll] which had allowed our soldiers to cross unseen by the Boers; and to the left, as the British began to advance along the plain parallel to the river was Paardeberg, a fair sized kopje that commanded an excellent view of both contending armies.

The British ground on this side of the river was bounded by the river on the right, which here flowed north and south, and on the left by the high ground and kopje.

The river where the Boers were ensconced turned westward at the end of the battlefield, and running south-west from it, was a donga, which afforded excellent shelter for them. In this way they had a part cordon around any final British advance which might be undertaken, and from this position they were able to enfilade those who got far enough up in the field.

After the crossing of the river, which was completed shortly after 9 o'clock, the hot rays of the sun began to steam on the soldiers' khaki clothes, and they moved on in so many apparently smouldering units.

Once across the river, their turn to the right led them in the direction they had to follow all day.

The training they had received at Belmont was at once put to use, and the companies went on the field extended at ten paces intervals between each man. "A" led, followed in turn by "C," "D" and "E," then came "B" and "G" in support, with "F" and "H" forming the reserves. Each company covered the width of the battalion, and properly extended they were mere dots on the veldt, with no man better target than the others.

With regard to the 19th Brigade, the Canadians were on the extreme right. The Cornwallis had two companies in support of the battery far to the left of the British ground, over the ridge, where was also placed the Canadian Maxim gun. The Shropshires were the Canadians' left-hand battalion, and later in the day the Gordons were also doing yeoman service on the left.

The Canadians — for we must follow them now — advanced as far as it was deemed safe and then crawling, they began what was a more onerous and tedious advance — though in the most expedient way. Where the ground before, from a distance, had seemed practically level, it was now found with a few folds in it, running parallel with the Boer trenches. These were heaven-sent breaks in the earth's flat surface, for, although they had seemed trivial, they were enough to hide the advancing regiment and to save the lives of the men who crouched behind them.

Zzz-Zzz-Zzz-Zzz-Zzz … the bullets from the Martini-Henri rifles first buzzed, like lightning humming-birds, over the heads of the front rows of Col. Otter's men, as those horrible well-aimed missiles came in abundance from the Boer marksmen. There the first of the Canadians were hit, at a distance of 1500 yards, when they showed their forms above the top of this rise of ground and came, for the first time, under fire. Soon, as the men crept up, as best they could, keeping cover wherever there was the slightest possibility, they began to hear the whistling ring of that excellent weapon, the Mauser rifle and carbine. Its report sounds just like a short exclamatory whistle that a person would use in the course of conversation.

Then again there was the whip-like crack of the explosive bullets, which the enemy used at times on that occasion. It was a queer mixture of marvelous sounds, as those slugs of lead were sent on their deadly mission, and no doubt the Dutchmen in their trenches were subjected to the same moral effect from our men's steady aim at the fringe of the trees ahead of them. Upon the hill to the left, Capt. Bell was having a little target practice with his single Maxim, which had been brought across the river, and the splashing rip of the quick-firing machine was a sort of consolation to our men. The wheel of one of the Maxims was broken on the far side of the river and it had to be left there for the time being.

The long drawn out "boom-boom" of the big guns on the other side of the river, which the Boers wee bringing to play on the British, seemed to be the backbone of all the heavy fire and to sustain the persistent rifle fire which was being sent from the trenches. What an aggravation it was to be continually fired at and still be unable to identify the shooters! There in the shade of the trees and piled up branches the Boers were able to look over the whole British field, and still the attackers could not see the Dutch riflemen, who so calmly laid in wait for them.

An hour before our flanks were thrown forward, with the centre resting, so that the Canadians' left came closer to the Boer donga, and the right shifted to the river and the trees which skirted the bank. Then the supports crawled up cautiously and added their strength to the firing line. New life was added to the front lines, and with here a sally to a piece of cover forward, and there a dash to some favorable ground in front, the whole firing line advanced to within, at the farthest, 700 yards of the enemy, the left creeping toward the donga, the centre looking square at the Boer trenches and the right out onto the clusters of trees on the high bank of the Modder. But this advance was not taken without the loss of life, for Royal Canadians dropped in every rush. The stretcher-bearers were kept busy attending to the wounded, where any chance was offered, and while this courageous section paid attention to disabled men and dying soldiers, the Boers paid marked attention to them. In one case, that where Capt. Arnold was being carried off the field, three of four stretcher bearers were hit while they bore him to the back of the lines.

Clumps of bushes and trees, instead of being any kind of protection, were the most dangerous places for men to go to, for, as if by actual measurement, the Boers had the range to a nicety. It was at one of those innocent-looking traps that Capt. Arnold of "A" Company received his mortal wound in the forehead while searching the enemy's position with his field glasses, and here also did a couple of privates die as soon as they had reached the fated spot. Private Findlay, of "C" Company, the first Canadian killed, fell shot through the heart at the spot where the "A" Company leader made his last stand.

There was no way that the Canadians could find the exact range, because they could not see where their shots fell among the trenches, but for the Boer it was different. One shot, and a puff of sand would give him an idea of how near he was to his mark and a slight adjustment of his rifle sight would give him an exact range.

How dear that day were the ant hills that the men had before on the march cursed for being in the way; and how welcome were a few stones for cover, that had formerly tripped them while on the trek! Everything that could hide even a part of a Canadian body was taken advantage of. In fact, for the slight opportunities of cover they had, the Canadians fought more after the fashion of the Boers than any other regiment I saw in South Africa. The Boers know best of any how to fight through that country, and the Royal Canadian Regiment, at least, followed his example as closely as they could.

Samuel McKeown Brown, With the Royal Canadians *(Toronto: Publishers' Syndicate, 1900).*

FEBRUARY 1900:
The Battle of Paardeberg, the Aftermath

Canadian newspapers were eager for any descriptions of the Boer War. Perkins, one of the volunteers who went to South Africa, does not gloss over the suffering of British soldiers and the Boers. Sending such letters home would be illegal in the First World War under Canada's censorship laws.

ALBERT PERKINS

Feb. 27 (Majuba Day) — Very lucky to be able to write. We are almost in the Boer lines and quite a few have given up and are passing to the rear. We laugh and talk with them. G Co. lost heavily. Herb Leavitt was shot right through with an explosive bullet. Yesterday right after writing we marched down the hill and took position on the river bank near the trenches. We had something to eat, then after dark took our position in the trenches. They are dug at night running at right angles to the river. At 2 a.m. we arose and advanced. We had gone about three hundred yards when orders came to entrench. We had only been at it a few minutes when we again got orders to advance. It was pitch dark and we had only gone about 100 yards when such a fire opened on us. I saved myself by a miracle almost. There was a perfect hail of bullets. We dropped like a flash, crawled and after a while got up and ran back to the trench, where we lay till some time ago. Then we advanced up this trench a hundred yards from the Boers. We have quite a lot killed. Our company suffered far the most. The Canadians did it all. Now it seems this crowd will surrender. Riggs, Scott, Withers, Johnston, and perhaps more of our company have been killed. Canadians did not receive support. Horrible work; Leavitt hardly expected to live. Boers surrendered to Canadians. Roberts said we did excellent work.

Am now in the Boer laager. Have tea, flour, meal, and have been cooking. Hundreds of rifles and tons of ammunition left here. Thousands of prisoners. Cronje took breakfast with Roberts.

G. Company took all the fire. Boers had families with them. Could get hundreds of souvenirs. Never felt worse than for Herb. Donahoe lost his leg. Men horribly shot; were within fifteen yards of trenches when Boers opened fire, and built trench less than 100 yards from theirs. Herb Leavitt walked over four hundred yards after he was shot.

28th. — Last night we lay around a fire and cooked. Walker made cakes, flour and oatmeal, fried in fat. I made tea. Not hungry, had a good sleep and I am going on fatigue. Found lots of rifles taken from British troops at Magersfontein. Most everyone has a kettle or pan. Boers have little kettles, pots galore (or had).

Albert Perkins, the Fredericton Daily Gleaner, *February 5, 1900.*

THE FIRST WORLD WAR

THE PUBLIC RELATIONS DISASTER OF THE BOER WAR TAUGHT THE BRITISH military that there was great danger in letting journalists move freely near front lines. The British, who still had control over the Canadian army, were determined to have a complete lock on information about the war. Between the Boer War and the First World War, they developed the world's first sophisticated multi-media propaganda machine, one that was the envy of their allies and their enemies. They also engaged in a ruthless censorship of articles, songs, photos and moving pictures.

War "reporting" was part of this propaganda system. The British had a stranglehold on censorship of war correspondence from the trenches because all telegrams and mail passed through London, where thousands of censors checked them. The British decided who could travel across the English Channel and to the Western front. Most "coverage" of the fighting in France and Belgium in the British and Canadian papers was actually propaganda issued by the British military. Very few reporters were allowed near the fighting — the British made it clear that any who might strike out on their own would be shot as spies. British reporters were kept penned up at British headquarters, far from the fighting, while Canadian journalists employed to cover the war were stuck in England.

The Canadian government named Max Aitken to be its official "eyewitness" to the fighting. Aitken, the Canadian newspaper baron, rarely visited the front and never got close to any real action. Instead, he worked in a London office with a staff of ten writers, rehashing military reports and giving them out to Canadian reporters. Aitken's Canadian War Records Office also employed photographers and camera operators to record "the front," although most of their work was staged behind the lines or in England.

Stories written in by Canadians stuck in England were vetted by the British Press Bureau. There was no point trying to report from neutral countries closer to the fighting. The Royal Navy severed the telegraph cables between Europe and the United States, partly to prevent the German side from being told in American newspapers. German reporters were able to get their copy out to American papers through the German government's press office in New York. Many U.S. papers, suspicious of the British lock on information and wary of London's propaganda, used the German reports.

Canadian newspapers suffered dreadfully in the recession that gripped the country in the years leading up to the First World War. The war began during a wave of newspaper closings and consolidation. Newspaper chains were just beginning to take shape, and only a few Canadian newspaper companies had the resources to send reporters overseas. They could afford to pay the salary of a journalist and the passage to England, but they could not cope with the outrageous fees of the telegraph companies. The publishers, faced with the choice of paying twenty-five cents a word or waiting eight to ten days for news to arrive by mail, chose the third option: taking news from the New York-based Associated Press, which was kind enough to find some stories with Canadian angles for its subscribers in Canada.

During the war, publishers decided they needed a Canadian news wire service. They organized The Canadian Press as a co-operative news sharing agency. Even so, they faced several obstacles that had to be overcome before Canadian reporters could make it to the front. It was possible to get reporters into less important fighting theatres like the Balkans, the African colonies and the Middle East, but Canadians wanted to read about the fighting in France, where their relatives and neighbors were deployed. They had to get clearance from the British propaganda system. The Canadian Press was subsidized by the federal government, so it had the wherewithal to send reporters overseas, but the journalists were selected by the government, not by the news agency.

In August 1914, the British Colonial Office offered to allow one Canadian reporter to file from the Western Front. That offer was quickly withdrawn when British authorities saw the *Times* of London's coverage of the retreat from Mons. So the first Canadian war correspondent did not arrive in France until March 1917. There were no Canadian journalists at Canada's most famous action of the war, the Battle of Vimy Ridge, and reports from the field were simply handouts from British army headquarters. The casualty lists told much more of the story than the bare-bones press releases.

Stewart Lyon of the Toronto *Globe* was the first Canadian Press reporter to file from the trenches. He got the job because of his talent and by offering to take a substantial pay cut, to $40 a week. Walter Willison, owner of the Toronto *News*, soon replaced Lyon and J.F.B Livesay, former assistant to Canada's domestic press censor. Ernest Chambers, took over in 1918. All three journalists, none of them boat-rockers, found themselves preoccupied with fights with censors, telegraph companies, and editors back home.

In place of real reporting, many people turned to the pulp propaganda books that appeared within a few months of the outbreak of hostilities. Some of them were created out of the imaginations of their authors. Others, like the work of Coningsby Dawson, were the work of gifted writers who lent their skills to the British propaganda system. Their books, usually aimed at an American audience as part of the campaign to bring the United States into the war, were underwritten by the British government. Some writers, like Dawson, saw the war as a sort of religious crusade, one that would not only stop the evil of "Prussianism" but would also cleanse society through the shedding of the blood of so many good young men. Books written by women, usually nurses who had seen some of the carnage of the front line, tapped into the feminist wave that had begun with the pre-war suffragette movement and had, through the war, pulled in working-class women to take the job of men in the factories.

The military also encouraged the creation of official and semi-official newspapers and magazines written and produced by members of the Armed Forces. Called "trench papers," they were usually put out by amateur journalists working at headquarters and rest areas. They sprang up at training camps, military hospitals, and on ships. Some were mimeographed or even typed with carbon paper. They provide an interesting insight into the minds of the people who were actually fighting the war, although the fingers of propaganda and censorship have left obvious prints on them.

After the war, even the senior members of the German High Command credited the British information control system with undermining the German war effort, defining the Germans as the aggressor power, and convincing politicians and citizens in the United States to abandon their neutrality and come into the war on the side of the British.

In the latter years of the war, Canada had its own domestic press censorship system headed by former newspaper journalist and British intelligence agent Ernest Chambers. He and his staff went through newspapers, magazines, music recordings, and films looking for anything that even vaguely portrayed the Germans and their allies positively. Ethnic newspapers, along with a handful of small English-language papers, were shut down. Under the War Measures Act, the censorship rules were steadily tightened to the point where it became illegal to discuss the origins of the war or to advocate a negotiated peace. The censorship lasted into 1919 as the government tried to quell any media support for Bolshevism and used its war powers to put down the labour unrest that flared up after the Armistice.

The readers of Canada were ill-served through the entire war, leaving both civilians and veterans angry and confused in the subsequent decades. Veterans returned to Canada shocked and troubled that people did not understand their war. Many could not accept the maudlin commemorations and the tacky attempts to sanitize and somehow moralize the war. Most, especially those who were not among the tens of thousands of wounded vets, simply tried to carry on. Others took to the bottle or lashed out by committing crimes. Civilians were afraid of the veterans. Liquor prohibition, brought in during the war, and tough new drug laws were aimed at the returning soldiers, and they knew it.

By the mid-1920s, people began pointing fingers. Walter Lippmann's *Public Opinion*, published in 1920, was a bestseller throughout the continent. Lippmann explained the British propaganda campaign and convinced many Americans that they had been manipulated and tricked into a war that was none of their business. They had been conned into accepting bogus stories of German atrocities committed against civilians. Proud British propagandists, who had convinced themselves there could never be another Great War, bragged in post-war memoirs about their coups. Americans read these books and became determined not to be fooled again. That attitude was to become entrenched in American society for the next two decades, with dire consequences for Britain and much of the rest of the world when Hitler engaged in aggression and atrocities that were beyond the imagination of the most skilled Great War propaganda writer. American — and many Canadians, especially in Quebec — believed the horror stories about the Nazis were cut from the same cloth as Britain's First World War propaganda. For many, it took the end-of-the-war revelations of Hitler's Final Solution to show there was, indeed, a wolf this time.

AUGUST 1914:
The Pressure to Enlist

Coningsby Dawson, who was born in 1883 and graduated from Oxford in 1905, was a writer who worked in the United States before the war. He sailed for England on a holiday three days before war was declared. Like so many of the Canadians who volunteered in the first weeks of the First World War, Dawson was British-born and had come to Canada with his parents in the massive wave of immigration that opened the Prairies during Sir Wilfrid Laurier's administration. Dawson returned to Canada in 1915, studied for several months at the Royal Military College, was commissioned as a lieutenant, and was sent to France in 1916. Dawson was seriously wounded in the arm at the Battle of Lens in June 1917. He spent the rest of the war writing propaganda books and briefing papers for Canadian officials. In this book, published about eight months before the end of the war, Dawson argued the blood-soaked trenches would someday be seen with the same awe and spiritual power as Christ's cross, and would redeem the sins of Western society. He continued to write about the war until 1922, when his flow of one or two books a year suddenly stopped. He published one post-war fiction novel, in 1934, and died in 1958.

Coningsby Dawson

At the Empire Music Hall in Leicester Square, tragedy bared its broken teeth and mouthed at me. We had reached the stage at which we had become intensely patriotic by the singing of songs. A beautiful actress, who had no thought of doing "her bit" herself, attired as Britannia, with a colossal Union Jack for background, came before the footlights and sang the recruiting song of the moment,

"We don't want to lose you
But we think you ought to go."

Some one else recited a poem calculated to shame men into immediate enlistment, two lines of which I remember:

"I wasn't among the first to go
But I went, thank God, I went."

The effect of such urging was to make me angry. I wasn't going to be rushed into khaki on the spur of an emotion picked up in a music-hall. I pictured the comfortable gentlemen, beyond the military age, who had written these heroic taunts, had gained reputation by so doing, and all the time sat at home in suburban security. The people who recited or sting their effusions, made me equally angry; they were making sham-patriotism a means of livelihood and had no intention of doing their part. All the world that by reason of age or sex was exempt from the ordeal of battle, was shoving behind all the rest of the world that was not exempt, using the younger men as a shield against his own terror and at the same time calling them cowards. That was how I felt. I told myself that if I went — and the *if* seemed very remote — I should go on a conviction and not because of shoving. They could hand me as many white feathers as they liked, I wasn't going to be swept away by the general hysteria. Besides, where would be the sense in joining? Everybody said that our fellows would be home for Christmas. Our chaps who were out there ought to know; in writing home they promised it themselves.

The next part of the music-hall performance was moving pictures of the Germans' march into Brussels. I was in the Promenade and had noticed a Belgian soldier being made much of by a group of Tommies. He was a queer looking fellow, with a dazed expression and eyes that seemed to focus on some distant horror; his uniform was faded and torn — evidently it had seen active service. I wondered by what strange fortune he had been conveyed from the brutalities of invasion to this gilded, plush-seated sensation-palace in Leicester Square.

I watched the screen. Through ghastly photographic boulevards the spectre conquerors marched. They came on endlessly, as though somewhere out of sight a human dam had burst, whose deluge would never be stopped. I tried to catch the expressions of the men, wondering whether this or that or the next had contributed his toll of violated women and butchered children to the list of Hun atrocities. Suddenly the silence of the theatre was startled by a low, infuriated growl, followed by a shriek which was hardly human. I have since heard the same kind of sounds when the stumps of the mutilated are being dressed and the pain has become intolerable. Everybody turned in their seats — gazing through the dimness to a point in the Promenade near to where I was. The ghosts on the screen were forgotten. The faked patriotism of the songs we had listened to had become a thing of naught. Through the welter of bombast, excitement and emotion we had grounded on reality.

The Belgian soldier, in his tattered uniform, was leaning out, as though to bridge the space that divided him from his ghostly tormentors. The dazed look was gone from his expression and his eyes were focused in the fixity of a cruel purpose — to kill, and kill, and kill the smoke-grey hordes of tyrants so long as his life should last. He shrieked imprecations at them, calling upon God and snatching epithets from the gutter in his furious endeavour to curse them. He was dragged away by friends in khaki, overpowered, struggling, smothered but still cursing.

I learnt afterwards that he, with his mother and two brothers, had been the proprietors of one of the best hotels in Brussels. Both his brothers had been called to arms and were dead. Anything might have happened to his mother — he had not heard from her. He himself had escaped in the general retreat and was going back to France as interpreter with an English regiment. He had lost everything; it was the sight of his ruined hotel, flung by chance on the screen, that had provoked his demonstration. He was dead to every emotion except revenge — to accomplish which he was returning.

The moving pictures still went on; nobody had the heart to see more of them. The house rose, fumbling for its coats and hats; the place was soon empty.

Just as I was leaving a recruiting sergeant touched my elbow. "Going to enlist sonny?

I shook my head. "Not to-night Want to think it over."

"You will," he said. "Don't wait too long. We can make a man of you. If I get you in my squad, I'll give you hell."

I didn't doubt it.

Coningsby Dawson, The Glory of the Trenches *(Toronto: S.B. Gundy, 1918).*

APRIL 22, 1915:
A Day With the Gunners at Ypres

William Boyd was a pathologist who worked as a medic with the Royal Medical Corps during the First World War. He became one of Canada's most successful pathologists after the war. He began teaching at the University of Manitoba in 1916 and wrote some of his profession's best textbooks. In 1937, he moved to the University of Toronto, and, in 1951, joined the faculty of the University of British Columbia. In 1968, he was awarded the Order of Canada. Boyd died in 1979. This piece was published in *With a Field Ambulance at Ypres.* The book, published in 1916, was subject to censorship of names of units and officers' names. It is a collection of letters home, so its contents were examined by both postal and press censors. This is an account of Boyd's visit to a forward artillery unit. A few hours after it was written, the Germans unleashed a gas attack on nearby French trenches.

The Canadian government distributed this picture with the caption "Over the Top: Canadians on their way to victory at the taking of Courcelle." In fact, it was likely staged in England, far from the fighting.

WILLIAM BOYD

There is no doubt about it when the gunners have a much better time of it than the infantry. They certainly live in greater peace and comfort, and their particular method of slaughtering men is full of scientific interest. As we passed one of the batteries we found the men engaged in a game of football. Suddenly the sharp sound of a whistle was heard. In a moment every man was a motionless statue. A hostile aeroplane was overhead, which would have once detected the gun position if the men had been moving about, whereas motionless they were invisible.

Our first visit was to one of the observation stations on Kemmel Hill. The hill is covered with trees, and amongst the trees are numbers of dug-outs, all used as observation posts by the various batteries, but quite invisible until you are actually upon them, so cunningly are they concealed. We reached the one for which we were bound, and entered. Inside were a couple of chairs on which we sat in comfort, and by means of a telescope suspended from the roof surveyed through a narrow opening in the wall the network of trenches spread out in the valley at our feet. It was glorious afternoon, ideal for observing, and there in front of us, spread out before our eyes, was a wonderful panorama.

Immediately opposite at a distance of a couple of miles were the German trenches, and over those lines the shrapnel was bursting in little fleecy clouds. Away to the left lay Ypres, like some dream city in the warm light of the sinking sun, with delicate wisps of mist eddying around its shattered spires. In between was Hill 60, where a furious bombardment was in progress. And yet with it not a living creature nor moving thing could be seen for miles, and the whole countryside seemed as deserted as the Sahara. But it was a Sahara swarming with moles, moles who live in burrows, who spied at one another through peep holes, in whose minds there was but one thought — to slay — and who shouted at each other with deep-toned voices, which carried but one message — death….

Every eye was strained at the enemy's trenches, and in a few moments we could see the flash and white smoke of the shell as it burst over the trenches, but it seemed ages before the noise of the explosion reached us. The first shell was short and a little high, so the range was corrected. The next was right for length, but still high; the fusing was altered. The third was just right, exactly above the trenches, and a murmur of satisfaction arose from a little group of watchers. Truly the gunner is a bloodthirsty man, and I must admit that I had certain qualms for the poor beggars in the trenches.

William Boyd, With a Field Ambulance at Ypres *(Toronto: The Musson Book Company/George A. Doran Company, 1916).*

APRIL 22, 1915:
"Canadians — Canadians — That's All!"

Harold Peat (1893–1960) was born in Jamaica and, as a child, moved to Toronto with his mother. He enlisted at the beginning of the war, but the military realized quite quickly that he was more valuable to the war effort as an author and propagandist. After serving with the First Canadian Contingent in its first actions, Peat wrote of his experiences in the internationally bestselling *Private Peat*. The book was made into a movie in 1918 by Edward José, with Peat playing himself. Peat spent the rest of his working life as a motivational lecturer and the manager of a speakers' bureau headquartered in New York City. He retired to Jamaica after the Second World War and ran a small hotel at Discovery Bay. This excerpt, describing the first gas attack of the war, was published in *The Great War in Verse and Prose*, a small, red canvas-covered book issued in 1919 as an Ontario school textbook. On April 22, the Germans attempted to crush the Ypres salient by sending a cloud of chlorine gas against lines of trenched held by the French. When the French line broke under this strange and terrifying new weapon, Canadian troops rushed in to close the gap. Two days later, the Germans used gas against the Canadian lines, but members of the First Contingent held their ground.

Harold Reginald Peat

The night of April twenty-second was probably the most momentous time of the six days and night of fighting. Then the Germans concentrated on the Yser Canal, over which there was but one bridge, a murderous barrage fire which would have effectively hindered the bringing up of reinforcements or guns, even if we had any in reserve.

During the early stages of the battle, the enemy had succeeded to a considerable degree in turning the Canadian left wing. There was a large open gap at this point, where French Colonial troops had stood until the gas had come over. Toward this sector, the Germans rushed rank after rank of infantry, backed by tanks and heavy artillery. To the far distant left were our British comrades. They were completely blocked by the German advance. They were like rats in a trap and could not move.

At the start of the battle, the Canadian lines ran from the village of Langemarck over to St. Julien, a distance of approximately three to four miles. From St. Julien to the sector where the British had joined the Turcos was a distance of probably two miles.

These two miles had to be covered, and covered quickly. We had to save the British extreme right, and we had to close the gap. There was no question about it. It was our job. On the night of April the twenty-second we commenced to put this into effect. We were still holding our position with the handful of men who were in reserves, all of whom had been included in the original grand total of twelve thousand. We had to spread out across the gap of two miles and link up to the British right wing. Doing this was no easy task. Our company was out first and we were told to get into field-skirmishing order. We lined up in the pitchy darkness at five paces apart, but no sooner had we reached this than a whispered order passed from man to man: "Another pace, lads, just another pace." This order came again and yet again. Before we were through and ready for the command to advance, we were at least twice five paces each man from his nearest comrade.

Then it was our Captain who told us bluntly that we were obviously outnumbered by the Germans, ten to one. Then he told us that, practically speaking, we had scarcely the ghost of a chance, but a bluff might succeed. He told us to "swing the lead over them." This we did by yelling, hooting, shouting, clamouring, until it seemed, and the enemy believed, that we were ten to their one.

The ruse succeeded. At daybreak, when we rested, we found that we had driven the enemy back almost to his original position. All night long we had been fighting with our backs to our comrades who were in the front trenches. The enemy had got behind us and we had to face about in what served for trenches. By dawn we had him back again in his original position, and we were facing in the old direction. By dawn we had almost, but not quite, forced a junction with the British right.

The night of April the twenty-second is one that I can never forget. It was frightful, yes. Yet there was a grandeur in the appalling intensity of living, in the appalling intensity of death as it surrounded us.

The German shells rose and burst behind us. They made the Yser a stream of molten glory. Shells fell in the city, and split the darkness of the heavens in the early night hours. Later, the moon rose in the splendor of springtime. Straight behind the tower of the great cathedral it rose and shone down on a bloody earth.

Suddenly the grand old Cloth Hall burst into flames. The spikes of fire rose and fell and rose again. Showers of sparks went upward. A pall of smoke would form and cloud the moon, waver, break and pass. There was the mutter and rumble and roar of great guns....

It was glorious. It was terrible. It was inspiring. Through an inferno of destruction and death ... we lived because we must.

Perhaps our greatest reward came when on April the twenty-sixth the English troops reached us. We had been completely cut off by the enemy barrage from all communication with the other sectors of the line. Still, through the wounded gone back, word of our stand had drifted out. The English boys fought and force-marched and fought again their terrible way through the barrage to our aid, and when they arrived, weary and worn and torn, cutting their bloody way to us, they cheered themselves hoarse; cheered as they marched along, cheered and gripped our hands as they got within touch of us. Yell after yell went upward, and stirring words woke the echoes. The boys of the Old Country paid their greatest tribute to us of the New as they cried:

"Canadians — Canadians — that's all!"

Harold Reginald Peat, Private Peat *(Bobs-Merrill Co., 1917). Reprinted in J.E. Wetherell, B.A.,* The Great War in Verse and Prose *(Toronto: A.T. Wildgress, Printer to the King's Most Excellent Majesty, 1919).*

NOVEMBER 1915:
Entertaining the Troops Before They're Sent to the Front

This article comes from a trench newspaper published by 2nd Army Troops Company, Canadian Engineers. Starved for news about themselves, Canadian soldiers started their own unofficial newspapers, which were usually printed on regular stationary or copied using carbon paper. The papers used military-issue paper and copying facilities, and the journalists were bound by military censorship, but the trench papers give readers an interesting look at front-line life. This article describes a send-off party in England for troops about to cross to the fighting front in France.

SERGEANT MITCHELL

It was the happy suggestion of our genial captain, that a farewell concert and luncheon [be held] on the eve of our departure for the front. The boys were all invited to bring their wives and sweet hearts, and if they did not have one of their own to bring one belonging to somebody else. There was a big crowd, but plenty of room for all, and they seemed to have plenty of room for all the good things on hand. Knowing that we could not pull the concert off without allowing Sergt. Cook to give us all a bad twenty minutes, with that rag time organization of his, which reminds one of a Chinese concert where all of the Chinamen are all drunk, we thought it better to know the worst at once, so we had him tear off a few spasms of something, assisted by Sapper Dunham on the bagpipes. Well! The audience remained and when Sapper Topping gave a splendid rendition of a solo entitled "Thora" we were on our way for an enjoyable time.

Lce. Cpl. Mar gave a splendid patriotic recitation which was followed by a more humorous reading, as an encore number.

The event of the evening was performed by Miss Nan McGregor (13 years of age) whose Scottish dancing and patriotic songs won for her the admiration of all present. Miss McGregor responded cheerfully to the many encores, and we were sure that our boys will not soon forget this excellent little entertainment.

Mr. C.A. Cook rendered several very fine baritone solos some of which were very humorous.

Number 2850 made his first little bow to the 2nd Army Troops Coy. as an entertainer, and it is safe to say that he is a marked man for future entertainments, after his very funny and well-rendered reading, entitled "The Ghost."

Sapper Murphy gave a good comic song that brought forth a good round of applause, after a few pleasant remarks from Cpt. Shaw, the chairman of the evening, everyone moved into the room adjoin where refreshments were served, consisting of ice cream, cake and coffee.

The floor of the concert room was cleared, and a large crowd finished the evening fun with dancing, everyone feeling that the farewell concert and dance was the most fitting way to spend with the boys of the 2nd Army Troops Coy who are on their way to do their worst.

Sergeant Mitchell, The Busy Beaver, *November 1915. Canadian War Museum, Archives Box 26 Per Box UG1 B879.*

DECEMBER 31, 1915:
Bill's Ghost Haunts the Trenches of Flanders

A great wave of patriotic book-writing, most of it jingoistic trash, flowed from the Great War. Murray's stories connected with the soldiers who had actually seen the front lines, combining humour with telling descriptions of day-to-day life. By effectively banning the press from the front, the British and French left it to the participants to tell the world about life in the trenches.

W.W. MURRAY

Back home, Bill had sung in the church choir and, such was his eminence and respectability, he had even been approached to run as town councilor. Bill was the quartermaster of our section, holding the exalted rank of lance-corporal, with pay while so employed. He was a righteous, trustworthy, conscientious man. Very rarely did he go on a toot, but when he did fall off the wagon, it was in a slithering sort of a way. All in all, Bill was one of the most gentlemanly lads I ever came across.

On New Year's Eve, 1915, we were at Ridgewood, between the Front Line and Dickebusch. The situation was quiet, Fritz was no more hostile than usual, and the night gave every promise of passing quietly. Rations had arrived, the rum was dished out and the camp slumbered.

Suddenly, Fritz took it into his head to liven things up. Just about 11 pip-emma he began crashing five-nines into the wood — not a very nice way to end the Old Year. A salvo burst right among the group of shelters which housed my section, and in alarm I crawled out to find what damage had been done. Several of the boys were already on the spot.

"Anybody hurt?" I demanded.

"Don't know yet, Sarge," said one of the chaps. "A 5.9 crashed into old Bill's shelter. We better get some shovels an' dig 'im out."

That was terrible.

We all scuttled around for shovels. Bill's shelter was the usual structure of slimy sandbags, with a few sheets of corrugated iron for a roof. What that five-nine hadn't done to it couldn't be told. The place was simply a reeking mess, everything collapsed.

Poor old Bill.

"Well, we've got to dig him out an' bury him properly," I said. "Let's get goin'."

We worked in the dismal, drizzling darkness, scooping out shovelfuls of muck, the while Fritz continued bursting H.E. and shrapnel all over the place. However, we finally got down to where Bill's body should have been, hoping, of course, that it wasn't there.

One of the lads, smaller than the rest, wormed his way over the slimy debris.

"Here's a bit of his greatcoat, Sarge," he said, his voice muffled among the debris.

"Any trace of the old boy himself?" I asked.

"Just a sec."

There was a long silence, and an ominous one. Finally the chap emerged attempting to extricate a large fragment of flesh.

"Blown to bits, Sarge," he whispered. "Shell got a direct hit on him. Dug this outs the bunk, where Bill had bin sleepin', covered with his greatcoat."

"Nothing more?"

"Nope. Blown clean to bits."

Well, we felt very uncomfortable, sad. What was to be done? The shelter was an utter wreck, and mixed among the ruins and the debris were small pieces of Bill. Best thing to do was simply to heap everything back, cover it over and let that be Bill's grave. I told the boys to bury the fragment.

Worming through the brush, I sought out the officers' shelters, and there reported to our own commander. He was extremely sympathetic. He paid glowing tribute to Bill's courage and integrity, to his fine spirit of comradeship. He recalled with feeling that on the days we managed to keep Bill sober there wasn't a better troop in the whole C.E.F. Furthermore — and I thought this quite a delicate point — it was a great comfort to know Bill was on the wagon when the Grim Reaper snaffled him.

Yes, sir, poor old Bill. When it was all over, I took the lads to my own shelter and handed them a tot of rum. We were discussing old Bill's virtues, saying how much the choir back home would miss him, and what a fine quartermaster lance-corporal he'd been, when the voices of some late revelers came floating up from the duckboards across Dickebusch Lake.

They'd been down in the village, celebrating the New Year, and were just returning, flown with red ink and grenadine.

"Sweet Adoline" and "The Long, Long Trail" were wafted to our ears, and the voices came nearer. We continued to pour forth eulogiums on Bill; but as the songsters got in among the shelters, I became uncomfortable. I saw the other boys getting a bit uneasy, too.

Without a word, I got up and crawled out of the shelter. Of course, it was pitch dark; but the roysterers were right home now.

"Hey, cut out that racket," I shouted. "Where d'ya think y'are? Cut it out."

"Happy New Year, Sergeant!"

The voice was the voice of Bill or his ghost.

"Who's that?"

"Well, fer cryin' out loud! Dontcha know yer own lance-corporal, Sarge?" hiccoughed the voice.

"Bill?"

"Bill — yes, none other than old Bill —"

The other boys were clustering around, and Bill approached. Sure enough, here he was, large as life. He was a bit rocky on his pins and swayed like a tamarack in a gale, but sure enough — there was Bill.

"Whatcha done to me dugout, Sarge?" asked Bill.

With puzzled wits I explained briefly. The bombardment, the collapse of the dugout, the finding of his greatcoat covering a fragment of flesh.

"You thought that bit of flesh was me, didja, Sarge? Whaja do with it?"

"Thinkin' it was you, Bill, we buried it," I said.

"Gee, that's tough, Sarge, I have to tell you; but that hunk of flesh you thought was me," said Bill, "was tomorrow's meat ration."

W.W. Murray, Five Nines and Whiz Bangs *(Ottawa: Legionary Library, 1937).*

JUNE 29, 1916:
The Last Letter Before Beaumont Hamel

Francis T. "Mayo" Lind earned his nickname by writing a piece for the St. John's *Daily News* complaining about the quality of cigarettes that Newfoundland soldiers were issued in the trenches. Readers responded by sending the troops plenty of Mayo brand cigarettes, which were a brand that was popular with Newfoundlanders. Frank Lind was thirty-five years old when he joined the army, and could have easily avoided war service. He fought at the Dardanelles, spent some time in Egypt, and was at the Western Front. Censorship and military discipline wouldn't allow him to write about the big push that was planned on the Somme, although he makes several allusions to it. Lind was one of the 780 Newfoundlanders who attacked at Beaumont-Hamel in the Somme on the morning of July 1, 1916. Only 110 men survived without wounds. Lind was one of the men who died. Beaumont-Hamel destroyed the Newfoundland Regiment as a fighting force. The waste of young men at Beaumont-Hamel is still mourned by the people of Newfoundland.

FRANCIS T. "MAYO" LIND

These Germans have a great fancy for putting up messages over their trenches for us to read. One day they put up "We sympathize with you in the loss of Kitchener." We did not know what it meant until the evening news came to us that Lord Kitchener and his Staff were drowned. How strange that the Germans should know more about it than we did; but they seem to know everything. No doubt the sinking of H.M.S. *Hampshire* was planned before she left England.

The other day someone saw a German digging and fired a shot at him; down drops Mr. Sausage, and held up his shovel signaling the results of the shot, and up he got to dig again, but he didn't signal the next shot — don't ask why!

Capt. Bert Butler is a hero, and never daunted. I think he is the bravest man I ever saw; he cares for nothing, and today he is going about, as happy as a lark, with a bullet wound in his cheek.

Our bombers have done great work, and are ready to do more when the time comes. Lance-Corporal Arch Gillam is in charge of 8 Platoon Bombers, and he has a good team with him: J. Pennell, F. Freake, T. Seymour, G. Abbott, N. Dean, G. Madore, and last, but not least, the unconquerable Joe Andrews. Joe came out to the Peninsula [Gallipoli, where Lind had seen action earlier in the war] and not getting enough of it there, he determined to do away with some Germans before seeing Newfoundland again, and here we find Joe Andrews going about like an armoured cruiser ready for action, and goodness help Germany when he gets going. He is a very accurate shot with bombs and rifle. Joe is also a good singer, and helps to pass many a weary hour when out for a rest.

Did I tell you about the mud here yet? Well, just a word; it is mud and slush from head to toe. We are quite used to it now, and would you believe it, we enjoy it. Yes, it is great fun, for believe me, a man can get used to anything, and when this bunch gets back they will be the hardiest men in the world. Here we face danger, awful danger, every hour, looking over the parapet sometimes during a beautiful clear sky, gazing across "No Man's Land" to the enemy's lines, perhaps just before dawn. It is wonderful how our boys have hardened to this life — shot and shells — and some shells you bet — flying all around them, yet not a flinch. Ah, I wish I could just, in imagination, take you into the trenches. I wish I could illustrate to you just what it is like, but I cannot. No pen could describe what it is like, how calmly one stands and faces death, jokes and laughs; everything is just an everyday occurrence. You are mud-covered, dry and caked, perhaps, but you look at the chap next you and you laugh at the state he is in; then you look down at your own clothes and then the other fellow laughs. Then a whizz comes across and misses both of you, and you both laugh together....

I will ring off for this time but I will write again shortly, when I hope to send you a very interesting letter. Tell everybody that they may feel proud of the Newfoundland Regiment, for we get nothing but praise from the Divisional General down. With kind regards.

Francis T. "Mayo" Lind, The Letters of Mayo Lind *(St. John's: Kellick Press and Creative Publishers, 2001).*

DECEMBER 25, 1916:
Behind the Great Advance

A year after their arrival in France, the writers of this trench publication were issuing a professional-looking magazine that lacked the rough writing and typographic errors of their first issues. Higher-ups had seen the value of this and other semi-official newspapers. *The Busy Beaver* had evolved from being the work of amateur soldier-writers to a piece of slick propaganda. Still, it was aimed at an audience that could see for itself whether the magazine was accurate in its news and its description of life on the front.

A Canadian soldier reads a trench newspaper published by fellow soldiers, Western Front 1917.

J.P.E.

The Province of Picardy is very beautiful. Nature seems to have chosen for her picture here a succession of closely-following hills and valleys — the hills, well-cultivated, sharply defined in the sunlight; the valleys, sheltered by the hills, with their winding roads and nestling shaded villages. And it is over these self-same hills and valleys that the great advance is pushing forward.

Let us stand on one of the main roads that lead up to the line. If you could picture this road in peace time you would see it on the high French gig, the peasant cart, and the occasional swift-moving motor. But what a contrast is its present state! To the eye of the watcher the scene is one of orderly confusion, to use a paradox. On one side of the road a steady stream of vehicles is ever pushing onward. Lorries, with their fanciful designs, preponderate. They are the mainstay of the Army. Limbers, G.S. wagons, guns, tractors, all are found here, halting sometimes, but making ground slowly and surely.

The country on each side of the road is full of men and transport. Everywhere one sees horse lines, backed by their orderly array of vehicles — limbers, tool carts, dot the hillside, like mushrooms in a field. And everywhere men. The whole country seems to swarm with them.

We are on the main road; in front lines lies a long, low ridge that the British went when the first barrage [of the Battle of the Somme] lifted on the morning of July 1. Strong points there were and many, but of these only the huge craters show where they have been lifted bodily off the map. Over the ridge the eye can only faintly follow the rough outline of where the Hun trenches were before the attack, of the trenches themselves little remain. They have been almost obliterated by the shell fire. You look at your map, "Halloa!" you say, "there is a village marked here." It should be right there, and a few short months ago you would have seen one of those well-to-do villages plentiful in this section of the country, with its costly farms and avenues of lofty elm trees. Reader, you see nothing — absolutely nothing — nothing to show that there has ever been a habitation here, except a few stray brick-bats among ragged tree stumps, and the unutterable chaos of shell holes. Over in front of us on the ridge the German shells are bursting, and all around us our own guns are hammering away.

Standing there on that war-torn spot, after a feeling of desolation, a wave of elation comes over you. Here, the Flying Corps people will tell you, was one of the most strongly defended sections of the whole line, a vast series of network trenches to surmount, on a naturally strong position. And we are over and beyond it, and going forward all the time. Look up in the air and you will see our own aeroplanes wheeling and circling; where are the Hun planes? Ask the Flying Corps. They will tell you that here the Fritz plane is a washout as far as the eyes of his army are concerned. Look at our guns! Just look at 'em! Did you ever see so many guns before? Just listen to the stuff going over, 12in. and 9.2in and 6in. — every caliber, all whistling their cheerful song to our own men in the trenches as they go over. And you cannot help but contrast the difference between now and two years ago. After the first battle of Ypres the popular legend has it that the infantry commander asked the C.R.A. of the supporting artillery how his guns had been working. "Fine," he replied. "Both guns are firing great." And what of the men themselves who are pushing the line ahead bit by bit? Reader, if you could stand with me and see the cheerful faces of a battalion going in — going in, hark you, to relieve a battalion that has probably lost many of its best — going in to face death and Blighties, mud and discomfort — you would join with me in that saying which has gradually become a by-word since August 22, 1914, when the first two corps took the brunt of the German drive. "We take our hats off to the Infantry!"

J.P.E., The Busy Beaver. *Canadian War Museum Archives Box 26 Per Box UG1 B879.*

EASTER 1917:
Canadian Troops Take Vimy Ridge

Stewart Lyon was the managing editor of the *Globe*. He was the first Canadian war correspondent in France, arriving in March 1917. He was required to file his stories to the newly-established Canadian Press wire service, a government-subsidized co-operative that shared news with most of the country's daily newspapers. Lyon missed the Canadian attack at Vimy Ridge, and no other Allied reporters were on the battlefield. Lyon put together his story from official statements issued by the press officers at the Canadian Headquarters. Vimy Ridge was the first attack launched by all the Canadian forces in France. While it was successful, the Allies lost the Battle of Arras, the offensive that encompassed Vimy Ridge. Still, Vimy was one of the most important Canadian actions of the First World War and eclipsed the Canadian successes at Ypres and Amiens in the public consciousness.

STEWART LYON

Canadian Headquarters in France, April 12 (via London) — From the last position held by them on Vimy Ridge the Germans were swept this morning (Thursday) after one of the most fiercely contested engagements in which the Canadians have recently taken part. This morning at 5:30 o'clock during a blinding snowstorm, an assaulting column was dispatched to drive the enemy from the height known as "The Pimple," occupying a dominating position on the ridge, to the northeast of Souchez. Though wearied by the constant struggle against the enemy and elements the last four days, the men responded splendidly. Swarming up the height, they attacked the enemy garrison, which included troops specially brought up to hold the position, among them the Fifth battalion of the Prussian Grenadier Guards.

The Germans fought under the peremptory orders to hold the position at all costs. The Canadians were not to be denied, however. Over the shell-plowed land and machine gun-fire, they climbed to the summit, and by 7 o'clock the flower of the German army were fleeing to the east and sought shelter in the village of Givenchy. This victory, the second within a week, gives our army absolute command of the entire ridge. Monday's success opened the way by the capture of Hill 145. That hill is the highest point on the ridge. It had to be secured before the attack on "The Pimple" could be made with any hope of success.

By today's win on the part of the Canadians, and the victory of the British, who carried Bois en Hache, on the west side of the Souchez River, the entire valley of Souchez is in our hands and we can look down on the enemy's positions in the plain of Cambrai.

Stewart Lyon, The Canadian Press, April 12, 1917.

OCTOBER 1917:
Night Attack on the Road to Passchendaele

Will Bird was a very lucky man. From Amherst, Nova Scotia, he was twenty-three years old and working as a farm hand in western Canada when the war broke out. He quickly returned to Amherst and tried to enlist but was turned down due to bad teeth. Angry and disgusted, he went back out west, and, months later, learned that his brother Steve had been killed in action in 1915. Bird again tried to enlist, and this time was accepted. He served with the 42nd Royal Highlanders of Canada in Flanders and France. He fought at Vimy Ridge, Passchendaele, and in the battles leading up to the end of the war, including the November 11 attack on Mons. Bird kept a diary of his time in the army which he rewrote into the best soldier's memoire of the war: *Ghosts Have Warm Hands.* After the war, Bird turned to writing full-time, publishing fiction and non-fiction books and magazine articles for periodicals in Canada and the U.S. He suffered a terrible loss when his only son was killed in the Second World War. In the post-war years, Bird

A Canadian soldier rebuilds his dugout after it was hit by an artillery shell. Passchendaele, 1917.

continued to write and lectured at Mt. Allison University in Sackville, New Brunswick. He died in Sackville in 1984, at the age of ninety-three.

WILLIAM R. BIRD

Word came to get ready. Every man was to have two Mills bombs to throw if need be. Baillee came and shook hands with me, a long hard clasp without a word spoken. Then I was amazed when Ira Black came and whispered he was glad we were on our way. The waiting was deadly and now we would have action and get from the hateful swamp when it was over. Then a sergeant came with a jug of rum and every man who would take it had a stiff jolt.

At least we found the road. It wasn't much. Shell fire had almost erased it in spots. We started in four little parties, McIntyre leading on the left. I was crawling directly behind him and told him that if I saw anything of the enemy I would pull his foot. Lugar was back of me, then Charlie Hale, Stewart, Mickey, Tommy, Brown and Johnson. On the other side of the so-called road was Clark, and back of him were Baillie, Ira Black, Jennings, a big man who disliked the French but who was religious and often got the boys to sing hymns, Neath and Flynn. The rest of the twenty-five followed in two groups.

There was quite a drop of bank on our left. McIntyre did not look left or right but kept scrambling along as fast as possible. I peered over the bank from time to time and suddenly saw three or four Germans raise their heads no more than twenty yards from us. I seized McIntyre's foot to signal him. He yanked it away and spoke angrily. The Germans fired instantly. A bullet creased the top of Lugar's head, slicing his scalp and causing him to be temporarily insane. Hale and I had to hold him down by main force, as had he raised he would have been shot. In our struggle Hale raised up higher than he thought and was likewise creased with a bullet. Now it was Stewart, the stretcher bearer, and I holding Lugar, but he began to quiet and the moment I could let go of him I threw my grenades over the bank. Both exploded as they went down and the Hun shooting stopped at once.

The next thing was to get Lugar's bombs to replace mine, which I did. McIntyre had never stopped and was quite a distance ahead. Clark's party kept up with him. Brown had crawled forward and now he and I left the group and ran to catch up with McIntyre. Machine-guns opened up on all sides. The night was an uproar. We dove into the mud and saw the signal go up for the Stokes support. The German maxim stopped firing and we jumped and started running again. There was a flaming white-hot instant — and oblivion!

When I recovered consciousness my head was splitting with pain and a terrible nausea had seized my stomach. The Stokes shell had dropped beside us, throwing me bodily across the road and knocking Brown down. He was rolled over on his back, feeling for wounds, as I saw him. All around us was the clamour of machine guns, bombs and rifles. I heard McIntyre shouting "Five rounds rapid!" Then his voice shut off abruptly. I discovered my nose was bleeding, and when I tried to get up I collapsed again with dizziness.

The burst of shooting stilled. There were no more bomb explosions. But far on our left another eruption of shooting began to dominate the night. Brown had tried to stand and had just slumped down again when we heard plunging noises in the mud and two dim figures came toward us, puffing and blowing, carrying something and grunting in conversation. They were Germans, big men, and had a machine gun on a tripod. They went past us, apparently thinking us dead, and set up their weapon about thirty feet from us. One man yanked at a long cartridge belt, while the other grunted something. I pulled the pin from one of my grenades, held it for a count or two, then hurled it at the Germans and flattened myself in the mud.

The bomb burst between the two gunners. Not a bit of metal touched Brown or myself. One German never moved but lay on his back, dead. The other pawed at his side feebly for a time, then was still. Brown and I struggled up, went over and made sure both Germans were dead, then heard a voice calling. We found a 42nd man in a shell crater, holding his left arm and groaning. He told us he was from "A" Company, that his group was lost and most of them had been killed or wounded. His left hand dangled, held only by a strip of skin. I cut the skin with my trench knife and bound up the stump with his field dressing, poured a bottle of iodine over it, slit a hole in his tunic and had him thrust his arm through it for support. Then I took off one of his puttees and made a tourniquet as best I could to stop the bleeding. We helped him from the crater and away he went, past the dead German gunners.

At that moment Clark came from somewhere behind us, trying to run and reeling all over the place. "C'mon!" he shouted, "Let's give them hell!"

His shout ended and he pitched into the mud ahead of us. He was dead when we tried to raise him. Another figure emerged from the murk. It was Neath. He said McIntyre was lying to our left, shot through the stomach and dying, unconscious. Neath wanted to get a stretcher and carry him out. We asked him where the others were.

"The party behind Clark's never came along after the shooting started," he said, "and I don't think the ones behind us did. The others are just ahead a few yards in a big shallow crater."

We went on and soon found the place, the limit of our advance, not one hundred yards from where I had yanked McIntyre's foot. Mickey and Old Bill Childs and Johnson were there, crouched low and taking quick shots at a German gun that streaked sparks a very short distance away. Its bullets tore at the crater lip. Brown gave me one of his bombs and we threw them at the same time. The bursts must have been right on the gun, since there was not another shot from it.

A look around showed us three figures still on the bank beyond Mickey. They were all dead: Baillie, his premonition proved correct, and Ira and Jennings, lying together, rifle in hand, all shot through the head by one sweep of the German gun. Beside them was another dead man, Sam Burnett. He had been with one of the rear parties. Neath came with a stretcher and Childs helped him get McIntyre on it. They carried him away, and Johnson went with them as relief in the carrying.

Suddenly I was sick again and vomited severely. Brown and Mickey stayed with me. There was comparative quiet in our sector, but heavy firing to both our right and left. Machine-gun bullets whined around so that we had to crawl, and when we were back a bit we found The Professor lying on the road bank, riddled with bullets. He was plastered with mud and had lost his glasses and steel helmet. Evidently they got lost in the darkness and there he lay, after years of study and culture, a smashed cog of the war machine, with no hope of burial save by a chance shell.

William R. Bird, Ghosts Have Warm Hands *(Toronto: Clarke, Irwin and Co., 1968).*

SPECIAL JOTTINGS FROM THE VINEGAR FACTORY

Knots and Lashings was the official newspaper for the officers and men stationed for training at Fort St. John, Quebec, on the Richelieu River southeast of Montreal. Like many young men, Canadian soldiers spent a considerable amount of time thinking about booze. When they returned from the war, many of them were angered by the tightening of Prohibition laws across the country.

"BEATRICE," *KNOTS AND LASHINGS*

Little sips of red-eye,
Little sips of bass,
Take away the senses,
And make a man an ass.

"Beatrice," Knots and Lashings, *Canadian War Museum Archives, Box 26 Per Box UG1.*

THE SECOND WORLD WAR

THE TWO DECADES BETWEEN THE END OF THE FIRST WORLD WAR AND the beginning of the Second World War saw a tremendous change in the attitudes toward war reporting. This time, Canadian news executives would not buckle under to British censorship. They would leave out information that would actually help the enemy, but they would not accept the handouts of official "eyewitnesses." This war marked the height of Canadian war journalism. Correspondents did not go to the fighting fronts as war tourists, they went embedded as officers, and, like the men they covered, they were at the front for months at a time. Matthew Halton, who worked for the *Toronto Star* in 1939, was one of the first to go overseas. He was sent to Finland to cover the Soviet-Finnish War in the winter of 1939–40 and sent back stories about the depredations of the Red Army that shook *Star* publisher "Holy" Joe Atkinson's faith in Marxism.

Gregory Clark, who had served in the trenches in the First World War, was sent by the *Star* with the first Canadian troops to leave Canada in December 1939, and was able to tour French and British units before the German offensive that began in May 1940. Clark took a look at the poor equipment and complacency of the British forces and the lousy morale of the French and realized the Allies were in deep trouble. Censorship kept him from sharing those observations with the Canadian public. Just before the German conquest of Western Europe, Clark returned to Britain along with Frederick Griffin and Claude Pascoe. The British high command became Griffin's beat. Clark went to France and arrived on the day that the German army violated the borders of the Netherlands, Luxembourg, and Belgium. Clark watched the evacuation of Dunkirk before finally fleeing France just ahead of the Wehrmacht. He returned to Canada to privately brief Atkinson of the situation, and the *Star* tailored its editorial position and its war coverage accordingly.

The *Star* recalled its four war correspondents. Halton went to Washington, where he continued to contribute to CBC and American radio networks. Halton was back in Europe in April to cover the fighting in Greece, but the Greeks had collapsed by the time he arrived, so Halton made for the Middle East. He saw some of the action of the now-forgotten war between British, Free French, and Vichy forces in Syria and Lebanon before heading to North Africa to cover the fight against the Italians and the Afrika Korps. Halton felt he had paid his dues in North Africa and expected to be the *Star*'s reporter in the Sicily campaign, but editor Harry Hindmarsh decided to give the assignment to Griffin and Clark. Halton angrily left the paper. It would be the CBC's gain. Quickly, though, Hindmarsh made a deal that Halton would contribute an article to each issue of the *Star Weekly* magazine.

Griffin arrived in Europe in 1942 and stayed overseas through the rest of the war, covering the Dieppe raid and the fighting in North Africa, Sicily, and Italy. Griffin went back to Allied headquarters in London and became the *Star*'s expert on over-all strategy. Gregory Clark concentrated on front-line reporting of the air war, an extremely dangerous assignment. Griffin and Clark were at Juno Beach on D-Day, with Griffin reporting from a troop ship and Clark watching the landing from an airplane a mile above the Norman coast. Clark stayed close to the action through the war, even in the weeks after his son was killed in action near the French coast. Griffin was with the Canadian army as it fought its way along the North Sea coast into Holland. He was replaced at Eisenhower's headquarters by Ross Harkness, who had stints in the field, including a brief assignment to General Patton's U.S. Third Army as it hooked up with Soviet forces in the last days of the war. Paul Morton tried to parachute into the Balkans to find Tito's partisans and cover the vicious fighting in the region that was part liberation, part civil war. Unfortunately, the operation was botched and Morton was unable to find Tito's forces. Wessely Hicks, a *Star* reporter who had left the paper to work as a Navy public relations officer, was allowed to return to the paper late in the war and work as a roving reporter in northwest Europe. William Kinmond arrived in the early fall of 1944 and was quickly captured by the Wehrmacht.

Allen Kent of the Toronto *Telegram* covered the Canadians' sweep along the North Sea coast and the tough fighting in the Scheldt Estuary.

Ralph Allen of the *Globe and Mail* covered D-Day and the northeastward march of the Canadians and also filed to *Maclean's* magazine, which he went on to edit after the war. Allen was probably the boldest and brightest of the correspondents, able to report the blood and mud fighting while writing tough analyses of strategic decisions and censorship.

The Canadian Press began planning its military coverage in the months leading up to the outbreak of the war. Gil Purcell, the young new general manger of the agency, went to London early in 1939, scouting locations for a London bureau and sizing up the real risks of war. The agency decided it would leave London with the British government if Nazi bombs made the city uninhabitable. Should London face destruction, married CP staffers would quickly be recalled to Canada and single men would take their places in whatever city the British government used as its temporary capital.

Purcell went overseas as an accredited correspondent with the First Canadian Division in 1939. He would soon jump to the army's public relations department. Eddie Johnson, head of the CP bureau in London, left that job to become the first Canadian correspondent accredited by the British. His replacement, Sam Robertson, was killed just months after his appointment. While he was travelling back to London from a short vacation in Canada, Robertson drowned when a German submarine torpedoed the troop ship *Nerissa*.

CP's staffers, who filed the bulk of the war correspondence carried in Canada's newspapers, had to deal with the British telegraph censorship system, which was both ham-fisted and uncaring of the deadline pressure faced by wire service reporters. The press was no longer stuck with the crippling telegraph rates of the previous war, which charged the equivalent of a labourer's daily pay for every word transmitted overseas. The per-word levy was cut by more than 80 percent and The Canadian Press wire service was finally able to afford the type of long analysis and news features that were published in American newspapers.

Beginning in May 1942, the wire service issued *The Canadian Press News*, a tabloid weekly, to Canadian soldiers, and gave free news copy to *The Maple Leaf*, the newspaper put out by the Canadian army's public relations department, which was made up of some of the country's best young reporters and editors. Film makers and print reporters in the Canadian forces were usually journalists in civilian life, and the army film unit often scooped their colleagues in other Allied units. They parachuted ashore before the main D-Day assault, and, because American cameramen were plagued with technical problems, almost all surviving D-Day film is from Canadian action at Juno Beach. The Canadians shot miles of high-quality front-line film during the Sicilian, Italian, and European campaigns, creating an impressive and important record that is still relied upon by historians and documentary makers.

Ross Munro, who would become CP's best war correspondent, arrived in London during the Blitz. CP had lured him away from a tempting offer by the Canadian army. He trained with Canadian soldiers in England, went with them on a raid to Spitsbergen in 1941, then to Dieppe, North Africa, Sicily, Italy, and northwestern Europe. By the end of the war, there were few Canadian soldiers who had seen as much action. Munro had become fairly adept at dealing with censorship and used a flaw in the system to scoop the world on the invasion of Sicily.

CP staff in London were hardly safe from the war: the agency's headquarters suffered direct hits during the Blitz and the neighbourhood surrounding it was destroyed. As the Allies opened more theatres of operation, war correspondents were added to CP's roster: D.G. Amaron, William Stewart, Foster Barclay, Louis V. Hunter, and Maurice Desjardin were accredited to the fighting fronts. They covered the Canadian army in Sicily and Italy, joined in the latter country by Doug Howe. William Boss, who went on to be an award-winning journalist in the post-war years and outlived all of them — he died in 2007 — came to CP after a stint in the army and covered the Canadians as they fought their way into Holland. Munro and Stewart went into Juno Beach with the Canadians, Stewart coming ashore first under nasty fire at Courseulles Beach. Munro had a slightly easier time at Bernieres.

Desjardins covered the entry of the Allies into Paris while his colleagues concentrated their attention on the Canadians holding the left flank of the Allied line in the west. Charles Bruce, the London bureau chief, talked his way onto a plane dropping supplies to trapped troops during Operation Market Garden. When his plane was shot down near Ghent, Belgium, Bruce was cut off from communications with his office. Finally able to find Allied help and to send a cable from Brussels, Bruce flew back to London expecting to resume his desk job. He arrived in London to find reporters had rifled his desk and were busy writing his obituary. His telegram had been lost in the great mass of war messages.

After covering the tough campaign in Holland and the plight of the starving Dutch people, CP staff watched German General Johannes von Blaskowitz surrender his forces in the Netherlands to Canadian general Charles Foulkes. Three days later, CP reporter Margaret Ecker, stationed in Paris, went to Reims to watch the unconditional surrender of the German armed forces to the Allies. She was the only woman correspondent in the room.

Canadians also found jobs with other countries' news agencies: radio reporter Rene Levesque with the U.S. Army's radio division and Charles Lynch with the British wire service Reuters. At home, reporters like Eric Dennis of the Halifax *Herald*, whose reporting set the standard for coverage of the Battle of the Atlantic, were as skilled as most of the overseas correspondents. Dennis was to see the war first-hand when he interviewed the survivors of the Nova Scotia to Newfoundland ferry *Caribou*, which was torpedoed in the Gulf of St. Lawrence in 1942. Many of them had lost their children in the disaster.

Radio news, listened to by nearly everyone in the country, was tough competition for the daily newspapers and The Canadian Press. Charles Bowman of the CBC went across the Atlantic with the First Canadian

Division in December, 1940. With only a few days' warning, he had to hurry to gather the equipment that he needed for recording the war and sending his reports to Canada. J. Alphonse Ouimet, probably the best engineer in the corporation, arrived at about the same time and developed the mobile studio vans that the CBC used through the war. He would later be one of the pioneers of television in Canada and would be a post-war president of the CBC. They were joined by Arthur Holmes. They made up the CBC team that stayed in London through the Blitz and sent home chilling reports on the destruction. Bowman went with the Canadians to Dieppe, then returned to Canada. H. Rooney Pelletier took his place as lead correspondent in London, but jumped to the BBC and was replaced by John Kannawin, who arrived in November 1942. He quickly built a stellar team of correspondents and engineers: Peter Stursberg, Paul Dupuis, Andrew Cowan, A.E. Powley, Lloyd Moore, Matthew Halton, Marcel Ouimet, Paul Barette, Benoit Lafleur, Joseph Beauregard, William Wadsworth, Bill Herbert, Clifford Speer, Fred McCord, A.E. Powley, and Laurence Marshall.

The CBC journalists were encumbered by pre-transistor technology. The tape recorder was a new invention. It was untrustworthy and the sound quality was often poor. Many reports were recorded on disks in the back of trucks that were converted into small recording studios. Correspondents went into battle with heavy portable units that sometimes worked and quite often didn't. Still, the CBC had better equipment than the American networks, and, with the help of the Canadians' skilled engineers, the CBC's reports were better than most of the radio news reports of any of the belligerent countries. British and U.S. networks ended up buying some of the recordings of battle to add to their own correspondents' work, and the sound recording system used by the CBC was so good that the British hired Bushnell and Holmes to drive around southern England recording the sound of German planes. The CBC records were used to train aircraft spotters and the soldiers who manned anti-aircraft guns. On the fighting fronts, these studio trucks got so close to the action that, by the end of the war, they were shot full of bullet and shrapnel holes.

Peter Stursberg, another former newspaper reporter, covered the Allied landing in Sicily. The CBC's reporting and engineering teams had made their reputations in Italy before the first Allied troops crossed the English

Channel. On D-Day, nine CBC correspondents went ashore in Normandy and stayed with the Canadian forces as they crossed Belgium, Holland, and entered northwestern Germany. Two weeks after the fall of Berlin, Peter Stursberg was in Berlin, where he visited the Fuhrerbunker and left with a souvenir knife and fork. Like many other reporters assigned to the fighting front, Stursberg sold stories to magazines like *Maclean's* and *Saturday Night*.

Most of the overseas correspondents became stars in Canada and went on to brilliant careers. Most of them had shown great personal courage, reporting skills, and writing talents. While Charles Lynch, among the least talented of them, would later discount their work as propaganda, they saw themselves as part of a mission to break the Nazi grip on Europe. Some did take on military authorities, but most were content to tell Canadians the stories of their sons and husbands at the front and report on the suffering of civilians in the liberated countries. They certainly had no reason to be ashamed of the work they left behind.

SUMMER 1936:
On Holiday with Hitler

Fascism had some appeal for Depression-weary Europeans and North Americans. Mussolini and Hitler seemed to offer stability, order, and a return to prosperity. They also had state-of-the art media skills, using modernist design and aesthetics that challenged the drabness of the 1930s. This article was published in a family magazine in November 1936. While not a military report per se, it illustrates the mixed messages Canadians received in the first half of the Third Reich's twelve-year run. The house guests at Berchtesgaden were to have unpleasant fates: Hitler killed himself as the Soviets closed in on his Berlin bunker in April 1945; Harvard-educated Hanfstaengl, who was in charge of courting the foreign press, fled Germany before the war and went to work for American military intelligence; Blomberg died in jail in Nuremberg after spending most of the war in disgrace and exile; Goebbels and his wife killed their six children and themselves in Hitler's bunker; Hermann Goring killed himself with cyanide a few minutes before he was to be hanged at Nuremberg; Alfred Rosenberg and Joachim von Ribbentrop kept their date with the hangman at Nuremberg.

W.G. FITZ-GERALD

Shall I ever forget that summer twilight on the terrace as a privileged guest of the Fuhrer — he whom Stanley Baldwin, Britain's Prime Minister, has called: "The only living man who can lift the shadow of Fear from Europe?"

It seemed incredible. For Hitler was wholly transformed. Here I saw this somber man laughing aloud as that musical giant "Putzi" Hanfstaengl, pounded out on the piano that most *un*-German of songs — "Hail, Hail, the Gang's All Here!" This he followed up with "The Sidewalks of New York" — with explanatory asides to the notable "gang" around our table, or else sipping coffee and liqueurs under canvas umbrellas outside....

The "Little Doctor" (our waggish Goebbels) boomed out funny (and naughty!) yarns with great vim and a voice much too big for his body. The ever-immaculate Ribbentrop chatted with Frau Hess about the queer folks he'd met in Paris and London salons. As for Hermann Goring — in easy suspenders, soft shirt and cotton shorts — he was in a sentimental mood. He's often like that after a heavy dinner!

Spread before Hitler himself was a mass of foreign newspapers and magazines. In these Alfred Rosenberg had marked a few cartoons and wisecracks with a red pencil.

"Look at this one," their victim chuckled. "Here I, as a 'hopeless' bachelor who preaches wedded love and baby-drives, am likened to a bald-headed barber touting his own hair-tonics!" And with a flabby hand he shot over the paper to Erick Raeder, who is today's "Von Tirpitz" of Germany's Navy.

But could *this* Hitler, I marveled, be the same mystic I'd seen swaying vast crowds in the open air, and with such hypnotic force that they imitated his every move with unconscious jerks? In those nervy orgies even the soldiers sobbed aloud, women and girls fell on their knees with shut eyes and folded hands of ecstasy!

Or again, I recalled Der Fuhrer in the Reichstag. There he used careful notes. Yet he worked up to a hoarse passion that brought beads of sweat to his resolute face; while both arms jerked up from the elbows, with fists clenched and the famous "browlock" wobbling in reckless disorder ... Was *that* racked Hitler tonight's gay "Squire," happy as a boy who forgot this school-grind in the play and pranks of a summer holiday?

I don't like to say he was in "hobo" rig. But there it was! On the floor beside him I spotted the brim of a battered hat upon which his big Alsatian, "Blonda," squatted to blink meekly. The old tweed coat Hitler sported was too tight and too short for him. His trousers were frayed; and between his knees stood a crooked fir branch picked up in the woods.

So this is the political idol by whom 65,000,000 Germans swear? His august name at least one mountain carries. So do the helpless rumps of cows and pigs on his neighbors' farms. And so do the white pavements of the Prinz Regentenstrasse in his beloved Munich, where adorers wear cute "printing"-shoes which leave *Heil Hitler!* greetings in black or blue letters at every step they take. Could homage go any further?

It can. For in Berlin's Unter den Linden I saw an awed crowd around the plate-glass window of a high-brow art-shop. What were they gazing at? At a new (and autographed) crayon portrait of their Leader, drawn by Carl Rosemann from special sittings given him in Breslau. *And that ikon was completely framed with pictures of Jesus Christ!* It was easily seen which was *the* Redeemer of Germany!

Our Squire's merry voice, too — could this be the same that moved the nations? Was it this man's nod which threw all France into armed panic; so that the "mole runs" of Andre Maginot (they cost $300,000,000!) were manned and gunned as though to repel a swarming invasion?

"No politics here!" was the cheery slogan tonight in this cool, airy place of green restful rooms, white furniture and easy-chairs of fine white plaited cane. The chalet is perched high on the forest-clad shoulder of a "German" alp. Yet the terrace where I sit looks straight into the Austria that is so dear to Hitler as his native land, and the scene of his hungry tramps in search of any job along Vienna's stately Ringstrasse.

Already the first lights of Mozart's own city (Salzburg) begin to glow and glimmer; it is barely ten miles off. Just below us, others of the party take turns at the long telescope which is forever turned towards Hitler's early haunts — especially Branau-on-the-Inn — "That little town" (which he mentions in the opening lines of "Mein Kampf") "on the frontiers of those two German states whose union appears to us younger men as a life-task to be achieved by any and every means." …

"This struggle," he remarked, "does take it out of me, and puts a great strain on my nerves. Mind, I'm not growing younger, and I have *everything* to do. I often fear that I give too much of myself in the emotional way. But my chance is *here*. And I feel that I am being led by some saving Fate, as a sleep-walker might be by a sure-footed friend who can see to the end." He recalled the rousing and kindling efforts of Gottlieb Fichte long ago, when Germany lay helpless under a conqueror's heel.

"But out here on these hills," he went on more calmly, "I'm in a different world. I can renew my forces and put off cares as I do my clothes."

W.G. Fitz-Gerald, "On Holiday with Hitler in His Summer Chalet," National Home Monthly, November 1936.

OCTOBER 29, 1941:
Canadian Press Legend Gil Purcell Loses a Leg

Gil Purcell was one of the most important Canadian journalists of the mid-twentieth century. He headed The Canadian Press but took a leave of absence to work as army public relations officer with the First Canadian Division. He was seriously injured during a botched training exercise in England. Purcell returned to CP in 1945 and was general manager until 1969. He was inducted into the Canadian News Hall of Fame in 1970 and died in 1987.

THE CANADIAN PRESS

Somewhere in England — Capt. Gillis Purcell, public relations officer of the Canadian Corps, suffered the loss of part of his left leg when he was struck by a supply canister dropped from a plane while on manoeuvres.

At the hospital this morning, doctors described his condition as "really excellent," explaining "he is out of the woods now and making a remarkable recovery."

The doctor in attendance said he had never seen "any man come through anything like that the way Captain Purcell has done."

The unit was on manoeuvres watching canisters being dropped by parachute. When one broke away, the medical officer of a Nova Scotia regiment was at the scene, and after administering first aid had the injured officer rushed by field ambulance to a casualty clearing station.

Before he was taken from the scene of the accident, Captain Purcell smoked a cigarette and chatted with officers. Both Major-Gen. G. R. Pearkes, commander of the First Canadian Division, and Major Gen. C. B. Price, commander of the Third Division, spoke to him after he was taken to the clearing station, 15 miles away, where he was placed in the surgery room within 45 minutes of the accident.

The Canadian Press, October 29, 1941.

NOVEMBER 25, 1941:
Matthew Halton Is Chased by the Afrika Korps

Matthew Halton is best remembered as a radio reporter, but he began his career as a newspaper journalist. In 1941, the *Toronto Star* dispatched Halton, who it called its "ace" reporter, and who was covered like a celebrity in the pages of his own newspaper, to Egypt to cover the desert duel between Erwin Rommel and Bernard Law Montgomery. This piece, written in a slit trench near the Egyptian-Libyan border, was held for two days by military censors. It appeared in the *Toronto Star* on November 28, 1941.

MATTHEW HALTON

With the British Forces in Libya — Your correspondent, sitting in a slit trench against Libyan wire at a place called Libyan Omar, far from where he was last writing, has, in the last 24 hours, seen the following:

Gen. Rommel's tanks roaring into this camp and being smashed by British 25 pounders firing across open sights.

Italians and Germans coming up to the car and asking to be taken prisoner.

Great R.A.F. bomber and fighter attacks against enemy gun and tank positions, visible to the naked eye.

And almost constant German shellings which have pitted our camp with hundreds of shell holes.

The day before yesterday, at noon, at a point some 30 miles south of Tobruk, we were caught by a bold roaming force of German tanks and chased 30 miles. To escape them we had 10 hours of nightmare in the dark, finding our way through German minefields to British positions at Libyan Omar, just inside the barbed wire line separating Libya and Egypt. As day broke we gasped and laughed with relief as we were challenged by Indian outposts. We were conducted into British lines to find ourselves in the very midst of another great battle. It continues as I write.

As war correspondents, we sought a real tank battle and we found it. Standing for two hours yesterday on the roof of this car — which now has been pierced in many places by shell and bomb splinters — I watched German tank attacks on this position decisively smashed by British guns. Wrecked tanks lie in the sand before me now.

After this week of terrible, unrelenting battle in which both sides suffered heavy losses in men, tanks and equipment, there was one strong force of German tanks left. They decided on a bold stroke: to burst through us or get around our left flank to the rear and harry our vast field of transports and whatever infantry they could find.

With them were lorried infantry — crack troops — and the Bechelon, that is their supply transport, carrying ammunition, fuel, water and food. This is the force which chased us and which British forces have largely smashed in a thrilling, almost hand-to-hand fight.

The Germans had with them batteries of mobile guns which are so carried that they can go into action the second their carriers halt. All yesterday morning, there was a violent, ear-splitting artillery duel as the enemy tried to knock out our guns before attacking our division with tanks and infantry.

For the first half of the morning, I had no slit trench and I lay on the ground. During lulls, we would dig our shallow, one-man trenches with pick and shovel. After one lull, we heard enemy guns explode, heard their evil whine rushing at us and flopped beside the car. One shell burst 40 yards away, one 30 yards, and one only 15 yards. Our car was hit three times. You can't walk anywhere in this lagger (corral) without seeing great and small jagged shell splinters.

Long before noon we were half blind and choking from cordite fumes and we couldn't see 100 yards. At noon there was a delicious respite. At half past two, the Germans charged forward from their position two miles away.

This was it. It was stand and fight now. It was win or die. It was up to our guns. In a few minutes, perhaps, lay the fate of our Libyan campaign. History itself stopped to watch this coming few minutes. As for the watching individual, his heart was hammering with excitement in the midst of the frightening pandemonium which now rent the blue sky. His thought of Churchill's description of the charge at Blenheim, of Tolstoy and Hughes' descriptions of the charges at Austerlitz and Waterloo. He calmed his nerves with an effort of will and steeled his courage as the tanks charged down the horizon, belching death,

Every man was in his position in case our big guns failed. If they did, it would be a fight to the death in our camp — a fight of men with machine-guns and grenades against tanks.

My friends and I stood on top of our cars in front of our infantry positions and machine-gun posts. British armoured cars rushed out to meet the attack and deflect it if possible. It was heroism plain and simple and for a time it succeeded. As a hundred tank shells burst among them, they veered left, and the enemy chased them out of sight. Ten minutes later a car came back well ahead of the enemy. The moment had now come for our guns.

Our batteries were well out in front, a quarter of a mile left and forward of where I stood. Their first burst fell short. Their second landed among the enemy. Twenty-five-pounders were firing across open sights at charging tanks, now coming down across our front and only half a mile away.

As the smoke cleared, we saw three enemy tanks out of 21 making this attack, going up in smoke. The rest came on, firing their powerful 75's so intensely that our batteries were lost to sight in great surging clouds of sand and smoke.

Oh, God, will the batteries hold? The next few seconds would tell whether they would be over-run after their historic stand. The withering volume of their fire hadn't ceased: it had lessened scarcely perceptibly and the whole plain was covered with erupting bursts rising 100 feet into the air. Enemy tanks were burning here and there.

And someone with me on top of the car jumped up and down and screamed "They've stopped them! They've stopped them! The ____s have stopped!"

What was left of the enemy had turned about face, full speed, and went roaring back. We saw them halt on the horizon two miles away as if forming for another attack. Our shells followed them and they disappeared from sight.

At that moment I trembled with excitement and jubilation as I had never done before. British gunners had charged forward, had stood to fight against odds, and had won the day.

During these awful, glorious minutes we could hear another tank battle somewhere on another side of our position. Later we learned that the enemy had made another tank attack almost simultaneously. It, too, was broken. In a few minutes the enemy lost at least 18 tanks. The enemy was broken. We were saved from disaster. It is unnecessary to describe how we felt.

In the smoking desolation, we saw one German tank nearer than the others. "Come on," said Ronnie Noble, a young English newsreel cameraman, "let's go out and look."

There was still firing; the enemy was still nearer the tanks than we.

"Another time, thanks," I replied. Noble, who had had his car practically taken out from under him the other day and had joined us, jumped into one of our three trucks and roared off into the battlefield with Cameraman Fred Bayliss — intrepid guys, these cameramen.

We watched them approach the tank. We could see the German force on their right and our hearts were in our mouths. But they got back all right. Bayliss brought back some very useful documents for the general and some wonderful presents for myself.

This morning he went out to the tank again. The last time they went, the tank contained only dead Germans. This time it contained three poor devils of Italians and the cameramen brought them in.

There are German and Italian prisoners everywhere in this camp. I have talked with dozens. The general has just told me that there are some Italian batteries on one of our flanks that have run out of ammunition and are trying to surrender. But every time they raise their hands and try to come out, the Germans machine-gun them.

"We'll attend to that machine-gun tonight," said the general.

Some prisoners have gone through, too exhausted to show anything but the horror in their eyes. But many Italians are delighted to be taken and curse everything connected with this war.

"Don't send us to India or Canada," asked one. "Send us, please, to London."

Matthew Halton, "Escaping Capture By Skin of Teeth: Halton Tells of Nightmare Hours With Death Belching From Horizon," the Toronto Star, *November 28, 1941.*

DECEMBER 1941:
Lost in the Mediterranean

John D. "Don" Shanahan, of Toronto, was a Royal Canadian Air Force sergeant, serving with the Royal Air Force, in charge of ferrying a Wellington bomber being ferried from London to Benghazi, Libya, via Gibraltar to help the British Eighth Army beat back Rommel. Lou Rymal, of Leamington, Ontario, the front gunner, was the other Canadian on the Wellington. The navigator was killed when the Wellington crashed into the sea southeast of Gibraltar, and the other five men climbed into a dinghy launched just as the plane was sinking. The dinghy stayed afloat for eight days, taking Shanahan on a horrific journey across the Mediterranean. Once ashore, the survivors were assisted by a French priest, but were turned in to Vichy French authorities by a doctor who treated one of the injured men. They stayed in a prison camp until the Allied invasion of North Africa in November 1942. A few weeks after his release, Shanahan was killed in the crash of an air mail plane in Scotland. *Maclean's* published this piece in its June 15, 1944, issue.

JOHN D. SHANAHAN

None of us had had any sleep from the time we pranged into the deck and we were getting so tired we were dopey. It took every ounce of will power to stay awake. Actually, during the entire nine days there were only about six hours when we could relax — and four of these were spent in paddling furiously while trying to reach the coast of Spain.

Finally the boys would drop asleep for a few seconds at a time, waking up when their heads jerked down. Then they'd ask me what time it was. My watch kept on going and I must have given the time thousands of times during those nine days. Johnny was not doing too badly. Either the first-aid bandages or the salt water had stopped the bleeding. George, however, was in really bad shape. Also he suffered more from the cold than the rest of us because he couldn't keep himself warm by working.

On the third day we'd given the injured men a mouthful of water each from Lou's flask. Lou and I stuck it out until the fourth day and then we took a mouthful each. Then we gave the rest of the water to the lads who had been hurt.

The evening of the fourth day, however, Lou and I were pretty thirsty. We'd read that if you soaked yourself in sea water, you wouldn't die of thirst, and we also wanted to see whether we could fix up some of the leaks on the underside of the dinghy. The wind dropped for about an hour just before sunset and nearly all of us went overboard to float in the sea. We fixed the worst leak in the dinghy. One of the guys chewed gum from his escape kit until it was all tacky. He used this with some Cellophane from a packet of cigarettes to make something like a blowout patch, which we crammed into the crack at the joint. It made a pretty good repair job.

Being in the water relieved our thirst to some extent, but it seemed to leave us awfully weak. At sunset we climbed into the dinghy and wrung out our wet clothes, trying to get them moderately dry for the night, working in a dopey haze because we were so exhausted.

Suddenly Johnny lifted a hand over his eyes and stared at the horizon. "I'm beginning to see things," he said. "That ship's duff gen, isn't it?"

Lou glanced up.

"Holy smoke, no!" he said. "That's pukka gen!"

A small freighter was poking across the horizon. It would come fairly close to us, we thought.

Immediately our exhaustion vanished. We started paddling on a course that we thought would intercept it. But presently we could see that the freighter would pass at least a mile off.

We built a human pyramid on the raft, with two of us below and one man on top waving a shirt. But the sun was setting directly behind us and we must have been hard to see. Next we lit a red flare — but that was also killed by the sunset. We really ran into tough luck with that ship. We had helio mirrors to flash, but with the sun sinking directly behind us we couldn't bring the reflection to bear on the freighter.

One or two of the boys absolutely refused to believe that the lookouts had not spotted us. They thought that the ship's skipper wasn't having any part of us because German submarines have used lifeboats and all kinds of other traps to lure ships within gun or torpedo range.

Finally the freighter crossed the horizon and night fell. With darkness the wind came again. Along came the big seas once more.

A couple of the boys lost heart now. George was the most affected. He'd been badly hurt and had a concussion besides. Johnny didn't feel any too good either. Both of them started to talk about their mothers and how they were going to pull through for their sakes. But they'd lost the fighting spirit.

The next morning we prayed to God for rescue. Before that, we'd only cursed our luck. Prayers helped. We were of different denominations, but we'd all join in on the Lord's Prayer. It got to be a regular thing to pray in the morning and again at nightfall. We'd recite the Lord's Prayer and then each of us would add a little prayer of his own.

On the fifth day, George wouldn't brighten up at all. He was in terrible pain and despondent as well. Lou Rymal's flask of fresh water was empty by now and we saw George sneaking little drinks of sea water.

Suddenly he handed me his escape kit with money and maps in it. Up until that time he had it in his tunic pocket. "This bothers me," he said. "Look after it, will you?"

Then he said he hoped the boys would get through all right.

I threw the kit back at him and told him not to be stupid. We'd all get through together.

He seemed to quieten down after that but some hours later methodically took off his Mae West and his leather flying jacket. He said he wanted to dry off. After a while he put his jacket on again and said he wanted to sit on the stern gunwale and stretch his legs a bit. Suddenly he heaved himself overboard.

We made a wild grab for him but he kicked himself free. I threw him my Mae West but he just waved to us and inside 30 seconds we lost sight of him.

This was a bad day. Now Johnny started going delirious. We tried to keep an eye on him to prevent him from following George but it was terribly difficult because we were so played out.

There were only three of us who were strong enough to do any work now: Lou and Tim and I. We tried to fix a schedule. One of us would pump for 10 minutes. Another would hold the sea anchor and the third would try to get a 10-minute nap.

In one of these I was dreaming of Niagara Falls — all beautiful fresh water — Suddenly I wakened with my mouth full of something. It was wet! It was salt water! I spat. I looked. Tim had gone to sleep at the pump and Lou, holding the sea-anchor rope, with his back to him, hadn't noticed it. The dinghy had leaked so much air in less than 10 minutes that it was barely afloat.

Lou and I started pumping and bailing like mad until the gunwales rounded out again. Tim was apologetic. We knew that he was pretty far gone and suspected he had been drinking sea water.

The night was really terrible. It seemed so long and cold and dark. Johnny mumbled and moaned to himself all night long. He talked baby talk and became delirious. He flung himself about wildly. The dinghy by now was braced together with a harness of ropes and neckties and was in a really precarious condition. But Johnny kicked at the ropes and lashings in his delirium and we couldn't stop him.

The sixth day dawned. We held our prayers and then looked at the compasses. The wind had turned again and now was sweeping us toward the African coast. We thought we could keep afloat for quite a while yet and had a good chance of making a landing if the wind kept up. So we started talking about what we might run into. Our chief worry was that we'd be washed up against a rocky cliff coast because North Africa is pretty mountainous. But mostly our talk was wishful thinking; trying to encourage ourselves to live; trying to give our minds something to chew on: to take them off our thirst and hunger.

The seventh day was wicked. It was still storming and we were being pitched up and down. I felt very low that day. I kept thinking of home and of mother and of everything that was swell back in Toronto. Then I realized that I was going the way Johnny and George had gone and that I'd better snap out of it.

By this time all the clothing I had left consisted of my under pants, vest and my service shirt. But despite the bitter temperatures, despite the wind, and spray I never caught cold, never once sneezed or coughed or had a sniffle. I shivered often. Lordy, how I shivered! I'd shake all over and my teeth would chatter like castanets — and then I'd get over my shivering and be almost comfortable for a little while. Later on doctors told me that I probably shivered so much and so hard that I warmed myself up as if I'd run half a mile.

On the eighth day neither Lou nor I could swallow the hard black chocolate left in our escape kit. We could grind it to powder between our molars but couldn't get it down. The inside of my mouth was as dry as an old shoe. In desperation, I dropped a chlorine water-disinfecting tablet into some of my urine, let it dissolve and then took a sip of it to wash the chocolate dust down my throat.

Tim and Johnny were barely alive — nothing more. We did our best to keep their heads out of the water washing about in the half-filled dinghy. We were too weak now to do any bailing.

On the ninth night Lou and I decided that we were too weak to paddle. We were too weak, also, to take spells acting as shock absorbers for the sea anchor. Besides our wrists were torn to ribbons from the rope. So we tried a new system. We tied the rope around our ankles and lay down in the water in the dinghy. Our leg muscles were still strong enough to take the drag from the sea anchor, even if our arms and wrists were not.

Gradually, that evening, the waves changed in nature. They became a huge rolling swell. Then we saw sea gulls. Soon after that Lou made a grab overboard at something floating in the water and came up with a handful of seaweed. We knew then that we were nearing shore.

Around 10 that night I saw a light on the horizon. For a while I looked at it steadily and kept on pumping, thinking that it was a planet just coming over the horizon. Then I saw another light. This was too good to keep to myself. So I shook Lou and pointed.

Lou was still half-asleep. He'd been dreaming that he was coming back from a raid on Germany. He looked up dopily, first at me and then at the lights.

"You're a lousy navigator if that is the best airport you can find," he grumbled. Then he dropped off to sleep. I shook Lou again and again. I got real mad at him. Finally he snapped out of his sleep and looked at the lights with intelligence in his eyes.

"Land," I shouted.

"Well, I'll be…," said Lou. "You're right."

We set to work then. We blew up all the Mae Wests and lashed them low on ourselves and the invalids in case we had to swim for it. We pulled up the sea anchor and scudded as fast as we could before the wind.

It was getting on to 11 p.m. now. We kept staring at the lights, wondering what they were. Later we found they were markers for the port of Mostaganem, a bit east of Oran in Algeria, and later used by the Americans as one of the landing ports for the invasion of North Africa.

But at the time the lights really put the wind up us. We figured, rightly enough, that where there were lights there must be a bad coast. Actually the coast *was* dangerous — huge rocks and cliffs. But for once our luck held. We hit a spot that was not too foul.

At the time, we didn't know our luck. All we knew was that the surf was breaking all around us. The white water started to break over the dinghy. We had to bail like mad and pump at the same time. We tried to rouse Tim and Johnny to help us or at least keep their heads out of the water by themselves.

But Tim was cold and stiff — and so was Johnny. We couldn't get a movement out of either of them.

That was the worst part of the trip. The suspense was terrific because we were certain the dinghy would be bashed into the rocks or against a cliff. We bailed and pumped and just when we thought we had things under control a big comber suddenly flipped the dinghy up and almost over. Lou was thrown overboard. I grabbed him and caught a handful of hair. When the next wave lifted his side of the dinghy I jerked forward and brought him into the boat. Lou splashed face down into the water and rolled over till his face was clear.

In about 10 minutes more we were on shore. By a miracle the dinghy made a crash landing on a bit of sandy beach. Lou and I got out and tried to stand. We fell flat on our faces. We crawled to the dinghy and the next wave helped us to push it farther up the beach. Then we collapsed in the sand.

Presently I looked at my watch again. It was four o'clock in the morning. Over to the east there was a faint greyness in the sky. Then Lou and I tried to haul Tim and Johnny out of the dinghy. But we soon gave up that effort. They were stiff. In the uncertain light their faces and hands looked bluish. We knew then that they were dead; that they had probably been dead for hours.

About this time a crazy delusion overpowered me. I was certain, somehow, that we were in the Bay of Fundy, where there are the highest tides in the world. Above us there was a 300-foot cliff. I had the feeling that we had to get to the top of this cliff before the tide came in and trapped us. It was all a lot of nonsense, actually, because at that point in the Mediterranean the tide is only about a foot.

But I suddenly started hounding Lou to climb that cliff. I felt the tide was lapping right at our heels. Lou, I guess, climbed just to humor me. But we were woefully weak, and it wasn't until six hours later that we stood on the top of the cliff.

It was broad daylight now and out of the shelter of the cliff we noticed that there was a strong wind blowing. Lou turned to face it.

"It's changed," he croaked. "It's blowing offshore now!"

John D. Shanahan, "Lost in the Mediterranean," Maclean's, *June 15, 1944.*

NOVEMBER 1942:
Japanese-Canadian Internee Expresses His Frustration in Poetry

The New Canadian, edited by Tommy Shoyama, was the only Japanese-Canadian newspaper allowed to publish after Pearl Harbor. Originally headquartered in Vancouver, it was forced to move to the internment community of Kaslo in the Kootenay Mountains in 1942. Shoyama was allowed to join the army in the last months of the war. He went on to a brilliant career in the Saskatchewan public service under Timmy Douglas, then moved to Ottawa where he ran several federal departments during the Trudeau administration. This poem was written by a young second-generation Japanese-Canadian man interned in the interior of British Columbia. Press censors refused to publish it, and it stayed buried in a box in Library and Archives Canada for sixty years.

ANONYMOUS

CINDERELLA
"Yea, curfew! Mediaeval!
Yeah, laughed like the devil!
No loitering for Japs
After taps!
    Aw, nuts!

"Yea … someone being playful!
Must hurt him something awful!
To see yellow Japs
Loitering after taps!
    Aw, nuts!

    "What's that?
    Rata-a-tat … Rat-a-tat

SUNDOWN TO SUNRISE: CURFEW ON ALL JAPS!

"What the…!
    Ah, hell!
        Seven p.m. now!
Go home like good lil Canucks!
        Aw, nuts!...

I am Canadian born!
    Hell, we've a right!
    A damn good right!

Germans, Italians and Japs…
Kick 'em out and we'll go!

        Sure!
            Sure!
                Sure!

When the Italians and Germans, they go!

Anonymous, The New Canadian, *February 15, 1943. Library and Archives Canada, Records of the Directorate of Censorship, Vol. 5976.*

AUGUST 20, 1942:
Horror on the Beach

Munro later told author Phillip Knightley that his Dieppe coverage was the only war reporting that cheated the Canadian people. Three years later, he could still not bring himself to condemn the raid outright, and spent several pages in his book *Gauntlet to Overlord* (1945) justifying Dieppe as a necessary rehearsal for landings in the Mediterranean and D-Day. Most of his Dieppe copy was badly butchered by the London-based British military censors. Munro's best account of the raid was published in *Gauntlet to Overlord*, which won the Governor-General's Award for Non-Fiction in 1946.

Ross Munro

The story of that blood-stained beach at Puits is a nightmare. Our boat was one of the last to make the beach as we passed close by the eastern headland, with the austere French church with its high steeple on the crest. We sailed in a cloud of smoke under the guns on the cliff-top, most of them anti-aircraft guns that crashed endlessly at our fighters and bombers carrying out more attacks.

Our coxswain tried to take us in to one section of the beach and it proved the wrong spot. Before he grounded he swung the craft out again and we fumbled the smoke to the small strip of sand which was the Puits beach. The smoke was spotty and the last thirty yards was in the clear. Geysers from artillery shells or mortar bombs shot up in our path. Miraculously we weren't hit by any of them. The din of the German ack-ack guns and machine-guns on the cliff was so deafening you could not hear the man next to you shout.

The men in our boat crouched low, their faces tense and grim. They were awed by this unexpected blast of German fire, and it was their initiation to frightful battle noises. They gripped their weapons more tightly and waited for the ramp of our craft to go down.

We bumped on the beach and down went the ramp and out poured the first infantrymen. They plunged into about two feet of water and machine-gun bullets laced into them. Bodies piled up on the ramp. Some staggered to the beach and fell. Bullets were splattering into the boat itself, wounding and killing our men.

I was near the stern and to one side. Looking out the open bow over the bodies on the ramp, I saw the slope leading a short way tip to a stone wall littered with Royal casualties. There must have been sixty or seventy of them, lying sprawled on the green grass and the brown earth. They had been cut down before they had a chance to fire a shot.

A dozen Canadians were running along the edge of the cliff towards the stone wall. They carried their weapons and some were firing as they ran. But some had no helmets, some were already wounded, their uniforms torn and bloody. One by one they were cut down and rolled down the slope to the sea.

I don't know how long we were nosed down on that beach. It may have been five minutes. It may have been twenty. On no other front have I witnessed such a carnage. It was brutal and terrible and shocked you almost to insensibility to see the piles of dead and feel the hopelessness of the attack at this point.

There was one young lad crouching six feet away from me. He had made several vain attempts to rush down the ramp to the beach but each time a hail of fire had driven him back. He had been wounded in the arm but was determined to try again. He lunged forward and a streak of red white tracer slashed through his stomach.

I'll never forget his anguished cry as he collapsed on the blood-soaked deck: "Christ, we gotta beat them; we gotta beat them!" He was dead in a few minutes.

The Germans were in strength on the top of the cliff and poured their fire into the gulch and on the slope which led up to the tops of the cliff crest. A high stone wall, topped with barbed wire, crosses the slope and Royals were dying by that wall.

From our battered craft lying in the centre of this wild concentration of deadly fire I could see sand-bagged German positions on the top of the cliff and a large house, with rows of windows, on the left side of the cleft in the cliff. Most of the German machine-gun and rifle fire was coming from the fortified house and it wrought havoc on the tiny beach. They were firing at us at point-blank range.

There was another smaller house on the right side of the break in the cliffs and Germans were there too. Some of the Canadians were able to return the German fire and they knocked off a number of the enemy. One German in his grey-green uniform toppled from one of the windows in the big house. Some of the less-well fortified positions were hit by fire from anti-tank rifles and Bren guns and Germans there were casualties.

Into the terrible German fire ran the men from our boat and I doubt if any even reached the stone wall on the slope, for mortar bombs were smashing on the slope to take the toll of those not hit by the machine-gun bullets that streaked across the whole beach almost continuously. Now the Germans on the cliff were turning their flak guns down on the beach. Our craft was the only one left.

Somehow, the Royals got the two heavy three-inch mortars in our craft down the ramp, as well as the ammunition, but they were never fired. They fell in the water as the crews were hit. The bottom of the boat was covered with soldiers who had been machine-gunned. The officer next to me, Jack Anderson of Toronto, was hit in the head and sprawled over my legs bleeding badly. A naval rating next to him had a sickening gash in his throat and was dying. A few who weren't casualties were firing back fiercely now from the boat. It was useless for them to try to make the beach. The way those men stood up and blasted back at the Germans, when they could feel even then that the attack at Puits was a lost cause, was one of the bravest things I've witnessed. Most of them received decorations later and well earned they were.

The naval orders were to land the troops and then pull off back to the sea, and the naval officer with us rapidly sized up the situation. It was useless to remain a sitting target on the beach.

Everyone who could be landed had tried to leave the boat. They had been cut down in front of our eyes. So the officer ordered the craft off the beach. The hand of God must have been on that little boat, for we were nosed up hard on the sand and yet when the engines reversed it slid back into deep water as if it had been pulled by something out to sea. In training, many boats used to stick on the beach and we had to get out and push them off but this time by a sheer miracle the craft cleared and slowly, ponderously swung around. There was an opening at the stern and through it I got my last look at the grimmest beach of the Dieppe raid. It was khaki-coloured with the bodies of boys from Central Ontario.

We limped a few hundred yards out to sea in the brilliant morning sunshine. The few of us in that boat still unwounded were numb with the shock of that fateful period on the beach. Of the eighty we had taken in there were about twenty of us left and more than half the survivors were wounded. A few Medical Corps lads with us were working on them and we all tried to help. There were shocking wounds. Some boys had been hit a dozen times with bullets or shrapnel.

Nobody had counted on casualties like this. We didn't know where to take the wounded. At first we thought we should land on the main beach and get them quickly to a dressing station we knew was to be set up in the town. But our wireless operator tried to check the main beach wireless station and there was no answer. That was the first hint we had that the attack on the main beach had gone badly too.

We did circle around to a point just off the jetty but came under machine-gun fire again and pulled back towards two destroyers lying about three-quarters of a mile from the main beach. We carefully got the wounded boys aboard one of them and into a doctor's hands.

For the rest of that morning one lost all sense of time and developments in the frantic events of the battle. Although the Puits landing had obviously failed and the headland to the east of Dieppe would still be held by the Germans, I felt that the main attack by three infantry battalions and the tanks had possibly fared better on the beach in front of the town.

Landing craft were moving along the coast in relays and the destroyers were going in perilously close to hit the headlands with shell-fire. I clambered from one landing craft to another to try to learn what was going on. Several times we were bombed too closely by long, black German planes that sailed right through our flak and our fighter cover.

Smoke was laid by destroyers and our planes along the sea and on the beach. Finally the landing craft in which I was at the time, with some naval ratings, touched down on the sloping pebble main beach which ran about sixty yards at that point to a high sea wall and the Esplanade, with the town beyond.

Smoke was everywhere and under its cover several of our ratings ran onto the beach and picked up two casualties by the barbed wire on the beach, lugging them back to the boat. I floundered through the loose shale to the sea-wall. There was heavy machine-gun fire down the beach towards the Casino. A group of men crouched twenty yards away under the shelter of the sea-wall.

The tobacco factory was blazing fiercely. For a moment there was no firing. It was one of those brief lulls you get in any battle. I thought our infantry were thick in the town but the Esplanade looked far too bare and empty.

There was no beach organization as there should have been. Some dead lay by the wall and on the shale. The attack here had not gone as planned either. A string of mortar bombs whanged on the Esplanade. The naval ratings waved and I lunged back to the boat as the beach battle opened up again. In choking smoke we pulled back to the boat pool.

Some other boats that had gone in to the beach were blown up. One tank-landing craft lay burning near the beach. The hulk of another floated aimlessly and deserted just off the beach. It had been bombed.

It was unbelievable to me even then that disaster had overtaken the units on the main beach. But the Essex, led by Lieutenant-Colonel Jasperson, had run into heavy fire as soon as they landed. They had got through the wire and to the sea-wall all right and there most of them were stopped. Some did make their way around the edge of the harbour and got into the town but the main force had to fight it out from the sea-wall. They were murderously mortared there and strafed and machine-gunned throughout the morning. But they fought on and on, until they had nothing left with which to fight. A handful of them got off in landing craft at the last minute but few craft got in to them.

The Royal Hamilton Light Infantry, commanded by Lieutenant-Colonel Labatt, were on the right side of the beach (the Essex landed on the left) and were also heavily opposed as soon as they landed. They got to the sea-wall and after heavy fighting drove the Germans out of the Casino on the western extremity of the beach. From there platoons worked into the town, fighting through the streets. Similarly with the F.M.R., who were put in on the main beach after the others had landed. Some of their platoons fought through the town too and some came back from those fiery streets. Lieutenant-Colonel Dollard Menard led the F.M.R.

The Calgary tanks, under Lieutenant-Colonel Johnny Andrews, had a bad time from the start. The tank-landing craft were large targets and German shell-fire blasted them as they beached. More than a squadron was landed and immediately the tanks struck the heavy shale. Some sank into it and were stopped right on the beach. Others wallowed through it, worked around by the Casino, got over the sea-wall, which is only a foot or two high there, sloping from about ten feet on the Essex beach. They fought on the Esplanade and at least a few of them broke into the streets of the town.

But German guns in the hotels and houses and entrances to the streets fired point-blank at them. The other squadrons were not landed but lay most of the morning off the main beach in their landing craft.

To the west of Dieppe at Pourville the landing fared better. The S.S.R. got ashore there without any opposition, climbed over the sea-wall and went into the town. They surprised the Germans in Pourville and established their little bridgehead before the enemy knew what was up. While the Germans were waiting for the Canadians at Puits and on the main beach, here at Pourville surprise was attained.

The S.S.R. got well established before the Germans began firing mortars on the town and the machine-guns on the hills on each side of Pourville opened up. The Cameron Highlanders, led by Lieutenant-Colonel Gosling, were coming in now and they had to run a gauntlet of fire in order to cross the beach and get into the town itself. They then made their way up the valley beyond, advancing along paths and a road nearly three miles inland towards the landing field, their objective. Meanwhile the S.S.R. carried out numerous attacks on pillboxes and machine-gun posts in the Pourville area that kept firing on the bridgehead. It was here that Lieutenant-Colonel Cecil Merritt, commanding officer of the S.S.R., showed such supreme gallantry in leading his regiment and personally attacking German posts that he was awarded the Victoria Cross — Canada's first V.C. of the war. He stayed on the beach after his regiment had withdrawn to the boats and fought alone until he was captured.

The two Pourville battalions realized that the main Dieppe plan had misfired in other sectors and late in the morning the withdrawal was ordered. The Camerons had done a magnificent job in going inland as far as they did. But without tank support and faced with the knowledge that the main landing in front of Dieppe had not been the success anticipated there was no purpose in their striking off towards D'Arques. Neither would they be able to withdraw as they were supposed to through the town of Dieppe. So around eleven A.M. they fell back on Pourville again, retracing their steps along the valley. Lieutenant-Colonel Gosling had been killed in the landing.

The S.S.R. were having a rough time by now, with the enemy mortar fire becoming more accurate and some machine-gun posts still belting bullets into the streets of the town. The landing craft now were moving in on Pourville, scores of them circling slowly off shore and then turning in to the beach, many of them grounding before they got there. The S.S.R. and Camerons came across the beach through the machine-gun fire and raced for the boats. They brought all the casualties they could. They even brought some prisoners.

I was in an assault boat which tried to go into Pourville; we got within three hundred yards of the beach when we were ordered along the coast to try to make the main beach and take off troops there. But I did get a glimpse of the Pourville evacuation.

It wasn't any nice ordered sight. The boats were having trouble. Many of them were under direct machine-gun fire. Some were sinking, with troops leaping back into the water. Batches of Canadians were on the fringe of the town among some trees on the inside of the sea-wall. Small groups of them hesitated there for a while; then they would leap over the sea-wall to the beach and scatter for the run over the pebbles to the water and the boats. There was the hammering sound of German machine-guns, the occasional sharp whang of the mortars and the knock-knock of the Brens. Smoke drifted over the beach in a long wispy trail as our craft turned for the main beach.

Then the German air force struck with its most furious attack of the day. All morning long, British and Canadian fighters kept a constant patrol over the ships and the beaches, whole squadrons twisting and curling in the blue, cloud-flecked sky. Hundreds of other planes swept far over northern France, intercepting enemy fighters and bombers long before they reached Dieppe. Reconnaissance planes kept a constant lookout on the roads from Amiens and Abbeville and Rouen where reinforcements could be expected. There were air combats going on practically all morning long. It was the greatest air show since the Battle of Britain in the fall of 1940, and the R.A.F. and R.C.A.F. had overwhelming superiority. The High Command had hoped the German air force would be lured into the sky and most of the enemy strength in western Europe came up.

They were given a thorough shellacking and the air victory at the time appeared to be the chief compensation for the raid. But Fighter Command's powerful air cover did not prevent German planes racing in over the ships and even strafing the troops on the beaches. Many of those aircraft that did make these daring sorties were shot down but they made it hot for those in the landing craft and on the destroyers.

Ross Munro, Gauntlet to Overlord: The Story of the Canadian Army *(Toronto: Macmillan, 1945).*

AUGUST 20, 1942:
Ross Munro Writes Dieppe on Smokes and Speed

Munro had a great vantage point at Dieppe, but the military did not expect the raid to fail. Munro had to out-think and out-last the censors to get his story out. His colleague, D.E. Burritt, describes the cat-and-mouse game, and how Munro's self-medicating allowed him to win his fight with the British press censors who controlled the telegraph cable lines out of London.

D.E. BURRITT

London, Aug. 20, 1942 — A tall, unshaven young man burst into the London office of Canadian Press early this morning, dropped his khaki-clad figure in front of a typewriter and began pounding out the journalistic history of Canada's part in the Dieppe assault

More than 12 hours later, Ross Munro, Canadian Press war correspondent, was still banging away at his machine, putting on paper an eyewitness story of the dramatic operation.

For hours on end the former University of Toronto student sat in his torn, blood-stained battle dress, ignoring food placed beside him. For three days and as many nights he had not been to bed and now as he sat typing from a scribbled sheaf of notes, he smoked endlessly and nibbled Benzedrine tablets given him by a Canadian medical officer to keep his eyelids open.

In his story Munro skipped lightly over the part where he changed from one craft to another a half-dozen times so that he might skirt the bullet-swept French beaches to make sure all regiments in his battle beat were covered.

He was apologetic that he had been unable to stay until the very end to ascertain whether any outfits were unable to return. It was much the same when he accompanied the expedition to Spitsbergen last year.

In the office today, he spoke all the time of the men he had accompanied, ignoring the fact that he had shared their perils.

"It's exciting," he conceded, "damned exciting. It's only now when I look back that I'm frightened."

D.E. Burritt, The Canadian Press, August 20, 1942.

OCTOBER 16, 1942:
The Sinking of the SS *Caribou*

Eric Dennis, whose family owned the Halifax *Herald*, was probably the most effective reporter covering the Battle of the Atlantic from the Canadian side. After the Navy turned down his request for enlistment, citing his health problems, Dennis worked the bars and rooming houses of downtown Halifax, ferreting out sailors who had survived sub attacks on the treacherous Atlantic crossing. The federal press censor in Halifax, H. Bruce Jefferson, often cut Dennis's stories to protect naval secrets, but he respected Dennis's skill. By the end of the war, Dennis's reporting was appearing, usually without a byline, in the *Toronto Star* and other large newspapers outside of the Maritimes. Dennis later went on to become a Parliamentary reporter in Ottawa. Dennis's byline was not on the original story, but Jefferson recorded Dennis's authorship in a memo he sent to Ottawa.

Eric Dennis

For five hours in the frigid early morning hours survivors clung desperately to rafts after a German submarine had torpedoed the steamship *Caribou* 22 miles outside Port-aux Basques, sending it to the bottom in three and a half minutes, said Miss Vivian Swinemar of Dartmouth, who, with Mrs. Gladys Shiers and her 14-month-old son, Leonard, were the only surviving Halifax and Dartmouth civilians on board.

One lifeboat was put afloat and the German submarine crew surfaced, hitting the boat and sinking it with its human cargo.

All watches stopped at 3:30 a.m. and Miss Swinemar, who was sharing a stateroom with Mrs. Shiers and her baby son, says it was then that a terrible shock aroused her, throwing her out of bed. Snatching the baby, she ran through the water which even then was pouring into the ship from all sides. Hindered by the weight of the baby in her arms, Miss Swinemar fell and was helped to the deck by a petty officer who saw her struggling in the water. Once on the deck she waited for Mrs. Sheirs, who had gone back to get two lifebelts in her cabin and then handed the baby to his mother.

The scene on deck was terrible beyond description, Miss Swinemar said. People were out of their minds with fear. One man ran at her "as if he were going to kill her" and jumped overboard when she screamed. Another man, desperate at the thought of drowning, clutched her and pulled her under the water. She thought she would never reach the surface again, but finally managed to loosen his grip. A woman, in a frenzy of terror, threw her baby overboard and jumped after it. Both were drowned immediately.

To Miss Swinemar, the rescue of baby Leonard seemed almost a miracle. To her knowledge, he was the only one of the several babies and small children on board that was saved. Miss Swinemar, Mrs. Shiers and Leonard were the last to remain on the ship and were sucked under by the current as it went down. Struggling frantically, Miss Swinemar was separated from her companions but finally managed to reach the surface and was picked up by one of the rafts. Two navy nurses were not so fortunate. One supported her companion, who appeared to have been injured or was unable to swim, as long as she could but was obliged to let her go before help came. Miss Swinemar believed practically all the crew, including the captain and his two sons, were lost.

The long vigil on the raft was heartbreaking, Miss Swinemar thought. Many of her 20 companions on the raft were only partly clothed and were suffering from the cold. One baby died.

Through it all, a wonderful spirit of bravery was in evidence. The survivors, exhausted and terrified, as they were, said the Lord's Prayer and then sang all the hymns they knew until a minesweeper came to their aid.

The crew of the minesweeper were "just grand" Miss Swinemar said. They gave hot drinks to everyone and the injured were bandaged.

"Just like a terrible dream" was the comment of Mrs. Gladys Shiers, another survivor of the torpedoed Caribou, when asked to describe her harrowing experience. Mrs. Shiers, with her son Leonard, was on her way to join her husband, who is stationed in Newfoundland. Mrs. Shiers was one of the eight women out of 35 rescued and Leonard, of the 22 children aboard, was the only one saved. Mrs. Shiers told of how, standing on the bridge of the ship with her baby in her arms, she felt the ship going down, saw a huge wave about to engulf them and then felt something strike her on the head, knocking her unconscious. She later learned from the other passengers that the baby had been torn from her arms by an explosion as the ship went under and had been pulled out of the water by an airman who had applied artificial respiration and then kept the child warm under his coat until picked up by a minesweeper. Mrs. Sheirs herself was badly bruised and had several cuts about the face and head. She was pulled out of the water while still unconscious and taken aboard one of the rafts. If it had not been for the lifebelt she was wearing, she would certainly have been drowned.

Mrs. Shiers told of the tragic experiences of her companions on the raft. One man had lost his wife and three children and a bride of two weeks had no knowledge of the whereabouts of her husband. A short distance away, they could hear a sailor, clinging to a piece of the shattered lifeboat, praying aloud. They tried to save him but he clung frantically to the wreckage and drowned before their eyes.

Frantic with anxiety about her son, Mrs. Shiers was again unconscious when the party was rescued by the crew of the minesweeper. When she recovered, the baby, wrapped in blankets, was brought to her by one of the sailors who had seen his name on the identification bracelet around his wrist.

Eric Dennis, the Halifax Herald, October 16, 1942.

JULY 11, 1943:
The Invasion of Sicily: "Say, Where is The War?"

After his escape from the Dieppe disaster, Munro must have been relieved when Canadian units came ashore in Sicily virtually unopposed. Certainly, the rest of Canada was.

Ross Munro

AN ALLIED COMMAND POST July 11 — (Delayed) — Canadian assault troops with a crack British formation on their right over-ran Pachino peninsula on Sicily and within 24 hours after their landing had established an invasion bridgehead.

It has been one success after another in this Canadian-British sector as the greatest combined operation in history is developing.

Canadians have now advanced into hilly country northwest and west of the fishing town of Pachino and major engagements are expected with probably more resistance than that put up by the Italian coastal defenders who staged only a mild fight when the Canadian and British forces first landed on the Pachino Peninsula, which is tipped by Cape Passero.

The past night and day have been one incredible series of incidents.

I landed alongside the first wave of assault companies of a famous Canadian regiment on a sandy beach at Costa Dell Ambra, four miles southwest of Pachino, at 5:15 Saturday morning.

The Canadian troops have been rushing ahead ever since. It is a tough job keeping up with them on two feet.

Casualties on the first day were very light. A colonel who heads a divisional medical service said less than 40 casualties have been reported to him so far. During my trip around the battle zone I saw only three wounded soldiers, who had been hit while cleaning out a pill box just before the beach defence collapsed.

There is a British hospital ship in our convoy now. It is lighted up at night.

[Allied headquarters in North Africa reported Monday a lighted British hospital ship had been sunk by enemy bombers but that the wounded had been rescued. There was, of course, no indication whether or not this was the same ship Munro reports as being with the Canadian convoy.]

The Italian beach defences which folded like a concertina were merely barbed wire and some machine-gun posts which fired a few bursts and then gave up. On our beach the enemy was obviously counting on a sandbar 15 feet off shore as a natural defence. But the Canadians surprised them completely by coming in in heavy surf and battling ashore through water to the waist.

Coastal batteries shelled the landing posts but the fire was erratic. The Canadians went through the beach defences in a matter of minutes and struck inland, mopping up groups of Italians en route. More than 700 prisoners, including 15 officers, have been captured already by the Canadians.

All day columns of prisoners poured down from the front, a happy-looking crowd, guarded by one or two soldiers.

The Royal Navy has been giving the troops magnificent gun support, and big and small warships lying close into shore bombard their targets with thundering salvoes which shake the peninsula.

During the day we saw no enemy aircraft. It seemed eerie not having any about.

The beach looked like a big traffic jam with tanks, guns and trucks plowing through the sand to roads leading inland. It was almost unbelievable to Canadians that this first stage could be so easy. But once the axis army gets reorganized to cope with this surprise descent on the coasts, there may be stubborn fighting.

There are some German formations in Sicily and the enemy has some tanks. The Canadians realize they met poorer Italian soldiers on the beaches and around Pachino — men of a coastal defence division — and they are not being misled that the road ahead will be easy. But everyone keeps asking themselves: "Where are the Italian navy and air force?"

I started this story of the first day in a slit trench on my cliff-top position and it is being finished now in the early morning aboard a headquarters ship. This is the story now of my trip onto the beaches, the assault and the follow-up.

Last night bombers attacked the troops near the beach and tried to hit our ships under the glare of dropped flares. The raid lasted only about 30 minutes and was not effective. Our ack-ack from ships and shore was terrific, filling the skies with red balls of tracer.

The troops were well dug in ashore and the bombers could not touch them except by direct hits. I watched the raid from the cliff top overlooking the bay, lying in a slit trench under a fiery curtain of flak.

The R.A.F. has been giving us fighter protection and you could hear the drones of Spitfires practically all the time during the day. Our ships have their barrage balloons up and look like part of the London scene.

Thousands upon thousands of troops poured on the bridgehead after the successful assault and vehicles, guns, stores and ammunition have been rushed in to the beaches.

This attack was the stuff that the men had prepared for in intensive combined operations training in Britain. Immediately after the exercises the convoy carrying assault troops sailed for the Mediterranean and they went right to these Sicilian beaches without being attacked by aircraft.

The entire 2,000 mile trip was made without any trouble — fantastic considering that we sailed in daylight right through the Sicilian Channel and the Malta Channel towards Pachino Peninsula with the whole invasion armada concentrated in one gigantic convoy.

The day before the attack we started heading in the general direction of Sicily and everyone was keyed to a high pitch. In the morning the wind started to kick up whitecaps on the Mediterranean which until then had been calm as a mill pond.

The wind rose steadily until by afternoon it was of gale proportions. By that time, we could see Malta. Our spirits sank, for we thought the operation would have to be postponed. Our small boats could not live in that sea. Some of the waves were 15 feet high and a heavy swell was running but there was bright, burning sunshine — and no message came telling us the job was off.

A colonel told us the attack was to go on. At last we were definitely on our way. There was quite a strong surface swell, though, and it wasn't going to be any sinecure landing on what everyone knew to be a tough beach with an sandbar stretching across the face of it.

During the evening (Friday, July 9), we learned from the headquarters ship that the Pachino airfield had been plowed up. Some thought that the Italians had somehow got wind of our attack. But security had been maintained 100 per cent. The attack was definitely a tactical surprise, according to headquarters staff officers.

Down in the mess decks the Canadians were preparing for their landing. They got their kit together, dabbed a little more oil on their weapons, sorted out grenades and loaded up with ammunition. They were having a whale of a time. In the sergeants' mess some N.C.O.s were playing cards and drinking soda pop — our ship was "dry" all the way. In the officers' lounge a British Tommy played a piano expertly, playing some lively tunes and a few melancholy ones.

The officers met in the lounge and were addressed by their colonel. Similar meetings were held aboard the other ships as the zero hour approached.

"We are on the eve of a night in history that will never be forgotten," said the colonel. "We will look back on this night and our children will. We will look back on it as the night that we started to put the skids to the enemy."

Then everyone repeated the Lord's Prayer and shook hands all around.

The meeting broke up. I went on deck and watched our convoy in the moonlight.

There was still no air attack. Unbelievable! At midnight we saw great flashes in the distance where Sicily lay. Our bombers were hitting their targets. Tracers reached into the sky. There were some coastal searchlights playing over the sea. We were too far out then to be bothered by them.

Earlier we had all been getting a little jumpy for it looked like suicide to try to land in the wild sea. We had the evening meal and were becoming reconciled to a possible postponement. But when darkness fell we were still heading to the southeast tip of Sicily.

Hundreds upon hundreds of other ships and warships were soon around us — the greatest convoy to ever sail to attack. There were ships as far as you could see. About 10 p.m. the wind suddenly dropped and the whitecaps disappeared. The gale had been one of those queer storms they get in the Mediterranean during the summer. Sometimes they do not last long, and this one didn't.

The high command gambled on the wind falling — undoubtedly it had the weather "taped" — and won. Then the big convoy broke up. The Americans headed off for the Gela beaches. We sailed right ahead under a first-quarter moon that gilded the ocean. The sky was clear and crowded with stars. It was a Mediterranean night of fiction and peacetime cruises.

I could hear our bombers droning over towards Italy. Some flares shot up from the shore. They were unnerving and lingering. I was going in with the naval command in a naval motor launch which was to guide the assault troops to the right beaches.

At 1 a.m. we went down the side of our ship in an assault landing craft and hit the swell which lifted us high in the air. We rocketed about and moved among the ships which were now anchored a number of miles off Pachino Peninsula. Finally we located our motor launch and clambered aboard. My trouble was that I had my typewriter waterproofed with adhesive tape for the plunge from the sandbar to the beach. Slowly the assault landing craft gathered around us for the run in. There were scores of these 40-foot craft bouncing around in the swell. Many of the troops were seasick in them.

Through a megaphone, our commander on our little, leaping motor launch told the flotillas destined for our beach to follow him and he started off. Other flotillas sped off noiselessly for other beaches. British Commandos were on the Canadian left flank and another British formation on the right.

Crack units were to land first and destroy a coastal battery. Ahead of us we could see a glare in the sky. The air attack and naval bombardment had set Pachino ablaze. Wooden buildings in the town of 15,000 population were burning.

To the left I saw tracer bullets and I could hear the bang of machine guns. Troops were landing. We crept in closer until we could see the low, dark coastline of Sicily in the shadows. It was a thrilling moment but a tendency to seasickness took the edge off it for many of the men. Some red flares shot up, lingered and snuffed out. The enemy was doing some kind of signaling. Tremendous explosions boomed out in the night. I think it must have been bombing far inland. We could see gigantic flashes.

On our right there were more flashes, but this time from seaward. Warships of the Mediterranean fleet were shelling positions on the peninsula. The noise was ear-splitting, though the ships were miles away. When the flashes occurred you could see the gleaming gun barrels lit up even at that distance. Tracers started to criss-cross our beaches.

Some Royal Canadian Engineers from Nova Scotia and two companies of an Ontario regiment were touching down ahead of us.

There were spurts of machine-gun bullets at their boats. Then I heard the Bren guns. The Brens have a distinctive knocking sound like a stick striking an oak door.

Canadians were in action.

Dawn was creeping up as I transferred from the motor launch to a landing craft for beaching. The typewriter was still tagging along somehow. Just then tank landing craft bringing up the first wave on an Ontario regiment came up and in we went. Naval craft were laying up a smoke screen for us, and gunfire from destroyer, a cruiser and a monitor dinned in our ears.

Some beach defences were still pegging away with their final shots before being wiped out. A coastal battery halfway between the beach and Pachino was firing with six-inch guns. Shells crashed in the seas around us. They were too close for comfort but they did not hit a thing.

Canadians were swarming over the beach and our craft leaped through the surf in smoke, confusion and noise. The landing craft hit the sandbar and stopped short. We piled over the side and plunged into four feet of water. My typewriter was dunked. I suddenly thought of Dieppe and wondered who would be writing the story because it looked plenty hot here.

But we waded frantically through the breakers and ran onto the beach. Troops swarmed off their craft and went through a tap in the wire defences which had been cut by sappers a few minutes before. Infantrymen were already spreading out in the sand dunes on the other side of the wire.

Not an enemy beach machine-gun was in action right here. More gaps were cut through the wire which stretched the whole length of the beach which was sandy and 50 yards wide from the beach to the dunes where the wire was located.

Canadians were firing to the right and the left and an occasional burst of enemy fire was heard from several hundred yards inland. The Canadians went for them. Beach organization was now being set up with the navy and army personnel working speedily.

I cleared off down the beach with one thought in mind — digging in for dive-bombing which, on the basis of a past disagreeable experience I thought was certain to come. I had no spade so I scooped out sand with my hands and a tin cup.

The sun was now up. Infantrymen with fixed bayonets were prodding bushes on the dunes. The first prisoner had been taken — a soldier in a pillbox. Apparently his comrades had run for it.

Canadians moved up a hill to the right of the beach and occupied it. Others scouted north and west. There was some firing from farmhouses among the vineyards on gently-rising land. There were stone walls around most of the fields. It was miserable farmland, though, with many rocks.

For half an hour, we waited tensely for enemy planes but they never showed up. The beach was organized now, and special British beach groups had the whole situation in hand.

Ross Munro, The Canadian Press, June 12, 1942.

NOVEMBER 24, 1943:
Soviet Girls, Canada Oil Run "Top of World" Lifeline

The northwest staging route was shrouded in secrecy through the early years of the war and its existence remains unknown to many Canadians. It was a string of airfields used by pilots shuttling planes and war materiel to the Soviet Union through Alberta, northern British Columbia, the Yukon, and Alaska. The planes were fuelled with gasoline refined from oil carried in the four-inch Canol pipeline from western Canada's first major commercial oil field at Norman Wells, Northwest Territories. Despite Ross Harkness's claims, the area was under effective control of the U.S. military, which even tried to maintain its own military censorship in the region.

ROSS HARKNESS

I have watched fleets of savage fighter planes bearing the Red Star of Russia scud across Canada's northland. Coming from U.S. factories in Buffalo and the west coast, they are flown by American pilots along the R.C.A.F.'s famous northwest staging route to Fairbanks, Alaska, there to be taken by Russian ferry pilots, most of them women.

The wicked-looking guns and cannon jutting from wings and propellers are fully loaded, ready for action if attacked on the long journey across Asia, or to go into instant battle upon reaching the German lines.

Now and then a squadron of huge bombers goes through, usually lightly-armed but with bellies full of jeeps, crated machine guns, or even a tank, its fuel tanks filled and guns already loaded. Because of the foresight of the R.C.A.F. and the Canadian government at spotting refueling bases at close intervals — and presumably the Russians did the same thing across Siberia — the bombers can carry capacity loads of armaments.

At Fairbanks, the Russians maintain a huge barracks for army ferry pilots, said to be the only military base maintained on U.S. soil by any foreign government. The shortest route across Siberia lies close to Jap-held territory. The Japs would not pass up a chance to shoot down a U.S.-piloted plane but so far have hesitated to attack a Soviet-flown machine.

I first realized the large volume of Soviet-bound air traffic when the R.C.A.F. bomber in which I was travelling with a group of newsmen pulled up beside a string of fighters at the Fort St. John air base 600 miles north of Edmonton. Beside each red-starred fighter stood an alert U.S. soldier, service revolver jutting from its holster, a Garand rifle in his hands. There were no pacing sentries but alert guards, more like the traditional backwoodsman than a soldier. One of them later told me he came from the Arkansas hills.

As we emerged from our machine, the guard of the nearest fighter stepped quickly between us and his plane. He told us to keep our distance. It was clear the U.S. intended those planes to get through.

While U.S. soldiers swarm all over the string of bases stretching from Edmonton to White Horse, Yukon, the airfields are completely under R.C.A.F. control. Once they enter Canada, the ferry pilots take their orders from the R.C.A.F. which tells them which route they are to follow, how high they must fly and, in fact, whether they are to fly at all.

The duty of the Americans is to guard the traffic, to refuel it, and to do any mechanical work required on the planes. While the U.S. soldiers are under their own officers for disciplinary purposes, each base is commanded by an R.C.A.F. squadron leader, and only R.C.A.F. personnel are allowed into control towers without permission of the Canadian commander.

Russia-bound planes have the right-of-way, and long before a squadron reaches the next scheduled stop other traffic has been warned to keep clear, airport guards are at their posts and the gasoline trucks have been wheeled out, ready to refuel our allies' weapons with the least possible delay. Similarly, when a Red Star plane is ready to take off, all other traffic must wait.

I stood in the control tower while an R.C.A.F. control officer dispatched five fighters. At the last minute one of them developed trouble, which the pilot radioed the tower could be fixed in half an hour. The officer ordered the other four to continue and held the fifth for the next flight.

The main route followed is Edmonton, Grand Prairie, Fort St. John, Fort Nelson, Watson Lake and Whitehorse in Canada and Fairbanks, Alaska. The northwest staging route is the great circle route between central North America and Asia and Eastern Europe. Following the only pass through the western mountains, it is believed this will be one of two great peace-time air routes of the world and its North American end is almost completely under Canadian control.

The entire chain of airways has been linked by gasoline pipeline with the Canol project. At present, planes are refueled at White Horse and other northern bases with gasoline pumped over the Skagway-White Horse Canol pipeline and then distributed to Watson Lake. When the refinery now under construction at White Horse is completed it is proposed to pump gasoline to all the other air bases through a pipeline already laid.

While the main Russian base is at Fairbanks, where they have a full complement of women mechanics and engineers to service the planes for their long flight across Siberia, they occasionally come as far south as Edmonton. The sight of a Russian air force uniform in Edmonton streets has already passed the novelty stage, but because of the popularity of the Russians, it still attracts immediate attention.

Ross Harkness, "Soviet Girls, Canada Oil Run 'Top of World' Lifeline," the Toronto Star, *November 24, 1943.*

DECEMBER 24, 1943:
There Is No Peace in Ortona

Matthew Halton, a former *Toronto Star* reporter, was one of the young war correspondents who went to Europe relatively unknown and returned as a star. Halton earned his fame by taking great personal risks. By the end of the war, he had seen more combat than many of the troops who went overseas. The CBC's war reporters were hampered by technology and censorship. The bulky recording equipment was difficult to lug around. Editing was done in a van that, by the end of the war, was shot up with bullet and shrapnel holes. The battlefield coverage was vetted by Canadian public affairs officers and by British censors in London, which was the choke point for material that was sent back to Canada by wire and on ships. This is a transcript of one of Halton's broadcasts from Ortona, Italy, where Canadians fought a bloody house-to-house battle for eight days against the elite German 1st Parachute Division, veterans of tough fights in Crete, Greece, and the Russian Front.

MATTHEW HALTON

This is Mathew Halton of the CBC speaking from Italy.

It is Christmas Eve. As I speak, there is still the hardest of fighting in Ortona and just beyond the Ortona Road on the left. I have never seen anything worse. Right now, in a deep ravine only half a mile from Ortona, some Canadian engineers are building a bridge under fire. I am now in safety, several miles behind there. But the fighting men are still in action and the engineers are still working on that bridge.

Here is a recording we made in a relatively quiet moment there today. While we were there, enemy mortar shells fell nearer, but not as we were recording, and I can't say I'm sorry. But you will hear a machine gun. A section of machine gunners was with the engineers to give them covering fire, and you will hear one of the Bren guns ripping away.

[Higher pitch to Halton's voice]

We're in this gully now. You can hear the engineers shouting in this gully just below Ortona, where western Canadian units are having one of the toughest fights of the campaign. Down in the gully, which is sometimes under enemy fire, there are more than a hundred Canadians ignoring whatever fire there is and doing this job so that the battle can get on. With me right now is Captain, Lieutenant Donald MacLelland of Vancouver, who is in charge of building this bridge, I think the largest the Canadians have put in, with a 170 foot span.

You're working sometimes in plain view of the enemy, aren't you, Lieutenant?

Lt. MacLelland: Yes, he can see us right from Ortona.

Halton: Has he shelled you much?

Lt. MacLelland: Not directly, but some have fallen rather near to me.

Halton: You've been driven off the job, yes? Well, I hope they don't start shelling for a few minutes.

Lt. MacLelland: Well, I hope they …

Halton: As I speak now, we can hear the machine guns, our own Bren guns, and the enemy's Schmeisers and Spandaus stuffing away at Ortona. Who is this older sapper? [Sounds of bursts of machine gun fire, obviously very close.] There you heard noises, fortunately not enemy. The blast you heard was a blast on the bridge, and the machine-gun was one of our machine gunners covering this position as the bridge is built. Among the sappers working here is Sapper Joseph Rome….

Lt. MacLelland: I'm sorry, I won't be able to say what his age is, the authorities might [unintelligible].

Halton: Well, anyway, I believe [burst of machine gun fire], there's the machine gun, the machine gun again, covering this bridge, as the bridge is built. Sapper Rome is, anyway he looks like quite an old man. Born in Carlisle, England, and when I asked him where he was from, he said "anywhere in Canada." There may be people listening to this who find it hard to believe that our sappers can build a heavy steel bridge with a single span of 170 feet across a blown gorge in a day or two, and do it under shell fire, and sometimes under machine gun fire. Yet this is done time after time by British and Canadian engineers. For security reasons, I cannot give you many details. I cannot tell you how the work is done, nor what enables it to be done. But it's a fascinating thing to watch, except when shells are falling. Shells have to fall right on top of these engineers before they go to ground. They're working against time, and with grim purpose, to help the infantry. The sooner the bridge is finished, the sooner our supporting arms can get to the forward infantry.

The men aren't talking much, though you hear them shout, "heave!" And you hear the quick orders of Sergeant William Prusk of Toronto, or Lieutenant Don MacLelland of Vancouver, or Major Evan Pritchard of Kingston. It's a beautiful piece of work, and a fine piece of gallantry, and to be with them for just a few minutes is to be better, come what may, while you're there.

This is Matthew Halton speaking from Italy.

Matthew Halton, the Canadian Broadcasting Corporation, December 24, 1943. CBC Archives, www.cbc.ca.

JANUARY 15, 1944:
How Do You Cover a War?

Frustrated with the tough British-run censorship system that throttled all news coverage coming out of the European theatre, Ralph Allen wrote this piece when he was home on leave. Allen was a staff reporter at the *Globe and Mail* and a contributor to *Maclean's* magazine. Later, he edited *Maclean's*, assembling a staff of star journalists that included Peter Gzowski, Robert Fulford, Peter C. Newman, June Callwood, and Trent Frayne. They joined Pierre Berton and several other brilliant reporters who had already been recruited to the magazine.

RALPH ALLEN

There are several main sources from which to gather news in the Mediterranean theatre, and several ways to get it out. The fountainhead of news is Allied force headquarters at Algiers. Every day, usually between 11 o'clock and noon, approximately 100 correspondents gather at press headquarters in the heart of the city to hear a public relations officer read the official communiqué which has been wirelessed from 15th Army headquarters in Italy.

Immediately after the communication has been read, the public relations officer delivers a 15 or 20 minute commentary, sketching in background and details from a sheaf of intelligence reports relayed from the two fronts by army signals. From this information the correspondents write their stories.

The stories are censored by army, air force and navy censors in an adjoining office and are usually on the cables within an hour.

The closer to the front you move, the harder it becomes to get a complete picture of what is going on in all sectors, the longer it takes to get a story back, the more confused and strict the censorship regulations become.

Copy at the front makes its way back by dispatch rider and plane to a cablehead at Bari, Naples, Algiers or perhaps Malta or Brindial, is censored somewhere en route, and transmitted by commercial cable or army signals to London, Washington or New York.

Depending on the state of the roads, the distance between the front and the nearest cablehead and the volume of traffic, a story written at the front will take from twelve hours to two days longer to reach the destination than a story written in Algiers.

Certain impulsive war correspondents have remarked from time to time that "censors are human after all." This is a theory that I do not care personally to challenge, although I am bound to say, in reply to numerous queries from inquisitive members of the newspaper industry, that any blind, overpowering gusts of passion for army censors which I have felt creeping up on me have usually yielded without too great a struggle to a more moderate emotion.

This is a fancy way of saying that I am not fond of the censors. To tell the truth, I am no more capable of writing a fair or reasonable sentence about censors than composing a brochure in praise of Brussels sprouts.

The first story I wrote from the Mediterranean theatre was a frail little travelogue in which I mentioned in passing, probably with the object of impressing the boys in the back room at home, that I had recently been sitting under a date palm in North Africa. The only deletion the censor made in the story was to cut out the words "date palm." From that moment on, I attempted to govern my actions by the conviction that all censors are maniacs, a hypothesis that has stood the test of time faithfully and well.

One time the censor passed the names of three towns which our troops had captured on the same road. The towns don't matter anymore, but let's say the sentence read: "The Canadians today took Capello and Broccoli and the intermediate village of Ravioli."

The only cut here was the word "intermediate." My contention was that, although the information that the Town of Ravioli lay between the Towns of Capello and Broccoli might well have been of use to the enemy, the enemy very likely had the information already, in view of the fact that he had lived in the vicinity for generations and probably had a map.

Once, groping for a purple passage to describe a rather nasty little battle, I wrote that a party of Canadian troops had "dashed into a capsule inferno." Never mind why I wrote that; let's just stick to the subject. Translated into cables, the gem dropped the article and read "dashed into capsule inferno." The whole phrase was deleted — and probably a good thing at that — the interesting point being that the censor appeared to be enforcing a standing rule and suppressing the mention of Capsule Inferno until its capture had been confirmed by official communiqué.

The grisliest thing that ever happened at a censor's desk was a joint adventure that befell Major Bert Wemp, the correspondent of the Toronto *Telegram*, and Wallace Reyburn of the *Montreal Standard*. Wemp mentioned in a story about the 48th Highlanders that they had fought at Vimy Ridge in the last war. The censor cut out the part about Vimy Ridge.

The episode appealed to Reyburn, who wrote a paragraph about it for his own paper. As he wrote it, the message boiled down to this: "Wemp wrote that the 48th Highlanders fought at Vimy Ridge in the last war, but when the censors got through with it all that was left was "The 48th Highlanders fought in the last war."

And when the censor finished with Reyburn's story on Wemp's censored story it read like this: "Wemp wrote that the 48th Highlanders fought in the last war, but when the censors got through with it all that was left was: 'The 48th Highlanders fought in the last war.'" Reyburn refuses to communicate with his office until the whole thing blows over.

Aside from sitting here and gnawing on a steel filing cabinet for the sheer pleasure of it, there is not much that anyone can do about censors. But there are a couple of angles to higher censorship policy which would stand review, assuming the army is interested in having the story of the war told as fully and as fairly as is consistent with security.

For one thing, it is ordained by the mysterious paladins who control censorship policy that decorations won in the field by members of the Canadian army cannot be mentioned in news stories until they have been officially posted in the *Canada Gazette*. This involves a delay of weeks or months, during which the news edge of the story behind the decoration is dulled, and other stories are constantly breaking. The result is that, although the official dignity of the *Canada Gazette* is protected, a soldier who wins a medal in the field does not often receive the prompt and full public honor which is his due.

It is also ordained that no battle casualty can be mentioned until his relatives have been notified that he is a casualty by the Department of National Defence. With the human impulse behind this ruling all war correspondents are in complete sympathy: no newspaper man who has served in the field would willingly give unnecessary pain or impose an unnecessary shock on the relatives of a dead or wounded soldier for the sake of a story.

Nevertheless, in practice the ban on mentioning names of casualties in front-line stories means that a soldier who is killed or wounded in action is often never identified by name in a newspaper story from the front.

Our soldiers aren't fighting for press clippings. Still, it is arguable that, so long as soldiers must be killed and wounded and their families must be told, it is at least as humane to tell the world that the young fellow got it as a hero than to send around a messenger boy with the official regrets of the Department of National Defence.

I am thinking now of a little battle in which 15 kids from this part of the country attacked a company of Germans. They got into trouble, but they kept going. Eight of them got back. Seven didn't. The story of one of them I remember particularly well. He was covering his section with a Bren gun. A German bullet smashed his foot. Badly hurt, weak, dazed with pain, he left his gun and crawled painfully over the battlefield to a ridge that gave him cover. He was safe now. He would live. A minute before he had been going to die.

And then the youngster lifted his head a little and listened to the dreadful sounds of battle a hundred yards ahead. He didn't have to see to know that on that fire-swept slope from which he had just found sanctuary his pals were fighting against terrible odds. The kid looked back over the valley that beckoned to life. Then, painfully, he crawled the other way, to where he had come from before. He found his Bren gun again and sprawled behind it with his broken foot and started shooting. He stayed with the gun, shooting, until he was killed.

The stories of this battle mentioned the names of the eight soldiers who got back. All the mother of the boy with the Bren gun heard about her son, at first, was that he was dead. If she knew what a magnificent son he had been, it was only because she had known it all along.

Ralph Allen, "How to Cover a War," the Globe and Mail, *January 15, 1944.*

JUNE 6, 1944:
Over the Rainbow

Alexander Gault McGowan was born in Manchester, England, and was an officer in Britain's colonial army before becoming a journalist. He wrote

Canadians land at Juno Beach, June 6, 1944. The work of the military's film unit and the Canadian war reporters assigned to cover the invasion ensured Canadian coverage was superior to that of the other Allies.

in India, Trinidad, and New York City and filed this little "brightener" to world newspapers on D-Day. Gault was captured by the Germans but was able to escape from a POW train. He stayed in Europe after the war and died in 1970.

GAULT MCGOWAN

An Air Base in Britain, June 6 — Allied troops landing in France were greeted with a giant rainbow which spread along the enemy-occupied coast for miles.

It was a heartening sign for the attacking infantry. The rainbow spread right across the combat zone only fading from view after thousands of men had seen it.

Gault McGowan, "Over the Rainbow," the Toronto Star, *June 6, 1944.*

JUNE 1944:
Quebec Soldiers Feel the Call of their Norman Heritage

Marcel Ouimet was one of the Canadian Broadcasting Corporation's best war reporters. He was appointed head of the news division of Radio-Canada, the French service of the CBC, in 1941 and sent overseas with David Halton to establish infrastructure of the CBC's war coverage. Ouimet went ashore with an advance party at Juno Beach an hour before the Normandy invasion officially began. After a distinguished career as a war correspondent, Ouimet returned to Canada, where he became one of the pioneers of domestic television.

MARCEL OUIMET

June 6th — and on the sandy beach of the once charming but now badly battered village of Bernieres-sur-Mer, a Canadian soldier lands. He's had to wade in, waist deep in the water, to lead the first column of the support company of his battalion to a dry spot. His battalion, the Regiment de la Chaudiere, is the only French-speaking unit on the assault. The battle has progressed favourably. The other companies are well in command already. A few shells and the odd bullet still are whistling by, but who cares? Francois has waited four years for this moment and his first words to a friend as he passes by are these: "*C'est beau la France*" — France is nice.

That day I was standing by the roadside when I heard those words, close to a group of wildly excited Frenchmen who had gathered about to see us come. They hadn't slept much. The bombing and the shelling had kept them all night long in their cellars or in their slit trenches. But now they wanted to greet the Canadians. The regimental patch on the Canadian soldier's shoulder soon attracted attention: "*Regiment la Chaudiere*," one mumbled, and then he cried: "*Tu parles francais?*" — "you speak French?" "*Bien oui, je parle francais*," — the reply came. "Yes, I speak French." "*Et tu viens d'ou?*" "Where is your home?" "*A Quebec*." With every word the Frenchman beamed. So he went on: "*Et quand serez-vous de Paris, la semaine prochaine?*" "And when will you be in Paris — next week?" The Canadian shrugged his shoulders and the reply came unexpectedly: "*Tet ben q'oui*" [*peut-etre bien que oui*] — the French Canadian colloquial expression which comes literally, "well, perhaps yes," which like so many other colloquial expressions has been preserved among French speaking Canadians and which this soldier, a direct descendent of a family deprived for centuries of most of its links with France, had chosen to bring back three hundred years later to the land of his forefathers. On hearing it the Frenchman had grown more excited. "But you are not a Canadian," he said. "You're French — you're a Norman like me." And instantly he proceeded to hug the soldier and to kiss him on both cheeks. Now, in Canada most of the French Canadian families have done away with the well-known French tradition of the accolade — of the affectionate embrace between men of the same blood and race. So the soldier was somewhat taken aback. Nevertheless, he, on the sixth of June, had succeeded in capturing the heart and soul of France.

Today, like many more of his compatriots, he has been on this continent for over three months. He has lived beside the French, mingling with them whenever his duties allowed him to do so. He has been invited into countless homes, and his rediscovery of his former motherland has been most interesting to witness. *C'est beau la France*! A short and simple phrase of the French Canadian soldier on his landing at Bernieres. Words which meant something to him then, but now they mean more. There is something concrete about them. The abstractness has gone. Yes, this country is quite a lot like he read in his history books: "That's my language they're speaking," he thinks. The village priest is still the inspiration, and the village church the centre of communal life. More since he began to rediscover France through Normandy, where the accents, customs and traditions, through their close association with those of French Canada, were the source of a series of striking impressions. Yes, some districts of Bayeux and Caen reminded him of his native towns: the tall church spires, the houses, the farms and their highly productive fields appealed to his imagination. He felt at home — much closer to home — and when he was forced to strike at other towns, somehow he felt badly. Something did tell him that in Normandy lay the foundations of his life and of his civilization. Why, on Sunday these people put on their best clothes and went to church. After Mass, they lingered in the square to exchange facts and ideas and inquire about the health of their respective families. These people liked to eat and to eat well, profusely. To eat a lot of bread, a lot of butter and a lot of cheese. But they didn't drink water. Instead they drank wine, cider and Calvados — their native apple brandy. Rediscovery of wine caused a severe headache to many of our lads.

And what about the Frenchman's attitude to his cousin from Canada? One of great interest. He can't help being amazed by the persistence in the Canadians of a great number of French traits. He likes him. He sympathizes more readily with him than with his British and American allies, for the simple reason that he can understand him and knows he is understood. So he has opened his home. He likes to have Canadians for a meal or for a drink, to provide him with a family atmosphere and with some friends-3,000 miles away from Canada.

"*C'est beau la France*," say the soldiers of Quebec. But centuries of attachment to their soil and to their homes will bring them back no less deeply convinced Canadians, to a great and grand country, their native land.

Marcel Ouimet, June 1944, CBC Archives. See also A.E. Powley, Broadcasting From the Front *(Toronto: Hakket, 1973).*

JUNE 15, 1944:
Lili Marleen

The lyrics of "Lili Marleen" were written in 1915 by Hans Leip (1893–1983), a school teacher drafted into the German army. The poem was set to music in 1938 and recorded by cabaret singer Lale Andersen (1905–1972). By 1942, the song was on the playlist of the German military radio station in occupied Belgrade, Yugoslavia, which had the wattage to broadcast throughout the Mediterranean and North Africa. Because of constant requests from German soldiers, the song was broadcast every night at 9:55, just before the station signed off. "Lili Marleen" became a worldwide radio sensation during the Africa campaign of 1942, when soldiers from both sides tuned in to hear it. An "official" English version was written by Tommie Connors. This did not prevent Allied soldiers from creating their own lyrics, including the versions below and a tune called "The D-Day Dodgers," written in 1944 by Canadian soldiers to show their contempt for "Zombies," draftees who refused to serve overseas.

PETER STURSBERG

A recent issue of the Middle East magazine, *Parade*, called "Lili Marleen" the song of the year. The Eight Army organ, The Crusader, asked British troops not to sing it because Yugoslav Partisans regarded it as a German killing song. The Nazis would sing it while marching hostages off to slaughter. However, I have heard that even Marshal Tito's men have their own version of "Lili Marleen," which just shows how the simple little tune has overcome national barriers and the worst hatreds of the war.

The Canadian soldier hears it so often, whistled by the Italians in the narrow alleyways of the towns and sung by the barelegged peasants in the fields, that he finds himself humming it, although he may not know what it is. Tommy Atkins, who was the first to spread "Lili Marleen," did not know the words when he originally heard it but wrote his own, which are still sung and tell the story of the tune.

There was a song the Eighth Army used to hear,
In the lonely desert, lonely sweet and clear,
Over the ether came the strain, the soft refrain, each night again:
With you, Lili Marleen;
With you, Lili Marleen.

We knew the music wasn't meant for us,
Husky the singer, blonde-haired Nazi huss,
But still the music sweetly came, each night again, the soft refrain:
With you, Lili Marleen;
With you, Lili Marleen.

A little later, after he had defeated Rommel's men, who were the first to claim the song, he added another verse:

Afrika Corps has vanished from the earth,
Smashed soon the swine that gave it birth,
No more we'll hear that lilting strain, that soft refrain, each night again:
With you, Lili Marleen;
With you, Lili Marleen.

Johnny Canuck has also written his own words. The Hastings and Prince Edward Regiment has a version of the song and I imagine other regiments have, too.

However, the universal appeal of "Lili Marleen" is not in its simple catchy little tune alone, but in the wistfully sentimental ballad which loses very little in translation from the original German and is certain to raise a lump in the throat of any soldier.

Outside the barracks, beside the heavy gate,
There stands a lamppost, and if it's standing yet,
We'll meet there once again, beside the lamppost in the rain,
As once, Lili Marleen;
As once, Lili Marleen.

The lamppost knows your footsteps, so lovely and so free,

Its light shines for you, but it's forgotten me,
And if I don't return again, who will stand there in the rain,
With you, Lili Marleen;
With you, Lili Marleen?

There is something elemental about this song. The lamppost shining in the rain — who does not remember a scene like that back home? And who has not met a girl beside a lamppost in the rain? The Canadian sings this song as an expression of a lonely man for the girl that he has left behind.

Peter Stursberg, "Lili Marleen," Maclean's, June 15, 1944.

JULY 4, 1944:
Matthew Halton Watches the Bombardment of Carpiquet Airfield

The airfield at Carpiqeut, on the outskirts of Caen, was one of the Canadian objectives on the first day of the Normandy invasion. The Germans, however, had dug in and had decided to make the ancient Norman city a killing ground. The 150 fanatical Nazi teenagers of the Hitler Youth garrison that held the airfield had built a bunker and tunnel system that sheltered them through the bombardment that Halton describes in his report. Carpiquet fell on July 5. Although outnumbered eighteen to one, the Hitler Youth soldiers at the airfield held on through three more days of vicious fighting. Caen itself was destroyed.

Matthew Halton

This is Matthew Halton of the CBC reporting from France. It's two minutes to five in Normandy. The sun hasn't risen yet over us or over the Germans, 800 yards away. It will rise on a fearful scene because at five o'clock precisely the Canadians are going to attack, and they'll attack with the largest concentration of fire ever put down on a small objective. It's hardly light enough to read these notes into the microphone. The morning is as soft and beautiful as a swan riding down a quiet river.

But just wait a minute.

I'm in a stone barn with a company of western Canadian machine gunners who are going to be in battle soon, drawing fire to aid the main attack. Plainly in front of me, not half a mile away, is the powerful German strong point of Carpiquet village and Carpiquet aerodrome, two or three miles west of Caen. That position has been a thorn in our side. We can't get Caen until we get Carpiquet. And now we're going to get it.

We can see Germans moving from time to time in the half light. We won't see them when the barrage begins.

Little white rabbits and baby ducks are playing at my feet. They don't know that this barn will soon be shelled and machine-gunned.

There's Carpiquet. There's the wood from which Canadian infantry and tanks are going to attack. And here are we, closer to Carpiquet than to the wood. The attack will come from right in front of us and toward us.

I've never had a better observation post for a battle and I dread what I'll see through this door. Many hundreds of guns will support the assault. No less than hundreds of field guns, twenty-five pounders, no less than hundreds of medium guns, and many heavy guns, and in addition the sixteen-inch guns of a British battleship and a monitor, which will throw their 2,000-pound shells from ten or twelve miles away, at sea.

And in addition to all that, many squadrons of fighter-bombers and rocket-firing Typhoons. This unimaginable barrage will move, followed by our troops and tanks. I wonder if the Germans over there can guess what kind of hell is about to break on their heads.

At five o'clock — and it's now about ten seconds to five, one, two, three, four, five, six, seven, eight, nine, ten, eleven, twelve, thirteen [sound of explosion], fourteen [multiple explosions] — here she goes. [Forty seconds of steady explosions.]

[Studio voice.] Since I spoke the foregoing words at 5 o'clock this morning, I've seen the most spectacular and terrible battle I've seen in many years of war reporting. I started out last night with Alec MacDonald, a CBC engineer, my French-Canadian colleague Marcel Ouimet and Capt. Jack Golding of St. Johns, New Brunswick. We were told it would be impossible to get a good view of the attack, but we got forward in the moonlight, to the forward companies of a regiment which was overlooking Carpiquet aerodrome.

We met Capt. Bill Matthews of Vancouver. He gave us a midnight meal of turkey, and then took us to Maj. Croft, who allowed us, in fact encouraged us, to drive our jeep and our recording machines right into his OP [observation post], right on top of the position that was to be attacked.

We were mortared getting in there. Sometimes the shells fell far away, and their coming sounded like a London air raid siren. Sometimes they fell a few yards away, and they came with a sobbing scream. Before five o'clock, at first light, we could see the hangars on Carpiquet airfield. For the next hour we saw hardly anything. A few minutes after the barrage started, the objectives below us and the fields were a great cloud of smoke and cordite.

In the following recording, you will hear the sounds of Canadian and German machine guns and German shells that fell on them and my attempt to describe something of what I saw. And above all, the incessant, earth-shaking and atrocious pounding of hundreds of guns. Fortunately for you, the sounds that are recording on a disk are quiet and tame compared to what we hear. Even bursting shells, which shook us and blasted us, sound pretty tame on a disk. Listen to this, and then imagine it ten times as loud.

[Sound of machine gun fire and explosions.]

[Halton's voice, recorded in the fighting, is higher and a bit more frantic than his studio voice as he describes what he sees.]

Twenty five minutes of, I think of, the most ferocious barrage I've ever seen. When I first spoke, we could see the aerodrome and we could see the hangars in the first light of dawn. We could see the German strong points. But now there is nothing but the fog of war. See, on this battlefield, one understands the meaning of the phrase "the fog of war."

I sit here, I stand here, in this observation post, with two or three Canadian officers, two or three Canadian privates, and watch and wonder. All we can see is smoke and the terrible bursts of flame as one of the huge naval shells falls on the enemy position. Occasionally, an enemy shell falls near us. You can hear, you can hear as I speak, the chattering, the hard stuttering of the machine guns. And now I can see German flares going up. The nervy Germans. He must be nervy now under a barrage of no less than scores of thousands of shells. Sending up his flares, he must be still thinking.

I can see tracer bullets from our machine guns going across our front. Now I can hear other machine guns farther away, from our troops, who are advancing. Some of our tanks are going across the front, too. So this is the morning, this is … after a night that was bad enough, this is the morning we waited for, a morning in France, a morning in which the fair fields of Normandy are torn and rent and split apart.

[Studio voice again.]

At seven o'clock, the smoke was clearing away and the sight we saw then was one I'll never forget. I looked at Carpiquet and was astonished by how many of the hangars and buildings were still standing. I looked at the open fields, over which our troops were coming, and the woods they were coming from, and as I stared, they came, and with them the black waddling tanks belching flame and high explosive shells, and the men, shooting their Sten guns from the hip as they came, and thousands of flaming red tracer rounds skimming the ground at what seemed a thousand miles a minute.

Matthew Halton, CBC Radio archives, www.cbc.ca.

AUGUST 16, 1944:
Nuns Fear Girls Kidnapped in the Falaise Pocket

Canadian war correspondents saw first-hand the toll that the war took on French civilians. Demoralized by the German conquest of France and ground down for four years by Nazi occupiers who stripped the country bare, the Allied invasion brought both hope and an even more desperate level of hardship. The Franciscan Sisters of Our Lady of Mercy were caught at one of the most violent actions on the Western Front, the closing of the Falaise Gap. Almost encircled by the Canadians, British, and Americans, an entire German army of 100,000 men fought desperately to break out.

RALPH ALLEN

A Canadian Army chaplain will say Mass tomorrow in the convent of the Franciscan Sisters of Our Lady of Mercy. The convent is in the hamlet of Tarps, three miles off toward Falaise.

Canadian soldiers follow a tank into action during the fighting to close the Falaise Gap, France, summer of 1944.

For the 12 nuns of the order, who defied a German evacuation decree and remained in the convent yesterday through a day of violent battle, it will be the most memorable and tragic Mass they have ever heard. It will be memorable because it will be the first Mass the pious sisters have heard in a week. Last Thursday the Germans forced the only priest in the district to join their stream of property-less refugees inside the Falaise-Argentan pocket. The Mass they will hear will be a tragic one, because it will also be a prayer for "les enfants."

"Les enfants" are the 120 orphan girls who are wards of the convent. Last Thursday the Germans drove every one away after first "requisitioning" all transport for themselves. The Mother Superior could not be sure what was best; she knew the armies were approaching. So she complied with the order and on a rainy afternoon three weeks ago 44 girls, some of them as young as four years, said tearful farewells and left for the south in charge of five of the youngest and most capable nuns. They departed on foot in a driving rainstorm. The only belongings they took were what they could carry.

There were of course, no railroad trains, and the Germans had commandeered every cart and horse for their own use. Their destination — if so forlorn an expedition could be said to have a destination — was Blois, a town in the centre of France.

A few days later, the Mother Superior was told that it was time for the other 76 girls to go. The SS officer who came to the convent made it plain that the order must be obeyed at once.

The Mother Superior herself and four other nuns accompanied this second group, which also left the convent on foot, but which, unlike the first group, was escorted by two armed guards, Most of these girls were old enough for factory work and, although the SS captain said the guards were only for their protection, the sisters who remained behind remembered uneasily that long before the Allies came to Normandy attempts had been made to persuade the older of "les enfants" to go to work in Germany.

At the convent no word has been heard of "les enfants" since the Mother Superior turned at the little blue signpost where the road bends and waved her farewell. At that time the 12 sisters who remained behind had not heard about the Falaise gap.

It is possible that some or most of them got through before the gap began to close or that they found their way through no man's land while the fighting to the south was still in a highly fluid state. "All we can do is pray," Sister Marie de Jesus, the assistant Mother Superior, said today.

Sister Marie de Jesus and the other nuns who greeted French-Canadian soldiers at the convent today represented 75 per cent of the entire civilian population of Tarps and Tassily and their surrounding districts when Canadian troops paused to take a fast census on their way to Falaise. Last Thursday the Germans drove every one away after first "requisitioning" all transport for themselves. The sisters flatly refused to leave and even SS troops weren't sure what to do about them.

While the battle raged outside yesterday, 11 of the sisters took shelter in the convent's basement. Sister Marie Agnes climbed to the top of the tower and kept watch during the long morning. Sister Marie de Jesus came often to the top of the stairway and called "Are the soldiers still there?" Each time Sister Marie Agnes looked out across the wall to where the Germans were firing from their trenches and said sadly: "Yes."

Early in the afternoon from her sentry post Sister Marie Agnes cried "Praise be to God. They have a different costume!" The battle was over and the convent of the Franciscan Sisters of Our Lady of Mercy was still undamaged.

While the sisters told their story to two Canadian newspapermen today, the French-Canadian army Chaplain Captain Giraud Marchand, Quebec City, came to pay them a visit. They told Captain Marchand about "les enfants" and they also told him about not having heard a Mass since last Thursday, and particularly about not having heard a Mass on Assumption Day, one of the holiest of all days to the French Roman Catholics. Captain Marchand promised to come and say a Mass tomorrow.

The Sisters thanked him.

Perhaps it would yet be well with "les enfants."

Ralph Allen, "Falaise Nuns Fear Girls Kidnapped," the Globe and Mail, *August 16, 1944.*

AUGUST 15, 1944:
Normandy's Deadly Harvest: "We Aren't Threshing Wheat This Time"

Munro filed this story six days before the Falaise Gap was closed and the German forces remaining inside had surrendered or been destroyed. While German defence on the edge of the Falaise Pocket was collapsing, German troops at the Gap — the last escape route out — fought hard to keep the Allied from completing their encirclement. While German tenacity won time to allow half of the 100,000 Nazi soldiers to escape the Falaise Pocket, a huge amount of weaponry, including hundreds of tanks and artillery pieces, was left behind by the Werhmacht. Canadian troops fought well but the weakness of their senior officers was shown clearly in the Falaise operation. The press, however, glossed over their failures.

German POWs march into captivity as Canadian soldiers look on. Falaise Gap, August 1944.

A Canadian soldier uses a burning tank for cover during the fighting to close the Falaise Gap in Normandy in the summer of 1944.

Ross Munro

With the 1st Canadian Army in France, Aug. 15 (CP Cable) — A Canadian officer said tonight Falaise might be entered within a matter of hours as troops of the 1st Canadian Army pushed forward through German defenses which appeared to be disintegrating.

Canadian guns are shelling the area all around Falaise, hammering roads that lead to and from the city and provide the Germans with a hazardous escape corridor from the pocket in which they have been caught in the west.

The Canadians are driving on the town from the north and northwest, with troops in the latter sector approaching from the Laize River valley. By late afternoon they were reported near Ussy, four miles from Falaise on a good road.

A staff officer at Canadian Army headquarters said there is no large scale movement eastward through the Falaise-Argentan gap which is well-blanketed with shellfire. But, he said, there are rough roads between Falaise and Argentan over which German columns could attempt to move. American troops are pushing northward in an effort to cut these possible escape routes.

This afternoon I watched Canadian tanks and infantry going forward rapidly along roads leading through the Laize River Valley northwest of Falaise. Great concentrations of Canadian artillery sent shells hurtling over their heads into German positions.

The guns were set among stooks of freshly-cut wheat and a Prairie soldier, wiping his moist forehead under the baking sun, remarked: "This is real threshing weather but we aren't threshing wheat this time."

Lieut. Forbes McLauchlin. 29, of Ganges Harbor, Salt Spring Island, B.C. said that although there was no firm line of defence the fighting was "damn tough," and another officer just back from forward areas said "The Nazis are fighting like bloody wolves all the way."

More and more Germans appeared to be surrendering, however.

Today Polish troops finally cleaned out the forest of Quesnay, east of the Falaise highway, where the Germans had resisted despite endless bombing and shelling.

The Laize Valley west of the highway is hilly and wooded, with steep banks leading down to cool, fast-flowing rivers. It is a hard country to fight through for it favors the defenders, but the Canadians penetrated with great speed.

Fighting in all sectors of the advance was particularly heavy yesterday and there were losses on both sides. One of the many stories of heroism concerned a Canadian tank officer who refused to come out of battle although he suffered a leg wound which broke a bone. He limped barefoot about his duties.

It is difficult to piece together a complete story of yesterday's fighting as many tanks are still in the line, but apparently at 11:42 a.m. Canadian tanks moved off from a start line between Robert Mesnil and Cauvicourt, east of the highway.

They went ahead of the infantry and remained ahead, until mid-afternoon when foot-troops pushed past them to take on German infantry positions.

The first break in German resistance came after noon when the Germans began surrendering in an area around Soignolles.

"They just stayed and fought until we got to them," said Lieut. McLauchlin. "They just threw down their weapons and came out in front of an Ontario tank regiment." The Jerries have been coming back all day. There are hundreds of them in the fields around here. McLauchlin did not cross the Laison River line until today and said that nearer to Falaise the Germans certainly were contesting ground with pockets of tanks, guns and nebelwerfers (multi-barreled mortars).

Ross Munro, The Canadian Press, August 16, 1944.

AUGUST 23, 1944:
The Canadians Capture Trun

By capturing Trun, the Canadians were close to sealing the encirclement of the German Seventh Army. About 50,000 Germans were trapped, but another 20,000 managed to escape by breaking through a weak section of the Allied line. The Allies would try to lay the blame for this on each other. The Americans accused General Montgomery of timidity, while he tried to pass the blame to the Canadians. Likely all of the Allies underestimated the German will to escape. There was also a fear among all of the western Allies of engaging the Germans in a bloody fight and sustaining First World War levels of casualties when this war seemed so close to its conclusion. Paris fell on August 28, the same day the story ran.

FREDERICK GRIFFIN

With the First Canadian Army in France, Aug. 23 — An Ontario regiment are the kingpins of Trun, where they held the gap against escaping Germans and where they captured a German general trying to get out by night in a tank. That was a hectic night as will presently appear.

The high road to Trun from Falaise was still dangerous in spots from fire from the Germans still caught in the pocket, so with Lieut. Dick Clayland of Montreal driving the jeep, I worked into Trun by back roads through Barou and Les Moutiers-Auge.

This was a country of peace, scarcely touched by the swift passing of war. A few miles away across the close fields and the wooded hills of this Bocage country, the German army was in its last death throes. The land there was one vast charnel-field of tanks, vehicles, guns, men and equipment blasted and rent by the swift, unrelenting power blows of our aircraft, our tanks, our guns and our infantry in an unforgettable, vengeful reckoning with the enemy.

But on this side, northwest of Trun, it was as peaceful this August day as Grey County and as beautiful. Such are the quick contrasts of this now fast war as it sweeps through its climax to its conclusion.

But while the land lay unhurt and lovely, with cows and crops, nevertheless there were many signs of war and of allied victory. Driving was as bad as coming down from Lake Simcoe next Labour Day.

The roads, all those roads, were thronged with thousands of our vehicles on the move with supplies and munitions for our marching armies. Convoys stretched for miles. So thronged were the roads that few refugees were on them. These might be seen in hundreds, working their pathetic way home on sidetracks and even streaming across fields. Unlike those whom I saw at the weekend, these were mostly peasants with heavily-laden carts. On top of immense loads of evidently everything they had been able to pack, perched children and women, including many elderly women. Many of them drove home their tired cows.

But let us hasten to Trun, a one-street country town of perhaps 1,000 population, which had been damaged, but not brutally like Buron or Tilly La Campagne. German prisoners were still pouring through, some on foot, some in our vehicles, some in their own. Those badly-beaten Nazis with only one desire, to get out and stay out of the war, passed virtually unguarded and almost unnoticed, so many have come by.

Here in Trun, I found this Ontario battalion not merely holding the town, but running it. The colonel paid high tribute to Elmer John Albert of Blind River, Ont., a French-speaking soldier who, given the job of setting up some kind of refugee control, had set up a rest centre in one of the wards of the town's hospice and had played the good Samaritan to all sorts and conditions of French people in distress.

I met the dark quiet Elmer who did not seem to think that he had done anything in particular. Said his colonel, "why, he put ladies in bed. He cared for the tired and sick all on his own. He scrounged for food for them and he gave them water to drink. I marked a map for him, showed him the roads safe for the refugees to travel on and Elmer sent scores of the happily on their way. All without sleep for 48 hours. A good lad, Elmer."

First man I ever met in Trun was L.-Cpl. William Kerr of Peterborough, the colonel's dispatch rider. Bill told me how he and Pte. Howard Bradley of Cornwall each on a motor bicycle had taken over one pocket of 1,000 German prisoners and with a truck in front and a truck in the rear carrying wounded had marched them back 14 miles to find a prisoner of war camp that wasn't full.

"Last night," said Bill, "one Jerry drove right in here with a U.S. jeep carrying three wounded pals, looking for a Canadian medical officer to attend them. He wanted to go back for more but we asked him to be good enough to stay with us. He stayed." A captured German doctor and two German medical orderlies were set to work by the colonel attending to their own wounded. He gave them a ward in the town hospital and let the go to it. They did a very good job, he said. He had just sent them back to a prisoner cage by truck before I arrived.

Altogether, he said, more than 3,000 German prisoners had passed through Trun alone, taken from the gap. They included the German corps commander Lieut.-Gen Menni.

Trun lies southeast of Falaise, about halfway across the Falaise-Argenian gap through which the Germans being squeezed to death in the Montgomery pocket sought to escape from the merciless rockets of the R.A.F.'s Typhoons, the lashing of our guns — British, U.S. and Canadian — and the incoming of our infantry.

Two nights ago at 7 a.m. this Ontario battalion took over Trun after our armor had pushed through it. In the dark of a very dark night lighted only by some fires in Trun, they took over the town and spread along 2,000 yards of front southeast along the road and the river Dives towards Chambois. Their job was to help close the gap and hold it against the grey hordes pressing to get out like fish from a seine net closing in. But this net was made of steel and the Canadians determined that none of them would get out.

Unknown to these Ontario men, when they took over that key stretch of road and river Lieut.-Gen. Menni and his staff were planning a breakout. Unknown to them this Wehrmacht brass had ordered four Tiger tanks and one Mark V filled with gasoline from other tanks that were to be left to their fate. With these and 100 SS men in half-tracks and backed by ordinary infantry on foot he meant to blast his way through the thin Canadian line.

The Ontario lads had scarcely dug in and they were not in position two hours when out of the dark a savage attack was launched at them in the line below Trun. The company commanded by Maj. O. Peterson of Peterborough bore the brunt of it, beat it off and captured the general.

The attack began with a blasting of the guns of the five tanks. Then followed a Donnybrook, according to the colonel, as the German infantry rushed the river followed by the five tanks with their precious general snuggled inside one of them.

They overran the company, cutting it off from its headquarters and disorganizing its signals. But the in the dark, the company second-in-command Capt. Jack Watt gathered the rest on high ground 500 yards back and reorganized. They waited until the German infantry was just 40 yards away, holding their fire, then cut loose with their machine-guns. They killed 75.

In the meantime from below, Maj. Peterson was plugging away at the tanks with his Plat gun. And also, from the high ground, two officers of an Ontario support battalion, Lieuts. Leatherdale and Howard Jackson, both of Ottawa, let the Germans have their fire. To cap it all Capt. Watts counter-attacked on the hamlet of Magney and retook it.

This company of eastern Ontario men did one grand job here two ago for the loss of one officer and six men dead and seven men wounded. When dawn came, they found the German remnants, those that were alive huddled in the sunken road to which they had been driven back. To our men's surprise the group included General Menni who was "just another Jerry" to them.

Altogether, inclusive of the general, they rounded up 400 prisoners plus, according to the colonel, the general's diary and other important papers, three fancy uniforms, a box of very good cigars, and some very "fruity" soap — all in his escape tank.

In addition to more than 100 Germans dead they "killed" three of the German tanks.

The general, a big fellow who spoke very little French, wore the Iron Cross of 1914 and 1939. He was brought to the colonel's headquarters just after first light. The colonel sent him back to a higher headquarters.

"Did you give him breakfast," I asked. "Heavens no," he replied. "I haven't had breakfast myself and besides I had no time at the moment to waste on generals. No, I just sent him on his way and glad to get rid of him."

Shortly after midnight last night the Germans staged another attempt to get through this unit's position. But they were hammered fearfully by their machine-guns and Canadian artillery cut them to pieces. According to the colonel, not one German succeeded in penetrating to their positions.

Such is a sample of the fighting that the Canadians have been doing in the mouth of the gap since they took Falaise. I asked the colonel, an Ottawa man, to tell me something of his regiment's job on the road to Falaise and beyond it to Trun. Things have been moving so fast and he was so tired, that he had difficulty giving me the events in sequence.

His regiment was part of the infantry borne in armoured carriers which, with tanks, attacked the valley of the Laison in the Canadian assault on the last German positions before Falaise which broke the Germans finally and let to the closing of the Falaise gap and the cutting of and cutting up of the German 7th army.

His battalion advanced 6,000 yards that day across the Laizon and was on its objective within minutes. They fought through a smoke barrage laid down by our guns to cover them, so thick that they could scarcely see.

The woods in the valley of the Laizon with the tanks using the roads, proved too thick to let the carriers through so the men jumped out of their vehicles and went through them on foot. On the way they knocked out one German tank with their six-pounder gun.

It was their first tank "killed" for sure and they did it surely — an anti-tank gunner's dream, according to the colonel. They only fired three shots at it. One plugged the turret, a second holed the driver's compartment, and a third the engine.

There was a stiff fight for the chateau some distance beyond the Laizon on high ground. With a Tiger tank, dug in on one side and the river on the other, it had to be carried by frontal assault.

One man did a great job there with his flame thrower. He was L.-Sergt. G.T. Gurnock of Carp, Ont., and his crew were L.-Cpl. Poitras and Gnr. E.T. Blair, Fergus, Dickinson of Listowel, Ont. and George Pigeau. Advancing under fire, they destroyed four enemy machine-gun nests and roasted out the infantry.

"The enemy ran out screaming," said the colonel. "It was the first time that I had heard Germans scream and it was not without satisfaction. That was the end of their position. After Gurnock got through there just weren't any more."

It was at the chateau that Cpl. Donald Richard N. Nicholas of Campbellford did a job of initiative, devotion and courage which, according to his colonel, really led to its capture.

"As his platoon was advancing," the colonel related, "it was pinned down by murderous fire from the direction of the chateau and its officer was mortally wounded. Without orders Cpl. Nicholas picked up his Bren gun, stood up and, shooting from the hip, advanced alone. He killed four Germans and his boldness caused 30 others to surrender."

Frederick Griffin, "Canadians Capture Trun, Close Falaise Gap," the Toronto Star, *August 28, 1944.*

AUGUST 24, 1944:
"It Is a Beautiful, Wonderful Day"

With the closing of the Falaise Gap, most of the remnants of the German 7th Army were encircled by Canadian, U.S., and Polish troops. At the same time, General George Patton's Third Army swept out of the Norman battlefields and broke through to Paris. Canadian soldiers concluded that the war was nearly over. A similar breakthrough had doomed the Kaiser's army in 1918, but Hitler's regime, purged of the professional officers who had shown their hand in the July 20 bomb plot and dominated by die-hard Nazis, was now fighting to survive. Its leaders knew their lives would not last much longer than the Third Reich. And the Allies were determined to firmly plant their feet on German soil, so that there would be no doubt this time that German militarism had failed.

L.S.B. SHAPIRO

With the British and Canadian Forces East of Falaise, Aug. 24 — (By Wireless) — "It's a beautiful, wonderful day," a Canadian corporal said — as he sat on top of his gun carrier by the side of the Trun-Falaise road. "It sure is a beautiful, wonderful day."

As a matter of fact, the rain was pelting out of a leaden sky, it was cold and everybody was caked with mud. But the corporal is entitled to some poetic license in the matter because this was the "beautiful wonderful day" he had been dreaming about for four years and a little thing like rain couldn't make it a whit less magnificent.

He had just heard General Montgomery's order of the day, stating that we had completely defeated the German armies in northwest France and that the end of the war is in sight. Besides, the corporal could see it for himself. The Falaise bag had been split wide open and Germans were rolling out of it like oranges — right into captivity. As he sat on his carrier fingering a Sten gun, Germans were streaming past in review, three abreast, hurrying to barbed-wire cages like marathon runners struggling the last, long mile. They were laggard and exhausted, yet they hurried.

They seemed frantic. They wanted to get out of the war — to be done with it — as though it suddenly had become too repulsive to bear.

The corporal wiped the rain out of his eyes and surveyed the prisoners stretching down the road as far as the eye could see.

"I can't believe it yet," he said. "It seems like only yesterday they were like supermen. I never thought I'd live to see them crack. And now look at 'em — coming in like a lot of blooming sheep. I'll bet there's been nothing so beat up since Sodom and Gomorrah." He lit a cigarette in the shelter of his carrier and continued, "You know what I call 'em? I call them Fritzies-in-a-Hurry. Some of 'em hurried into France from Russia. Then they hurried into line around Vipers. After a while they hurried into trying to escape through Falaise. And now look at 'em — hurrying like hell to get to the cages. Fritzies-in-a-Hurry, that's what they are.

"And now they say the war's nearly finished. That's hard to believe, too. It's become like normal to us fellows by now, I've been in uniform for five years. Do you know I've got a daughter back in Canada who begins going to school in a couple of weeks and I've never laid eyes on her, I wonder how's it going to be when I get back — my little girl saying to me 'How do you do?'"

He inhaled deeply on his cigarette, the trace of an expectant smile played on his lips. The rain poured down. Prisoners shuffled past moodily. But for this fleeting moment the corporal was in another world.

L.S.B. Shapiro, The Canadian Press, August 24, 1944.

AUGUST 24, 1944:
"Seeing Those German Dead, I Am Very Happy"

The Canadians fought hard to complete the encirclement of the German 7th Army in the farm country behind the Normandy beachhead. Historians still argue over the extent of damage to the 7th Army and its equipment. While thousands of German troops did escape the trap, thousands more perished or surrendered, ending any real chance of throwing the Western Allies back into the sea. After the murder of surrendered Canadians by Hitler Youth fighters and the tough combat around Caen, Canadian correspondents joined with the troops in rejoicing at the sight of the burned and broken remains of a German army that many of them had feared was superior in training, equipment, and motivation to their Allied opponents.

FREDERICK GRIFFIN

With the Canadian Army in France, Aug. 24 — I drove for miles through the most fearful cemetery that Western Europe has ever known and only saw a fraction of it. This was the cemetery of the 7th German Army, or that considerable portion of it which was trapped in the Normandy gap and slaughtered.

There died an army. There died Hitler's last hope of holding the Allies. It lies rusting and rotting in roads and fields, in lanes and orchards with a horrible finality. We only wish Hitler might be made to see every mile of these stinking miles of death, of the pitiable impotence of the gray men with the black faces lying in the churned mud, of these men whom he willed to their slaughter, as he willed the slaughter of so very many men, women and children who only wanted to live their little lives in peace.

I only wish that all men who dream of war, who talk of glory or the grave, who aim at conquest through killing, might see these charnel fields of Normandy. They would have to see it now and soon, for not only are the human dead being buried and the animal dead being burned, but nature is already beginning to assert her power to cleanse her earth of this foul thing.

Never, surely, has so much havoc to men, animals and machines been packed into such space. Some roads are impassable with the mass of smashed German machines and materials and detours have to be made through the fields. In other places, in order to let through the onrush of our mighty military machine which is pounding and hounding Hitler to his early doom, bulldozers have simply pushed the smashed, burned and rusting junk of tanks, guns, half-treads, troop carriers and staff cars off the roadside. Hundreds of such vehicles lie to one side, overturned in ditches and gullies.

If anyone wondered about the power and accuracy of the RAF and the RCAF, of the medium bombers and fighter bombers, or the deadly contribution to victory of the rocket-bearing Typhoons, he need wonder no more after seeing this wholesale precise havoc in the twisting lanes, in the leafy orchards through fields and along the hedge rows where the fleeing Germans sought to conceal themselves.

Here is the evidence of how our air forces and our artillery flailed relentlessly at the Germans trying to get out of the net, scourging them with rockets, cannon-fire and shells in this gauntlet of unparalleled destruction. A good many of the debts the Nazis owe us were paid off in this Normandy pocket and in the Falaise-Argentan gap which the Canadians, with the Poles, closed by winning down through fast to Trun and Chambois.

Time was when I was greatly moved by death. But today I saw here massed and monstrous German dead lying gross in the ditches, dying like maggots in the mud of the roadside without a qualm. Foul to the nostrils but not to the eyes. Offensive to the senses, but not to the soul. This, I felt, was our vengeance on the Germans who were without pity for their fellow men; who even now are killing English folk in the cites and the country with the inhuman flying bombs.

It is hard to tell you and difficult to describe what I saw for miles and hours today when with Lieut. Les Callan, the Star's cartoonist, as companion and with Lieut. Dick Haviland as conducting officer and jeep-driver, I got lost in a jungle between dead Germans and our own tanks.

I asked Callan, a very gentle, kindly man, what he thought of it all. "Put me down as saying I did not see enough dead Germans to satisfy me," he said. "But I like horses and I was downright sorry to see so many dead horses. You can see that many of them have died literally in the traces, doing their best to get these Jerries out. That's what hurts me — these dead horses."

He was right: We saw in the relatively small area in and around the gap we were able to visit, not just scores of horses dead, but hundreds of horses. You will not find one horse-drawn vehicle in our magnificently mechanized armies in France, but the Germans, for all their vaunted mobility, which we have turned into immobility, used very many horses to draw guns and transport.

Near a group of dead horses a small red calf rubbed itself against an apple tree and an old white horse grazed undisturbed. On all sides the living and the dead showed close together in vivid contrast. The countryside was little disturbed by the slaughter which had swept like a thunderstorm across it. There was little evident damage. Most farmhouses seemed unhurt, though dead cows, dead horses lay at many a doorstep or the foulness of Germans lying in nearby lanes poisoned the air sweet with the scents of harvest.

Peasant women worked in vegetable plots and men worked in the fields as if this smear of German wreckage and of German dead lay a thousand miles away instead of under their eyes and noses. I saw many cases of peasant women rummaging through a litter of German garments, squatting down right by German dead and retrieving what trousers, shirts and linens they might find serviceable. The French are realistic, logical and thrifty, and no doubt they got many a useful thing. They were not hunting souvenirs as our troops, British and Canadian, were. Many of them were culling over the debris for treasure.

And many Yanks in tin hats up from their sector south were indulging in regular rubbernecking expeditions throughout the area. It was all certainly a sight to be seen, however awful a sight, that was a sermon on the littleness of man and the monstrousness of war.

We drove down the mouth of the gap as it began from Falaise, taken by Canadians, to Argentan, which the United States had won eventually. About three miles short of Argentan we cut across by a side road northeast toward Trun, which had been one of the back roads the Germans had used in their attempt to sneak out of the gap.

Reaching Trun, we drove southwest toward St. Lambent-sun-Dives and Chambois, the axis along which the Canadians had driven to close the gap and hold it against the Germans. Approaching St. Lambent, we began to come on the real slaughter, and from there to Chambois and then north on the roads and in the fields for miles, it was indescribable. Literally hundreds and hundreds of every kind of German vehicle, from Panther tanks to farm carts and tiny trailers and bicycles, smeared the roadsides and showed along hedgerows and in fields and orchards in a gargantuan messing.

How they were spotted and destroyed with such accuracy by the airmen and our gunners in thick bocage country bowered with leafage, passed my comprehension. But spot them they did, and smash them they did, mercilessly.

St. Lambent and Chambois, two villages cluttered with German wreckage and with dead horses and dead Germans along fences; in gutters, hedges, even on the doorsteps of stores and homes, were roaring crossroads where it seemed the Allied armies met, British, Canadians and Poles in tanks and carriers, U.S. troops in jeeps, all in a coming and going of traffic to hurry the war's end.

We drove up the road from Chambois northeast toward Vimoutiers, meaning to make a circular swing around across the back of our rapidly-moving front. But we did not get to Vimoutiers, could not get to Vimoutiers.

First of all, the German wreckage so thickly clattered the back roads, dirt roads we would call them in Canada, that in places not even the bulldozers could clear it. As a result there were diversions for our armor through fields and woods.

I was grimly savagely happy at having seen that smashing of the Germans, that terrible reckoning by our men and our powerful machines with the Nazis in their own coin a hundredfold.

I hate war and I think killing is madness, but seeing those German dead I am very happy.

Frederick Griffin, "Vaunted 7th Army Rusts and Rots in Normandy," the Toronto Star, *August 24, 1944.*

SEPTEMBER 1944:
The Van Doos Fight Their Way Across the Marano River

The Quebec public was split on Canadian participation in the Second World War, but the francophone Royal 22nd Regiment, the Vingt Deux or "Van Doos," attracted tough men who fought hard to maintain the fearsome reputation of their regiment. In the weeks after D-Day and the closing of the Falaise Gap, the Canadians fighting in Italy had good reason to resent the shift in media and public attention from their theatre to western Europe. The fighting was still tough and the hilly Italian geography favored the defenders. After another ugly fall and early winter in Italy, the Canadians who had battled their way from Sicily to the upper part of the Italian boot were transferred to join the rest of the Canadian army, just in time for the grim assaults in the Low Countries. Boss outlived the rest of his colleagues on CP's war reporting team. He died in 2007 at the age of ninety. Boss was a well-educated and inquisitive Renaissance man who spoke eight languages. Boss remained footloose for a decade after the war, travelling and writing in Europe, then covering the Korean War, before eventually settling down into a public relations job.

Canadian soldiers roast a pig under the hot Italian sun in the summer of 1944.

WILLIAM BOSS

With the Canadian Corps on the Adriatic, Oct. 17 — This story takes you back to the night of September 13, when the Royal 22nd Regiment approached the Marano River. Then follow the four days during which the regiment battled its way through the heaviest shell and mortar fire ever experienced by the 8th Army.

It ends the morning of Sept. 18 when the exhausted battalion was pulled out, after having established the Marano crossing, made a deep bridgehead beyond and making secure part of the San Lorenzo-San Martino Ridge, second last obstacle to the Lombardy Plains.

Read the story as though every sentence were punctuated with a shell-burst, or eight mortar bombs in your immediate vicinity. Every minute brought its packet to the Van Doos. "Never before had so much been dumped on our heads," commented Major Gaston Poulin of Quebec after the battle. "To come through that alone required nerves of steel."

The spearhead through the inferno was a company under Capt. Simard, Quebec. Simard's men saved the day when other companies under Majors Poulin and Henri Tellier, Montreal, established the original crossing of the Marano, then were pushed back.

New attacks failed. Finally Simard came through, either drove the Germans back or by-passed their strongpoints. He reached a high ridge overlooking the regimental objective so quickly that other Van Doo companies didn't catch up with him until next day.

Later, in the final attack on San Martino, Simard smashed through again. Once launched, his company never stopped. Enemy pockets and strongpoints were overrun without pause. The actual Marano crossing was made by companies under Majors Poulin and Tellier. In the pitch dark the route to the river was followed by compass bearings from the stars. Yet Poulin made no mistake. His men, and Tellier's following close behind, reached the appointed crossing-place, prepared their attacks. But each was minus two platoons.

Lieut. Francois LaFleche, Ottawa, and Lieut. Mark Devlin, Quebec, were skirmishing with a fortified house up the river, while, a little behind, one of Tellier's platoons had become engaged. The two had only a company strength between them, and two headquarters.

Storming the opposite bank they advanced to a high point several hundred yards beyond. Resistance was heavy. The mortaring and artillery became furious. From the flanks, and especially behind, near the river, they were taking a beating.

The arrival of LaFleche and Devlin with their platoons, supported by six tanks, helped out. A strong machine-gun post was attacked by LaFleche with his platoon and two tanks. Just within range his tanks were knocked out. The houses were also sheltering two Panthers.

After LaFleche had been drawn back, Poulin and Tellier withdrew to bring artillery on the Germans. Casualties had been heavy. Another attack went in — again unsuccessful. Then the Three Rivers Colonel sent companies under Simard and Major L. Fremont Trudeau, Quebec, to by-pass the strongpoint, and leave it for Poulin to clean up.

While Trudeau and Simard sped past, Poulin, with only 40 men and LaFleche left among his officers, attacked again. Again he failed and his last officer went out wounded. The fourth time, he went around the sore spot, encircled it, but the enemy eluded the pocket in the darkness. The action had cut Poulin's company to 35, including himself and his Sergeant Major.

Meanwhile Trudeau and Simard were forging ahead until Trudeau tangled with a large chateau, occupied in strength — the Chateau des Verges. Simard pushed on to the objective, 3,000 yards ahead. Trudeau took on the castle. But the Colonel brought in Tellier's company to tidy up the chateau, ordered Trudeau to push on without further loss of time.

Until Tellier arrived Trudeau maintained the pressure. Lieut. P.P.E. Larochelle, Three Rivers and Peterborough, Ont., cleaned out a couple of houses around the chateau and took some prisoners. Lieut. Claude Gagnon's (Rimouski) platoon handled another. Then, two Tigers were discovered. Of the six self-propelled guns and three tanks sent to help them, three guns and two tanks were shot up.

The place was inferno of bursting shells, flaming tanks and wounded men. Medium artillery supporting the regiment silenced the enemy until Tellier's company arrived to help Trudeau get about his own job.

By-passing the trouble, Trudeau's men advanced 2,500 yards and finally found themselves on Simard's right. But they were strongly counter-attacked by tanks supported by infantry. Trudeau retired 500 yards to a ditch, reorganized and launched a new attack later in the morning which gave him back the group after an hour.

Simard's men had been virtually alone since going ahead the night before. And at 5:30 in the morning, Lieut. B. Pelletier of Ottawa, liaison officer with the tanks for the action, spotted two Tigers forming up for another counter-attack with more than 50 infantrymen.

In less than three minutes Simard had an artillery barrage dead on the spot. There was no counterattack. But the Tigers, and two others which approached unheard in the noise of battle and invisible in the close country, knocked out three of his four tanks during the morning. Trudeau's men were welcome when they finally came up on the right at 11:45.

By now the regiment had a deep bridgehead across the Marano. Tellier had cleaned up the Chateau Des Vergers, Poulin had reorganized and received reinforcements. Both were ready for new roles. Trudeau and Simard were 3,000 yards ahead on a ridge overlooking San Martino, the final objective. The afternoon attack on the little village was another of those speedy Royal 22nd assaults which knife through to an objective, then clean up the enemy pockets later.

At 2:30 there was a terrific artillery barrage. Then the infantry went in supported by a fresh tank squadron. The French-Canadians sped through. Mortar consistently fell behind, serving only to spur them on. Tank and machine-gun posts opened as they came up, were silenced without diminishing the impetus of the push or else were left behind for Poulin's company to clear out.

Halfway to the objective, Poulin's company consolidated, Simard's and Trudeau's took short breathers, then sped on. The next 1,000 yards went smoothly, infantry and tanks co-operating beautifully, despite the enemy's furious defense.

Later, when a strong line of machine-gun posts slowed things, Simard shouted: "It's only 50 yards, boys. 'Rien que cinq cent verges,' let's go. It's the brigade objective!" Before he'd finished the men were away. An artillery barrage helped them with the position ahead, and by bounds and spurts, they brought themselves to San Martino's outskirts half an hour later.

Trudeau's company on the right had been no less speedy. Lieuts Gagnon and LaRochelle literally carried their platoons as they dashed ahead. At the outskirts, Simard's company held firm while Trudeau's cleared the town of its paratroopers in what the commanding officer later described as a "fast" battle, then retired to the hilly outskirts again where they consolidated for the night with Simard.

The position was bad, there was insufficient cover, they were exposed constantly to enemy fire, and in a poor spot if counter-attacked. They just had to sit, taking everything the enemy threw, able to give him little in return. One platoon emerged with but six men.

After a day of this, Major Poulin, whose company had been reduced to 35 when pulled out after the Marano crossing, was ordered to make an evening attack on a ridge to the left of San Martino. Though launched in the face of "Moaning Minnies," Poulin's attack went in on the double,

A Canadian sniper takes aim in Italy, 1944.

Van Doo style. Tanks roared up from behind, went on with them, and 10 minutes later the position was theirs.

First on the objective were Poulin himself, Pte. Romeo D. Dupras, Montreal, signaller, and Pte. Laurent Chamberland, Quebec, with his mortar, but no ammunition left. That evening attack of more than 800 yards succeeded without a single casualty and in 15 minutes. The morning of the 17th brought a counter-attack and three Panthers with companies of infantry forced Poulin to withdraw just 150 yards down the slope. British tanks eventually arrived at noon to support him. Then, in a lightning, seven-minute attack, the Germans were toppled off the hill, and the French-Canadians took over to stay.

Three more enemy assaults were repelled that afternoon. Directing medium gunfire, Poulin knocked out two of the three Panthers taking part. In the evening a suspicious lull in the mortaring suggested to Poulin the enemy might try a night infiltration. The Germans did … only to walk into a pocket formed by the depleted platoons, then have the full benefit of an artillery concentration the young Major had prepared for them. Not one escaped.

The Royal 22nd Regiment was relieved next morning, Sept. 18. Its epic achievement on the Marano and on the San Lorenzo-San Martino Ridge was recognized by Prime Minister Churchill and Gen. Sir Oliver Leese in special messages,

And only when it was all over did they remember that their-most bitter battle in this war coincided with the anniversary of Courcellette, epic French-Canadian achievement in the First Great War.

William Boss, The Canadian Press, October 17, 1944.

SEPTEMBER 20, 1944:
The Liberation of Brussels

Pierre Dupuy had an interesting career. He was the second-ranking Canadian diplomat in Paris when the Nazis conquered France in the spring of 1940. Accredited as Canada's senior diplomat to the collaborationist Vichy regime, Dupuy travelled three times to unoccupied France between June 1940 and October 1942. These trips appear to have been made at the behest of Winston Churchill, whose government had broken relations with Vichy in the summer of 1940. Dupuy eventually became Canada's ambassador to France and ended his public service career as the chief executive of Expo '67. He made this broadcast for the CBC, invited by the radio network because of his pre-war familiarity with the Belgian capital.

PIERRE DUPUY

The town was given up to rejoicing. Large crowds in the boulevards sang, cheered and danced. They were deliriously happy. Elderly people smiled behind their tears. They could not yet believe that they were free. The young people laughed triumphantly because they had escaped the clutches of the Gestapo. Brussels showed few evidences of the war. The British advance was so quick that the Germans had no time to destroy it. Only a few houses, occupied by the Gestapo, have been burned, in all probability to destroy their incriminating documents. This is why the Palais de Justice was burnt out. Here and there could be seen an abandoned motor car which had been stolen by the Germans in their rout. It was indeed a rout. It was described to me by Belgian friends who during three days and three nights saw the vanquished troops pass under their windows.

What a change since 1940. No more goose-stepping parades and gone the arrogant young Nazis marching towards their conquest of the world. These troops were nothing more than a crowd of unshaven, exhausted men, without arms and in ragged uniforms. Many of them were riding stolen bicycles, some without tires. Others were riding two and three together on farm horses or donkeys. Some of the staff cars, lacking petrol, were drawn by horses. Push carts and even baby carriages were used for transporting the loot.

It is not difficult for you to imagine the feeling of our Belgian friends at the sight of this disorderly retreat. They dared not show their emotions while the enemy remained. Two young girls, who dared to laugh, were killed by a German officer. Immediately after the last of this lamentable cortege had passed, Belgian flags appeared.

But it was still too soon. German armoured cars turned back again, to fire on the flags in impotent rage. Finally they disappeared in the distance forever. Brussels was free again after four years of physical and moral suffering bravely endured.

I stopped to talk to a brave Belgian of sixty years of age, who was standing outside a shop where the following notice had been put in the window: "Closed for Victory." He told me that the most terrible thing during the German occupation was the constant menace of the Gestapo. "We were like people condemned to death but who didn't know the date of their execution. One after another, people disappeared. Nearly every morning at about five o'clock I was awakened by the heavy boots of the SS on their way to arrest someone. Were they going to knock at my door?

Oh M'sieu, you will never understand the joy that it will give me to be able to say: It is not the Gestapo, but only the milkman."

Pierre Dupuy, the Canadian Broadcasting Corporation, September 24, 1944. Reprinted in A.E. Powley, Broadcasting from the Front (Toronto: A.M. Hakkert Ltd., 1975), 132.

SEPTEMBER 1944:
Georges Vanier Returns to Paris

Georges Vanier was the first diplomat to return to Paris after the Liberation. He and his family barely escaped the fall of France in 1940. After the Allied break-out in Normandy and the capture of Paris, Vanier, who had been a hero in the First World War, resumed his post as Ambassador to France, accompanied by diplomat Saul Rae, whose son Bob would have a distinguished career in politics. Vanier would become Canada's second Canadian-born and arguably its most popular governor general. Clark covered the war for the *Toronto Star* and lost one of his sons in the fighting. After the war, he went to work for the Toronto *Telegram* and became one of the country's most famous humorists. He was awarded the Order of the British Empire for his war reporting and, near the end of his career, was presented with the Order of Canada for his humour writing. A few days before this piece was written, Clark's twenty-three-year-old son Lieutenant Murray Clark was killed in action on the English Channel coast between Calais and Boulogne.

Gregory Clark

"VANIER is coming!" The announcer was Saul Rae, in civvies that looked as if he had slept in them. And he had. Two days and nights. Saul Rae had had difficulty getting into the Scribe Hotel, our press headquarters. The captain at the door, a lithe Parisian in a turtleneck sweater with a captured German Parabellum nine-millimetre pistol strapped across his stomach, was letting nobody enter the Scribe except us war correspondents, Canadian, American, British, Russian, Italian, Chinese and, of course, Free French.

But Saul finally convinced the captain, who was a typewriter repairman in normal times, that he was indeed Saul Rae, of the External Affairs Department of the Government of Canada, and that he had important news for the Canadian war correspondents inside.

And there was Saul in the Scribe lobby, not looking at all like a career man but rather like a scholar who had slept in his clothes in this Paris that was in the delirium of its liberation: Paris gone nuts.

"Vanier is coming," he announced to us.

"When? Where?" we shouted, all ten or fifteen of us.

"Le Bourget. This afternoon."

Saul cleared his throat.

"He is coming," he said, "as Ambassador to France!"

He did not need to say any more. Georges Vanier, holy Moses, that lovely old one-legged Van Doo, the pre-war Canadian Minister to France, coming here to this pandemonium, France liberated, France risen from the dead, a French-Canadian coming as the first Canadian Ambassador to the land his fathers left 250 years before. And at such an hour, such a time!

Saul looked at us and we looked at Saul in a kind of luminous silence.

Then the youngest of us, a lad whose education had been sadly neglected, but who was a whale of a good front-line reporter, said mildly:

"Who's Vanier?"

In the awful silence, the gang with wry smiles turned to me, the old man, to reply.

"Who's Vanier! Son, there was a war one time, a war you wouldn't know about, and Vanier was in it. He was in a unit known as the Van Doos. Yeah? The same as the Van Doos we have now, only different. Younger, if you know what I mean. And Vanier got the Military Cross. Then he got the D.S.O. Then he got a Bar to the Military Cross, which isn't very common. After you get D.S.O.s, you're usually up where you aren't in a position to get any more Military Crosses. He lost his leg in a far-off, ancient battle, one with Nineveh and Tyre and Thermopylae, called Passchendaele ..."

"Aw, Greg, come on!" cried everybody, and we lunged for the door of the Scribe to rout out our jeeps and trucks, and to load the cameras and pile in the recording gear for the radio recordings, and everybody yelled:

"Where's Le Bourget? How do we get ..."

But there at the head of the cavalcade to guide us was Saul Rae in a beautiful black French limousine, shining like patent leather. Where in the world had he got a car in this gasless, carless, tumultuous pandemonium of Paris?

Le Bourget was like a painting by Salvador Dali. The Germans, in a last insane frenzy, had blown it to pieces, dynamited its runways, dragged vast loads of concrete wreckage on to the open space of it, and with unbelievable spite had smashed and mutilated all the beautiful buildings of the airport.

But even in delirium, the Parisians had somehow bulldozed a few paths amid the ruins. And on those narrow mean paths, aircraft were landing, one a minute, two a minute: British, American, Canadian and French.

We all formed up in style behind Saul Rae, who was still wearing his rumpled civvies.

Air Marshal Arthur Tedder's plane landed.

Air Marshal Tedder had no transport into the city.

There was Saul Rae's patent-leather limousine waiting.

"Sir," said Saul, brokenly, "take my car."

He had a Corsican driving it.

"Get back fast," hissed Saul in the Corsican's ear.

One, two; one, two, every minute the planes floated into the ruins of Le Bourget, transports, bombers, fighters. One, two; one, two a minute, waddled out and roared away.

It would be 4 p.m. The bright sun of Paris was shining.

"Look!" yelled Saul Rae.

The plane approaching was a medium bomber. But on either side of it, keeping pace with it, curvetting, zooming, split-essing, caracoling like outriders to a royal procession, were two Spitfires, little, shiny, sparkling Spits.

"What do you say?" cried Saul Rae, facing us.

It was Vanier. And from the gunport on the starboard side of the bomber somebody had stuck out a small flag.

Red, the Jack in the corner, and the coat of arms! The medium bomber trundled up. The Spits landed back of it.

Gen. Vanier came down the steep ladder, meant for boys of nineteen, twenty, his wooden leg first. Mrs. Vanier came down next.

Next came Vice-Admiral Percy Nelles, of the Royal Canadian Navy.

"Percy," said Gen. Vanier, "should not be here. But when we were leaving London a few minutes ago, we said, 'Percy, why not come along with us? You can return on the plane.' So he came."

Mrs. Vanier, whom last we had seen four years before, in the Port of Plymouth, where she and her four children had been landed off an Argentine frozen-beef ship, having escaped from Bordeaux the day France fell, leaned down to the rubble of the ground of Le Bourget and picked up a handful of it and pressed it to her breast.

"I regret," said Saul Rae, "that the conveyance I had secured for Your Excellency was taken by Air Marshal Tedder."

A trim small French officer in blue-grey stepped in among us.

In French he addressed Gen. Vanier:

"I am Capt. Gudin des Pavillons of the Spahis. May I present M. Michel Fontaine of the Quai d'Orsay? We are to escort you to your apartment in the Ritz."

"Would not the General prefer to ride in my jeep?" I suggested.

"I think," said Vice-Admiral Nelles, "I'll just run into town and pay my respects to Thierry d'Argenlieu, the head of the new French navy."

"We'll have lots of room in our jeeps," we chorused.

At which moment, Saul Rae's Corsican came swooping back on to the cinders in the patent-leather limousine.

"Well, thank you, gentlemen," said General Vanier.

We escorted him and his lady and Vice-Admiral Nelles to the blue-grey car of Capt. Gudin des Pavillons of the Spahis, and the long black car of Saul Rae and his hawk-faced Corsican.

The General was still holding the little $1.49 Canadian ensign on its little stick. Oh, yes; I forgot. It was he who had stuck it out the starboard gunport of the bomber.

"I think," he said, rolling it up on its stick as he bowed awkwardly to get his Passchendaele leg into the small but formal blue-grey car of the captain of Spahis, "I think I'll have this framed."

Gregory Clark, War Stories *(Toronto: Ryerson Press, 1964), 134–38.*

SEPTEMBER 30, 1944:
Liberating a Gestapo Prison in Belgium

Brought up to be cynical about British atrocity stories from the First World War, Canadian troops and reporters were shocked when they came across evidence that the Nazis had committed far worse crimes than anything the Kaiser and his troops had been accused of by even the most creative British propaganda writer.

MATTHEW HALTON

Breendonk — I hate to tell atrocity stories, because I've been telling them for so long. Much the same story that I now tell, I told ten years ago about concentration camps in Germany. But there are still people who ask if the cruelties of the Gestapo can be as bad as they say, and I think the concentration camp should be, in part, described. In this camp, several thousand Belgian and other resistants have been imprisoned at different times during the German occupation. Hundreds of them were tortured and killed in this camp. Before being shot or hanged, each man or woman had to build his or her own coffin. The bodies were taken to Brussels for cremation. Before the victims were murdered, their clothes were taken from them, and these clothes, many of them soaked with blood, were carefully ticketed and put away on shelves in a depot. And you can still see them there if you can bear to go in.

Breendonk prison is an obscene place. But on the walls of the cells you can read an inspiring story of human greatness and courage. You can read the words that have been scratched on the walls by tortured and dying men. Things like this: "Long Live England; Speed the Victory."

There in that place of evil memory, you wonder for a moment if there is any hope for a world which can produce such monstrosity. And then you see those scrawling inscriptions on the walls. Carved there by men and women [some of the names are those of women] after tortures too hideous to describe. And you know then that while there are devils in some men, there are gods in others.… That is a bit of the story of Breendonk. Part of the story of what we are fighting. And what we are fighting is not Germany alone. There are mad dogs in every country. The chief torturer at Breendonk was not a German. He was a Belgian fascist. The Belgian Resistance told me that the Belgian fascists were just as fiendish as their German masters of the Gestapo. The German military commandant of this area protested against the Breendonk tortures. So the point is that while there are mad dogs in every country, in Germany the mad dogs are in control.

Matthew Halton, the Canadian Broadcasting Corporation, September 30, 1944. CBC Archives (available through www.cbc.ca).

OCTOBER 11, 1944:
Rescuing the Dogs of War in the Scheldt Estuary

By the time Canadian soldiers reached the Scheldt Estuary, which blocked the Allied shipping route to the vital port of Antwerp, Belgium, they were battle-toughened veterans. Still, no experience or training could prepare them for the tough fight to clear the Scheldt. Not only were they up against Germans who had no avenue of escape, they faced units of Soviet deserters who had joined the Nazis. For those men, there was no surrender. They faced death in the mud of the Scheldt or by Stalin's firing squads.

ALLEN KENT

With the Canadians at the Scheldt Estuary, Oct. 11 (Delayed) — A single company of Canadians, not many more than a hundred in number, and most of them Toronto boys, last night closed the trap on 15,000 Germans in the Dutch Islands at the mouth of the Scheldt, and by seizing the neck of land which joins Walcheren and South Beveland to the Holland mainland they sealed the doom of 7,000 more enemy soldiers south of the river mouth.

Capture of the narrow causeway was effected at last light yesterday by infantrymen of an Ontario unit led by Major T. F. Whitley, pre-war Toronto bank manager.

The daring exploit was the final chapter in a strange story of the unit's quite unscheduled advance toward the last supply and escape route for

22,000 Germans, an advance that involved all four companies in the unit and necessitated a hurried revision of official plans which did not call for such a success until days later.

It all began last Sunday afternoon, when the unit's dog company was sent out as a reconnaissance in force, with orders to explore the enemy strength in the region of the South Beveland neck and if possible to pick up prisoners.

Under the command of Major D. S. (Tim) Beatty of Toronto and Sault Ste. Marie, the dog company moved westward on a dyke road across inundated fields, and then swung north. They had gone two miles and had almost reached the base of the neck before they hit stiff opposition, and then they were nearly cut off by a sudden enemy counter attack.

More to protect the men of the dog company than anything else, the commanding officer ordered A Company under Major H.W. Caldwell, of 14 Walker Ave., Toronto, into action. Enemy bombardment of both groups was heavy, but by nightfall A Company reached a point just short of the dog company's position and on Monday morning Caldwell's men moved onward to take the offensive against the enemy.

But the artillery and mortar fire laid down as a preliminary to the attack put the Germans to flight.

They had pulled away completely and A Company took new positions closer to the Causeway. It was at this at this stage that an opportunity was seen for exploiting the surprising success which had come from the original recce party. The corps and division commanders held hasty conversations, plans were altered, and the unit was told to firm up its hold on the territory preparatory to a thrust aimed at the capture of the neck of land.

Yesterday afternoon Major G.J.S. Ryall, also of Toronto, led his C Company to a forward position and, with strong artillery and mortar support, they captured Woensdrecht, a town at the base of the South Beveland neck. The town was taken in a bayonet charge that netted 90 frightened prisoners.

Then, at seven o'clock last night, just before dark, the final assault was made. From the town, C Company was able to plaster the Causeway with good supporting fire, and Major Whitley led B Company to the attack. It did not take long. One hundred-odd Toronto and Ontario men sped forward on foot, determined to capture the only road and rail lines which connect the Dutch Islands with the mainland. It was not quite dark when they were successfully astride the communications lines and had completed the isolation of thousands of Germans. In the effort they took 100 more prisoners.

Ultimately it was the element of surprise that accounted for the victory.

The prisoners, most of them low category pioneer troops, who were supposed to be building fortifications to prevent just such a thrust, said the Germans had been taken completely by surprise. They said the fighting troops had all fled to the Island, handing them guns at the last minute and telling them to fight as best they could.

And actually the pioneers had fought hard before they gave up.

The significance of the achievement in the capture of the south Beveland Causeway can hardly be overestimated. It means that the thousands of Germans fighting desperately to hold their positions and prevent use of the port of Antwerp by the Allies are not only trapped but — far more important — cut off from all supplies and reinforcements.

The only alternative route for supplies or escape is the hazardous water crossing to other Dutch islands, and even this unlikely method is prevented by our Typhoons and Spitfires.

That the enemy realizes his predicament was evident today in the strength of his counter-attack against the Canadians, who have straddled the narrow isthmus, but they are now holding their positions with greater strength.

Allen Kent, "Canadians Rescue Dogs in the Scheldt," the Toronto Telegram, October 13, 1944.

OCTOBER 12, 1944:
"If Their Brains Matched Their Guts They'd Be Causing Us a Lot More Trouble"

Ralph Allen, like almost everyone on both sides of the fighting lines, knew it was just a matter of time until Hitler's regime collapsed. Like many soldiers, he could not understand why so many young men were willing to throw their lives away on a futile defence of Germany. At the same time, he, along with the Canadian troops fighting in northwest Europe, was enraged that the Germans seemed eager to take so many other people down with them. He tries in this piece to explain their tenacity to a Canadian audience.

RALPH ALLEN

Biervliet, Holland, Oct. 12. — Fully sold at last on the propaganda myth that took five years to become a reality, the non-Nazi, non-SS, "nonpolitical" male German today is willing to pay with his life and is paying to delay the last constrictions of his country's encirclement.

If this is the twilight of the Wehrmacht only its blood-red sunset is visible to the Allied soldier who fights the Wehrmacht in the front-line towns of Western Europe. Biervliet is the newest of these front-line towns: Its oldest battle scars are not 48 hours old, its newest as fresh as the quick warning spit of the last 15-centimetre German shell. The Canadian soldiers who captured it yesterday after a four-hour attack and held it through 12 more hours of German counterattacks, move through its battered little streets as warily as the frightened civilian inhabitants who have stuck it out so far in their cellars.

The nearest Germans are 500 yards from the outskirts. In these respects this new-won hinge of the Canadians' Scheldt Estuary bridgehead is no different from 100 other front-line towns on the route from Bernieres-sur-Mer to the German border. But Biervliet is different in one respect. They talk about different things here than they talked about in the other front-line towns. Here they talk almost exclusively about the enemy.

Not merely about his weapons and his tactics, but about his unpredictable battle-moods.

The mood in which the average and even the sub-average German soldier of today is fighting could never have been predicted by those who believed that the degree of savagery with which the individual German fights bears direct ratio to his indoctrination. Still less could it have been predicted by those optimists who have clung all along from the beginning to the venerable theory that the German is a bully and all you have to do to make him quit fighting is to rough him up a bit, and show him you are stronger.

The Germans who are opposing the Canadians in the Scheldt bridgehead are not especially well indoctrinated. And natural bullies or not, they are taking a beating and taking it with a sullen and Spartan fatalism which might have been borrowed straight from the young fanatics of the Hitler youth.

They don't fight especially well for they are not particularly well trained and their staff work on the lesser levels is confused and liable to primitive errors. But they fight bravely, and the important thing to remember is that, among the bravest are inferior physical specimens who two years ago would have been thrown into labor battalions classed as unfit for combat service.

Three months ago when his officers commanded this bottom of the barrel list of German soldiers to hold his position or die, the soldier answered, "How, lieutenant?" And then surrendered.

In three months Eisenhower has done what Goebbels couldn't do in five years. He has persuaded the male German that his country is really fighting for survival. Some of them will surrender, of course. But far more pitiful than the voluntary prisoners is the soldier of the 64th infantry division who was captured on patrol near Biervliet Thursday morning. The German private, while being marched back under an armed guard, made three attempts to escape. The guards humanely kept him captive. But when he reached battalion headquarters and was put under a new guard he tried to escape again, running headlong down an open street in full view of scores of armed fanatics.

This time he was killed — successful suicide at the fourth attempt.

"These aren't SS men," Major Bill Strickland of Toronto, who commanded the Ontario troops that took Biervlet, said today, "but we haven't seen anything like them since Caen; they just don't seem to care whether they live or not. They are dangerous.

"They've got more artillery than they've used against us in the entire campaign. Last night, for the first time since the second front started, I heard them lay down such a heavy concentration of medium and heavy shells that I thought for a minute it must be our own guns firing. Around Caen they had more mortars than they're using here, but here they have more guns."

A senior officer who was in direct command of the entire bridgehead operation in the early phases said later: "I have seen more dead Germans, in this little piece of Holland than I had seen anywhere else since we closed the Falaise gap. The Germans counter-attacked last night all along the little front. And when they weren't attacking they were prodding at us with strong fighting patrols.

"They took a bloody nose at Biervliet and over on the right below Hoodfplaat they worked into a regular little massacre. They're making us fight for every foot of ground but they're not very good with their counter-attacks. Their technique is bad.

"They're not very well co-ordinated. They bring all their artillery down and then after about 15 minutes' dead silence the infantry comes over, about 50 or 60 men at a time, standing up and charging right into our machine guns. Occasionally they overrun a section or a platoon, but mostly it's straight murder for them, and when they do attack through for an initial success they don't seem to be ready to exploit it.

"If their brains matched their guts they'd be causing us a lot more trouble — and they've been causing us plenty as it is."

The dike-honeycombed borders of the estuary are good defense country. "There's always another dike," said Capt. J. A. Ferguson of Galt, who commanded a company in the attack of Biervliet. "You scrambled over one after a hell of a fight and there, 50 yards ahead, is the next one slightly more thickly populated than the one you just left. And you can't just clean up a dike and leave it behind you.

"You put a strong guard on it or the Jerries will turn up in your rear again. Their strong suit is infiltration."

That the Germans are confused is apparent by the disjointed frenzy of their reaction. There is evidence that they have both sent reinforcements into the area of our bridgehead and even moved some of the troops who were there before the reinforcements arrived. So far most of their counter-attacks — which now run up into the dozens — suggest only the bewildered desperation of men who sense that they are being trapped and are trying to fight their way out.

"But even where the Germans are trying to get away," another officer said, "they're not fleeing solely from fear. They're trying to get away in the hope that they may fight us again somewhere else."

The figure that stands limned in the blood-red sunset of the

Wehrmacht is not a figure whose emotions need interest us except where they effect the progress of the war.

The thing that needs concern us is that disillusioned and embittered, confused and tired though he may be, he is still a very dangerous man and fighting him is still a hard and dangerous business.

Ralph Allen, "If Their Brains Matched Their Guts, They'd Be Causing Us a Lot More Trouble," the Globe and Mail, *October 12, 1944.*

OCTOBER 14, 1944:
His Body Was a Notebook for Nazi Cruelty Story

Paul de Martigny, born in Quebec in 1872, was a member of the Canadian Parliamentary Press Gallery, working for La Patrie, before taking a job as La Presse's European correspondent in 1936. From there, he reported on the rise of fascism and the fall of France. Despite the prognosis of his Nazi captors, he lived until 1951. Ross Harkness tracked him down a few weeks after the liberation of Paris.

ROSS HARKNESS

PARIS — Paul de Martigny is an old Canadian newspaper man trained in the Ottawa press gallery, so when he tells of the horrors of imprisonment in the famous Bosancon internment camp he does not speak from memory alone. He has the day-by-day notes of an experienced reporter to guide him.

Not that he needs notes. His hands and legs, so gnarled and twisted by rheumatism, as to keep him almost always indoors, remind him of the 106 interned Canadian nuns grubbing in foot-deep mire for stray lumps of coal and sticks and roots with which to build a small, feeble blaze against the coldest and dampest winter the Vosges district has known.

That constant gnawing in his stomach, like ever-present hunger, recalls the 45 women who died in one day from being fed poisoned food and the scores of other innocent people who died similar deaths in the year that he was locked up with them.

His wasted form and failing vision are constant reminders of the brutal Prussian camp commander who finally kicked him out with neither home to go to nor means of subsistence because, said the Prussian, "you are going to die and my men have enough graves to dig."

But he didn't die, and that was three years ago, said Mr. de Martigny. He and Mrs. de Martigny found shelter in the garret studio of Henri Beau, famed French-Canadian painter and longtime friend.

It was at Christmas, 1940 that the Germans took him. As resident European correspondent for the Montreal *La Presse* since 1936, he had a comfortable apartment and a wide circle of friends among officialdom.

"I was shaving," he recalls, "when the knock came. I had just called to my wife that the coffee was perking when a French gendarme who knew me well summoned me. I was wanted at once at the office of the mayor. I thought little of it because I had often been called upon as an interpreter.

"I was dressed only in an old pair of trousers and I hurriedly slipped on an old jacket. I never saw the rest of my clothes again, and that's all I had to wear in unheated barracks during that bitter winter."

Hardly was de Martigny out of sight down the street when another gendarme asked his wife to accompany him.

"Bosancon was a French army barracks built to accommodate 2,500 troops," de Martigny said. "After France fell, they locked up 30,000 prisoners of war there. On three days' notice the commander was ordered to move the 30,000 and clean up the place to receive 3,000 internees.

"He cleaned it up by shoveling the filth out the windows into the yard. He didn't scrub the floors or disinfect the place, he didn't even sweep the floors and we civilians were dumped into that foul den.

"The tortured prisoners of war had been kept under constant lock and key in quarters so crowded that they could scarcely have been able to lie down all at once and for a breath of air they had broken the windows. In all that bitterly cold winter the windows were never repaired and many of us died of pneumonia."

The food, he said, was not only insufficient and unpalatable, it was positively poisonous, and was seldom more than half-cooked. The whole camp was swept by dysentery and scarcely a day passed without deaths. In one day alone, 45 women died.

"We protested to the commander but he laughed at us. It was fit food for British swine, he told us."

This disregard for sanitation and cleanliness seems characteristic of the Germans. Apparently the master race relights in demonstrating its own superiority by forcing its victims to live in filth.

Among the internees was a cultured Englishwoman with her 18-year-old idiot son. The guards delighted in torturing the mother by playing pranks on the boy. She spent most of the time in tears, de Martigny recalled. "The more she wept, the more they teased. Nothing more demonstrated the bestiality of the Nazis. Their excuse for locking them up was that he was of military age and might escape to England to fight. But he was so helpless they had to lock his mother up with him."

Also with them was a mother and her crippled son, also imprisoned because he was of military age.

As the cold intensified the prisoners were driven to desperate means to keep warm. Anything that could burn was used, even partitions were torn down, but because of the broken windows it was impossible to heat the barracks.

Several times de Martigny was called before the commandant and asked whether he was French or Canadian. "I was told that if I said I was a Frenchman and not a British subject, I might be released," he said. "The commandant gave me long talks on the way the British ill-treated Canada and the way English-Canadians ill-treated French-Canadians.

"Finally I told him: 'Sir, I might have a French name and I may speak English with a French accent, but my family has been Canadian for four centuries and British for nearly two. De Martigny is one of the proudest and most famous names in French Canada and there has never been a traitor among us. My every heartbeat is British.'"

De Martigny was soon to be released anyway. Cold, bad food and hardship had undermined his health.

"The commander called me in one day and said he was letting me and Mrs. de Martigny go," he related. "He told me in the most callous manner imaginable that since I was sick and likely to die any day he felt safe in releasing me. He said the city of Paris could bury me and save his men the trouble.

"He said Der Fuehrer regarded a newspaperman as more dangerous than an entire battalion of soldiers because a newspaperman is trained to observe and is experienced in scheming to get his story out. He warned me that I must never speak English, must not write or receive letters, must never discuss the war with friends, must never be seen with any of the English-speaking people still at liberty, must be off the street by sunset and would be shot if found on the street in an air raid."

In spite of these warnings, however, de Martigny managed to smuggle his diary out of the camp. The de Martignys returned to Paris to find a German colonel living in their apartment and all their possessions commandeered. Somehow Henri Beau learned of their straits and sent word that they would find a key to his studio, where they lived until the Allies freed Paris.

Ross Harkness, "His Body Was a Notebook for Nazi Cruelty Story," the Toronto Star, October 14, 1944.

OCTOBER 23, 1944:
"Tried to Murder Me, Then Took Me for His Mother"

As Canadians cleared the Scheldt Estuary and fought their way into Holland, the coverage, like the fighting, became gruesome. Most of the Canadian correspondents filed stories of heroes and tough guys working the front lines. These showed Canadians' anger and frustration at being sent to fight in the desolate, dangerous dike country, and their grim determination to get the job done.

ROSS HARKNESS

Beyond the Leopold Canal, Holland — During the 10 terrible days and nights that the Canadians held and enlarged the Leopold Canal bridgehead, the village of Blezen was obliterated house by house and almost brick by brick. It was there that Lieut. (now Capt.) Dick McGlove of Winnipeg, a six-foot-two Paladin who once, when in water up to his chin, took two bullet holes in his tin hat without injury, and without going under, dreamed up an odd and practical device for knocking down houses that the Germans had turned into miniature fortresses.

Boys look on as Canadian soldiers fix a tank track in Holland, spring of 1945.

This was to wire in or tie with a string a number of incendiary and blast grenades into the vanes of a Piat mortar bomb and then shoot the whole contraption at a house held by the enemy. This deadly missile would drop on such a house with the effect of a sack of explosive onions, blowing out the walls and then setting the place on fire. By way of retort, the Germans sent over kerosene bombs so that the village battle went on in a succession of blazing ruins.

An outstanding job was done by Sergt. "Buck" Ryan, a trapper and dog sled driver from around Flin Flon. His specialty was to land mortar bombs on a house not 30 yards away, first by low-angle shooting, then by firing them straight up in the air which almost brought them back down on Buck's own head.

It was on this same tough Buck Ryan that a young German prisoner picked up when he came running in with his hands up. This lad of not more than 16 came in like a crying child. He threw his arms around Ryan sobbing "I want my mother."

Buck hasn't been so astonished since the war began. "I'm not your mother, you son of nothing," he said as he knocked the German off his shoulder. "Why, two minutes ago," he said indignantly, "this sob sister was trying to murder me with a gun. The nerve of the bloke — taking me for his mother!"

Ross Harkness, "Nazi Took Me For His Mother," the Toronto Star, *October 23, 1944.*

OCTOBER 30, 1944:
Opening the Sea Road to Antwerp

Antwerp was vital to the Allies. It was one of the few North Sea ports in Allied hands. If the water approaches to Antwerp were open to shipping, the port could have been used to supply the British Army's thrust into Holland and northern Germany. The Wehrmacht, using German conscripts and former Soviet prisoners enticed or forced into the German army, fought hard against Canadian troops to keep the Scheldt Estuary closed. The arrival of Minesweeper 78 was proof that the Canadian blood spilled along the Scheldt had, in fact, opened the river.

RALPH ALLEN

Antwerp, Nov. 30. — The plump vessel's only shield against complete anonymity is the letter 78 splashed across her bows, and even if she had a name it would never crowd the Santa Maria, the Golden Hind or the Victory out of the textbooks. But for one grey and gentle anxious day His Majesty's Minesweeper No. 78 was the most important ship in the world. Seventy-Eight was the first Allied ship to dock at Antwerp.

Her skipper, a Dover man, Lieut. John Crane, brought her into port.

Fortunately, even when she is poking her way through an uncharted minefield, with much of the navigation done by instinct; the ship isn't the best target in the world. The Germans' Walcheren guns dropped several big coastal shells uncomfortably close, but that was all.

Nothing hit H.M. Minesweeper 78 from the land and H.M. Minesweeper 78 hit nothing in the water.

Today Crane's round little ship and scores of others like it are still patrolling a bleak and dangerous beat that winds for 50 miles from the docks of Antwerp to the North Sea, and they are finding that the navy's half of the Battle of the Scheldt has much in common with the army's. The job is cold and monotonous, with sudden perils. Progress is seldom spectacular. The job has had its delicate aspects

When Lieut. Crane came in, closely followed by other ships of the flotilla, navigation charts were all but obsolete. Two or three pre-war Belgian pilots who had taken refuge in England in 1940 went along, but they found the tricky river bed, which the Germans had neglected to dredge, had shifted almost beyond recognition.

"We just kept our fingers crossed," said one of the skippers. "The guns bothered us quite a bit, but they didn't hit anything. We just crawled along, taking it very easy, and here we are."

The story of the navy's share in the Battle of the Scheldt would sound a lot more exciting if it were possible to go more deeply into details. There have been casualties, and, undoubtedly, there will be more before the strategic harbor can be put to its maximum use.

"Minesweeping is just like fishing," the skipper told me. Sometimes you wait a long time, but if your patience and your health hold out you always get something. With a wryly dramatic smile, the lieutenant-commander pointed to the floor of the wardroom as his frail wooden craft bobbed on the harbor swell. "According to information which I have no reason to question, we are sitting on top of a German mine right now,'" he said. "Have a drink."

Ralph Allen, "Opening the Sea Road to Antwerp," the Globe and Mail, *October 30, 1944.*

NOVEMBER 1, 1944:
Did British Complacency Cause the Bloody Battle of the Scheldt?

Allen is very kind to General Montgomery in this piece, which he wrote the day after Minesweeper 78 opened the sea route to the vital port of Antwerp. Rather than see the Arnhem offensive as a failure that drew British strength away from the coastal ports at a time when the Allies desperately needed them for supply transport, Allen tells his readers that Operation Market Garden was an important and successful strategic move. In reality, Montgomery and his supporters should have cleared the way to Antwerp before taking on the risky and futile lunge for Arnhem. How important was the port? Important enough to be, after London, the city that took the second-largest number of hits by the Nazi's V2 ballistic missiles. In the end, the Canadians paid a high price for Montgomery's stalling. The Germans and their Soviet POW fighting units fortified their strong-points between Antwerp and the sea, flooded the low land around them, and fought ferociously against the Canadian soldiers who were sent into the Scheldt Estuary to clear them out.

RALPH ALLEN

Antwerp, Oct. 31 — As the long and complicated battle for Antwerp neared its close today it left behind a trail of glory for the men who fought it and pointed ahead to a trail of headaches for the historian who will someday allot its place in the textbooks.

This highly important battle will also become a highly controversial battle — perhaps the most controversial battle — of the Second World War. As they argued over Passchendaele and Haig's Somme offensives, military experts will still be arguing over Antwerp 20 years after its soggy battlefields have heard their last shot.

The battle for Antwerp will be a second-guesser's delight.

There can never be any doubt that for the soldiers who carried out the operation and for the local commanders who directed its intricate details the battle has been a triumph of ingenuity and courage.

But when the time and opportunity come to examine the battle's more astral planes, to fit into perspective against grand strategy, the arguments will begin. The basic facts about the Battle of Antwerp bristle with invitations to debate.

The two basic facts are these:

1. On Sept. 4 the spearhead of Gen. Dempsey's 2nd British Army, completing its epic dash from the Seine, took the great port intact before its stunned garrison or the beaten rabble fleeing through them could muster anything approaching formal resistance. This swift and almost bloodless capture, in an undamaged condition, of a harbor that in peacetime handled 40 million tons of shipping a year, constituted the greatest windfall of the second front. With the racing Allied armies already severely strained by supply lines almost half a continent long, it came at a heaven-sent time.

2. Today, on Oct. 31, the great harbor has still to unload its first ship. It has yet to supply a single shell or a gallon of petrol to any of the six Allied armies whose whole tempo of movement has been interrupted by the problems of supply.

Allowing a few more days for the mopping up of Walcheren Island and the south bank of the Scheldt and a reasonable period for the sweeping of the port's heavily mined approaches, it seems likely that the final time lag between Antwerp's fall and its serviceability to the Allied war effort will be something like two or three months.

The real food for controversy lies not in the fact that it has taken so long to free Antwerp for shipping, but in the fact that, under a different strategic program, the job might have been done more quickly.

Until its latter phases the battle for Antwerp held a low priority in the Allied general strategy. The fall of the city happened to coincide roughly with two other events of the highest strategic importance, the 2nd Army drive for the Rhine supported by the combined parachute army through Nijmegen and Arnhem and the American thrust into the Siegfried Line near Aachen.

With the fall of Antwerp the Allied High Command found itself approximately in the position of an entrepreneur who has planned a two-ring circus and is suddenly confronted with an arena in which there are not two rings but three.

To mount a full-scale offensive on the sea approaches to Antwerp would have meant diverting supplies and possibly manpower from

Nijmegen or Aachen. The decision could not have been easy for it involved not only mathematics but philosophy.

The optimist's choice was to concentrate on the Arnhem and Aachen thrusts in the hope that the enemy, already confused and off balance, could be struck decisive blows at either or both of these decisive points in his trembling defenses.

The pessimist's choice would have been to strive for a quick clean-up at Antwerp, in the expectation that before we could hope for final victory in the Battle of Germany we would first have to gain final victory in the battle of supply.

The choice that was ultimately taken was the optimist's choice.

Whether it was the best choice it is much too early even to guess.

The Aachen and Nijmegen thrusts did not produce decisive results in themselves, but they have given us a bridgehead over the Lower Rhine and a breach in the Siegfried Line.

It was the appreciation of two months ago that set the pace for the battle of Antwerp. For the first month it was scarcely a battle at all, but a series of company, battalion, and, occasionally, brigade actions that erupted over a front that sprawled from Zeebrugge to the outskirts of Antwerp itself. A month after we took Antwerp German soldiers were still sitting a few hundred yards away in Merem and the attenuated Canadian forces holding the city could take no more aggressive action to dislodge them than to send out an occasional fighting patrol.

Stretched along the Channel coast from Le Havre to the Leopold Canal, short of ammunition, the 1st Canadian Army was in no position to mount a real offensive on the Scheldt.

The historians will doubtless ask along with the larger questions, whether it was wise while doing virtually nothing to free a major port that had been captured undamaged to expend a large-scale effort on a series of smaller ports whose docks were known to be all but destroyed. It is these and other highly debatable points still beyond the scope of public discussion that guaranteed the Battle of Antwerp's place as one of the most controversial battles of this war.

Ralph Allen, "Did British Complacency Cause the Battle of the Scheldt?" the Globe *and* Mail, *November 1, 1944.*

DECEMBER 4, 1944:
The Heroism of The Argylls

This piece is typical of Ross Munro's war correspondence. It's tailored to a hometown audience, this time of the Hamilton-based Argyll and Sutherland Highlanders. Munro names many of the soldiers and recounts acts of individual heroism. Munro does little to explain the regiment's actions in the context of Canadian and Allied strategy, but he works hard to instill pride in the Argyll and Sutherlands. Soldiers, editors, and readers loved this kind of reporting, and Munro would tailor his stories and rework them so he could send hometown hero pieces to newspapers across Canada. All of them were thick with the names and hometowns of soldiers and officers. For an agency like CP, which needed cash infusions from its member papers to cover the cost of sending reporters into the war zones, Munro's prolific, specially crafted reports were vital to keeping publishers' wallets open.

Ross Munro

With the First Canadian Army, Dec. 4, (CP) — The Argyll and Sutherland Highlanders from Hamilton have had some amazing achievements in the western European campaign.

There was a three-day period at St .Lambert sur Dives in the Trun gap when two depleted companies of Argylls, totaling only 70 men operating with tanks of the South Alberta Regiment, captured 3,000 Germans.

Maj. Ivan Martin of Toronto led one of the companies and he was killed there. Maj. Gordon Winfield led the other and was wounded.

The Germans tried to break through St. Lambert many times and the Canadians mowed them down. That town was the graveyard of the Seventh Army. There was no slaughter in all the Trun gap like there was at St. Lambert.

After Trun, the Argylls drove to the Seine and then to the Somme, which they crossed near Abbeville, pushing on to St. Omer and Bruges in Belgium. Then they fought on the canal at Moerbrugge southeast of Bruges. Maj. Robert Mackenzie of Sarnia took his company across the canal first, ferrying them over in relays in a single rowboat.

The rest of the battalion also crossed in rowboats and when they started to clear the town, they found strong forces of the German 4th Division were holding it.

It was this division which later fought for a month in the Scheldt pocket until it was wiped out.

No bridge could be erected and the Argylls were practically cut off from supplies. The shelling went on for 36 hours and Capt. William Findlay of Red Deer, Alta., the artillery representative who had been with the Argylls most of the time, said it was the heaviest he had seen.

The Germans counter-attacked at least four times in one day. Finally the Royal Canadian Engineers got a bridge over the canal and the South Alberta Regiment rumbled into Moerbrugge with its tanks.

The two infantry units and the tanks then drove the enemy out of the town and back to the Leopold Canal.

Later, after Eschen was captured, the Argylls were ordered to cross the canal north of Bergen. Maj. Gordon Armstrong of Barrie personally carried out a night reconnaissance, swimming the icy waters of the canal to find out what the area on the other side was like.

Then he and Capt. Pete McCordic of Toronto led their companies over the canal and a firm bridgehead was established.

Ross Munro, The Canadian Press, December 4, 1941.

FEBRUARY 1945:
Keeping the Secret of the Transfer of the First Division from Italy to Northwest Europe

Canadian journalists kept the biggest secret of the Canadian forces in Europe: the pullout of the 1st Canadian Corps from their tough slog up the Italian mainland and their redeployment in northwest Europe. Not only did reporters stay quiet, some continued to file fake stories datelined from the Italian front. Radio correspondents continued to broadcast from Italy to keep up the volume of "chatter" needed to convince the Germans nothing had changed. Weeks after the Canadian force arrived safely and was deployed, correspondents were free to report on the big switch.

WILLIAM BOSS

With the 1st Canadian Army in Northwest Europe, April 23 — The 1st Canadian Corps, veterans of Sicily and Italy, and the 2nd Canadian Corps, veterans of fighting in France, Belgium and Holland, have been reunited under the command of Gen. H. D. G. Crerar, within his 1st Canadian Army. Announcement that the two corps — five divisions and two armoured brigades — were finally fighting in the same operational theatre was doubly historic.

For one thing, the enemy knew nothing of the move. And for another, this was believed to be the first time that a corps, complete with everything required to keep a formation in the field, had been taken out of the front line in one theatre and transferred intact to another front 1,000 miles away, ready for action.

The same guns which smashed the German's Lamone river line in Italy last December now are in action in northwest Europe, fired by the same crews. The same tanks which cleared the enemy from Valle Di Commacchio now are pursuing the beaten foe in northwest Europe.

Where British units had become an integral part of the 1st Infantry Division and the 5th Armoured Division, or where British officers were key members of a headquarters team, they, too, were transferred to the new theatre. The troops didn't know when they were pulled from the line last February they were heading for a link-up with the 2nd Corps. Only officers kept in the picture were selected personnel in various headquarters.

These privileged few were highly elated. They saw in it something the troops had been harping about for a long time.

They didn't feel the fighting on the northwestern front would be any harder or any easier. But they figured their fighting would receive more recognition in the new locale. In Italy they felt they were forgotten children and their deeds, as dangerous and bloody as those elsewhere, were not as highly regarded because they were not engaged in a principal theatre.

Decision to make the transfer was taken at Malta last February 4. During the joint conference there of chiefs of staff which preceded the "big three" meeting at Yalta, withdrawal of certain troops and their employment in a more decisive theatre was agreed upon.

Lt.-Gen. Charles Foulkes, of London, Ont., received the news at Field Marshal Alexander's headquarters. Gen. Foulkes dispatched senior officers to inform Gen. Crerar and by February 11 the move was under way.

While the 1st Division continued to hold a sector of the Senio River front, the 5th Armoured Division "got mobile." The 1st Canadian Armoured Brigade was stopped in its tracks on an overland haul from the Bologna sector to the concentration area of a British corps . The brigade was turned around, brought closer to the Canadian area and held until time to move toward a west coast port.

The 1st Division held their line on the Senio until the rear areas had been reasonably cleared. Then they quietly disengaged and were relieved without the enemy knowing what was brewing.

By that time the remainder of the corps was on the west coast, waiting to be ferried to Marseilles, whence they journeyed overland to join the 2nd Corps.

The Germans were kept entirely in the dark about the move by the security-conscious Canadians. Shoulder flashes, Canada patches, cap badges and other insignia all came down. Vehicle tactical signs and divisional markings were painted out. The magnitude of the operation called for the utmost secrecy.

The men were not fully informed but knew something big was on and shut up tightly.

Withdrawal from the line into concentration areas was explained as the revival of an earlier plan to rest the battle-worn Canadians.

Such a plan had been talked about. It was an open secret that advance parties had arranged for billets and recreational accommodations in a certain area and then had been recalled. That it should be reinstated aroused no conjecture.

The move towards ports was another matter. This, the troops were informed, was explained by the fact that they were going into areas in reserve of the 15th Army Group. This was technically true, but once the soldiers marched aboard ships they were told the whole story.

Civilian chatter was more feared in Italy than in France as a security break. Aside from the greater political differences, Italians are generally a curious and gossipy folk, capable of "spilling the beans" with the best will in the world.

William Boss, The Canadian Press, April 23, 1945.

MARCH 17, 1945:
The Luftwaffe Sinks "Hoodoo" Ship Carrying Refugees

The Second World War created millions of refugees from all sides of the fighting lines. Fred Backhouse reported the killing of two Canadian sailors who lost their lives while ferrying refugees from Antwerp to England.

FREDERICK BACKHOUSE

London, March 17 — The Belgian liner *Ville de Bruges* was a "hoodoo" vessel from the time she left New York until she became a battered burning wreck at the mouth of the River Scheldt near Antwerp, Canadian survivors of the bombed ship said tonight.

The 13,689-ton ship, formerly the United States liner *President Harding*, was bombed by a German plane after leaving Antwerp with fifty families of refugees from war-engulfed Belgium. The survivors told of the deaths of two Canadian and two Belgian seamen during the bombing.

The Canadians killed were identified as David Donn, about 53, of Peter Street, Hamilton, and Daniel Duffy, formerly of Montreal.

While company officials were silent at the request of authorities, crewmen who asked to remain anonymous asserted that misfortunes started a day out of New York, from where the ship sailed after being sold to a Belgian company, when an unnamed seaman died.

Then, as the *Ville de Bruges* neared Europe, her engines broke down for several days and she had to be towed into Falmouth, England. Subsequently Duffy, who later died in an Antwerp hospital, was stricken with a mysterious illness. Then came the bombing.

One old salt said: "I guess changing her name placed a curse on her."

About fifty of the sixty-three Canadian survivors, who reached London by train with hundreds of other refugees today, were dressed in an amazing assortment of clothes.

They had lost all their possessions.

Husky seamen were dressed in rainbow-colored jumpers, blue denim overalls, ill-fitting peasant clothes supplied by the kindly people of Antwerp and one even wore a swanky green silk blouse.

The adventure was only half over for the seamen when they got ashore from the bombed ship. They made their way to Ostend by truck and rail.

"We had been at Ostend what seemed only a couple of minutes when German bombers swooped over the city," said one crewman. "We all ducked for shelter but far as I learned no bombs were dropped."

Donn was the first assistant engineer. It was believed he was overcome by fumes after the bomb explosions. Duffy died in hospital twenty-four hours after the ship was attacked.

Harold Relland, ship's carpenter, of Toronto, said: "Just before the bomb hit us the pantryman was about to go into the galley to get butter for breakfast. Luckily he didn't get there, because the bomb fell right in the galley and exploded."

Alex Robinson, 23, radio operator of London, Ont., also paid tribute to the behavior of the passengers.

The vessel left New York in March on her first trip under the Belgian flag and was in Antwerp about eight days.

All refugees told of ruthless attacks either in the Low Countries or on the rescue ships that brought them to Britain. British women with babies held close in their arms and Irish priests were among them.

One man reported that parachutists who came down in Belgium included women. They used transparent cellophane parachutes and were dressed in sky-blue overalls, so that they were almost invisible in the air. They burned their parachutes as soon as they landed.

Belgian vigilance against the invaders was indicated by an Irish priest, member of a party of five from St. Anthony's College in Tournei, Belgium. On arriving at a Belgian channel port, the priest said, he was shadowed on suspicion of being a disguised parachutist. As he walked to church he saw signals pass between a French officer and someone on the street. Footsteps sounded behind him, keeping pace with his own. He knew he was being trailed.

He entered the cathedral. As he knelt in prayer the caretaker came up and murmured that police wished to speak to him. He was able to prove his identity and they retired.

Telling how German planes repeatedly attacked the fleeing groups, the priest said mothers had crouched over their sleeping children to act as living shields. Other women told how one person had been arrested as a spy when he was caught waving a flashlight to direct the raiders.

Two Catholic Sisters, members of the Ursuline Order, reported that 170 nuns were evacuated from their convents in Belgium. Sick women were among them. Hundreds of laymen who had taken refuge there also fled.

"As Britons," said one of the nuns, "we are proud of the wonderful work the navy has done to rescue refugees, and we express our gratitude to them."

Survivors of the *Ville de Bruges* were picked up and brought to Britain with Dutch and Belgian refugees. The ship is now lying, a gutted wreck, on the bank of the River Scheldt twelve miles below Antwerp. She was bombed by a German plane Tuesday morning shortly after leaving Antwerp with many families, mostly British, aboard. All sixty-four passengers were landed safely after the bombing.

James Gibson of Montreal, boatswain of the ship, described the experience as follows:

"We left Antwerp at 4 a.m. Shortly after 6 a.m. a Nazi plane flew overhead and when about 200 yards away let go with machine guns. Fortunately all passengers were below deck and no one was hurt.

"About an hour later three bombers appeared and one swooped down to a height of about 150 feet and let go a bomb. It hit us aft, went through and exploded in the side of the ship, blowing it out.

"Three of the crew below were killed and a fourth died later in hospital from shock. The steel bulkhead by the ship's hospital protected the passengers' quarters and they were unhurt.

"The passengers, all women except five, behaved extraordinarily well and after the first shock calmed down and mustered for roll call on deck."

Gibson said smoke swept down the ship as they beached her to land the passengers. "While we were getting them ashore," he continued, "we were afraid the Nazi planes would come over and machine-gun us again but luckily a French air patrol came along and kept watch."

The crew lost all its belongings in the vessel, which was still burning ten hours after the attack.

Frederick Backhouse, The Canadian Press, March 17, 1945.

MARCH 13, 1945:
A Hero Goes Down Fighting

This is one of the dozens of short stories of local heroes that Munro filed to papers across the country as the Canadian army moved through France, Belgium, and the Netherlands. Hopefully, as Ralph Allen argued at the beginning of 1945, these stories gave families and friends of dead soldiers some reason to believe their lost one had died with glory and had made the enemy pay dearly. These kind of heroic pieces were popular with the public and with soldiers, and were relatively easy to research and write. Through the war, Canadian correspondents had a tenuous grasp of the big picture, but they compensated by writing glowing tales of the front-line fighting man. This would be no war of trenches and grinding attrition. Reporters looked for men of action who helped push the line fighting forward to Germany.

Ross Munro

With 1st Canadian Army in Germany, March 13 — Sergeant Aubrey Cosens of the Queen's Own Rifles of Canada, a Toronto unit, was killed on the grim battlefield at Keppeln, 1½ miles north of Uedem, in front of the Hochwald line. The story of his heroism is one of the finest in the numerous infantry exploits in that struggle, as savage as anything the Canadians have known on the western front.

The sergeant came from Latchford, Ont., and had also worked in Timmins, Ont. before joining the army. He was made a sergeant with the Queen's Own and before dawn of February 26 he moved forward over flat farmland with a platoon of D Company, which was the battalion spearhead, to capture ground east of German-held Keppeln.

Six tanks of the 1st Hussars, of London, Ont., were operating with the infantry. The platoon reached its first objective through withering machine-gun fire but casualties were suffered. The platoon officer was severely wounded and Cosens took over immediately, re-organizing the men in a covering fire group.

He knew the position had to be held at all costs and that the Germans in three houses nearby must be driven out. So he ran 25 yards across the flat ground under intense fire and climbed on top of a 1st Hussars tank. Sitting at the front of the turret he directed the tanks' fire against the enemy positions he had spotted.

The Germans, who were tough paratroopers, formed up for a counter-attack but the gallant sergeant was still riding. The Sherman tank, its guns blazing, was directed into the middle of the Germans. Those who survived fled.

Then Cosens, perched on the tank, took on three two-storey houses. He ordered the tank commander to ram the first house, which drove the enemy into the open, where they were shot up. He leaped from the turret and ordered the tank to follow him to the next house where the Sherman again smashed down the wall and the sergeant plunged into the building to kill six paratroopers there. The third and last building also was rammed by the tank and Cosens raced into the wreckage alone to clear that house.

Four of his men then came up to hold the ground won and the heroic Cosens began to move back to report to the company commander. He had not gone 50 yards when a sniper hit him in the head. He died a few minutes later on the smoking, roaring battlefield of Keppeln.

He had himself killed at least 20 Germans and taken as many prisoners. His name is listed among the great of the Queen's Own Rifles, which has produced many heroes since it landed in Normandy on D-Day last June.

Ross Munro, The Canadian Press, March 13, 1945.

APRIL 18, 1945:
"Liberated Reporter Hates Nazis, Turnips and Ersatz Coffee"

William Kinmond, a thirty-year-old *Toronto Star* reporter, was the only Canadian war correspondent captured by the Germans during the Second World War. He was captured on September 8, 1944, while heading toward Antwerp in a Jeep. Early reports suggested Kinmond was killed in action. Because Kinmond and the rest of the Canadian accredited war correspondents were given the honorary rank of captain in the Canadian army, Kinmond was held in a camp for officers. Kinmond later joined the *Globe and Mail*, where he became the paper's China correspondent in the mid-1950s. He won a National Newspaper Award for feature writing in 1957.

THE *TORONTO STAR*

London — William Kinmond of the Toronto Star, the only Canadian correspondent taken prisoner by the Germans in this war, arrived in England yesterday 25 pounds lighter than when captured seven months ago, and with intense hatred of ersatz coffee, turnips, black bread and Germans.

Captured Sept. 8 while en route to Antwerp, which he had been told incorrectly was liberated, the 30-year-old correspondent was confined to Oflag 79 with British, Canadian and U.S. officers. They were freed from the camp, just outside Brunswick, last Thursday by the U.S. 9th Army.

Also released were John Talbot of Reuters who was captured in a German paratrooper's raid on Marshal Tito's headquarters in Yugoslavia and John Smyth of Reuters, captured at Arnhem.

Brunswick, when last seen by Kinmond Saturday, had no house or building standing. He said the destruction caused by Allied planes and artillery was "simply unbelievable."

Kinmond said his treatment at the Oflag (officers' camp) was better than at stalags where non-commissioned officers and men were housed. Food was poor, but none of the prisoners was ever mistreated.

The high point in his seven months in the camp was the day of the Arnhem airborne operation. Terrific excitement swept the camp as Allied planes and gliders roared over it and officers optimistically ran a pool on the date of their anticipated liberation.

Toronto Star reporter William Kinmond recuperates after being liberated from a German POW camp. He spent seven months in captivity after he was picked up by a German artillery unit near Antwerp.

Later, when the Germans sent a special propaganda agent to the camp to tell the prisoners that the Arnhem operation had ended in disaster, the prisoners at first didn't believe him. When they learned it was true, there was a corresponding depression.

Kinmond, like other recently liberated prisoners, told how older and older men were assigned to guard duty as the Germans scraped the bottom of the manpower barrel. In recent months, he said, the guards had become increasingly apathetic but as far as he knew none had attempted to fraternize with the prisoners.

Kinmond was captured within a few days of his arrival on the front. After witnessing the liberation of Brussels, he went to Ghent and then headed to Antwerp.

At a wayside café where he rested, the proprietor insisted on serenading him with "Yankee Doodle Dandy." Kinmond's jeep ran right into a German self-propelled gun a few hundred yards up the road from the café.

"I don't know whether to laugh or cry," said Mrs. Kinmond, a member of the *Star*'s classified advertising staff, when the first word came on Saturday that her husband had been freed. "I was terribly worried," she added, "because I heard that the area where he had been interned had taken some terrible punishment."

Last September Kinmond had dashed by plane and train across France to report the liberation of Belgium. After he was captured, 42 days elapsed before his fate was made known.

A member of the *Star* staff since 1934, Kinmond had many adventurous newspaper assignments. He hunted polar bears in the Arctic and reported the trial on Belcher Island of eight Eskimos charged with killing eight of their compatriots in a religious frenzy. He was sworn in as a juror.

He enlisted in the R.C.A.F. on May 29, 1943, and in June, 1944, was honorably discharged. Rejoining the *Star* staff, he went overseas the following month. His parents, Mr. and Mrs. Joseph Kinmond, live in Uxbridge with his sister, Carol Ann.

"Liberated Star Reporter Hates Nazis, Turnips and Ersatz Coffee," the Toronto Star, *April 18, 1945.*

MAY 2, 1945:
Canadians and Germans Work Together to Save the Starving Dutch

After the collapse of Operation Market Garden in September 1944, the

German military and civil administration in Holland turned on the Dutch people. Railway workers who had gone on strike during the failed British lunge for Arnhem were brutally punished and food rations for the entire country were cut to starvation levels. As the Germans fell back to the populated areas along the Dutch coast, they opened the dikes, flooding farmland and destroying the country's transport system. By late winter 1945, the people were reduced to eating garbage, tulip bulbs, weeds, and wild animals. The occupiers, cut off from Germany, looted farms of livestock and seed grains.

In April 1945, it was obvious to even the most die-hard Nazi, including Arthur Seyss-Inquart, the Nazi Reichskommisar of the

A member of the Army Film and Photo Unit records an interview between Canadian war correspondents and a German soldier deployed to guard food donated by Canada to feed the starving Dutch. Holland, April 1945.

Netherlands, that the war was over. Seyss-Inquart knew that his personal survival was bound up with Hitler's, as Seyss-Inquart had betrayed his home country of Austria by engineering the Nazi putsch and had brutally governed Bohemia. Still, in April, one of the most dramatic scenes of the war took place in Amersfoort when German and Allied officials met to discuss ways of working together to get food to the starving Dutch civilians. The Allies were determined to rescue the Dutch, while the Germans, still bound by their loyalty oath to Hitler, were violating the Fuhrer's orders against negotiating with the enemy. Senior Canadian, American, and German officers gathered in the Amersfoort town school, broke into groups, and planned out the movement of food by land, water, and air. But the atmosphere was

German soldiers guard cases of Swift's Premium Stewed Steak destined for starving Dutch civilians during a truce in Holland, April 1945.

not always pleasant. At least twice, officers in the room quipped that Seyss-Inquart would end up in front of a firing squad. In fact, he was hanged October 16, 1946, after being found guilty at the Nuremberg War Crimes trial. The bizarre situation — a humanitarian food drive run by Canadians and German soldiers who were very much still at war — began while Hitler was still alive and continued for ten days, until the German forces in Holland surrendered on May 7.

WILLIAM BOSS

With the 1st Canadian Army, May 2 — High-ranking Germans from the enemy's Netherlands Command intimated during the course of negotiations with Canadian authorities on supplying food to the Dutch civilian population that the talks had wider possibilities, not excluding the possibility of surrender.

Maj.-Gen. Harry W. Foster of Winnipeg and Picton, Ont., commander of the 1st Canadian Division, who was one of the group conferring with the Germans April 28, said he could transmit the news to the proper authorities. A despatch from Ross Munro, another CP war correspondent, said a captured German officer asserted Wednesday that Admiral Karl Doenitz had ordered troops facing the Western Allies to cease fighting and to withdraw to the east to oppose the Russians. The report was attributed to a Canadian Army source. The despatch said there was no confirmation or further information.

Luxembourg radio said Wednesday night a German capitulation in Holland was imminent. The radio, which is Allied-controlled, said reports from the 1st Canadian Army front indicated armistice negotiations have been in progress more than 24 hours.

Reports reached Canadian Army Headquarters, through Dutch refugees and German deserters, of an uncontrolled civilian demonstration at Utrecht Monday. The German garrison was said to have watched Utrecht citizens shout and wave Netherlands flags without taking any disciplinary action. The demonstration was said to have been related to rumors the war had ended.

It may also have been connected with plans to deliver food to Dutch civilians, negotiations for which have been going on since April 25.

The negotiations began after Gen. Eisenhower, Allied Supreme Commander, said it was planned to drop food from airplanes over German occupied Holland, the population of which has been reported near starvation.

After messages had been exchanged for several days, a German delegation crossed the Grebbe Line to a rendezvous in no man's land, west of Wageningen. Gen. Foster listened to the German delegation, headed by the Judge Advocate-General of the Netherlands, which made suggestions regarding routes to shipment of food.

Another meeting was held April 29, at which Allied representatives included Lt. Gen. Charles Foulkes of London, Ont., commander of the

Canadian snipers pose in a foxhole in Holland in the spring of 1945.

1st Canadian corps, senior staff officers of the 21st Army Group, Allied Supreme Headquarters, and the Netherlands military government, and Prince Bernhard of the Netherlands.

A third meeting was held later, attended by Arthur Seyss-Inquart, Gauleiter [Nazi governor] for Holland, at which military matters related to the food movement were quickly settled.

The first convoys consisting of several hundred trucks, loaded with food, began to move at 7 a.m. today, from the Canadian lines across no man's land in front of the Grebbe Line. They were headed for an unloading depot.

William Boss, The Canadian Press, May 2, 1945.

MAY 4, 1945:
58 10-Ton Trucks Needed to Shift Gold Nazis Stole

In the last weeks of the war, *Toronto Star* reporter Ross Harkness was intrigued by the rumors of vast amounts of treasure being found by the Allies in mines, trains, and other hiding places throughout the former Third Reich. Nearly seven decades after the end of the war, art historians and investigators are still trying to track down and repatriate looted artifacts and artwork.

ROSS HARKNESS

PARIS — The value of German gold and treasure found in the mine at Meckers was vastly greater than the wildest guess of the most imaginative reporter. This was disclosed by Col. Bernard Bernstein, deputy chief of the financial branch at Allied headquarters. The treasure was so great it required 58 10-ton trucks to move it to a place of greater security and it took 22½ hours to load the gold and jewels alone, he said.

"It was like an Arabian Nights treasure cave with valises and chests bursting and overflowing with precious and semi-precious gems, rooms filled with gold ingots and rare objects of art and cotton bags stuffed with foreign currency and coins," he said.

The gold, originally estimated at 100 tons, was nearer 200, he said, while further search of the mine's galleries revealed the loot of the S.S., stolen from the ravaged countries of Europe, stuffed into 87 valises, some of them as big as trunks and some of them so full they couldn't be closed and some even burst at the seams.

"There was silver plate, silver and gold cigarette cases, watch cases, spectacle frames and wedding rings," he said. "There were gold and silver fillings wrenched from the teeth of the dead in concentration camps. There were sacks like 10 pound flour bags filled with precious and semi-precious jewels of every description. There were pearls, both loose and in necklaces. There were bank notes and coins of every country. There was everything conceivable of value that might be looted."

The S.S. treasure was being held by the Reichsbank under agreement between one of the big bank officials and heads of the S.S., which made the bank an accomplice of the S.S. in robberies. The bank had already melted down some of the gold, possibly rings and settings from which gems have been removed, and a number of nuggets of recently-melted gold were among the spoils.

Many of the gold bars had been recently cast. Evidently they were gold ingots stolen from occupied countries and melted down to remove identification marks. Most of it was hidden in the mine between mid-February and mid-March, about the time the Reichsbank decided to move to Weimar as the safest place in Germany. Ironically, Weimar was captured before Berlin.

Some records of the Reichsbank were found with the gold, and some minor officials, including a not-so-minor head of the precious metals branch, were rounded up. From them the Allies learned of scattered deposits of gold and notes all over central Germany. At Halle was found 63 bags of foreign currency, including many old, large-size U.S. dollar bills.

"These could only have been looted from private hoardings, for financial houses did not keep these bills," Col. Bernstein said.

At Cobourg gold was found buried in private gardens and under chicken coops. Silver bullion was found hidden in a forest. Other gold and currency was found at Erfurt, Naumberg and elsewhere. At Hof, ecclesiastical treasures were found, but whether they were from German churches or Poland has not been established. German churches often hid their treasures in national caches.

Ross Harkness, "58 10-ton Trucks Needed to Shift Gold Nazis Stole," Toronto Star, May 4, 1945.

MAY 7, 1945:
The German Army Surrenders in Holland

With Hitler dead, the Russians holding Berlin, and the unoccupied parts of Germany shrinking to a few isolated pockets, Hitler's designated successor, Karl Doenitz, authorized the surrender of German forces in their last holdouts in the West, including Holland. General Johannes Blaskowitz, the German commander, was placed in charge of maintaining order in territory occupied by the Germans. The Wehrmacht took the opportunity to collect and execute at least two German deserters who mistakenly came out of hiding, believing themselves to be safe. During the surrender negotiations, Blaskowitz tried to distance the German army from the Nazi S.S. This did not prevent the Allies from trying Blaskowitz as a war criminal, but the general killed himself by jumping from a balcony in 1948, on the day that his trial was scheduled to begin.

Ross Munro

The German surrender was received by Gen. Foulkes in the lobby of a battle-wrecked hotel at Wagningen, west of Arnhem, and the German commander of the 25th Army agreed to all surrender terms without dispute. Divisional headquarters of both occupying formations will be set up close to headquarters of the German Corps which occupied these districts. Headquarters of the 1st Canadian Division will move to Hilversum, close to Blaskowitz' headquarters.

For the time being, German forces will remain where they are and retain personal weapons such as rifles, pistols and machine-guns.

After the Canadian Corps moves in they will be moved to concentration areas and disarmed.

In the days after the Nazi surrender, German rifles were stacked like cordwood.

"In the Netherlands now there is only one authority and only one person to issue orders and that person is me," Gen. Foulkes declared. "No orders will be issued by German civilian authorities in Holland from now on."

When Gen. Foulkes inquired about SS forces in the German army, Blaskowitz said criminals in the S.S. already had been disarmed and put in prison and that 400 Germans had been put with the S.S. force to ensure there was no trouble. Blaskowitz said his men had been ordered to remove all demolitions from dikes prepared for destruction.

Accompanying Gen. Foulkes at he conference were Brig. George Hitching, of Montreal; Brig. P. Gilbridge, of London, Ont., and Major Darly Kingsmill, of Toronto. Capt. George Molnar, of Montreal, was interpreter.

Prince Bernhard of the Netherlands, also with Gen. Foulkes' party, wore on his battle dress the battle patches of the 1st Canadian Army.

While photographers recorded in the flood-lighted room, war correspondents watched.

Blaskowitz sat directly opposite Gen. Foulkes as his heavy-lidded eyes flitted balefully from the table to the Canadian commander as Gen. Foulkes slowly read the terms of the instrument of surrender.

Gen. Blaskowitz asked when the German forces would be moved out of Holland and Gen. Foulkes replied they would be moved as soon as possible into Germany by way of the Zuider Zee causeway.

Ross Munro, The Canadian Press, May 7, 1945.

MAY 7, 1945:
The Final Surrender at Reims

Ross Parry was a reporter for the *Maple Leaf*, the military newspaper edited by J.D. Macfarland, who later went on to a career as editor of the Toronto *Telegram* and editorial director of the Toronto *Sun*. Parry, like all but one journalist at Reims, observed the news blackout. He was scooped by Edward Kennedy of the Associated Press, who broke the embargo. The anger of this colleagues and military authorities destroyed Kennedy's career. Of the Germans in the room, Hans-Georg von Freideburg killed himself two weeks later, while Alfred Jodl was hanged on October 16, 1946, after being found guilty at Nuremburg of war crimes.

A scruffy group of German soldiers, many of them old men, are escorted to POW cages by a lone Canadian soldier on a motorcycle in the winter of 1945.

Ross D. Parry

Supreme Forward Headquarters, Reims, May 9 — It is hardly possible for me to express my feelings as I witnessed Germany's complete and final surrender.

It was like a stage drama. The characters seemed unreal. Yet it lacked the trimmings a theatre setting would have provided.

It was difficult to absorb at the moment the true significance of the events. I tried to think of the number of people it would affect, of the number of my comrades it would save from death and suddenly — like all things — it became personal and I thought how my mother would feel.

After a night of anxious waiting as surrender talks went on in a room above us, we were finally called to the war room of Supreme Headquarters, the same room that only last week Gen. Eisenhower and his commanders were directing the all-out and final fight against the Reich. I wound up sitting about 12 feet from the surrender table, around which in a few minutes Allied and German representatives would end the war.

Great lights flooded the room as cameramen prepared to record this greatest moment in recallable history. The light was dazzling as it reflected from the cellophane-covered battle maps of Europe that covered all the walls. Still there were the pins and cardboard signs and arrows which showed the present position of all belligerent air, sea and land forces. The white ceiling added to the brilliance of the room and the only relief was the heavy red carpet on the floor.

In the centre of a room about 20 by 40 feet, was a table, a plain, wooden affair with a cracked top. Around it were 14 chairs, 11 on the far side and at both ends for Allied representatives and three on the near side for the German surrender delegation. The table, which reminded me of an oversized Canadian dining room piece, was about 20 feet long and eight feet wide. It was bare except for a black, double-holder ink stand, a microphone for an official recording of the proceedings, a couple of "liberated" German china ash trays — which weren't used, because no one smoked — and at each place a pad and a yellow pencil.

After waiting 15 minutes, anticipation reached such a point it was almost impossible to think straight and I wondered if I could remember what I was about to witness.

At 2:34 Monday morning, while the people of Reims slept peacefully in their beds, Lieut.-Gen. Walter Bedell Smith, U.S. Army, allied chief of staff, entered the room, followed by the chiefs of staff of the British, U.S., French and Russian forces, empowered by their governments to accept unconditional surrender.

For a few minutes they seemed a bit mixed about who was to sit where, although there were place cards at each seat. When it was fairly straightened out — the minutes seemed like hours about this time — they talked quietly and cracked a couple of inaudible jokes which caused general laughter. It hardly needs to be said that they looked happy about the whole thing.

Gen. Smith, with folded arms, kept an eye on the door but turned occasionally to speak to Admiral Sir Harold Burroughs, Allied naval commander, on his right, and to look around the room at cameramen vying for vantage spots.

The Soviet representative, General Susloparov, chief of the Russian mission to France, was on Gen. Smith's left, and he stood quietly talking with a Russian interpreter, a junior officer, and once his face broadened into a wide smile, but if it was joke, it was all Russian to me.

Lieut.-Gen. Sir Francis Morgan, deputy chief of staff and the man who did the original planning for the invasion of Europe, was three places to the right of Gen. Smith, and, during the waiting period, talked with Adm. Burroughs and exchanged wisecracks with cameramen around the corner of the table. In exactly four minutes a British officer stepped into the room, nodded to Gen. Smith and immediately there was silence.

At 2:39, Col.-Gen. Gustav Jodl, German chief of staff, entered, followed by Gen.-Admiral Hans Georg von Friedburg, commander-in-chief of the German navy, and Maj. Wilhelm Oxenius, personal aide to Jodl.

Jodl, short of stature and gray of face and hair, walked stiffly and determinedly to the table. His face and eyes showed neither emotion nor expression. He seemed determined to carry the tradition of a Junker's control of emotion to this bitterest of all ends and maintained a marble countenance throughout. He stood opposite Gen. Smith for a moment, clicked his heels, bowed slightly and sat down with von Friedeburg on his left and Oxenius on his right. The Allied representatives sat down after the Germans were seated.

On the table before Gen. Smith lay a folder in which were the unconditional surrender terms and instructions to the German government and the chiefs of staff. Camera bulbs were flashing like brackets of rockets and the steady whine of movie cameras provided a sound back-drop. Over this noise I could not hear distinctly all that was said.

Gen. Smith spoke quietly in short, to-the-point sentences. He asked Jodl if he was ready to sign unconditional surrender terms, to which the German nodded. Jodl does not speak English well, and Maj.-Gen. K.W. Strong, British member of the allied intelligence staff, did the interpreting between Gen. Smith and Jodl.

Gen. Smith handed the documents across the table to Jodl. They were plain, legal-sized paper in an ordinary Manila folder.

"Will you please sign the original document first and the four copies afterwards," Gen. Smith instructed.

Jodl picked up a pen and signed the document without hesitation and handed it to Gen. Strong, who returned it to the allied side of the table for the signature of Gen. Smith on behalf of the Supreme Commander. Gen. Susloparov on behalf of the Soviet high command and Gen. Francois Sevez for the French high command. They signed as witnesses to Jodl's signature.

Other documents involving the terms and instructions to the German government concerning land, sea and air forces were signed in a similar way. The signing started at 2:40 and lasted five minutes.

After Jodl finished, he seemed to slump in his chair, putting one hand in his tunic pocket, then resting both hands easily on the table, but there was no relaxing of that Prussian face.

"I want to say a word," he said in English, and then delivered this little speech in German:

"With this signature the German people and the German armed forces are, for better or worse, delivered into the victors' hands. In this war, which has lasted more than five years, both have achieved and suffered more than perhaps any other people in the world. In this hour I can only express the hope that the victors will treat them with generosity."

Then he turned sharply and walked from the room, followed by von Freideburg and Oxenius and a few minutes later by the Allied representatives.

Jodl was then escorted formally to the office of Gen. Eisenhower, who had not taken part in the formal surrender. As he entered Gen. Eisenhower's office for the first time at 2:55, he stopped, heel-clicked to attention, bowed slightly and shifted to face both the supreme commander and Air Chief Marshal Sir Arthur Tedder, deputy supreme commander, across the desk.

The conversation again was brief. Gen. Eisenhower asked Jodl if he understood and was ready to enforce the surrender terms. Jodl answered that he did and would. With that he left the office and was seen no more.

In Gen. Eisenhower's office, cameramen gathered for a victory picture with Tedder and Smith. The supreme commander held the two pens used for the signing of the surrender in a V-for-victory sign.

Ike was happy and gay now that it was all over and he joked with the cameramen and officers. It was in this mood at 3:46 that he recorded his victory speech to the world from the "peace room" of supreme headquarters.

Ross D. Parry, "The Maple Leaf," the Toronto Star, *May 8, 1945.*

MAY 8, 1945:
The Canadians Arrive in Appeldoorn

The liberation of Appeldoorn was one of the most heartening and uplifting moments in the Canadian army's campaign in Europe. The people of the town were starving, the German defenders, who must have known their fight was useless, had used the natural defences to turn the town into a fortress. Everyone in Apeldoorn that week carries grim memories of the attack. The editor's mother-in-law and her sister, who were small children at the time, were hiding with their mother in a pit near the edge of the town on the night of the attack and were almost crushed by advancing tanks. Their father had already been killed in a German concentration camp in reprisal for the murder of a Wehrmacht officer.

WILLIAM BOSS

With the Canadian Army in Holland, May 8 — When the Royal Canadian Regiment chose 4 a.m. to capture Apeldoorn last month the townsfolk made it a pyjama party.

For some days the 1st Canadian Division had been trying to get into the city, but the Germans had thrown up a perfect perimeter defense.

Had it been a German locality, upward of 200 Lancasters would have been loosed upon it and the place leveled. But it was Holland, and it was desired to spare the town as much as possible.

During the latter phases of the battle, companies of the Royal Canadian Regiment, under Majors Dennie Jotcham of Montreal, Eric M. Hills of Sussex, N.B., and Captains Harry Davies of St. Thomas, Ont., and E. K. Wildfang of Kitchener, Ont., were flush with the east bank of the canal which snipped about a third of the city away from the remainder. The Germans lined the other side.

While the enemy heated up the Canadian side with Spandau and mortar fire, the RCR's replied with Brens, Stens and their own mortars.

A field battery under Major Ralph Hoar of Calgary and a squadron of tanks from the Three Rivers Regiment took part in the firing.

On April 17, the Halifax commanding officer became tired of the deadlock. His request for close air support was granted and a squadron of rocket Typhoons was sent over the German bank and the enemy panicked and decamped to the centre of the town, three blocks away.

A two-man patrol sent over in the evening brought back prisoners who said they had been left behind to blow up the locks and a large garage inside the town. That settled it.

Major Jotcham's men were first over after Major Hill's company made a tactical seizure of the lock itself. Jotcham's penetrated right into the heart of the city, consolidating around a five-road junction.

Davies seized the town hall, Hills occupied the right town centre and Wildfang firmed up in the southern section.

By then it was 4 a.m., but that made no difference to Apeldoorn. Citizens flocked out of doors in night attire to welcome their liberators.

Patrols were hastily organized with civilian guides and in no time 160 German stragglers were rounded up, bringing the prisoner total to 1,229 for the operation. It was the RCR's [Royal Canadian Rangers] who, two days earlier, had overrun the grounds of St. Joseph's Hospital outside the city to free a number of wounded Allied prisoners, including 12 Canadians.

German wounded taken in the hospital numbered 799 at the final count and medical staff totalled 85.

The same day Jotcham's company made a spectacular bid to force their way into Apeldoorn by riding in on Sherman tanks of the 1st Hussars, but the bridge was blown by the enemy when they were within 30 feet of the span.

Commanding the headquarters company of the RCR was Major Frank Darton, Halifax. Lieut. D. C. Martin, Kirkland Lake, Ont., commanded mortar and anti-tank platoons of the support company.

William Boss, The Canadian Press, May 8, 1945.

MAY 9, 1945:
Death Has Walked at Their Side

Matthew Halton elegantly describes the war-weariness of soldiers who had finally finished the grim and inglorious job of crushing the Third Reich.

MATTHEW HALTON

During long weary years, and during hours that seem like years, one sometimes wondered if the carnival of death wasn't a nightmare from which one would happily awake. And now the nightmare is over, one has to wonder if it isn't a pleasant dream from which we shall wake to find the usual mad mornings of blood and death. Today the sun rises as it hasn't risen for nearly six years, and soldiers I have talked to don't quite know what to do about it. They shave and have breakfast. They clean their guns. They try to brush the mud off their clothes. They ask if there is any mail. After all, they've lived strange and dangerous lives. It's hard to believe that no shells will come screaming over. It's hard to believe that if they stand up in the open that no one will shoot at them. Death has walked at their side. It's hard to believe, for a day or two, that the nightmare is over and they can drink the wine of life.

Matthew Halton, May 9, 1945. The Canadian Broadcasting Corporation Archives, www.cbc.ca.

VE-DAY:
A Censor Describes the Halifax Riot

H. Bruce Jefferson, a long-time journalist in Nova Scotia, was the government's press censor in Halifax during the Second World War. Jefferson was a packrat who, from his room on the top floor of Halifax's Lord Nelson Hotel, acted more like a spy than a censor. He photographed convoys and warships as they came and left the city, kept tabs on all of the U-boat attacks in the northwestern Atlantic, was wired into Halifax's busy gossip grapevine, and, months before the Halifax Riot, predicted there would be trouble at war's end.

The trouble started on May 7, when the news of the German surrender was expected that day. The city government responded to the good news by ordering liquor stores and taverns to close. At the same time, the navy gave shore leave to sailors in the ships that lined the harbour and filled Bedford Basin. During the riot, Jefferson wandered the city looking for material to send to his superiors and colleagues in Ottawa. Jefferson blamed the riots on the snobbery of Halifax business owners and residents who, he believed, had no qualms about fleecing soldiers and sailors stationed in Halifax while, at the same time, snubbing them. The riot ruined Admiral Leonard Murray's career.

While this memorandum was circulated among the press censors in the days after the riot, it is published here for the first time. Jefferson went to work for the Nova Scotia government after the war, but had slipped back into newspapering before his death in 1970.

H. BRUCE JEFFERSON

Because the weather forecasters predicted rain for tomorrow, the Halifax committee had decided not to await Churchill's announcement of VE day, but to shoot their fireworks at George's Island this evening.

The display began about 2100 hours, and Citadel Hill was absolutely jammed with thousands of people watching the affair, which lasted for nearly two hours.

As soon as it was over the crowd began to come down from the hill, serious rioting broke out on a downtown street. First I saw of it was a dull glare over Barrington Street, where they had set fire to two street cars, and upset a police patrol car, letting the burning gas run over the pavement.

Through the open window we could hear the crash of glass as window after window went in, and soon over the roofs we could see the crowd breaking into the Sackville Street liquor store.

About 2 a.m., I got a car and toured the devastated area, which did not look too bad at that time, broken glass being the main item. Three of the liquor stores bad been looted, and about 250 RCN shore patrolmen were gathered around the fourth, on Agricola Street in the North End.

This had not been touched.

By this time the rioters had gone home, and nothing more happened Monday night.

During the late evening I passed stories for Dennis, Ken Chisholm (*Globe & Mail*) and several others, all somewhat lurid and placing the damage at $1,000,000.

May 8, 1945.
This morning had several enquiries from locals and wire services about coverage of last night's riots, which I assured them were wide open, as no security was involved.

In the afternoon I attended a short garrison drum-head service of prayer and thanksgiving on the Garrison Grounds, back of the Citadel, and just west of the old Atlantic Command HQ.

There was quite a large turnout of troops of all branches (Navy, Army, Air Force and women auxiliaries) but they did not show any particular enthusiasm over the business — as it turned out, their thoughts must have been with their brethren down town.

Coming down Sackville Street, near the corner of Barrington, our ears were greeted with the now-familiar sound of falling plate glass. I spent some time observing the scene from various angles, and it kept getting worse and worse as the afternoon advanced. When most of the plate glass had been smashed, people climbed into the windows and kicked in the glass or thin wood backs of the show windows, and entered the stores. In some cases goods were thrown from upper windows to the crowd below, in others the stuff was merely carried out.

Generally speaking, the service men, principally navy although there were lots of Army and Air Force boys, too, took the physical and other risks of breaking and entering, while the civilians cheered them on and carried off the loot.

There was absolutely no interference with them by city or service police or RCMP. There was so much going on that it was like a 43 ring circus, and no one person could begin to follow all of it. For example, one Barrington Street crowd broke into Eaton's store, and for a time it looked as if nothing was being taken, but in the meantime another crowd had obtained entrance through Granville Street, and were carrying goods away by the ton through rear doors and windows.

It was the same everywhere.

As we passed the corner of Granville and Sackville, some people were looting the best shoe store in town. A man would appear at a window up two or three flights, with half a dozen shoe boxes in his hands, and throw them down to pals below. On the way down the boxes would open and the shoes get scattered, and then one fellow with a number seven worth $15 a pair would be hunting for somebody else who had the mate and vice versa.

There were all kinds of comic incidents, such as the old lady who must have been 75 or 80, with her dress covered with old war medals, who came up the car tracks arm-in-arm with a young airman, each drinking from bottles of beer and singing lustily. Later they did a sort of square dance in the intersection of Sackville and Barrington, and one of the locals took and printed a picture of it. In some ways it reminded me of a scene from the French Revolution movies.

I forgot to mention that when I came out of the [Lord Nelson] hotel shortly after noon on my way to the Garrison Grounds, I noticed a number of beer parties beginning on the lawn around the Cornwallis statue across the drive from the Nova Scotian. Other sailors kept arriving with cases on their shoulders, and I vaguely wondered how they had been able to save it from the night before. It turned out that they were even then looting [Alexander] Keith's Brewery, and as we went up South Street more sailors kept arriving, and a standard salutation was, "Well, I see the liquor store is open today, after all."

At one point a civilian came dashing down the line to warn the sailors that RCN patrol trucks were touring the city snatching cases back from sailors, and that they had better get rid of the boxes at once. This proved to be a racket. When the sailors would rush to hide their boxes under verandahs, etc., other civvies would call them away on one pretext or another, while still others made off with the cached beer.

One man told me he was looking for hard liquor but was unable to locate any. Some friends invited him into have a drink of beer. While they were chatting, a policeman who knew him came in and said: "What are you doing here?" He said: "Having a drink of beer." The cop said: "O.K. but let me have that box of brandy you're sitting on."

One of the last places attacked was Birks' [jewellery] store, and they made quite a mess of it. While watching the crowd go through Birks', I ran across A.D. MacNeill, former owner of the *Glace Bay Gazette* who sold that sheet to the U.M.W. when he had to retire on account of ill health, and learned for the first time that A.D. has been living since October at 129 Spring Garden Road.

It was at this time (about 1855 hours) that I heard a horn car coming through the crowd, and a voice which I recognized as that Admiral Murray commanding the service people to go home to their barracks. For a moment I thought that he must have made a record of the kind sometimes used in these cars, but in a few seconds, I heard an impromptu remark from the horn which showed me that the Admiral himself was on board, and when the car came past I recognized him in the front seat.

The gist of his remarks were:

"This is the Commander-in-Chief, Admiral Murray, in person. The mayor of Halifax has declared a curfew effective at 8 p.m. Any service personnel found on the street after that hour will be subject to the full penalties of the law."

Some sailor must have interjected a wisecrack as the car went by, as the Admiral said: "This is the Commander-in-Chief speaking — and that's not funny at all." I did not hear the statement attributed to him by the *Chronicle* and *Star* and others to the effect that "You don't want to get caught with loot, do you?" or words to that effect. From the general tenor of his remarks, I would gather that if he did make such a remark it was only ambiguously worded, and meant that they would not want to expose themselves, etc. for staying after 8 p.m.

The Admiral came around several times, completely circling the district, and there were slight variations in his remarks each time. For example, someone must have asked if this applied only to service people, because on his second circuit he took pains to specify civilians as well as personnel were subject to the order. (Which, incidentally, I am informed by one of the brightest legal minds in Cape Breton is all baloney and has no standing in law whatever.)

However, the bluff, or whatever it was, worked. As soon as the Admiral came around the first time, all service people on the spectator side of the street began to move away toward barracks, etc. and within a short time even the rioters departed, except for a few in the stores who possibly could not hear the horn or had not taken in what it said.

To my mind this indicates that if similar action had been taken earlier, the whole business could have been avoided. It was the slowness of action that permitted the chief destruction to occur.

I have been told that while there was some desultory activity in other parts of the city, on Gottingen Street and elsewhere, no damage of importance took place after the admiral made his rounds. Thousands were still AWOL but were parked with beer cases in such dark spots as Point Pleasant Park, Camp Hill Cemetery, etc.

The job was a very thorough one, and cleaned out the various business areas completely. Barrington was smashed and looted on both sides from the Convoy Cafe (which is between the Nova Scotian park and Morris Street), for a distance of two miles to the end of the store district above the Dockyard. Gottingen is smashed from Cogswell to Stadacona. The East-West streets like Spring Garden Road and Quinpool Road escaped attention altogether. But all the hill-side streets lying between Brunswick and Water street in the old city were cleaned out in toto.

Woods' — the place Jacques was asking about — was the only downtown store to escape glass damage or looting. Why, Lord only knows as their clothing prices were terrible. They took no chances on a second visitation and boarded them up right away. Everything else along there was smashed.

The crowd also smashed some of the windows in the Mounties barracks (old Halifax Hotel) not the plate glass lobby windows, but smaller panes in the adjoining Julien section. There were all kinds of queer sights, such as looters using the RCMP verandah to lay out their dresses, stockings, etc. and pack them into neater bundles for carrying. Cash registers lay all over the streets with their keys bent and twisted.

(I picked up a brand new quarter on the curb in front of the little Ideal store, where some fellow was busy bagging up sugar for himself out of a bin beneath the counter.)

When we went home to dinner, a sailor's dream was being enacted on the front steps of the Nova Scotian. A captain (four striper) was standing in stiff dignity waiting for a taxi, with a sailor in a jersey haranguing him and the crowd on the Navy and what he thought of it. In front of the captain in civvies was an old jovial veteran of the last war, with one leg and crutches. Both the veteran and the sailor were pretty drunk, and behind the captain was an open-mouthed audience of retired duchesses from the hotel hanging on every word. The sailor, however, was good-natured and polite, although drunk, and refrained from any really naughty language. The conversation as I came up was going something like this:

Old Vet: "Now, me lad, you shouldn't be carrying on like this. Remember you are a member of the Silent Service."

Sailor: "To hell with the Silent Service. I wasted three years and a half in it, and they can take their silent service and put it you know where."

Old Vet: "Tut, tut. That's no way to be talking in front of your captain."

Sailor: "He ain't my captain and you can put him you know where."

Old Vet: "You wouldn't talk like that to him if you were on the quarter deck."

Sailor: "I ain't on the quarter deck, and neither is he, and you can take your quarter deck and put it you know where."

Old Vet: "Have you no respect for your superiors in rank? Don't they teach you any discipline in the Navy?"

Sailor: "They ain't my superiors except in rank, and I've seen all the captains and admirals I want to see for the rest of my life, and you can take your captains and admirals and you can put them you know where."

The sailor carried an open bottle of rum in his left hand and never lost his polite leer and this went on and on until the skipper's taxi finally arrived and he left in a cloud of dust, much to the chagrin of the aforesaid dowagers and duchesses who apparently were getting quite a kick out of it. Similar scenes were going on all over town, although there were no attacks on officers with the exception of Commander Smith, who was found on King's campus with his head bashed in, but there is some uncertainty whether this was an accident or someone settling up old scores.

Although I did not see it myself, I understand that some of the CWACs and Wrens also distinguished themselves in the "Battle of Halifax," which was a long while getting here but turned out to be a lulu when it finally arrived.

I heard one yarn about two Wrens who were fighting half a dozen sailors in a vacant lot bounded by a board fence, lined with spectators who applauded lustily as one side or the other scored a particularly telling point.

The harbor side of Citadel Hill staged the biggest beer picnics in the history of the city, and there are some almost incredible, but apparently well-authenticated yarns about genuine "orgies" which went on in such public places as Grafton Park and Cornwallis Park (in front of the Nova Scotia Hotel).

One of the features on the Commons was a nude dance put on by members of several of the services. Apparently old Robespierre and the boys would have felt right at home in the Warden of the Honor of the North on May 7–8/45.

A lot of this stuff no doubt will come out at the official hearings.

We had very few submissions on this event, in fact mostly enquiries, from the newspapers and services. The wire censors (as old soldiers mostly) were shocked beyond words, and frequently referred the flamboyant stuff that was being sent out in query and story form by various local feature writers at last free to give full rein to their natural instincts in the matter of exaggeration.

I passed everything, telling the boys that there is no censorship on this. I had a particularly strong kick about Eric Dennis including rape as one of the features of the day, and I think this is a fake, or at least based on very slight grounds, as no such charge has appeared since in local courts. All accounts of the day's activities agree that this would have been a work of supererogation.

Neither of the locals had intended to publish today, but on account of unusual circumstances, both *Mail* and *Star* put out extras replete with editorials, stories and pictures.

The *Mail* blew rather hot and cold, one front page editorial deploring the incident and demanding vengeance and recompense, while another took pains to point out that the whole Navy should not be blamed for the actions of a comparatively small number.

The *Star* rather stole the show with a front page editorial actually naming Admiral Murray as the person responsible for the whole business by reason of his alleged failure to take prompt and vigorous action to stop the rioting before it got started again on the second day.

In the evening, over at CHNS [Canadian Headquarters Naval Services], Admiral Murray made a short statement in which he maintained that naval personnel were only a small part of the shock troops and that civilians were primarily to blame for both breaking and looting.

He was followed at 1900 hours by Mayor Butler, who followed the *Star* lead in naming Admiral Murray as the chief cause of the trouble, demanded compensation, and added the charge that many of those (provosts) sent to quell the rioting had in fact deserted to the rioters.

(Mr. Pickering, an old soldier who works upstairs, had predicted this very result if small pickets were used against the rioters, saying that the same thing happened in 1900 when Halifax troops sent on a similar errand hid their rifles behind fences and joined in the disturbances. He was through Boer War troop riots in Newcastle and Durban, South Africa, in 1899, Halifax riots in 1900, and additional local riots in 1917, 1918 and 1919, and qualifies as something of an expert on the subject.)

H. Bruce Jefferson, May 11, 1945, Library and Archives Canada, Records of the Directorate of Censorship, Vol. 5960.

THE KOREAN WAR

THE *HUFFINGTON POST* ARTICLE BELOW THAT WAS WRITTEN BY PETER Worthington five decades after the Korean War shows the frustration of veterans about the lack of public awareness of their "forgotten war." Korea was a difficult war to cover. Canadians had some grasp of the geography of Europe, but Korea was a far-off place that very few Canadians had ever visited. Korea was portrayed as a police action, a front line in the struggle to contain Communism. For the first time, Canada was not fighting as part of a British imperial force. Our troops were part of a United Nations mission. The goals of the operation were unclear. While, at one point, U.N. troops controlled much of North Korea, the U.N. mandate did not include the destruction of the North Korean state and its Communist regime. The war eventually evolved into a stalemate, with short, tough battles for high ground in the borderlands between North and South Korea.

It was a difficult war to cover. Reporters wandered quiet areas of the front and, from time to time, found themselves in great personal danger when North Korean and Chinese troops attacked Allied positions. The great Allied attack of the war, Douglas MacArthur's seaborne attack at

Inchon, was an American operation. MacArthur and most of the rest of the U.N. generals were headquartered in Tokyo, so in Korea news was massaged and manipulated by MacArthur's team of public relations officers. Another great drama of the war, the firing of General MacArthur and his replacement by Matthew Ridgway, was a Washington political story.

Probably as important as Canada's confusing role in Korea and the dominance of American military and political leaders was the fact that the fight in Korea asked almost nothing of Canadian civilians. There were no war bonds drives, no rationing, no official censorship, no fight over conscription. The country was prosperous, busy, wealthy, and oblivious. Korean stories, including lists of the dead, were stuck in the back pages. Radio reports were filed from confusing places that meant nothing to Canadians. There were very few Korean war-themed movies. Television was not yet able to bring the war into Canadians' homes. It ended with a truce, not a treaty; the status quo, not victory. All of these factors combined to make Korea the war for the little brothers of the heroes of the Second World War.

APRIL 26, 1951:
Outflanked, Encircled Pats Won't Quit

The material in brackets regarding censorship rules was inserted into the copy by CP editors.

WILLIAM BOSS

West Central Sector, Korea — The Chinese had enough. They withdrew. Throughout Tuesday night and part of Wednesday, the Communist hordes attacked U.N. positions on a steep hill on this west central sector of the flaming Korean front. They out-flanked and encircled these troops who had until now met only token resistance as they advanced northward.

But they failed to break a line held by such stalwarts as the sergeant who flung his empty rifle like a spear into the face of the enemy. Or the young company commander who coolly ordered mortar and artillery fire on his own position when his men ran out of ammunition.

(Boss, covering the Princess Patricias in Korea, cannot mention "Canadian troops" or individuals he sees in action because of censorship regulations.)

(Reuters news agency in a Tokyo dispatch reported that a Canadian battalion fought its way out of a Red trap on the west-central sector Thursday. Reuters said the Canadian battalion, along with a Belgian unit, were cut off when the Chinese threw in heavy forces against a new Allied line south and southwest of Yonchon.)

These troops held steady as rocks as enemy masses assaulted their hill from the front, from the flanks and finally from the rear when the flanks gave way under the sheer weight of numbers. By 6 a.m. yesterday, the enemy had had enough. He withdrew down the hill and dug in.

But he was only 100 yards away, screened by a thick curtain of smoke, and building up for another attack. But for the time being, the enemy had been turned back.

I counted 17 dead Chinese within inches and feet of those troops, and approximately 50 graves of enemy buried in the heat of battle. There were uncounted enemy dead where the intended read and flank attack was thwarted.

It was a hard-won victory. Time and again the Chinese rushed the U.N. front line position, and at one time the ammunition of one defending company ran out. And then a young captain, fighting his first action as a company commander, ordered his men into slit trenches and called for artillery and mortar fire upon the hill.

For three hours, the guns of three field regiments and two battalions of mortars rained upon the position as the captain coolly gave fire directions. It was too much for the Chinese. They moved back.

Wave upon wave, following the orders of whistles and bugles to the split second, the enemy hordes emerged into late Tuesday night. It was suicidal, but it evoked this tribute from one sergeant:

"They're good. They were on top of our positions before we knew it. They're quiet as mice with those rubber shoes. There's a whistle. They get up within ten feet of our positions and come in.

"The first wave throws grenades, fires its weapons and goes to the ground. A second does the same, and a third comes up. They just keep coming."

This was the sergeant who hurled his bayoneted rifle like a spear when his ammunition gave out. Another hurled his bayonet at the foe. The sergeant's company held out by dividing the slim remaining supply of ammunition until the enemy pressure eased.

The young captain's company was supplied yesterday by "flying boxcars" which made air drops of supplies.

William Boss, The Canadian Press, April 26, 1951.

SEPTEMBER 1952:
The Van Doos Are Shelled in Korea

Harry Pope, the son of Lieutenant-General Maurice Pope and a Belgian countess, served in Europe in the Second World War with great distinction. Taken prisoner in Italy while trying to save a wounded soldier, then-Lieutenant Pope escaped from a POW transport truck eleven days later. Pope remained in the army as a staff officer, and commanded a company of his own regiment, the Royal 22 (Van Doos) in Korea. There, he was awarded a Military Cross. After the Korean War, Pope joined the staffs of CCF/NDP politicians Hazen Argue and Tommy Douglas and later worked for the federal government in the mid-1960s, examining the issue of foreign ownership. After his stint in Ottawa, he taught economics at Ryerson Polytechnical Institute and was a frequent NDP candidate. Pope died in 2000.

WILLIAM HENRY POPE

Hill 159, which "C" Company I R22eR occupied for September 1952, faced the enemy to the north and to the west. Thus we were a salient in the enemy positions which dominated ours, especially from the north, where the enemy occupied Hill 227. The enemy could very well see all my company HQ, which was placed on the reverse slope, just below the crest of 159, between the two tanks that were on the crest itself.

The shells that came our way every afternoon were big ones, either 155 mm or 210 mm, all missed the tanks during this month. But they did not miss the company. The shells landed on the forward trenches in front of the tanks, on my HQ, and at the bottom of the hill, where I would have placed our kitchen, had I wished to find new cooks at the end of each afternoon. The shells also landed in the garbage dumps where we put our empty food tins, because, without a kitchen, we ate only "C" rations. Finally, the shells that did not land in front or on the crest of 159, or again completely at the bottom of the reverse slope, landed in the Rosebowl.

This Rosebowl was a circle of sand, maybe 60 yards in diameter, surrounded, except to the south, by two of my platoons and my HQ. No one strolled there during enemy shelling.

We started our month on 159 with maybe 60 men, half the regulation number. Apparently in the great Ottawa HQ (NDHQ) no one had realized that the departure from the battalion during the summer of the last Korean Special Force volunteers would leave gaps in the autumn. Since the company was losing one man killed or wounded every three days, after a month we were down to 50.

I was perfectly aware that, in the event of an enemy attack, my company would die in place: the position could not be successfully defended by a company at less than half strength. Of course, I did not tell my platoon commanders of my "appreciation of the situation," or the battalion commander. It was not his fault that the imbeciles of Ottawa were unable to count.

There was nothing to be done except to do our duty the best that we could. Among other things, this meant 100 percent stand-to in the trenches all night long: no one slept at night. So, at about 0600 or 0700 hours, after a tin of Spam, it was bedtime. But there again it was the hour of the grand visit of the generals, who all seemed to prefer spending a few minutes at the front line when the enemy had the sun in its eyes and therefore offered no fire.

I was not happy about these visits, probably because the generals always found the same things to criticize in my command: my men had not shaved, there were empty food tins scattered all over our famous Rosebowl, I did not have a steel helmet.

I told them that my whole company, like civilized men everywhere, shaved on getting up early in the afternoon, to the sound of the start of the daily enemy shelling. As for the empty food tins, the generals would have to ask the enemy to stop shelling our garbage dumps. My steel helmet of 19 May 1944 had saved my life on the Hitler Line, but I suppose in Korea I had decided that it was worth it to take a small risk if that made my men a little happier: "It can't be very dangerous, if the captain doesn't wear a helmet!" Or possibly it amused me to be different. Probably mostly that!

Well, one day after another grand visit that had interrupted our breakfast, I decided to settle the matter of the garbage and also indicate to the big chiefs the proper visiting hours.

The next morning, at about 0700 hours, consternation at battalion HQ: Hill 159 is on fire! Is it a surprise enemy attack? I was called to the phone (signalers re-laid the wire in the evening after the enemy shelling).

"No," I replied, "everything's fine here."

"And the smoke, then?"

"Yesterday you ordered me to clean up my hill. I'm doing it with my three man-pack flame-throwers. I've torched all the garbage dumps."

"But you're giving away your position to the enemy!"

"It's the enemy that put his ****** shells in our ****** garbage dumps in the first place. The enemy knows well, too well, where we are."

William Henry Pope, MC, Leading from the Front: The War Memoirs of Henry Pope (Waterloo, ON: The Laurier Centre for Military Strategic and Disarmament Studies, Wilfrid Laurier University Press, 2002).

NOVEMBER 11, 2011:
"I Didn't Expect Anything When I Joined the Army and That's Exactly What I Got — Nothing"

Writing sixty years after the Korean War, journalist Peter Worthington, who went to Korea as a young lieutenant, captures the frustrations of the veterans of Canada's "forgotten war." After Korea, Worthington, son of a Canadian general, went on to become one of the country's best foreign correspondents, then was one of the founders of the Toronto *Sun* newspaper.

PETER WORTHINGTON

Ever since Canadian soldiers first saw action in Afghanistan in 2002, respect and appreciation for our military has grown across the country.

In the past, such recognition has usually been confined to Nov. 11, Armistice or Remembrance Day. Yet admiration, even affection, for our soldiers has spread to the everyday — witness the re-naming parts of Highway 401 as the Highway of Heroes, marking the route those killed in Afghanistan take when their bodies are flown into Trenton for transportation to Toronto and to hometowns beyond.

It's something of a cliché to say that reverence for our military is unmatched since the days of World War Two, but I'd argue the feeling the country exudes today was absent in WWII.

In WWII, it seemed everyone of military age was in uniform. It was the thing to do. No big deal, no fuss when someone "joined up."

I was of that wartime generation who couldn't wait to go to war. Like many teenagers, I feared the war might end before I was old enough to enlist.

Most Canadians today weren't alive when WWII was fought. I was 12 years old when the war started, and a sub-lieutenant in the Fleet Air Arm when it ended. At age 17 I joined the navy (the army took boys at age 18), went overseas, caught the last year of the war, but was never shot at.

Unfulfilled, I later joined the army and served as a platoon commander with the Princess Pats in Korea, as well as a battalion intelligence officer, and then flew with U.S. Mosquitos (6147 Squadron), marking Chinese targets with coloured smoke for U.S. strike aircraft to bomb.

During Korea, the Canadian public — and media and politicians — didn't give a hoot about the military. Few soldiers expected otherwise. Soldiers used to joke: "I didn't expect anything when I joined the army and that's exactly what I got — nothing."

It's often forgotten (if it was ever known) that in WWII young men joined the military because it was inconceivable that they wouldn't. Many of their fathers and uncles had served in WWI. Now it was their turn.

There was a sense of adventure, mixed with patriotism. Germany, again! Most kids had played war games in the between-wars period, and most were curious about the real thing. Everyone knew war was dangerous, but youths felt invulnerable. If anyone was to be killed, it'd be someone else.

In the Korean War, I felt lucky to be going at someone else's expense. Adventure and curiosity. How would it feel to be shot at? What was an artillery barrage like? Would there be hand-to-hand fighting? All the stuff we saw in movies, read in books, were told by veterans. We all expected to survive.

Many who enlisted for Korea had missed out on WWII — or had served in "the war," and were dissatisfied with civvy life.

A saying at the time was that those who enlisted were "too lazy to work, too timid to steal." No soldier I knew ever expected the country — citizens back home — to either understand or care about them. Or show gratitude or appreciation. We were soldiers for our own reasons, not for any expectations that we were serving the country's interests.

Soldiers were wryly amused when the *Vancouver Sun* published the same story about Korea, on the same page, every day for a week — and didn't get one complaint. When troopships left for Korea, there was no fanfare; likewise, there was none when troopships returned a year later.

Casualties were noted in small type deep in the paper. Even in the post-war era of peacekeeping, casualties were fill-in items. Not like today, when casualties occurred in Afghanistan, it's a lead news item and the nation takes note.

Canada had over 60,000 killed in WWI, over 40,000 in WWII, over 500 in Korea. Those who served in Korea resented (and still resent) it being called by some "a police action."

Some 40,000 Americans were killed in Korean fighting, and maybe a million South Koreans. It was a terrible war — and a strange one: When the Second Battalion Princess Pats were the first Canadian unit to fight in Korea, it was a fluid, mobile WWII-type of action. By the time I was there, it was WWI trench warfare, with mostly patrols in the no-man's-land valley, being shelled and periodically attacked by the Chinese. A defensive war, and unsatisfying.

Most WWII and Korean veterans — whose numbers are fading fast — never experienced the appreciation today's soldiers get. Most feel that such respect is long overdue, and welcome it for those who came after.

After WWII everyone seemed to be a veteran. Nothing special. Canada was generous with veteran grants and provided free education. I went to university, thanks to veteran grants, and also got $60 a month to live on.

I didn't feel entitled to anything, but was thankful to get something. I suspect my feelings were pretty typical. It was only later that I realized with shame that Canadian Indians who had served with me, many of whom were better soldiers than I, got few veteran benefits on discharge.

But that's another story for another day.

Peter Worthington, The Huffington Post, www.huffingtonpost.ca, November 11, 2011.

PEACEKEEPING AND PEACEMAKING

THE KOREAN WAR HAD SHOWN THAT CANADIANS WERE WILLING TO serve under the United Nations and would be satisfied with fighting for peace, rather than victory. Then-External Affairs minister Lester Pearson used the Korean precedent to offer U.N. "peacekeepers" as a buffer between Israel and Egypt as part of the solution of the 1956 Suez Crisis. Canadian soldiers took part in missions all over the world. Some were small and intense, like the 1990s mission to Sierra Leone during its ugly civil war. Others, like the Canadian mission to Cyprus, were large-scale deployments lasting years. Covering a peacekeeping mission had its challenges. The military took many reporters to Cyprus on trips that were more like vacations than journalistic missions. Other places were so dangerous that few reporters were willing to risk their lives for any length of time. And, as in the case of the Rwandan genocide of 1994, many editors and reporters simply did not understand what was happening until the situation was out of control. In the post-Second World War era, foreign reporting was priced out of the hands of many Canadian news organizations. They began to rely more and more on foreign wire services for text and photos, and news gathering organizations like the British Broadcasting Corporation, the big three U.S. television networks and, after the late 1980s, Atlanta-based Cable News Network (CNN) to fill column inches and air time. Still, Canadian reporters, given the chance, showed they were as good as their foreign colleagues at finding and telling stories.

SEPTEMBER 1973:
The Night the Brothel Burned

Australian-born Jack Cahill, one of the best Canadian foreign correspondents of the 1970s, was a frequent visitor to Vietnam in the twilight years between the signing of the U.S.–North Vietnam peace agreement and the fall of Saigon in 1975. His coverage of the collapse of the South Vietnamese regime and his own harrowing escape won him a National Newspaper Award. Cahill had a remarkable eye for detail and a talent for spinning phrases. He died in 2005.

JACK CAHILL

There are some great hotels in Asia. The old Repulse Bay Hotel in Hong Kong is one of them, with its huge rooms and antique furniture, its running room boys, and the marks of Japanese bullets from the World War II invasion still on some of the thick cement walls.

While we were looking for a permanent home and office on the island, my family and I lived for four months at the Repulse Bay. We had two rooms, paneled in rich wood, with ceilings about fifteen feet high. We overlooked the long, pure white beach, with its constant crowd of ice cream and hot dog devouring Hong Kong Chinese, who seemed desperate, for some reason I have never understood, to tan themselves.

Beyond the beach the fleets of local fishing junks spread their nets and the old, unpainted junks, down from Canton or other parts of the Communist mainland, sometimes passed by. Their crews strained at long oars when the wind was still but usually their patched and faded red sails billowed in a breeze.

The balcony of the Repulse Bay is one of the world's best places to eat and the setting among the world's most exotic. But even the best French food becomes a bit boring after a few months so that we came to prefer the simpler meals of the coffee shop or the steaks barbecued on the hotel's broad lawns in the balmy evenings.

Raffles in Singapore, once the rambling, white second home of the British planters, is a little run-down now, with an occasional cockroach and furniture that is old without being antique. It is still a nice place to stay if you can manage to ignore the lines of tourists who gawk at you, clutching their complimentary Singapore Slings, as you dine in the magnificent dusk of the open-air Palm Court, with its starched linen and candelabra, green lawn and waving palms.

My favorite is the old section of the Oriental Hotel in Bangkok, where the two-story rooms — comfortable living area below and bedroom above — overlook the muddy river. One can watch a stream of sampans, loaded with fruit and flowers, dead pigs and people; the long, narrow, motorized ferries, low in the water with workers and tourists; and at night the twinkling lights and cooking fires of the adventurous city.

The Taj Mahal in Bombay is magnificently ornate and efficient, its foyer constantly crowded with the rich of the poor land and their beautiful ladies in flowing saris. The new Sheraton in the same city is perhaps even more luxurious in a more modern way. You can see, from the plush comfort of your suite, hordes of ordinary Indians in a shanty town almost directly below, sleeping in the heat under slanting scraps of galvanized iron, making their homes in packing cases, gathering in big families around a cooking fire with small bowls of rice, their meal for the day. As you sip your Scotch you can see the women carrying on their heads the pitchers of water from some dirty well and you can ponder the plight of these people, who live on less in a year than you have to pay for a night at the hotel.

Hotels like these help the foreign correspondent.

In the back of his mind he knows he can usually escape to one of them, often to dine in considerable style in some places with a bottle of reasonable wine, while he contemplates what he will write about those real people in that other world he works in. This ability to escape gives him a troubled conscience sometimes. But in a strange way the blatant contrast can also encourage his sympathies and enforce his objectivity. At least he realizes that he is a very fortunate fellow indeed.

However, not all hotels in Asia are oases of riches and luxury in a desert of poverty and under-privilege. The Majestic Hotel, for instance, in Can Tho in the Mekong Delta of Vietnam, is different.

Photographer Boris Spremo and I checked into the Majestic one evening in 1973, partly because we had been told it was to become the headquarters for the Canadian forces assigned to the ICCS peacekeeping force in that area, and partly because it seemed to be the only hotel in town.

We were tired. We had tried to sleep the previous night in an abandoned barracks at Saigon's Tan Son Nhut airport. This was because the Vietnamese, for some reason, would not let us near the area of the airport where the Canadian peacekeeping forces were setting up their main headquarters. They had arrested a Canadian photographer and thrown him in jail. We were smuggled into the airport on the floor of an ICCS car and hid in the abandoned barracks so that we could catch the chopper to Can Tho in the morning.

The barracks was full of mosquitoes and the few thrown-away mattresses in it were full of fleas so we didn't sleep except for a few minutes on the flight. We were told when we landed that the chopper had run through a few rounds of ground fire as we slept.

At the Can Tho air base we had picked up a jeep with a Vietnamese driver who spoke fairly good English and we spent most of the day at another airport on the outskirts of the town trying to interview a group of about a hundred female Viet Cong soldiers. The women were squatting glumly in their black pyjama suits under conical hats on the hot tarmac, waiting to be flown to North Vietnam in the first stage of a prisoner exchange.

At first the American officers wouldn't let us near them but after hours of negotiation they allowed us to interview a Canadian captain who was in charge of policing the exchange and he agreed to turn his back while we talked to the women through the driver-interpreter, providing Spremo took no pictures.

All the women would do was snarl at us. Some of them spat. None of them would say a word. But Spremo managed to shoot a few pictures from the hip, the first Western pictures of the prisoner exchange and the first in many years of Viet Cong women soldiers.

When we asked the driver what they had said when he approached them he look embarrassed and said it wouldn't exactly translate. But when we asked him to try anyway, he told us, "They said I was a running dog of the Yankee imperialist bastards. You were the shit of the earth and we should all fuck off.

"I've never met any Viet Cong women before," he said with a note of distress in his voice. "They are not very nice."

The driver, who chewed constantly on a dead grasshopper, as many Mekong Delta men do for some narcotic reason, eventually drove us between the open sewers that line the highway to the town. On its outskirts, not far from the American base, he pointed to a ramshackle shack bearing a big sign in English proclaiming "The Happy Fuck."

"Number one bar that," he said, chewing on his grasshopper. "Hell of a good place. Not very pricey."

When we got to the Majestic Hotel, a four-or five-storey building across the dusty main road from the Mekong River, he described it similarly and, we should have realized, ominously. "Number one place," he said. "Not very pricey. Lots of fun place."

When Spremo and I checked in we were given the numbers of rooms on the second floor, but no keys. And when I began to open the door to my room a shrill voice shouted something in Vietnamese which sounded similar to the remarks of the Viet Cong women at the airport.

While I was contemplating this situation, Spremo emerged from his mono across the corridor clutching his nose and looking strangely pale.

"I try to go to the bathroom," he said in the thick Yugoslav accent he hasn't lost in two decades in Canada. "I open the door and the smell knocks me over. So I slam the smell in so it can't get out. I think there is something dead in the bathroom. Do you have a bathroom?"

"I don't know yet," I told him. "There's somebody in my room."

We went to the clerk on the first floor who had booked us in and told him there was something dead in Boris' bathroom and somebody alive in my room and he shrugged and told us to wait a while and he'd fix it up. Then after about five minutes he told us to go back to our rooms. Now mine was empty except for two cockroaches as big as frogs in the corner. They were too big to stomp on because of the mess they would have made. And there was a rat running round inside the glass lampshade. It made the already dim light come in oddly varying intensities as it moved around the bulb.

There was a small, low bed in the room with a dirty cover and that was all except for a door with peeling paint leading to a bathroom. I opened it with great care. There was a hole in the bare and filthy cement floor for a toilet and a rusty pipe in a corner with a shower attachment.

A woman knocked at the room door while I was surveying the bathroom and asked if I wanted her to stay. She was very fat and she didn't seem to have any teeth and she got quite upset when I told her to go away. Spremo was upset too when he knocked and he looked even paler than before.

"I open the door again just a little bit," he said. "And the stench you wouldn't believe. There is something dead in there, maybe some*body*. I not open the door again. Do you have a bathroom?"

Boris used the bathroom and emerged looking a little better. "You cheated," he accused me. "You took the room with the good bathroom."

"Boris," I said, "I have become convinced that, in general, this is not one of the better hotels." I showed him the rat in the lampshade.

The food wasn't very good either in the restaurant on the ground floor, mainly rice with a shrimp or two in it, and while we were eating the kitchen exploded and the building caught fire. Jets of fire spurted suddenly toward our table, as if from a flame thrower. The kitchen was a yelling mess of brown men and burning fat. We ran into the street.

Spremo can be an excitable fellow especially if anything occurs that might stop him doing his job, and the first thing he thought of, maybe the only thing, was his precious collection of cameras hidden under the bed in his room.

He ran through the hotel's main entrance up the staircase and although it was the opposite of common sense I followed him. The stairs were on fire and we were scorched a bit as we ran down them, clutching cameras, typewriter, and notebooks.

Then we stood in the street and watched the arrival of a fire brigade consisting of scores of shrilly vocal men towing galvanized tanks of water on hand carts.

There is something funny about a burning brothel. Maybe there shouldn't be, but there is. It is not the deshabille of the emerging clientele, but the expressions on their faces. This is a strange mixture of shock and shame, combined with false attempts at casual unconcern and complete detachment, probably unseen on the human face except in these circumstances. There is also no gallantry in a burning brothel. The men, all of them Vietnamese or Chinese, because the Majestic was obviously an institution for wealthier locals, charged first down the burning stairs, pulling up pants and pushing the girls aside so that the towels some of them had wrapped around their bodies were ripped away and they were running around with only two hands and three or four places to put them.

Despite their primitive equipment, the yelling fire brigade managed somehow to confine the fire to the restaurant and staircase and part of the first floor of the hotel and put it out after an hour or so, so Spremo and I were able to return to our rooms to sleep. But Boris never did open his bathroom door again. And I tried not to disturb the rat and the cockroaches. Twice during the night I managed to be polite in rejecting disheveled ladies who seemed to be going for fire sale prices.

There are many great hotels in Asia and the image of the foreign correspondent living the luxurious life, even covering the wars from the comfort of his suite, is sometimes justified. But the Majestic in Can Tho is not one of these hotels. And unfortunately on some jobs there are just as many Majestics as there are Taj Mahals.

Jack Cahill, If You Don't Like the War, Switch the Damn Thing Off! (Toronto: Musson Book Company, 1980).

MARCH 19, 1994:
Canadians Observe a "Crazy" War-Ravaged Croatia

Steven Ward

As midnight approaches, Sierra Charlie 22 is one of the spookiest spots along the Krajina frontline.

The Canadian UN observation post is shrouded in darkness, wedged between Serb artillery positions, a nightly observer to shelling that brightens the sky and shakes the ground in this region of southern Croatia.

Corporal Claude Alie, from Gracefield, Que., monitors the sound of distant mortar, warming his hands by a kerosene stove. The small but cozy post, protected by 4,400 sandbags, overlooks the Serb-Croat line three kilometres away.

"You can really feel it when all hell breaks loose, but we don't see the people being killed," says Cpl. Alie, 28, peering through a laser night-vision device at two Serb tanks.

Today is a relatively quiet day: 39 mortars and 20 artillery shells have been fired by the warring sides, plus 1,000 rounds of machine-gun fire. It was a lot worse before a ceasefire in December.

This stretch of Krajina, where Serbs fight for an independent state, is a military mad house.

The Canadian post, one of five in the area, is circled by Serb mortar, artillery and tank positions. Each day, the Serbs fire on Croat positions to the west, and each day the Croats respond in kind.

The volleys go back and forth over the heads of the nine-member Canadian section that mans the post and its attached house.

Over the past five months, the heavily guarded post has come under fire several times. Shells have exploded in the former front lawn, leaving gaping holes and shrapnel strewn around the area.

"This is the hottest point in the Krajina," adds Sergeant Marc Lavalle of Quebec City. "We are a target. The Serbs don't want us here."

In the darkness, Corporal Jean-Francois Lizotte of Rimouski, Que., walks a foot patrol around the post, ringed by razor wire and trip flares.

An eerie white light shines on a small UN flag atop the house so gunners hopefully won't fire on the post.

Inside the house, soldiers watch a television on top of a fridge filled with pop and cold beer. A picture of retired major-general Lewis MacKenzie, former UN commander in Sarajevo, hangs on a wall.

The kitchen has a supply of seven days' food in case the road to the section's company headquarters, a 20-minute drive away in Benkovac, is cut by the Serbs.

"Here your day is never really over," says Cpl. Lizotte, 23. "You have to be prepared for anything. Nobody drinks a lot of beer here because a round can come in at any time, and you could get an injury anytime."

For the young Canadians, this daily pattern, carried on for the past three years, is a baffling exercise in futility.

"It's a crazy, part-time war," Cpl. Lizotte says. "Some nights we sit here and speak about how lucky we are that nobody has been yet killed or injured."

Steven Ward, The Canadian Press, March 19, 1994.

DECEMBER 1994:
A Desperate Struggle to Help Amid Sarajevo's Living Ghosts

At Christmas 1994, the *Toronto Star* asked Canadian peacekeepers to write letters to the paper. The newspaper published a full page of descriptive letters from Canadian forces personnel stationed overseas. Dr. Peter Vaughan wrote of his harrowing work trying to help civilians wounded in the siege of Sarajevo, Bosnia, and in other parts of Yugoslavia.

Dr. Peter Vaughan

It was a quiet day in Sarajevo, and the smell of corpses was in the air.

The ambulance outside the hospital had so many bullet holes through the windshield it could be a sieve for straining souls. The gun-toting soldiers hanging around have a carrion stench about them. My doctor friend said, "It is very difficult to say no to someone who is carrying a gun that you will not take their child out of the country."

I recently returned from a United Nations High Commissioner for Refugees mission. Aboard Canadian and Royal Air Force Hercules C130s, we flew food and medical supplies and evacuated sick and wounded from Sarajevo in Bosnia-Herzegovina and Split in Croatia.

The snow over the Dinaric Alps as we flew over the former Yugoslavia reminded me of the solitude of the Canadian Rockies. My serenity was shattered by the pilot's voice on the intercom. We are now at 5,000 feet — five minutes from touchdown. Shots have reportedly been fired near the airport. We abort the sorties and return to our base in Ancona, Italy.

On board are two Bosnians going home, one of them a child still recovering from injuries. The child's eyes, enormous with anxiety, stare at me in the roaring hollow of the C130.

The war is more than just a matter of staying alive: It's choosing where you want to die.

In Sarajevo, I shudder as the armored car turns toward the hospital on the route called "sniper alley." Everyone here runs as if late for an appointment, but it is already too late: They are running for their lives. The front lines of the war are to my immediate right where the snipers use modern rifles with sophisticated sites to shoot old men, women and children. I was told snipers are paid in Deutschmarks — 200 per child, 400 for adults, 600 for UN and 800 for media. A Canadian doctor must be worth at least DM 700.

At the hospital, in the non-sterile burn unit, a brother and sister cling to life. They were burned when their home was blown up by a mortar shell that punctured a gas tank, killing their grandmother and burning the boy, age 12, over 60 per cent of his body, and his 10-year-old sister more than 50 per cent. The little girl has internal bleeding that required emergency abdominal surgery and resection of a portion of her small bowel which further complicates her recovery.

Farther up the valley, a river winds its serpentine course to the mountains where salmon spawn. But for Sarajevo, a city which stands among the rushing rivers, its old buildings and families as they have been for hundreds of years, time is running out.

Dr. Peter Vaughan, the Toronto Star, *December 24, 1994.*

JULY 1999:
Louise Arbour Investigates War Crimes in Kosovo

Toronto-born Michael Ignatieff was a top-tier journalist and an accomplished academic before returning to Canada to take up politics. Ignatieff led the Liberal Party in the 2011 election. After his party placed third, Ignatieff gave up the Liberal leadership and accepted a position with the University of Toronto. He has resumed his journalism work and has become a commentator on Canadian political and foreign policy issues. Louise Arbour was a judge on the Ontario Court of Appeal before being appointed to investigate charges of brutality by police and guards during a riot at the Kingston Prison for Women. She was then appointed by the United Nations as an investigator of war crimes. Soon after this article appeared, Arbour was appointed to the Supreme Court of Canada. In 2004, she left the court to resume her human rights and war crimes investigation work.

Michael Ignatieff

Celine is a small village on the road between Prizren and Djakovica in western Kosovo. It is a hot July morning and about a hundred villagers are waiting for a helicopter to land in the meadow beside what remains of the local school. It has been torched: the roof timbers are lying among charred children's desks. The red and black Kosovo flag flies over the ruins.

A clutch of brown-faced schoolchildren are standing against a rope line, holding bunches of wilting flowers picked from their family's gardens. They have been told that an important woman is coming to see them. They do not know who she is, but they like the idea that she is coming in a helicopter and so they peer up into the sky and cock their ears for the sound of rotor blades.

The older men of the village sit on the meadow grass in a circle, smoking, running their fingers through their mustaches and staring at the mountains across the valley. They are wearing the kelesche, the conical cap of Albanian country people. The women, in their best white embroidered dresses and kerchiefs, sit in a separate circle, talking among themselves. One of them wipes away tears with the back of her hand.

As the sun rises in the sky, camera crews begin to arrive: young people in wraparound sunglasses, shorts, T-shirts and Caterpillar boots. They are from CNN, Reuters, Sky and Channel Four Television from London, plus the *Washington Post*, National Public Radio, and Deutsche Welle Radio.

About forty yards from the cameras and reporters, on the other side of the rope line, there is a Dutch armored personnel carrier with signalers inside talking on the radio phone. Next to the APC are a couple of military tents with camouflage nets spread between them. Inside one of the tents, a heavy-set man in white shirt and chinos is poring over a map. He looks glumly at the gathering of the TV crews, lights a cigarette and come out to talk to them. His name is Bill Gent and he is in charge of the forensic team — pathologists, archaeologists, anthropologists, ballistics specialists — who are digging in the ravine behind Celine.

After a long wait, a Huey with German markings comes up over the hill behind the village, circles twice and settles down gently beside the school, while Dutch soldiers positioned on the perimeter duck and shield their faces from the rotor blast. A short female figure wearing black glasses, her shoulders hunched and head bowed, steps down from the helicopter and, with a small entourage following behind, approaches the villagers, gathering against the rope line. Louise Arbour doesn't like scenes like this: she is a criminal prosecutor, not a celebrity, yet she plunges into what the scene requires, taking the bouquets held out by the children, stroking their cheeks, clasping some of the hands held out to her and saying over and over: "Thank you, thank you." Kosovo has been in NATO's hands for a month. Since then, the troops, together with Arbour's investigators from the International Tribunal at The Hague have been finding "sites" everywhere. The whole of Kosovo, she has been quoted as saying, was "one vast crime scene." She had been up in the French sector that morning at Mitrovica and next she will be visiting a site near Gnilane where the Canadian RCMP is digging; now she wants to see what her team has found at Celine. She gets into Bill Gent's Land Rover and they drive down the hill, followed by the reporters' jeeps. The villagers stay where they are: they know what there is to see. But the crews don't: they push and shove each other to get a shot of Louise Arbour looking down into the pit and slowly shaking her head.

I do not go down in the ravine — I know what is there. So I wait for her to return. When she comes back up to the forensic team's tent, she does not look shocked or dismayed, just tired. The crowd is about fifty yards away, watching her every move. While she has not said she will bring them truth and justice, that is what they expect. I ask her whether there isn't something cruel about these expectations. How likely is it that she or anyone else will find the men who killed the villagers of Celine — twenty-one of them — for no other reason than that they were Kosovar Albanians?

She thinks about this, hands on hips, head down and then says fiercely: "We have no choice. We owe it to these people. If there are expectations, we just have to meet them."

They are calling her over to the rope line, and she duly goes and shakes hands, and bows her head in thanks, and then her staff turns her towards the helicopter — rotors now whirring up the dust — and she climbs aboard, and is suddenly airborne, whirling overhead. A tiny hand is just visible waving down at us and then the chopper wheels around and vanishes behind the next hill.

Michael Ignatieff, Virtual War: Kosovo and Beyond *(Toronto: Viking, 2000).*

THE FIRST GULF WAR

Saddam Hussein's invasion of Kuwait on August 6, 1990, started a chain of events that led eventually to both the 9/11 attacks on America and, eventually, the destruction of his own regime. Until that time, Hussein had been an ally of the United States. His war with Iran had lasted nearly eight years, until the summer of 1988, and had tied down the anti-American Iraqi regime in bloody stalemate that had cost the Iranians 400,000 casualties. Hussein's attack on Kuwait enraged the Saudis, who feared the loss of a friendly neighbour and worried about further Iranian aggression. The Saudis asked for U.S. help and offered bases along the Saudi-Kuwait and Saudi-Iraqi frontier. This move was used as potent propaganda by Osama bin Laden, who built his al Qaeda network by claiming the Americans had imposed themselves on Arabia, the cradle of Islam.

Canadian pilots were deployed at Qatar for bombing runs against Iraqi positions. A Canadian supply ship was also dispatched to the region.

During the build-up to the invasion of Kuwait, Operation Desert Shield, Canadian reporters tended to be headquartered at the Canada Dry air base in Qatar. This proved to be frustrating when the military imposed long news blackouts, ordering soldiers and air crews not to talk to them. Journalists were also concerned that Iraqi missiles carried chemical and bacterial weapons, a fear that was shared by soldiers and civilians in the targeted area.

Once Operation Desert Storm began, some Canadian reporters were able to report from the fighting lines and from Kuwait City. Journalists had considerable freedom in the battle zone and were able to move among Canadian and American military units. Some of the best reporting was done after the war was over, when Southam News reporter Anne McIlroy toured the war zone and reported on the environmental damage — much of it deliberate — in the Kuwaiti oil fields and the Persian Gulf.

FEBRUARY 27, 1991:
Canadians "Bombing the Hell" Out of the Republican Guard

BRIAN KENNEDY

CANADA DRY ONE, Qatar — CF-18 fighter planes are "bombing the hell" out of Iraq's Republican Guard, a military official said today.

But military sources told The Canadian Press some senior officers and pilots in Qatar are annoyed that Canada's contribution to the war is not being told.

The official, who could not be identified because of a news blackout, said Canadian pilots have been pumped up for days flying low-level bombing missions first in Kuwait and now in Iraq.

"They feel we are contributing by dropping thousands of pounds of bombs on Baghdad's bully boys in the desert," he said.

The Republican Guard, considered Iraq's best fighting force, has been concentrated in south-eastern Iraq, north of the Kuwaiti border.

He said the pilots and the personnel on the two Canadian bases feel the war will be over within the week.

"We have been blowing through the Iraqis like they were nothing. It's like driving through the desert with nothing there."

Canada, which has 24 CF-18s based in Qatar and a three-ship naval force headquartered in Bahrain, switched to an offensive role in the crisis when the ground war in Kuwait started last Sunday.

He said the pounding that Iraqi troops are taking from the coalition forces and the swiftness of the ground campaign had prevented Iraq from using chemical weapons.

A news blackout was imposed once the huge allied land, air and sea offensive began and reporters have been denied access to the two Canadian air bases in Qatar.

"They (officers) feel we are not getting credit for what were doing in the air especially at this crucial time," a source said.

In a telephone interview from command headquarters in the island country Bahrain, Capt. Rod Gray said the three-day-old blackout would continue until orders from Ottawa were sent to change it.

"Don't blame us for the blackout," he said. "Blame Ottawa."

A military communiqué stated Canada's field hospital at the front in Saudi Arabia was fully operational.

The communiqué said surgical teams at the hospital were already treating wounded Iraqi PoWs, captured during the battle for Kuwait.

In the Qatari capital Doha, military officials said there were no Scud alerts during the night.

However, one officer said four Scud missiles landed in and around Qatar late Monday night and early Tuesday morning.

The officer said one landed on the outskirts of Doha, another further north in the desert and two came down south of the capital, one in the Gulf the other in the desert.

"Several soldiers on duty and some new recruits at Canada Dry One saw a missile fly by," he said.

A Qatari Ministry of Information spokesman would neither confirm nor deny four Scuds exploded in and around the tiny country.

Initial reports had only two scud missiles coming down in Qatar.

Brian Kennedy, "Canadians 'Bombing the Hell' Out of Republican Guards," the Ottawa Citizen, *February 27, 1991.*

MARCH 23, 1991:
The Spoils of War: Iraqi Soldiers Carried Away Kuwait's Heritage

MOIRA FARROW

The strong sunshine of the Middle East, filtering through the latticework of a concrete canopied roof, makes patterns of light and shade on the floor of the interior courtyard at the Kuwait National Museum.

It's a scene of tranquil beauty until that moment when the first Iraqi army truck roars to a halt outside and soldiers, shouting instructions and encouragement to each other, crash through the doors of the elegant building.

Moments later more trucks arrive, and the museum's galleries are soon filled with men hurling delicate and priceless works of art into cardboard boxes.

The trucks, loaded with loot, vanish into the traffic of Kuwait City; the carefully selected treasures of Sheik Nasser Sahah al-Ahmad al-Sabah carted away to an unknown destination.

The museum's entire 7,000-piece collection of Islamic art — a gift from the sheik in 1982 — was gone when coalition forces reached Kuwait City earlier this month. It is now part of the spoils of the Persian Gulf war.

The treasures themselves, collected in many parts of the world and brought together by the sheik in his homeland, represented every type of craftsmanship. There were silk and cashmere carpets dating back to the 16th century, delicate enamels, jewel caskets inlaid with ivory and rare woods, centuries-old manuscripts painted in glowing colors, ceremonial daggers from Moghul India encrusted with diamonds and rubies, 800-year-old bronze basins and ewers, gold dinars from the time of the Crusades, gold bracelets and ear ornaments, fine porcelains from every corner of Araby, ancient astrolabes and compasses — in total, one of the world's pre-eminent collections of Islamic art.

And the loss of the al-Sabah collection is only part of the tragedy. Twenty kilometres off the coast of Kuwait City lies the small island of Failaka where, since 1958, archeologists have been excavating a Hellenistic fortress buried in the sand for some 2,300 years.

"It's one of the most important sites on Earth for the mingling of eastern and western cultures," says archeologist Joan Connelly, an assistant professor of fine arts at New York University and an expert on this excavation.

On the low-lying, sandy island, fringed with a few date palms, archeologists have worked for years to reveal the mud brick foundations of a moated fortress that was once a bustling city filled with temples, little houses, narrow streets and throngs of people.

Excavated columns bear witness to that critical meeting of cultures — pillars with Ionic-style capitals and distinctly Persian pedestals.

Now, it's doubtful that the columns are still standing. Much of the material excavated at Failaka since 1958 was in storage at the Kuwait National Museum, and the island itself was heavily bombed during the Gulf War.

"It's a great tragedy — this fortress survived for 2,300 years and it's possible it was wiped out in one afternoon," says Connelly. "It breaks my heart."

Kuwait's triple loss — the 7,000 treasures of the al-Sabah collection; the artifacts from Falaika, including sculpture, coins and pottery that were at the Kuwait National Museum for safekeeping; and the island site itself, where east met west more than 300 years before the birth of Christ — is a serious blow. But more than priceless art objects, the country has lost a large part of its cultural heritage.

"It's like a thief going into your bedroom and stealing your wedding certificate and your children's birth certificates," explains Hanna Kassis, professor of religious studies at the University of B.C. "Your sense of identity has gone.

"The purpose of a national museum is not just to be a showplace of expensive things. It's a place where a society assembles, with the help of specialists, the items which give hands-on access to its identity."

Michael Ames, director of UBC's Museum of Anthropology, puts it this way: "You can repair oil wells, rebuild buildings, but you can't replace a national cultural heritage."

So many times throughout history people have learned the truth of these words. Think of proud Carthage and Corinth, ground to dust by Rome during the Third Punic War in 146 BC, the Incas and other Mesoamerican empires stripped of their gold by the Spanish in the 16th century, the religious art of native North Americans carried away by greedy collectors in the last 100 years.

During the Second World War, both sides lost cultural treasures in addition to the incalculable loss of human life. The new cathedral of St. Michael's in Coventry is a beautiful structure, but it can never replace the 14th-century basilica that was destroyed by German bombs in 1940. And the reconstructed Baroque buildings in Dresden will only ever be attractive copies of the original ones smashed by Allied bombs in 1945.

"For a nation it's like losing all the reference points that bind a people together," says George Macdonald, director of the Canadian Museum of Civilization in Ottawa. "Objects like the al-Sabah collection are reality anchors; looking at them is a way of communicating with your ancestors. Now that dialogue has been broken in Kuwait."

Macdonald believes that a culture is defined by "a whole package of esthetics" — precisely what the Kuwait museum contained before August 1990. A nation that loses its past also loses its directions to the future.

No one knows for certain what happened to the contents of the great museum in Kuwait City. British reporter Robert Fisk, writing in the London Independent shortly after Kuwait was liberated, described a ravaged, burning landscape that was "Hieronymous Bosch courtesy of the Iraqi army."

He wrote of walking through the "smoking embers" of the National Museum, outside of which a collection of "historic wooden boats had been burned to cinders." He said there were cartridge cases in the forecourt of the museum and bullet holes in its cracked walls, and that its national treasures had been looted.

The Islamic wing, added Fisk, "lay in ruins."

It was this wing, known as the House of Islamic Antiquities, that contained the 7,000-piece al-Sabah collection. According to scholar Marilyn Jenkins of New York's Metropolitan Museum of Art it "ranked with the other great Islamic collections of this art in Berlin, Leningrad, London, New York and Paris."

Islamic art developed over 1,300 years up to the 18th century in an area that extended from Spain and North Africa to Pakistan, India and the borders of China. It included such ancient Arab cultural centres as

Baghdad, Cairo and Istanbul. And its variety of design was enormous — everything from geometric patterns to calligraphy, from flowers and fruit patterns to animal figures. The materials used were as diverse as the design: wood, earthenware, porcelain, glass, wool, stone, rock crystal, forged and precious metals, gem stones.

A glance through the collection's glossy catalogue, published in 1983, shows how tragically easy it must have been to walk off with this art.

"We've heard accounts from colleagues that witnesses in Kuwait saw Iraqi army trucks backed up to the doors of the museum; the collection was thrown into cardboard boxes and that's the last we've heard of it," says Jack Rutland, director of exhibitions for the Trust for Museum Exhibitions in Washington, D.C. "It's devastating — just imagine what we'd feel if that happened to our own Metropolitan Museum."

Imagine what British Columbians would feel if all the Emily Carrs were stripped from the Vancouver Art Gallery or all the Haida carvings stolen from the Museum of Anthropology? The city would lose its visible link to what writer Allan Fotheringham once described as the "little village on the edge of the rainforest."

One fragment of good news for Kuwait is the fact that 107 items from the collection were on tour in the Soviet Union when Iraq invaded in August. The display has since moved to the U.S. for a five-city tour and opened March 16 in the Kimbell Art Museum in Fort Worth, Texas.

Canadians will get a chance to see the art when it comes to the Museum of Civilization in Ottawa in 1992.

The items on tour are a microcosm of the al-Sabah collection, spanning 1,000 years. There's a 10th-century marble column from southern Spain, for instance, its capital carved to represent a pale mass of tendrilling flowers; and from the 14th century, a basin raised from a sheet of Syrian bronze and inlaid with silver filigree; and a star-patterned Ushak carpet in shades of rust and sienna from 17th-century Turkey.

In his catalogue notes, Nasser explains how the objects in his collection had been scattered all over the world until he gathered them together in Kuwait — "near to their place of manufacture."

The artifacts from Falaika that were stored at the museum and the excavations on the ancient fortress itself have fared no better than Nasser's collection.

Joan Connelly explains that plans for a special gallery to house the Falaika treasures had been stalled since 1985, but were about to get going again when the war started. She says she still hasn't confirmed whether the objects in storage were also stolen by the Iraqis but she does know what happened to the little island off the coast. "It was heavily bombed," she says. Coalition bombs thundered down on to Failaka because it was occupied by Iraqi troops.

Angie al-Salem of the Citizens for a Free Kuwait, based in Washington, has even worse news: "Failaka was completely destroyed by the Iraqis before the bombing."

Connelly, for whom the excavation of Failaka is an abiding passion, says the small island (14 kilometres by five), with its woods and fresh water supply, was an ideal place for a military stronghold in ancient times. That's why the fortress was built there by the successors of Alexander the Great after his death in 323 B.C.

But the fortress was as vulnerable as it was valuable. It was buried under only a metre of sand and built of mud bricks.

As Kuwait struggles to rebuild itself, there is an optimistic and a pessimistic view of what may have happened to its cultural treasures.

"My hope is that the objects taken from the museum were properly packed and put in a safe place," observes Esin Atil, Islamic art historian at the Smithsonian Institution. "Maybe they are now in the hands of Iraqi scholars who will give them the same love and care as they give to precious objects from their own country."

Atil and other scholars hope the museum's collection will eventually be returned to Kuwait as part of the ceasefire conditions agreed to by Iraq.

Atil, who has held many of the museum's treasures in her hands, pondering their history, says: "When you pick up any object from the world of Islam you feel it is incredible it has survived so many turbulent times. And now this war. I can only hope there is peace again one day for all these treasures."

Moira Farrow, "The Spoils of War: Iraqi Soldiers Carried Away Kuwait's Heritage," Vancouver Sun, March 23, 1991.

NOVEMBER 24, 1991:
Mopping Up the Gulf War Mess

After the fighting was over, Southam News environment writer Anne McIlroy spent a month in Kuwait and Iraq examining efforts to clean up the devastation of Kuwait and southwestern Iraq. McIlroy also filed stories on the impact of the war on Iraqi women.

Anne McIlroy

SABRIYA OIL FIELDS, Kuwait — The lakes of heavy, black crude sink into the desert and stretch for miles. Where there are no lakes there are pools. Where there are no pools there is sludge.

Oil is everywhere in the flat northern reaches of Kuwait, blackening the sand, killing the vegetation, filling the air with a heavy, sickening smell. It is even worse in the south, where the oil well fires that darkened the country for eight months were the most intense.

The inferno is out but the thick, gooey legacy of Saddam Hussein's retreat from Kuwait lingers. Kuwaiti environmental officials are hoping to suck up the oil and refine it. But for now, they're still assessing what to do with the 252 oil lakes, many covering suspected mine fields.

"We have to find out how deep it's getting, and how it is affecting the food chain. We can't know that now," says Ibrahim Hadi, secretary of the Environmental Protection Council in Kuwait. He says as much oil fell back to earth from the oil fires — black rain from the dense, grey clouds — as was spilled into the Gulf during the six-week war that started in mid-January.

And that spill, let loose by Allied and Iraqi bombs during the war, was the largest in history.

Even the most conservative estimates now put it at 20 times the size of the 1989 Exxon Valdez disaster off the coast of Alaska: Four to eight million barrels in the Persian Gulf compared to 250,000 in Prince William Sound.

But while thousands of people worked to clean up the formerly pristine Alaska site, only a few hundred are involved in the Gulf, already heavily soiled from a long history of major spills. In this part of the world, dig in a beach and you find layers of oil from previous accidents.

As in the past, this time little is being done to clean up the oil, although the International Maritime Organization, a United Nations agency, has funded projects to test flushing methods.

"The effectiveness of the cleanup is really questionable," says John Walsh, an American-based environmentalist with the World Society for the Protection of Animals who toured the Saudi coast this fall.

He says the oil is matting on the surface, having a disastrous effect on productive intertidal zones and coastal marshes, which serve as fueling stations for migratory birds.

Tens of thousands of birds, which visit the Gulf during their migrations every year, have already been killed, says Walsh.

The mangroves, a critical nursery for sea life, have also been badly damaged.

"I think the mangroves may be totally beyond any recovery at this point," says John Robinson, with the National Oceanographic and Atmospheric Agency in the United States.

The Saudis have been criticized for being indifferent to the spill and caring only about a stretch of shore where the royal princes like to hunt rabbits.

Aramco, the Saudi Arabian oil company, has done much of the work so far but has refused to allow even Saudi environmental officials on the coastal land where the oil lies.

But there has been some progress. The Saudi government — which had said it shouldn't have to pay for the cleanup — recently pledged almost $500 million for a 15 to 20 month operation.

Saudi officials have defended their country's efforts. So far, 1.5 million barrels have been recovered, mostly to protect desalination plants, where sea water is transformed to drinking water.

The Saudis say another 1.7 million barrels are left on shore. Some scientists fear that huge amounts of oil, made heavy with sand and dust, have sunk to the bottom.

The combination of hydrocarbons in the oil, and chlorine used in the region's 16 desalination plants, could produce compounds hazardous to humans, says Randy Thomas, a Canadian environmentalist who went to Kuwait immediately after the war to assist in the cleanup.

But Badria Al Awadi, secretary for the Gulf countries' Regional

Organization for the Protection of the Marine Environment, says there is no reason for fear.

"We have been testing, and have no evidence that there is a problem."

Another invisible health threat may have been left by the allied armies. The United Kingdom's Atomic Energy Authority recently reported that 40 tonnes of depleted radioactive uranium was left in the battlefields of both Kuwait and Iraq.

Used in tens of thousands of armor-piercing rounds fired at Iraqi vehicles by allied tanks, the existence of the uranium has not yet been made public in Kuwait, although it could be a health risk and may seep into the food chain and water table.

Still another threat lies in the long-term impact of the smoke from the oil fires that Kuwaitis breathed for eight months.

Haluk Ozkaynak, with the Harvard School of Public Health, says that 10 per cent more people in Kuwait than usual will die this year because of the smoke. His study is based on the health effects of pollution in New York, and he says it is a conservative estimate.

But the long-term impact is still unknown. The World Health Organization is funding a study of 400 households in Kuwait.

"For now, the chronic implications, six months, nine months down the road is a hard thing to address," says Ozkaynak.

Meanwhile, some scientists have speculated the impenetrable smoke plume — that blocked out the sun over Kuwait for months and blackened snow in the Himalayas — will have a cooling effect on the entire region and delay the monsoon season in India.

But in Kuwait, the focus is on the kind of damage you can see. Reconstruction is proceeding at break-neck speed, the most visible signs of the war are in the desert, where hundreds of burned out armored personnel carriers lie in the sand, some spray painted with messages like "I love you, Mary."

In the south, hundreds of reinforced holes in the desert — Iraqi bunkers — are just as their inhabitants left them: with filthy bedding, Rambo cologne boxes, maps, records, boxes of magic markers and combat manuals, showing how to do everything from making a fist and firing an automatic weapon to committing suicide.

Near the Burgan oil fields, personnel files complete with pictures lay scattered in the dirt — perhaps the men who set the oil wells on fire or the hundreds of corpses firefighters buried in the desert.

The hot wind is filled with dust and the smell of oil. Turning around slowly, all you see is destruction.

Tony Burgess, a desert ecologist from Arizona who visited the region as part of a Friends of the Earth assessment team, says it could take centuries to recover. The worst-case scenario is that it never will.

Bolstered by the speedy international effort to put out the oil well fires, Al Badria and other Kuwaiti officials don't fear the worst. But they say it will take time and billions of dollars to mitigate the environmental impact of the Gulf War.

"When you destroy a building, you build it again. But when you hurt the environment like this, it can take generations," says Al Badria.

"I don't think it will ever be the same again."

Anne McIlroy, "Ecological Legacy of the Gulf War Sill Unknown in Iraq, Kuwait," the Ottawa Citizen, *November 21, 1991.*

AFGHANISTAN

CANADIAN COVERAGE OF THE AFGHANISTAN WAR CAN BE BROKEN DOWN
in two phases. The first began very soon after the attacks of September
11, when the Northern Alliance, with Western air support and help from
special forces teams, including Canadian snipers, began its drive to expel
the Taliban from Afghanistan. In this confusing period, journalists had
considerable freedom of movement and most believed the Afghan people
were happy to be "liberated" from the oppressive Islamist regime. On
March 4, 2002, the illusion that Western reporters were somewhat safe
in "liberated" areas came to an abrupt end when a man threw a bomb
or grenade into a car carrying *Toronto Star* reporter Kathleen Kenna,
her husband Hadi Dadashian, *Star* photographer Bernard Weil, and
their Afghan driver. The explosive landed under Kenna's car seat. The
explosion left her near death. Fast evacuation by American forces and
numerous surgeries saved her life.

In the second phase of the war, most Canadian reporters were housed
in the relative safety of Kandahar air base. A few, like Matthew Fisher
of CanWest (now PostMedia) News and Scott Taylor, publisher of *Esprit*

de Corps magazine, declined the military's protection and reported from Afghan cities and towns. Even the 20,000 military personnel at Kandahar airfield could not offer complete protection. The base was hit with sporadic rocket fire. Some reporters went on missions with Canadian soldiers at considerable risk to their own safety. On August 22, 2007, Radio-Canada reporter Patrice Roy and his camera operator-editor Charles Dubois were travelling in a military vehicle that was heavily damaged after hitting a roadside bomb west of Kandahar. Dubois had sustained a severe leg injury, while Roy was treated for shock. On December 30, 2009, just a few days after U.S. troops arrested a man for the attack on Kathleen Kenna, Michelle Lang of the *Calgary Herald* was killed along with four Canadian soldiers when an improvised explosive device was set off under their vehicle. Lang's colleagues covered her "ramp ceremony," the loading of coffins of fallen Canadian troops, onto a plane to return her to Canada.

NOVEMBER 11, 2001:
Advance of the Northern Alliance

Michael Petrou, a young reporter at the *Ottawa Citizen*, and a handful of Canadian journalists travelled relatively freely in territory held by the Northern Alliance as its troops captured Kabul and spread out through the country. With the support of U.S air support and special forces, along with Canadian JTF2 soldiers and army snipers, the Northern Alliance was able, at least temporarily, to drive al Qaeda and the Taliban out of Afghanistan. This gave Canadian reporters the opportunity to do some of the best front-line reporting in the war. Petrou returned to Afghanistan as a *Maclean's* magazine correspondent.

MICHAEL PETROU

Only people with nowhere else to go have remained in this village, whose inhabitants live literally in the shadow of war: When the sun sets in the west, nearby hills controlled by the Taliban block the sun and eclipse their homes.

Then the shooting starts.

"It is difficult to live here. The Taliban are always shooting at us," says Adbul Haq, whose mother was shot in August while tending the family's backyard garden.

The Taliban's closest trenches are almost two kilometres away. The chances of hitting anyone from such a distance are low, but this is not much consolation to Mr. Haq or others whose loved ones have died here.

Even as Mr. Haq speaks, squatting outside his house, shells are exploding in nearby fields. Mr. Haq estimates that more than 300 villagers have moved out over the past year. He fled, too, but couldn't find a job; he has no family outside Jilemkhar. He returned, and now lives in his mother's house.

"We have to live here," says Afkar Khan, another villager who left and came back. "We can't live in Hodja Bahauddin. There are no homes there and there is no work."

There is little work in Jilemkhar, either. And the houses here are primitive shelters of mud and straw. But it is difficult to leave your home when that is all you have. "I worry about my safety," says Ali Murad, a farmer who grows potatoes, rice and wheat.

"A few days ago they shot right over there," he says, pointing at a patch of grass and thorn bushes across the street. "Sometimes the bullets and bombs land right in my field."

Despite the dangers, Mr. Murad has no plans to leave. "I have a wife and seven children. My family would like to go somewhere else, but where can we live? We have been here for 45 years.

"Last year the Taliban surrounded this village. Some people fled to Hodja Bahauddin and I ran too. But I came back."

~~~

There is a road from Jilemkhar to the front-line trenches occupied by the Northern Alliance, but no one uses it: It runs through open fields, exposed to shells and stray bullets. Instead, villagers use a sunken creekbed that winds its way to the front; there, they are invisible to snipers.

But someone needs to work the fields. Today it is Mir Mahamad. A grown man with the thin, frail body of a 12-year-old, Mr. Mahamad wears rubber boots and an over-sized coat. An ethnic Uzbek in a village where almost everyone speaks Dari, he is lonely, even by the standards of a ghost town.

When I approach Mr. Mahamad, he is digging his wooden plow into the broken earth. Two massive oxen, yoked together, are pulling the plough. "I am afraid here," he says. "The Taliban drop bombs and shoot machine-guns here. But this is my job. There's nothing else I can do.

"Twenty days ago a Taliban bomb landed in the next field. I threw myself on the ground. Whenever the Taliban shoot, I hide."

I have been speaking with Mr. Mahamad for 15 minutes. Already my guide is getting edgy: We are in an open field with no cover.

~~~

Soldiers take turns spending the night in the trenches near Chagapay. But it is impossible to sleep there: The Taliban are too close. Even during the day it is impossible to relax, although the soldiers try, sharing food, cracking jokes and trying to ignore the explosions around us.

Most of the heavy shells are landing well in front of us or behind us. Mortars, however, can demolish a trench. And they are terrifying.

In the trench opposite ours the Taliban begin their mortar attack. The shell makes a loud, hollow bang when it is fired. Then there is 10 seconds of silence as the shell arcs high above our heads and begins its descent. It is enough time to seek cover. Enough time to feel sick. Enough time to pray. Soldiers near me wrap their arms around each other and huddle as deep in the trench as they can. I curl up into a ball with my arms around my head and my face pressed between two Kalashnikov assault rifles.

A few more seconds pass like heart beats, then a dull explosion is heard safely behind us. We unravel ourselves and pass around a bag of nuts and raisins. It is now early afternoon. Those in the trench now will be here until dawn, when they are to be relieved.

"I can't sleep here," says Gulboden, a Northern Alliance soldier whose black beard is flecked with grey. "All night I lie with my gun over the trench and I watch. I sleep for about three hours in the morning.

Michael Petrou, the Ottawa Citizen, *November 11, 2001.*

MARCH 28, 2006:
Law and Order, After a Fashion, in Kandahar

Christie Blatchford, one of Canada's best crime writers and newspaper columnists, won a Governor General's Award for Literature for her book on the Canadian mission to Afghanistan, *Fifteen Days: Stories of Bravery, Friendship, Life and Death from Inside the New Canadian Army*, published in 2007 by Doubleday Canada.

CHRISTIE BLATCHFORD

It was just a month ago that the so-called "night letter" was posted on the front gate of the Mir Bazaar Primary School in the south end of this demented and sprawling city.

A notorious instrument of terror in this part of the planet, the letter was addressed to both students and teachers, headmaster Mahmood Khan said yesterday. He filed the original with the Education Department and ultimately with the Afghan National Police, but keeps a copy of the incident report.

A rough translation of the note is as follows: "Don't come to school. If you don't stop, you will be killed like the others who are not following orders of the Taliban."

Overnight, the students and teachers disappeared, Mr. Khan said. He appealed to the government, and soon a little ANP checkpoint was established next door.

The ANP is as yet an imperfect police force — many officers aren't trained and have little equipment, and many, as with those at the school checkpoint yesterday, haven't been paid in months — but it nonetheless provides a measure of law and order in a country accustomed in its recent history to virtually none.

In this instance, it was enough: The students — 410 of them in Grades 1 through 6 — and 13 teachers came marching back as soon as it was safe to do so. Now, there's a waiting list of youngsters who want to come here, as there is for schools all over Afghanistan, which has one of the lowest literacy rates in the developing world and an education system decimated by almost three decades of war and insurgency.

The fact that only four weeks ago, the Taliban was still threatening people — and still had clout enough to do it successfully — is a useful reminder that despite the long periods of relative calm in this part of the country, Kandahar city remains a very dangerous place.

It's a lesson not lost on the Canadian soldiers based at the Provincial Reconstruction Team compound on the outskirts of the city. A satellite operation of Kandahar Air Field, where most of Canada's 2,000 troops are stationed, the PRT is staffed by about 250 infantrymen from the Princess Patricia's Canadian Light Infantry, Second Battalion, Bravo Company, which is based in Shilo, Man.

Like all the Canadians here, B Company has a complicated mission with two heads — the first, to bring security to Kandahar city, because without that there is nothing, and the second, to engage Afghans in the rebuilding of their own nation and help them do it.

The visit to the Mir Bazaar school yesterday — the school is like virtually everything else in Kandahar, a city that appears modelled after a 1950s-era North American motel strip in that virtually all of it is low-lying and one-level, but here built of mud, with the school classrooms resembling baseball dugouts — was a "psy op."

That's short for "psychological operation," because Lieutenant Ryan Palmer, a 24-year-old reservist with the Calgary Highlanders, was along to hand out a propaganda sheet (with a colourful comic strip urging locals to report terrorist activities, explosives finds and the like) and gifts of notebooks, red pencils and Afghanistan puzzle maps to the impoverished school.

But despite its secondary purpose, the patrol was like any other in Kandahar city — intense, fraught with peril, chaotic and not a little confusing and terrifying to both soldiers and locals alike.

Kandahar is Afghanistan's second-largest city. Its streets and alleys range from so narrow that army vehicles are but inches from the nearest mud walls to wide roundabouts into which all manner of traffic — donkey carts, the motorized rickshaws known as tuk-tuks, the vast fleet of dented yellow and white taxis, lavishly decorated jingle trucks with their colourful skirts, motorcycles and bicycles, wheelbarrows, horse and buggies and legions of gorgeous darting children and other pedestrians — flows at speed and with abandon and steely resolve to claim the right of way.

Kandahar province is the most illiterate in this nation; the National Risk and Vulnerability Assessment done three years ago by the World Food Program on rural Afghanistan — and four of five Afghans live in the countryside — revealed that of those citizens over the age of six, only 12 per cent of males in this province and zero per cent of females were able to read and write.

That means that the Canadian convoys can post "stay away" signs on their vehicles — those bringing up the rear of every convoy do now, and since the fatal shooting earlier this month of a local man during a night patrol, these signs are being improved — until the goats come home, and a great portion of the population will never have a clue what they say.

The Canucks here have improvised rather brilliantly, although making much more nerve-wracking work for themselves than shooting first and asking questions later would ever cause.

On our psy-op yesterday, for instance, Private Nick Kerr, a 24-year-old from Victoria, B.C., who was the gunner in the turret of my G-wagon, kept a load of full water bottles within reach, and whenever a vehicle came too close or failed to yield, he would wing one of these out at the offending car.

In addition, although Pte. Kerr was armed to the teeth — a general-purpose machine gun mounted in the swiveling turret and the Canuck's standard-issue rifle at hand — his weapons of first resort were his stash of water bottles and his biggest, loudest voice.

"*Wa dariga,*" he yelled. "*Sha ta sa! Sha ta sa!*" — or in English, "Stop" and "Stay back."

It requires great patience and restraint to do this, for Kandahar is the former stronghold of the Taliban; suicide bombings, ambush and improvised explosive devices, or IEDs, are real and proven threats, and that which appears benign here is not always so.

Yet Pte. Kerr used his own smarts, and with the cool and seasoned voice of patrol commander, Sergeant Jason Pickard, guiding him over the radio — calmly evaluating everything within view with a comforting, "It's okay, there are kids in the car," or "The guy on the motorcycle was on that cell before we arrived," or "Nothing in that wheelbarrow" — all ended well.

We were able to visit the Mir Bazaar school, and another, a private English-language school near Kandahar U which is, that rarest of facilities here, actually co-educational, with 11 female students out of about 40, including sisters Yalda and Salda, respectively 13 and 11, both of whom plan to be doctors, like their mother.

The girls and I chatted. The pencils and gifts were given out. I engaged in a necklace exchange with a handsome and flirty teenager wearing an ANP uniform; when it was over, I had the interpreter tell him that in Canada, such an exchange meant we were now married, and that he was very unlucky to have a very old wife, setting off howls of laughter. It was all fun and games in the hot spring sun, with no one and nothing the worse for wear but for Pte. Kerr's voice, which by the time we returned to the PRT was a thin rasp.

The National Investigation Service probe into the shooting of that poor Afghan almost three weeks ago is winding to a conclusion. I think it is frankly a miracle that in these difficult and complex circumstances, Canadian soldiers have not reached for their weapons — their real ones, their guns — many more times.

Christie Blatchford, "Law and Order, After a Fashion, in Kandahar," the Globe and Mail, *March 28, 2006.*

JUNE 27, 2008:
"I Was Very Happy When I Killed People"

Alex Panetta, a member of Canadian Press's Ottawa bureau, was a member of the CP team that was deployed in Afghanistan throughout the war.

ALEXANDER PANETTA

A former Taliban fighter has provided a gripping first-hand account of being secretly trained by members of the Pakistani military, paid $500 a month and ordered to kill foreigners in Afghanistan.

Mullah Mohammed Zaher offered a vivid description of a bomb-making apprenticeship at a Pakistani army compound where he says he learned to blow up NATO convoys.

He's one of three former Taliban fighters introduced to The Canadian Press by an Afghan government agency that works at getting rebels to renounce the insurgency.

Zaher insists he was neither forced to go public with his story nor coached by Afghan officials, whose routine response to terrorism on their soil is to blame Pakistan.

Pakistan officially sides with the West against the insurgents and vigorously denies that it aids the war on terror.

A report produced for the Pentagon and released this month by the Rand Corp., a U.S. think-tank, claims individuals in the Pakistani government are involved in helping the insurgents.

Zaher has not seen the 177-page report. But he made claims that supported its conclusions — and offered new details.

He described how men in army fatigues housed, fed, paid and threatened insurgents into carrying out attacks on foreign troops.

Most startling was his description of the repeated warning from Pakistani soldiers about where trainees would be sent if they refused to fight: Guantanamo Bay.

Two other former insurgents said they were aware of colleagues being trained in Pakistan, but said such fighters were part of an elite minority.

Mullah Janan said he heard that some of his Taliban comrades had received training in Pakistan, with many more receiving shelter or medical treatment across the border.

When infighting broke out between Taliban factions, Janan said, mediators from Pakistan even came across the border to help.

Zaher said he was among the elite minority being trained.

He said he arrived in 2003 for his first of several training sessions at a walled military compound in the Nawakilli area outside Quetta, Pakistan.

He said he was greeted warmly by men in military fatigues, introduced to his fellow trainees and taken to a building where for the next 20 days he would eat, sleep and learn the finer points of waging jihad.

He said he remembers only the last name of the man in the khaki uniform, Khattak, who presided over the orientation session.

The man told his pupils their homeland had been invaded again by non-Muslims, just as it had been by the Soviets in the 20th century and the British in the 19th.

Zaher said the group was told that the infidels had been stopped before and they must be stopped again.

"You are supposed to get good training here — and you are supposed to go and kill them there," Zaher recalled being told.

"We have to kick their asses out of Afghanistan and send them back to their own country … We have to fix mines for them, destroy them and get them out of Afghanistan."

Zaher said he learned to produce a variety of explosives. They ranged from a crude bomb with wiring and fertilizer stuffed into a plastic jug, to more sophisticated remote-controlled devices: "I can even make a bomb by buying stuff at the bazaar — for $10."

Zaher said he attended three sessions at the compound, lasting from 20 days to two months.

On a typical day, the half-dozen trainees would have breakfast at 10 a.m., lunch at 2 p.m., and spend every other waking hour learning how to kill foreigners.

Zaher said he doesn't know how many soldiers died from the bombs he planted on roads in Zhari, Panjwaii, Khakrez and Maywand districts of Kandahar province. And he said he has no idea whether the vehicles he blew up were Canadian, American or British.

He showed no remorse.

On the contrary, his dark eyes softened, his smile sparkled and his nasal voice quivered with excitement as he listed the places where he had ended enemies' lives.

"Sure, I've killed many foreigners," he said. "I was very happy when I killed people. That was supposed to be my task — and it made me very happy."

Zaher said he doesn't know much about Canada except that it's a foreign country.

The Canadian military began moving operations from Kabul to Kandahar in August 2005, initially establishing a provincial reconstruction team. By February 2006, some 2,000 Canadian troops had arrived and taken charge of security in Kandahar province.

Zaher said he left the insurgency about two and a half years ago — around the time the Canadians entered Kandahar in force.

He wanted to come back home.

Upon being offered amnesty under the Afghan government's reconciliation program, he crammed his family and a few possessions into their Mazda minivan, rolled out of Pakistan in the middle of the night and moved into Kandahar city's District 6.

Zaher has since trimmed his once-bountiful beard and turfed his turban in favour of a white skull cap. But he eagerly showed off old pictures of himself holding rocket launchers, AK-47 assault rifles and dressed in trademark Taliban garb.

The Rand Corp. report offered several reasons why certain elements in the Pakistani government would support the Taliban.

Islamic militancy is only one of those factors, wrote Seth Jones, the report's author.

His report said Pakistanis want to continue exerting more influence in Afghanistan than their arch-nemesis, India — an emerging economic superpower that has helped bankroll a number of construction projects including Afghanistan's new parliament building.

Jones suggested some people in Pakistan may want to hedge their bets in Afghanistan in case of a NATO defeat, maintaining close ties to the rebels as a backup plan.

Mullah Mohammed Zaher says he's a former Taliban commander who was trained in Pakistan. Briefly, here's what he says he did:

2001: Loses job as a Taliban commander when regime collapsed.

2003: Tired of being harassed by local officials hostile to the Taliban, he moves his wife and 10 children to Quetta, Pakistan. He is urged to visit a Pakistani army compound in Nawakilli, outside Quetta. He says he is paid $500 a month, given a motorbike and a rent-free house, and trained to kill foreigners. For more than two years, he criss-crosses the border, planting bombs against NATO convoys in Kandahar province.

Winter 2005–2006: He leaves the insurgency, moves his family back to Kandahar city under an amnesty program.

Alexander Panetta, The Canadian Press, June 27, 2008.

DECEMBER 27, 2009:
The Justice I Want for Captive 783

Kathleen Kenna started her career at the *Toronto Star* as Ontario regional reporter, then moved through the ranks as assistant city editor, assignment editor, and entertainment editor. She accepted a posting as the *Star*'s India bureau correspondent just a few months before the 9/11 attacks. Kenna roamed Afghanistan in the opening weeks of the war with her husband, Hadi Dadashian, *Star* photographer Bernard Weil, and an Afghan driver. On the road from Kabul to Gardez a man threw a bomb into Kenna's car. The blast nearly killed her. She was given so much blood by the Americans who rescued her that Kenna's blood type changed from O positive to O negative. After years of surgery and therapy, she returned to university to learn how to work with injured war vets. Two days after this piece was published, reporter Michelle Lang of the *Calgary Herald* was killed by an improvised explosive device.

KATHLEEN KENNA

I was flat on my back for my first bone density screening recently, when the technician asked, "What is THAT?"

"Oh," I said. "I forgot to tell you about the shrapnel."

She showed me the scan: There were more than a dozen chunks of something sprinkled inside my abdomen.

It's fascinating, in a way.

Eight years after being ambushed in an alleged Al Qaeda attack while covering the Afghanistan war for the *Star*, I can still be surprised by its impact on my life.

The bits are parts of the vehicle, and perhaps the grenade or improvised explosive device, remaining from that March 4, 2002 attack.

They looked different than the last time I had a torso X-ray, for my final reconstructive surgery in 2003.

That time, the technician gasped and rushed to fetch help.

Her reaction seemed alarming enough, until the radiologist appeared, checked the X-ray, and also gasped.

"What is THAT?" she asked.

Despite more than a dozen surgeries on three continents after the attack, I had not seen any X-rays of the damage that left me permanently disabled.

I looked at an image that appeared to be a flurry of snowflakes.

Fascinating.

My trauma surgeon at Vancouver General Hospital — who had removed shrapnel from places I won't mention — later explained the "snowflakes" were too tiny to be removed.

Dislodging them would just create more risks, he explained.

No problem — it's not as if I ever want surgery again.

I'm sharing these anecdotes because of the pending trial of Abdul Zahir.

He's a man alleged to have been one of several attackers who lobbed an explosive device into a jeep in which I was travelling with my husband, Hadi Dadashian, *Star* photographer Bernard Weil, and an Afghan driver.

We were returning from an afternoon of interviews with villagers near Zirmat, southeast of Kabul. They were digging wells in the desert, in the shadow of aerial bombers.

Zahir is alleged to have been involved in the attack, which almost killed us.

We know little about the man tagged as "Guantanamo Captive 753."

He's estimated to be 37 years old. According to the Pentagon charge sheet, Zahir is an alleged Al Qaeda translator and "money courier," who allegedly worked with the Al Qaeda leadership.

Zahir is alleged to have paid Al Qaeda and Taliban terrorists. The conspiracy charges against him state that he willingly joined Usama [*sic*] bin Laden and was committed to murder and others acts of terrorism against Americans.

He was captured in Afghanistan in July 2002, and has been held at Guantanamo Bay since then.

For almost eight years, we have all waited for justice.

We don't seek retribution. We've made it clear we cannot identify our attackers.

We seek real justice, not a contrived justice.

My conscience is divided: As a woman committed to social justice in everyday life, I want a public trial at a court where the defendant would enjoy the same rights to which we're entitled under American and international law. As someone horribly wounded, then disabled, by the explosion, I want as fair a trial as possible at a time of war.

But war changes how justice might be served.

Ordinarily, a citizen must be "read his rights" at the time of arrest, or the charges might be dismissed at court. A prisoner-of-war may not have had any such notice of rights, given the nature of the battle zone, and the conditions of arrest.

We know nothing about Zahir's arrest, but he was held at Guantanamo without charges for almost four years — far longer than is normally allowed under peacetime law.

Unlike those awaiting criminal trials, Zahir was held without access to a lawyer of his choice, without a chance to tell his family his whereabouts.

He wasn't charged with war crimes until Jan. 2006: attacking civilians, aiding the enemy, and conspiracy.

I don't believe in indefinite detention without trial.

However, with all the legal challenges to the Guantanamo detentions, and the military commissions that would try some of the detainees, my expectations for justice have cooled.

The Pentagon has assured us, almost annually since his arrest, that this would be the year of Zahir's trial.

My husband and I hoped this meant true justice would be served, and also hoped it brought us all closer to the shutdown of Guantanamo. We agree with Vice-President Joe Biden's assessment of the prison camp as one of the best recruiting tools for terrorists.

We're not lawyers, nor armchair arbiters of how the men of war from Afghanistan should be treated by the United States.

After living in a war zone for months in Afghanistan, and closely following the war's progress since then, we have strong convictions that any prisoner-of-war should be treated with dignity, and afforded all the rights guaranteed by the Geneva Conventions and international human rights laws.

It's what we would demand for any Canadian, American or other citizen — whether combatant or aid worker — captured and held in a country of war. It's what we want for Zahir and all the Guantanamo detainees.

We don't know if Zahir was waterboarded or subjected to any of the other awful interrogation methods reported on so vividly by media worldwide. We hope not.

We believe that he has met privately with teams from the International Commission of the Red Cross (ICRC), and that his needs and comfort are met in ways similar to that of prisoners in American prisons.

The International Commission of the Red Cross keeps such visits confidential, but we are satisfied with their assurances that Guantanamo inmates can write to their families, send photos, and have minimal contact with the outside world.

We were encouraged by President Barack Obama's declaration that he would close Guantanamo by late January, 2010.

There are no easy solutions to the transfer of detainees — witness Obama's admission that the U.S. can't meet that closing date — but we don't want Zahir released without trial.

He is, after all, alleged to have been involved in the attempted murder of four unarmed civilians in our vehicle.

I can't guess the attackers' motives: Perhaps men in his neighbourhood that day saw all intruders as the same and lashed out. The nearby aerial bombing — in a mountainous region where Osama bin Laden was believed to be hiding — had drawn streams of fighters alleged to be Al Qaeda, and we might have appeared to be just another part of that war mix.

We were heartened earlier this year, when President Obama announced that every case of the Guantanamo detainees would be reviewed, and the military tribunals suspended pending further review.

Although this added many more months, and perhaps years, of delay to Zahir's anticipated trial, we appreciated the opportunity for more fairness — for another review of the evidence against one of our alleged attackers, and a re-assessment of the military commission system.

Military tribunals have been used by the United States since the Civil War, yet I'm uneasy about the amount of secrecy and classified information that might be involved.

Unlike the criminal system we would face if charged with attempted murder, Zahir doesn't have the same chance to answer evidence against him. There may be classified evidence that he won't be able to see, for reasons of national security.

Unlike American criminal defendants at court, Zahir's lawyers can't cross-examine everyone who offered information against him.

While information gained through torture is no longer admissible (as it was under President George Bush's administration), hearsay and hearsay-on-hearsay evidence still might be deemed admissible by the military judge overseeing Zahir's trial.

Its source could be kept secret, to protect American and allied soldiers, intelligence officers and others here and overseas.

Because of such controversial differences, military tribunals have been decried as "kangaroo courts."

Can a trial of an "enemy combatant" be fair if the judge, jury, prosecution and defence lawyers are all from the same military fighting in the detainee's country?

We were pleased with the announcement of upcoming trials in New York of Khalid Sheik Mohammed, self-proclaimed architect of the 9/11 massacre, and four other self-avowed terrorists, all current Guantanamo detainees.

This trial opens the door to justice for the rest of the detainees, their victims and the families of their victims.

It might speed the military trial of Zahir. Or it might provoke more legal challenges that lead to more delay.

I am confident it will help the world see more clearly the motivation of self-proclaimed terrorists, and the dangers of their ideology to all of us.

We share the security concerns of some families of 9/11 victims who oppose bringing the five detainees to New York, but we still welcome open trials.

A just people should not fear true justice.

Kathleen Kenna, "The Justice I Want for Captive 783," the Toronto Star, *December 27, 2009.*

DECEMBER 29, 2009:
Civilians Flock to Kandahar for Experience, Pay

The day after this story was published in the *Calgary Herald* and other papers in the CanWest chain, Michelle Lang and four Canadian soldiers were killed in an improvised explosive device blast.

MICHELLE LANG

Last month, hair stylist Vanessa Mead packed up her scissors and her life in Fredericton to try her hand at a new job: combat barber.

The 25-year-old now spends her days giving close-cropped haircuts to soldiers at the Canadian Forces' barber shop at Kandahar Airfield. She's only been here four weeks, but Mead has already donned a flak vest and flown to a forward operating base where she gave troops on the front lines a trim.

"It's an adventure," says Mead of her decision to leave New Brunswick for a six-month job in a conflict zone. "I wanted to help, even in a minuscule way."

Mead is one of nearly 4,500 civilians from around the world who have left family and their home countries to work at Kandahar Airfield, the massive NATO military base in this southern province of Afghanistan.

They deliver pizza, work construction and provide a long list of other services that keep the airfield — which is the size of a small city at a population of 20,000 — running smoothly.

For some contractors, money is the motivating factor behind their move to Kandahar Airfield. Companies are willing to pay people top dollar to put their lives on hold and live in Afghanistan for several months — or longer.

Other civilians say they were looking for a new experience and wanted to do their part to support the soldiers here.

Sandy Keeler was inspired to come to Kandahar after she became friends with Capt. Trevor Greene, the Canadian soldier who was seriously injured in 2006 when he was struck in the head with an axe during a meeting with village elders.

Keeler, who met Greene while she was working in Vancouver with a brain injury organization, now works for the military's personnel and family support services in a variety of roles.

"For me, it's not the money at all," said Keeler. "For me, it was Capt. Trevor Greene. I feel honoured I was selected to come."

But leaving worried family and friends behind in Canada is often tough, although civilians who come to Kandahar Airfield quickly realize the base is relatively safe — except for an occasional rocket attack.

Marry Morrow, a grandmother from Kingston, Ont., said her daughter frets about her safety.

"She hears stories on the news and thinks there are all kinds of things going on here," said Morrow, who works as a switchboard operator at the airfield's communications centre.

Morrow admits she was "shocked for about a week" when she first arrived last May. The drab, rocky base with endless rows of tents and shipping containers had none of the greenery she was accustomed to at home.

For the most part, though, Morrow is enjoying her time here. The noise from fighter jets doesn't disturb her sleep and she spends her free time reading and watching television – just like at home.

"The people here are great. There are so many different cultures," she says. My plan is to stay until June of 2011."

Surprisingly, recruiting contractors to work here isn't as difficult as it may seem. Jan Kwasniewski, who manages part of the Canadian Forces' personal and family support services, said he has filled the 77 available civilian jobs at Kandahar Airfield until August of next year.

Of course, not every employee comes to Afghanistan works out but Kwasniewski notes "that's true of every job."

Most complete their six-month stint with no problems and some employees want to come back. "I have people who have been here three times," he says.

Kwasniewski said the wages are higher at home for comparable jobs, but he doesn't say how much higher. It doesn't hurt that a portion of his employees' salaries are tax-free. "Some do come for the money," says Kwasniewski, "but a lot of people say they come for the adventure."

Michelle Lang, "Civilians Flock to Kandahar for Experience, Pay," the Calgary Herald, *December 29, 2009.*

DECEMBER 11, 2010:
Taliban By Conviction or Convenience; Afghan Hearts and Minds not Easily Swayed

MURRAY BREWSTER

The man in the white cloak and turquoise striped turban didn't want to be photographed, and pleaded that his name remain a secret.

That's always a sign around here, but not necessarily a good one.

"If you write my name, by the evening my throat will be slit," the villager with anxious eyes said through an interpreter. A young boy of about 10 stood at his elbow.

"Not only me, but they will kill my family. The Taliban know my face."

Just moments earlier, the man had stood shoulder to shoulder with the governor of Panjwaii district in an interview with a western journalist. He'd given his name and offered his support to Haji Baran, who'd come to put the Afghan government's stamp on this enmeshed little corner of Kandahar province.

He was introduced by the district chief as a supporter of the Taliban with two sons active in the insurgency, prompting nearby Canadian military officers to scribble furiously in their notebooks. The man — in his 40s and well-dressed, compared with his companions — said he believed in his heart the future was with the government.

"I have 100 per cent confidence in Haji Baran, the district leader, that he will support me and keep the promise he has made," the man said.

Whether the man was Taliban by conviction or convenience wasn't clear.

Baran said he'd received assurances that the man would "support us until the day he has one drop of blood left in his body."

The words were no sooner out their mouths before the man started to tiptoe backwards.

The scene neatly captures the conundrum NATO faces as it pushes westward in Kandahar province into former Taliban stronghold areas such as Zangabad, which was taken over this week by Canadian troops.

The soldiers will be slowly clawing their way through the region known as the Horn of Panjwaii over the next few weeks.

The bigger strategy is to push governance and development aid through the narrow window of calm that has overtaken southern Afghanistan with the arrival of winter. Once there, the people who've lived under the sandal of the Taliban for years will come to accept their federal government.

But turning over the former insurgent haven will require more than just armoured vehicles and truckloads of dollars.

Canadian Brig.-Gen. Dean Milner was cautious in his assessment.

"There are those who want to reintegrate because they realize we have the momentum," he said. "The time is right for this country to move on."

Baran, a wily tribal elder and former militia commander, offered up his own form of personal immunity for the Taliban and supporters willing to submit and join the reconciliation.

"I have given them full assurance that I will protect you and the Afghan government will protect you," Baran told them. But he also added a warning to NATO forces.

"I can tell you it will make me sad, it will make me angry, if they are touched and being bothered."

At a sparsely attended public meeting held on the grounds behind a madrassa — or school — dating from the Taliban era, Zangabad elders sat cross-legged, sipped Diet Pepsi and listened to Baran make his pitch.

But the shadows of the hard line Islamist movement were everywhere.

The walls of the school, now occupied by Canadian troops, were etched with ghostly slogans urging the faithful to pray five times a day and describing Shiite Muslims as infidels. The Taliban is a Sunni movement.

Baran recalled the days when the Taliban would execute people by hanging them in the trees on the grounds.

At least two of the 17 men attending the meeting were thought to be Taliban spies. They asked few questions and offered even fewer answers when queried by curious Afghan soldiers and interpreters.

"I did see some Taliban representation," Baran said. "I can tell about 50 per cent of these people have either been insurgents or they have been involved with the insurgency, (but) they are more than welcome to come and reconcile with the Afghan government."

Earlier in the day, four insurgents had gone door-to-door in the freshly taken village and warned residents not to attend Baran's meeting.

Instead of the usual cacophony of demands for schools, medical clinics and wells, the biggest ask in Zangabad was for the release of prisoners.

A patrol of newly arrived troops from the 1st Battalion, Royal 22e Regiment battle group took up to five prisoners in the region earlier this week, two of which turned out to be bona fide insurgents. The Taliban's deputy shadow governor for the province was also apparently picked up in a special forces raid a few days ago.

One man at the public meeting complained his two sons had been taken in a raid on the family compound.

"We will make sure and investigate about these detainees we were not aware of," Baran said. "We'll find out after the investigation whether they were innocent people. If they are found guilty and were committing crimes, then the Afghan government will deal with them."

Milner conceded that sometimes Canadian troops have detained the wrong person, but they work quickly to rectify the mistakes.

"Ninety per cent of the time we're right in who we take," he said. "As you know, sometimes there are insurgents around here planting IEDs and we have pretty clear evidence. But there are some times and I have actually handed back some detainees."

Murray Brewster, The Canadian Press, December 11, 2010.

NOVEMBER 12, 2011:
Nothing Induces Melancholy Like the Skirl of a Lone Piper

Matthew Fisher, son of Second World War veteran and Press Gallery dean Douglas Fisher, became an expert on the Afghan War by sloughing off the protection of the military and risking his life wandering the country. Fisher remained in the country longer than most Western journalists and earned the respect of his peers and combat soldiers. In this piece, Fisher ably sums up the mixed feelings of troops and reporters as they prepared to leave Afghanistan at the end of the Canadian combat mission in Kandahar. Fisher tallies the country's losses and leaves the reader to decide whether they're confident the effort was a waste of blood and money.

Matthew Fisher

I have lost count of how many times I have heard a piper's lament for a fallen Canadian at Kandahar Airfield. At a guess, it must be more than 50 times.

My mother served in the Royal Canadian Navy in Britain during the blitz. My father landed at Normandy and found his way across the Low Countries and into Germany by the spring of 1945. Their best friend, Tom Miller, a Halifax navigator whose bomber was shot down twice, was the first Canadian to be receive the George Medal — from King George himself — and subsequently spent four years as a prisoner of war.

So, Canada's many wars were much discussed in our household and Remembrance Day was always of special importance. But Remembrance Day only became extremely personal for me when I got to Afghanistan, where I have attended scores of ramp ceremonies in Kandahar and several Remembrance Day memorials, including the last one Friday.

I first arrived in Kandahar in April 2002 a few days after the first four Canadians to die in Afghanistan were killed in a friendly-fire incident at Tarnak Farms. The dynamic was much different back then. The Taliban were regrouping in Pakistan at that time and that first Canadian mission was mostly about scouring the mountains for Osama bin Laden and his hideouts.

In October 2003, Robbie Beerenfenger and Robert Short became the first two Canadians to die in combat in Afghanistan and the first to die in an improvised explosive device attack — the IEDs that were soon to become infamous as the Taliban's weapon of choice.

I had a nodding acquaintance with these two soldiers, but they were friends of Stephen Thorne of The Canadian Press, who did a great and brave job of reporting Canada's early years in Afghanistan, when there was little media or political interest in the conflict.

The next Canadian to die was diplomat Glyn Berry in January 2006. Only a couple of weeks before Glyn was killed by a suicide bomber in Kandahar City, we had been roommates in a mud hut high in the mountains near the Pakistani border on a madcap undertaking with a squadron of Royal Canadian Dragoons. It was impossible to not get caught up in his exuberance.

Soon after Glyn was killed, Canadian combat troops moved back to Kandahar in large numbers for a combat mission. At the same time, the Taliban returned to the South in strength and, almost immediately, Canada's death rate accelerated rapidly and public interest in Canada's first war since Korea became much more intense.

Coverage of ramp ceremonies in Kandahar, guards of honour at Canadian Forces Base Trenton in Ontario and convoys of hearses travelling on Canada's Highway of Heroes became commonplace, as one Canadian died every 10 days on average between the spring of 2006 and the summer of 2010. That was when, with substantial U.S. help, Canada finally pushed the Taliban out of the fighting districts to the west and south of Kandahar City and the casualty rate began to drop.

Inevitably, I knew quite a few of the Canadian soldiers who have died here. One of them was Maj. Yannick Pepin, who spoke very eloquently after the deaths of several of his sappers before the combat engineer was killed himself in an IED strike a few weeks later.

I also knew Michelle Lang, the *Calgary Herald* journalist who was killed along with four Canadian soldiers when their vehicle detonated a huge homemade bomb on a muddy road south of Kandahar City on Dec. 30, 2009. Optimistic, cheerful and brimming with excitement for her work, Michelle had been my Christmas replacement. In her short time in Afghanistan, she had already greatly impressed the troops.

Except for a few months in 2006, when two Canadian battle groups were heavily involved in close combat in Kandahar, it has been a highly impersonal war, fought largely with IEDs and suicide bombers on one side, and increasingly on the other by unmanned aerial missile platforms that launch rockets from the sky.

As in other wars, the Canadians fought well in Afghanistan in often very difficult circumstances. They behaved humanely and with dignity. After a slow start, their sector in Kandahar was largely pacified months before the last combat troops were withdrawn in July.

Since the combat mission began 5 1/2 years ago, tangible progress has been made by Canadian soldiers, diplomats and development specialists in schooling and health care and Canada spent $50 million on a project that has provided water to give Kandaharis a chance to flourish economically. Furthermore, the original goal of preventing al Qaeda from running terrorist training camps in the South has been realized.

For that cause, 158 Canadian soldiers and two civilians have given their lives. Was their sacrifice worth it? I think so, although their sacrifices are a tragedy and I understand the excruciating sorrow of their families and friends who will always ache for them.

Along with hundreds of others, I remembered all of Canada's Afghan war dead one last time at Kandahar Airfield on Friday. I shall think of them often, but from this day on I hope to never again hear the skirl of a lone Canadian piper playing a dirge in Afghanistan.

Matthew Fisher, The Canadian Press, November 12, 2011.

IMAGE CREDITS

Page 40: Carte de Nouvelle France, Jésuites, 1657, *Novae Franciae accurata delineatio*, Bressani, Francesco Giuseppe (1612–1672).

Page 53: Courtesy of the Royal Ontario Museum.

Page 54: Courtesy of the Royal Ontario Museum.

Page 76: Courtesy of the Royal Ontario Museum.

Page 87: Steel image by T.B. Welch in Charles J. Peterson, *Military Heroes of the War of 1812* (Philadelphia: William A. Leary & Co., 1849).

Page 113: Alexander von Erichsen. Courtesy of the Fort Erie Museum, Ridgeway.

Page 116: Alexander von Erichsen. Courtesy of the Fort Erie Museum Ridgeway.

Page 118: Alexander von Erichsen. Courtesy of the Fort Erie Museum, Ridgeway.

Page 121: Courtesy of Library and Archives Canada, C-00261.

Page 125: Courtesy of Library and Archives Canada, C-003458.

Page 148: Courtesy of Library and Archives Canada, PA-130112.

Page 159: Courtesy of Library and Archives Canada, PA-002402.

Page 163: Courtesy of Library and Archives Canada, PA-002217.

Page 215: Courtesy of Library and Archives Canada, PA-131506.

Page 225: Courtesy of Library and Archives Canada, PA-115568.

Page 228: Courtesy of Library and Archives Canada, PA-116586.

Page 228: Courtesy of Library and Archives Canada, PA 132192.

Page 242: Courtesy of Library and Archives Canada, PA-201345.

Page 246: Courtesy of Library and Archives Canada, PA-130610.

Page 264: Courtesy of Library and Archives Canada, PA-137140.

Page 280: Courtesy of Library and Archives Canada, PA-170777.

Page 282: Courtesy of Library and Archives Canada, PA-133320.

Page 283: Courtesy of Library and Archives Canada, PA-134415.

Page 285: Courtesy of Library and Archives Canada, PA-141723.

Page 289: Courtesy of Library and Archives Canada, PA-151925.

Page 291: Courtesy of Library and Archives Canada, PA-142103.

BY THE SAME AUTHOR

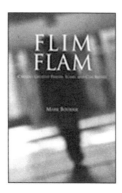

Flim Flam
Canada's Greatest Frauds, Scams, and Con Artists
9780888822017
$17.99

Flim Flam explores the world of Canadian white-collar crime, a place inhabited by hustlers, wild gamblers, and crazy dreamers. It takes the reader to the Vancouver Stock Exchange, where dream salesmen have peddled wild stories of easy money, through the "moose pasture" scams of northern Canada, to the con artists who have been drawn to Toronto's financial district. Along the way, you'll meet crooked politicians, a young con man who confessed to a church congregation after he was "born again," disbarred lawyers, and the creator of a huge paper fortune who was left with nothing but a wolfskin coat when his real estate empire fell apart.

Greed is a powerful motivator that has taken some Canadians down strange roads. Some have ended up pocketing millions, but many more of Canada's con artists have self-destructed, taking with them the fortunes of the people they bilked. In the end, they've usually fooled themselves, too.

Flim Flam shows that Canadians aren't nearly as dull as we'd like to believe. When it comes to conning each other, we have some of the most colourful and interesting hucksters in the world. This book contains stories from all regions of the country. It will appeal to business and true-crime readers, as well as people who are students of human nature.

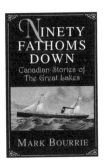

Ninety Fathoms Down
Canadian Stories of the Great Lakes
9780888821829
$17.99

Ninety Fathoms Down is the first collection of Canadian stories about the Great Lakes, the inland seas that shaped the development of Ontario. This fascinating book explains the history of the Canadian side of the Great Lakes by telling the stories of people whose lives took dramatic turns on the vast lakes. In these pages you will meet people like Paul Ragueneau, the Jesuit priest who tried to save thousands of starving Hurons in 1650; the seventeenth-century dreamer Rene-Robert Cavalier de La Salle, whose luck always let him down; and Lt. Miller Worsley, who takes revenge on the loss of his little supply ship Nancy by capturing two of the American warships that sank his schooner in the War of 1812.

The Great Lakes have been a stage for courage, gree, misfortune, and murder. *Ninety Fathoms Down* fills an important void in Ontario's popular history by using the theme of the great waterways to show the development of central Canada.

DUNDURN
www.dundurn.com

Visit us at
Dundurn.com
Definingcanada.ca
@dundurnpress
Facebook.com/dundurnpress

Harold Fre

The Young Emperor
Germany

Harold Frederic

The Young Emperor, William II of Germany

1st Edition | ISBN: 978-3-75235-169-9

Place of Publication: Frankfurt am Main, Germany

Year of Publication: 2020

Outlook Verlag GmbH, Germany.

THE YOUNG EMPEROR, WILLIAM II OF GERMANY

By Harold Frederic

WILLIAM II.

THE YOUNG EMPEROR

WILLIAM II OF GERMANY

*A STUDY IN CHARACTER DEVELOPMENT
ON A THRONE*

BY

HAROLD FREDERIC

Author of "In the Valley," "The Lawton Girl," &c., &c.

WITH PORTRAITS

NEW YORK
G. P. PUTNAM'S SONS
1891

CHAPTER I.—THE SUPREMACY OF THE HOHENZOLLERNS.

I n June of 1888, an army of workmen were toiling in the Champ de Mars upon the foundations of a noble World's Exhibition, planned to celebrate the centenary of the death by violence of the Divine Right of Kings. Four thousand miles westward, in the city of Chicago, some seven hundred delegates were assembled in National Convention, to select the twenty-third President of a great Republic, which also stood upon the threshold of its hundredth birthday. These were both suggestive facts, full of hopeful and inspiring thoughts to the serious mind. Considered together by themselves they seemed very eloquent proofs of the progress which Liberty, Enlightenment, the Rights of Man, and other admirable abstractions spelled with capital letters, had made during the century.

But, unfortunately or otherwise, history will not take them by themselves. That same June of 1888 witnessed a spectacle of quite another sort in a third large city—a spectacle which gave the lie direct to everything that Paris and Chicago seemed to say. This sharp and clamorous note of contradiction came from Berlin, where a helmeted and crimson-cloaked young man, still in his thirtieth year, stood erect on a throne, surrounded by the bowing forms of twenty ruling sovereigns, and proclaimed, with the harsh, peremptory voice of a drill-sergeant, that he was a War Lord, a Mailed Hand of Providence, and a sovereign specially conceived, created, and invested with power by God, for the personal government of some fifty millions of people.

It is much to be feared that, in the ears of the muse of history, the resounding shrillness of this voice drowned alike the noise of the hammers on the banks of the Seine and the cheering of the delegates at Chicago.

Any man, standing on that throne in the White Saloon of the old Schloss at Berlin, would have to be a good deal considered by his fellow-creatures. Even if we put aside the tremendous international importance of the position of a German Emperor, in that gravely open question of peace or war, he must compel attention as the visible embodiment of a fact, the existence of which those who like it least must still recognize. This is the fact: that the Hohenzollerns, having done many notable things in other times, have in our day revivified and popularized the monarchical idea, not only in Germany, but to a considerable extent elsewhere throughout Europe. It is too much to say, perhaps, that they have made it beloved in any quarter which was hostile before. But they have brought it to the front under new conditions, and secured for it admiring notice as the mainspring of a most efficient, exact, vigorous, and competent system of government. They have made an Empire with it—a magnificent modern machine, in which army and civil service and subsidiary federal administrations all move together like the wheels of a watch. Under the impulse of this idea they have not only brought governmental order out of the old-time chaos of German divisions and dissensions, but they have given their subjects a public service, which, taken all in all, is more effective and well-ordered than its equivalent produced by popular institutions in America, France, or England, and they have built up a fighting force for the protection of German frontiers which is at once the marvel and the terror of Europe.

Thus they have, as has been said, rescued the ancient and time-worn function of kingship from the contempt and odium into which it had fallen during the first half of the century, and rendered it once more respectable in the eyes of a utilitarian world.

But it is not enough to be useful, diligent, and capable. If it were, the Orleans Princes might still be living in the Tuileries. A kingly race, to maintain or increase its strength, must appeal to the national imagination. The Hohenzollerns have been able to do this. The Prussian imagination is largely made up of appetite, and their Kings, however fatuous and limited of vision they may have been in other matters, have never lost sight of this fact. If we include the Great Elector, there have been ten of these Kings, and of the ten eight have made Prussia bigger than they found her. Sometimes the gain has been clutched out of the smoke and flame of battle; sometimes it has more closely resembled burglary, or bank embezzlement on a large scale; once or twice it has come in the form of gifts from interested neighbours, in which category, perhaps, the cession of Heligoland may be placed—but gain of some sort there has always been, save only in the reign of Frederic William IV and the melancholy three months of Frederic III.

That there should be a great affection for and pride in the Hohenzollerns in Prussia was natural enough. They typified the strength of beak, the power of talons and sweeping wings, which had made Prussia what she was. But nothing save a very remarkable train of surprising events could have brought the rest of Germany to share this affection and pride.

The truth is, of course, that up to 1866 most other Germans disliked the Prussians thoroughly and vehemently, and decorated those head Prussians, the Hohenzollerns, with an extremity of antipathy. That brief war in Bohemia, with the consequent annexation of Hanover, Hesse-Cassel, Nassau, and Frankfort, did not inspire any new love for the Prussians anywhere, we may be sure, but it did open the eyes of other Germans to the fact that their sovereigns—Kings, Electors, Grand Dukes, and what not—were all collectively not worth the right arm of a single Hohenzollern.

It was a good deal to learn even this—and, turning over this revelation in their minds, the Germans by 1871 were in a mood to move almost abreast of Prussia in the apotheosis of the victor of Sedan and Paris. To the end of old William's life in 1888, there was always more or less of the apotheosis about the Germans' attitude toward him. He was never quite real to them in the sense that Leopold is real in Brussels or Humbert in Rome. The German imagination always saw him as he is portrayed in the fine fresco by Wislicenus in the ancient imperial palace at Goslar—a majestic figure, clad in modern war trappings yet of mythical aspect, surrounded, it is true, by the effigies of recognizable living Kings, Queens, and Generals, but escorted also by heroic ancestral shades, as he rides forward out of the canvas. Close behind him rides his son, Fritz, and he, too, following in the immediate shadow of his father to the last, lives only now in pictures and in sad musing dreams of what might have been.

But William II—the young Kaiser and King—*is* a reality. He has won no battles. No antique legends wreathe their romantic mists about him. It has occurred to no artist to paint him on a palace wall, with the mailed shadows of mediaeval Barbarossas and Conrads and Sigismunds overhead.

The group of helmeted warriors who cluster about those two mounted figures in the Goslar picture, and who, in the popular fancy, bring down to our own time some of the attributes of mediaeval devotion and prowess—this group is dispersed now. Moltke, Prince Frederic Charles, Roon, Manteuffel, and many others are dead; Blumenthal is in dignified retirement; Bismarck is at Friedrichsruh. New men crowd the scene—clever organizers, bright and adroit parliamentarians, competent administrators, but still fashioned quite of our own clay—busy new men whom we may look at without hurting our eyes.

For the first time, therefore, it is possible to study this prodigious new Germany, its rulers and its people, in a practical way, without being either dazzled by the disproportionate brilliancy of a few individuals or drawn into side-paths after picturesque unrealities.

Three years of this new reign have shown us Germany by daylight instead of under the glamour and glare of camp fires and triumphal illuminations. We see now that the Hohenzollern stands out in the far front, and that the other German royalties, Wendish, Slavonic, heirs of Wittekind, portentously ancient barbaric dynasties of all sorts, are only vaguely discernible in the background. During the lifetime of the old Kaiser it seemed possible that their eclipse might be of only a temporary nature. Nowhere can such an idea be cherished now. Young William dwarfs them all by comparison even more strikingly than did his grandfather.

They all came to Berlin to do him homage at the opening of the Reichstag, which inaugurated his reign on June 25, 1888. They will never make so brave a show again; even then they twinkled like poor tallow dips beside the shining personality of their young Prussian chief.

Almost all of them are of royal lines older than that of the Hohenzollerns. Five of the principal personages among them—the King of Saxony, the Regent representing Bavaria's crazy King, the heir-apparent representing the semi-crazy King of Wurtemberg, the Grand Duke of Baden, and the Grand Duke of Hesse-Darmstadt—owe their titles in their present form to Napoleon, who paid their ancestors in this cheap coin for their wretched treason and cowardice in joining with him to crush and dismember Prussia. Now they are at the feet of Prussia, not indeed in the posture of conquered equals, but as liveried political subordinates. No such wiping out of sovereign authorities and emasculation of sovereign dignities has been seen before since Louis XI consolidated France 500 years ago. Let us glance at some of these vanishing royalties for a moment, that we may the better measure the altitude to which the Hohenzollern has climbed.

There was a long time during the last century when people looked upon Saxony as the most powerful and important State in the Protestant part of Germany. It is an Elector of Saxony who shines forth in history as Luther's best friend and resolute protector. For more than a hundred years thereafter Saxony led in the armed struggles of Protestantism to maintain itself against the leagued Catholic powers.

Then, in 1694, there ascended the electoral throne the cleverest and most showy man of the whole Albertine family, who for nearly thirty years was to hold the admiring attention of Europe. We can see now that it was a purblind and debased Europe which believed August *der Starke* to be a great man; but in his own times there was no end to what he thought of himself or to what others thought of him. It was regarded as a superb stroke of policy when, in 1697, he got himself elected King of Poland—a promotion which inspired the jealous Elector of Branden-berg to proclaim himself King of Prussia four years later. August abjured Protestantism to obtain the Polish crown, and his descendants are Catholics to this day, though Saxony is strongly Protestant. August did many wonderful things in his time—made Dresden the superb city of palaces and museums it is, among other matters, and was the father of 354 natural children, as his own proud computation ran. A tremendous fellow, truly, who liked to be called the Louis XIV of Germany, and tried his best to live up to the ideal!

Contemporary observers would have laughed at the idea that Frederick William, the surly, bearish Prussian King, with his tobacco orgies and giant grenadiers, was worth considering beside the brilliant, luxurious, kingly August. Ah, "gay eupeptic son of Belial," where is thy dynasty now?

There is to-day a King of Saxony, descended six removes from this August, who is distinctly the most interesting and valuable of these minor sovereigns. He is a sagacious, prudent, soldierlike man, nominal ruler of over three millions of people, actual Field Marshal in the German Army which has a Hohenzollern for its head. Although he really did some of the best fighting which the Franco-German war called forth, nobody outside his own court and German military circles knows much about it, or cares particularly about him. The very fact of his rank prevents his generalship securing popular recognition. If he had been merely of noble birth, or even a commoner, the chances are that he would now be chief of the German General Staff instead of Count von Schlieffen. Being only a king, his merits as a commander are comprehended alone by experts.

There is just a bare possibility that this King Albert may be forced by circumstances out of his present obscurity. He is only sixty-three years old, and if a war should come within the next decade and involve defeat to the German Army in the field, there would be a strong effort made by the other subsidiary German sovereigns to bring him to the front as Generalissimo.

As it is, his advice upon military matters is listened to in Berlin more than is generally known, but in other respects his position is a melancholy one. Even the kindliness with which the Kaisers have personally treated him since 1870, cannot but wear to him the annoying guise of patronage. He was a man of thirty-eight when his father, King John, was driven out of Dresden by Prussian troops, along with the royal family, and when for weeks it seemed probable that the whole kingdom of Saxony would be annexed to Prussia. Bismarck's failure to insist upon this was bitterly criticised in Berlin at the time, and Gustav Frey-tag actually wrote a book deprecating the further independent existence of Saxony. Freytag and the Prussians generally confessed their mistake after the young Saxon Crown Prince's splendid achievement at Sedan; but that could scarcely wipe from his memory what had gone before, and even now, after the lapse of a quarter century, King

Albert's delicate, clear-cut, white-whiskered face still bears the impress of melancholy stamped on it by the humiliations of 1866.

Two other kings lurk much further back in the shadow of the Hohenzollern —idiotic Otto of Bavaria and silly Charles of Wurtemberg. Of the former much has been written, by way of complement to the picturesque literature evoked by the tragedy of his strange brother Louis's death. In these two brothers the fantastic Wittelsbach blood, filtering down from the Middle Ages through strata of princely scrofula and imperial luxury, clotted rankly in utter madness.

As for the King of Würtemberg, whose undignified experiences in the hands of foreign adventurers excited a year or two ago the wonderment and mirth of mankind, he also pays the grievous penalty of heredity's laws. Writing thirty years back, Carlyle commented in this fashion upon the royal house of Stuttgart: "There is something of the abstruse in all these Beutelsbachers, from Ulric downwards—a mute *ennui*, an inexorable obstinacy, a certain streak of natural gloom which no illumination can abolish; articulate intellect defective: hence a strange, stiff perversity of conduct visible among them, often marring what wisdom they have. It is the royal stamp of Fate put upon these men—what are called fateful or fated men." * The present King Charles was personally an unknown quantity when this picture of his house was drawn. He is an old man now, and decidedly the most "abstruse" of his whole family.

* "History of Friedrich II, of Prussia," book vii. chapter vi.

Thus these two ancient dynasties of Southern Germany, which helped to make history for so many centuries, have come down into the mud. There is an elderly regent uncle in Bavaria who possesses sense and respectable abilities; and in Würtemberg there is an heir-apparent of forty-three, the product of a marriage between first cousins, who is said to possess ordinary intelligence. These will in time succeed to the thrones which lunacy and asininity hold now in commission, but no one expects that they will do more than render commonplace what is now grotesquely impossible.

Of another line which was celebrated a thousand years ago, and which flared into martial prominence for a little in its dying days, when this century was young, nothing whatever is left. The Fighting Brunswickers are all gone.

They had a fair right to this name, had the Guelphs of the old homestead, for of the forty-five of them buried in the crypt of the Brunswick Burg Kirche nine fell on the battlefield. This direct line died out seven years ago with a curiously-original old Duke who bitterly resented the new order of things, and took many whimsical ways of showing his wrath. In the sense that he scorned

9

to live in remodeled Germany, and defied Prussia by ostentatiously exhibiting his sympathy for the exiled Hanoverian house, he too may be said to have died fighting. The collateral Guelphs who survive in other lands are anything but fighters. The Prince of Wales is the foremost living male of the family, and Bismarck's acrid jeer that he was the only European Crown Prince whom one did not occasionally meet on the battlefield, though unjustly cruel, serves to point the difference between his placid walk of life and the stormy careers of his mother's progenitors. Another Guelph, who is *de jure* heir to both Brunswick and Hanover—Ernest, Duke of Cumberland—has a larger strain of the ancestral Berserker blood, but alas! no weapon remains for him but obdurate sulkiness. He buries himself in his sullen retreat at Gmunden in uncompromising rage, and the powers at Berlin have left off striving to placate him with money—his relatives not even daring now to broach the subject to him.

And so there is an end to the Fighting Bruns-wickers, and a Hohenzollern has been put in their stead. Prince Albert of Prussia—a good, wooden, ceremonious man of large stature, who stands straight in jack boots and cuirass and is invaluable as an imposing family figure at christenings and funerals—reigns as Regent in Brunswick. So omnipotent are the Hohenzollerns grown that he was placed there without a murmur of protest—and when the time comes for the Prussian octopus to gather in this duchy, that also will be done in silence.

Of the sixteen remaining sovereigns-below-the-salt, the Grand Duke of Baden is a fairly-able and wholly-amiable man, much engrossed in these latter days in the fact that his wife is the Kaiser's aunt. This makes him feel like one of the family, and he takes the aggrandizement of the Hohenzollerns as quite a personal compliment. The venerable Duke Ernest, of Saxe-Coburg-Gotha, has an active mind and certain qualities which under other conditions might have made him a power in Germany. But Bismarck was far too rough an antagonist for him to cope with openly, and he fell into the feeble device of writing political pamphlets anonymously against the existing order of things, using the ingenuity of a jealous woman to circulate them and denying their authorship before he was accused. This has, of course, been fatal to his influence in the empire. Duke George, of Saxe-Meiningen, is another able and accomplished prince, who has devoted his energies and fortune to the establishment and perfecting of a very remarkable theatrical company. The rest are mere dead wood—presiding over dull little country Courts, wearing Prussian uniforms at parades and reviews, and desiring nothing else so much as the reception of invitations to visit Berlin and shine in the reflected radiance of the Hohenzollern's smile.

The word "invitations" does indeed suggest that the elderly Prince Henry XIV, of Reuss-Schleiz, should receive separate mention, as having but recently abandoned a determined feud with Prussia. It is true that Reuss-Schleiz has only 323 miles of territory and 110,000 people, but that did not prevent the feud being of an embittered, not to say menacing, character. When the invitations were sent out for the Berlin palace celebration of old Kaiser Wilhelm's ninetieth birthday, in 1887, by some accident Henry of Reuss-Schleiz was overlooked. There are so many of these Reusses, all named Henry, all descended from Henry the Fowler, and all standing so erect with pride that they bend backward! The mistake was discovered in a day or two and a belated invitation sent, which Henry grumblingly accepted. On the appointed day he arrived at the palace in Berlin and went up to the banqueting hall with the other princes. Being extremely near-sighted, he made a tour of the table, peering through his spectacles to discover his name-card. Horror of horrors! No place had been provided for him, and everybody in the room had observed him searching for one! Trembling with wrath, he stalked out, brushing aside the chamberlains who essayed to pacify him, and during that reign he never came to Berlin again. Not death itself could mollify him, for when Kaiser Wilhelm died the implacable Henry XIV, who personally owns most of his principality, refused his subjects a grant of land on which to rear a monument to his memory. But even he is reconciled to Berlin now.

Thus with practical completeness had the ancient dynasties of old Germany been subordinated to and absorbed by the ascendency of the Hohenzollerns, when young William II stepped upon the throne. Thus, too, with this passing glance at their abasement or annihilation, the way is cleared for us to study the young chief of this mighty and consolidated Empire, to examine his personality and his power, and, by tracing their growth during the first three years of his reign, to forecast their ultimate mark upon the history of his time.

CHAPTER II.—WILLIAM'S BOYHOOD

WILLIAM II. AS A BOY.

(From a photograph by Reinh. Graz, Berlin.)

The young Emperor was born in the first month of 1859. The prolonged life of his grandfather, and the apparently superb physical vitality of his father, made him seem much further removed from the throne than fate really intended, and he grew up into manhood with only scant attention from the general public. There was an unexpressed feeling that he belonged to the twentieth century, and that it would be time enough then to study him. When of a sudden the world learned that the stalwart middle-aged Crown Prince had a mortal malady, and saw that it was a race toward the grave between him and his venerable father, haste was made to repair this negligent error, and find out things about the hitherto unconsidered young man who was to be so prematurely called upon the stage. Unfortunately, this swift and unexpected shifting of history's lime-light revealed young William in extremely repellent colours. Many circumstances, working together in the shadows behind the throne, had combined to put him into a temporary attitude toward his parents, which showed very badly under this sudden and fierce illumination. "Ho, ho! He is a bad son, then, is he?" we all said, and made up our minds to dislike him on the spot. Three years have passed, and during that time many things have happened, many other things have come to light, calculated to convince us that this early judgment was an over-hasty one.

So far as I have been able to learn, the first hint given to the world that there was a young Prince in Berlin distinctly worth watching appeared in the book "Sociétiê de Berlin. Par le Comte Paul Vasili," published at the end of 1883. This volume was, perhaps, the cleverest of the anonymous series projected by a Parisian publisher to make money out of the collected gossip and scandal of the chief European capitals, and utilized by more than one bright familiar of Mme. Adam's *salon* to pay off old grudges and market afresh moss-grown libels. The authorship of these books was never clearly established. There is a general understanding in Berlin that the one about that city was for the most part written by a Parisian journalist named Gerard, then stationed in Germany. At all events, the evidence was regarded at the time as sufficient as to warrant his being chased summarily out of Berlin, while the book itself was prohibited, confiscated, almost burned by the common hangman. Perhaps Gerard, if he be still alive, might profitably return to Berlin now, for to him belongs the credit of having first put into type an intelligent character study of the young man who now monopolizes European attention.

"The Prince William," said this anonymous writer, "is only twenty-four years of age. It is, therefore, difficult as yet to say what he will become; but what is clearly apparent even now is that he is a young man of promise in mind and head and heart. He is by far the most intellectual of the Princes of this royal family. Withal courageous, enterprising, ambitious, hot-headed, but with a heart of gold, sympathetic in the highest degree, impulsive, spirited, vivacious in character, and gifted with a talent for repartee in conversation which would almost make the listener doubt his being a German. He adores the army, by which he is idolized in return. He has known how, despite his extreme youth, to win popularity in all classes of society. He is highly educated, well read, busies his mind with projects for the welfare of his country, and has a striking keenness of perception for everything relating to politics.

"He will certainly, be a distinguished man, and very probably a great sovereign. Prussia will perhaps have in him a second Frederic II, but minus his scepticism. In addition, he possesses a fund of gaiety and good humour that will soften the little angularities of character without which he would not be a true Hohenzollern.

"He will be essentially a personal king—never allowing himself to be blindly led, and ruling with sound and direct judgment, prompt decision, energy in action, and an unbending will. When he attains the throne, he will continue the work of his grandfather, and will as certainly undo that of his father, whatever it may have been. In him the enemies of Germany will have a formidable adversary; he may easily become the Henri IV of his country."

I have ventured upon this extended extract from a book eight years old because the prophecy seems a remarkable one—far nearer what we see now to be the truth than any of the later predictions have turned out to be. "Paul Vasili" continues his sketch with some paragraphs about the Prince's vast penchant for lower-class dissipated females, concluding with the warning that if ever he comes under the influence of a' really able woman "it will be necessary to follow his actions with great caution." All this may be unhesitatingly put down to the French writer's imagination.

There is no city where more frankness about talking scandal exists than in Berlin, yet I have sought in vain to find any justification for this view of the Kaiser's character, either past or present. The impression brought from many talks with people who know him and his life intimately is that this special accusation is less true of him than of almost any other prince of his generation.

William's boyhood was marked by one innovation in the family traditions of a Hohenzollern's training, the importance of which it is not easy to exaggerate. His father had been the first of these royal heirs to be sent to a university. He in his turn was the first to go to a public school.

It is a solemn and portentous sort of thing—this training of a Hohenzollern. The progress of the family has been one long, sustained object lesson to the world on the value of education. No doubt it is in great part due to the influence of this standing example that Prussia leads the van of civilization in its proportion of scholars and teachers, and has made its name a synonym for all that is thorough and exhaustive in educational systems and theories. The dawn of this notion of a specially Spartan and severe practical schooling for his heir, in the primitive and curiously-limited brain of the first King Frederic William, really marked an era in the world's conception of what education meant.

We have all read, with swift-chasing mirth, wonder, incredulity and wrath, the stories of the way in which this luckless heir, afterward to be Frederic the

Great, got his education stamped, beaten, burned, frozen, almost strangled into him. The account reads like a nightmare of lunatic savagery—yet in it were the germs of a lofty idea. From the brutal cudgeling, cursing, and manacling of Frederic's experience grew the tradition of a unique kind of training for a Hohenzollern prince. The very violence and wild barbarity of his treatment fixed the attention of the family upon the theory of education—with very notable results.

Historically we are all familiar with the excessive military twist given to this education of the youths born to be Kings of Prussia. The picture books are full of portraits of them—quaint little manikins dressed in officers' uniforms—stepping from the cradle into war's paraphernalia. The picture of the Great Fritz beating a drum at the age of three, of which the rapturous Carlyle makes so much, has its modern counterpart in the photographs of the present child Crown Prince, clad in regimentals and saluting the camera, which are in every Berlin shop window. But another element of this stern regimen, not so much kept in view, is the absolute dependence of the son upon the father, or rather the King, which is insisted upon.

We know to what abnormal lengths this ran in the youth and early manhood of Frederic the Great. It did not alter much in the next reign. In 1784, when this same Frederic was seventy-two years old, a travelling French noble was his guest at a great review in Silesia. There was also present the King's nephew and heir, who two years later was to ascend the throne as Frederic William II, and who now was in his fortieth year. Yet of this forty-year-old Prince the Frenchman writes in his diary: "The heir presumptive lodges at a brewer's house, and in a very mean way; is not allowed to sleep from home without permission from the King."

The results in this particular instance were not of a flattering kind, and among the decaying forms of the dying eighteenth century—in an atmosphere poisoned by the accumulated putridities of that luxurious and evil epoch—even the Hohenzollern of the next generation was not a shining success. He was at least, however, much superior to the other German sovereigns of his time, and he had the unspeakable fortune, moreover, to be the husband of that Queen Louise who is enshrined as the patron saint of Prussian history. It was she who engrafted a humane spirit upon the rough drill-sergeant body of Hohenzollern education. She made her sons love her—and it seems but yesterday since the last of these sons, a tottering old man of ninety, used to go to the Charlottenburg mausoleum on the anniversary of her death, and pray and weep in solitude beside the recumbent marble effigy of the mother who had died in 1810.

The introduction of filial affection into the relation between Hohenzollern parents and children dates from this Queen Louise, and belongs to our own century. Before that it was the rule for the heirs of Prussia to detest their immediate progenitors. From the time of the Great Elector, every rising generation of this royal house sulked, cursed under its breath, went into opposition as far as it dared, and every fading generation disliked and distrusted those who were coming after it. Nor were these harsh relations confined to sovereign and heir. Wilhelmine, Margravine of Baireuth, records in her memoirs how, at the age of six, she was so much surprised at being fondled and caressed by her mother, on the latter's return from a prolonged journey, that she broke a blood vessel. * It seems safe to say that down to the family of Frederic William III and Louise, no other reigning race in Europe had ever managed to engender so much bitterness and bad blood between elders and juniors within its domestic fold. The change then was abrupt. The two older boys of this family, Frederic William IV and William I, lived lives as young men which were poems of filial reverence and tenderness. The cruel misfortunes of the Napoleonic wars made the mutual affection within this hunted and homeless royal family very sweet and touching. Perhaps the most interesting of all the reminiscences called forth by the death of the old Kaiser was furnished by the publication of the letters he wrote as a young man to his father—that strange correspondence which reveals him resolutely breaking his own heart and tearing from it the image of the Princess Radziwill, in loving obedience to his father's wish.

<pre>
* "Memoirs of Wilhelmine, Margravine of Baireuth,"
   translated by H.R.H. Princess Chri of Wilhelmine, Margravine
   of Baireuth, translated by H.R.H. Princess Christian,
   London, 1887
</pre>

This trait of filial piety did not loom so largely in William's son, the late Frederic III, as one or two random allusions in his diary show. And in his son, in turn, its pulse beats with such varying and intermittent fervour that sometimes one misses it altogether.

Young William, as has been said, was the first of his race to be sent to a public school, the big gymnasium at Cassel being selected for the purpose. The innovation was credited at the time to the eccentric liberalizing notions of his mother, the English Crown Princess. The old Kaiser did not like the idea, and Bismarck vehemently opposed it, but the parents had their way, and at the age of fifteen the lad went, along with his twelve-year-old brother Henry, and their tutor, Dr. Hinzpeter. They were lodged in an old schloss, which had been one of the Electoral residences, and out of school hours maintained a considerable seclusion. But in the school itself William was treated quite like any ordinary citizen's son.

It may have been a difficult matter for some of the teachers to act as if they were unconscious that this particular pupil was the heir of the Hohenzollerns, but men who were at the school at the time assure me they did so, with only one exception. This solitary flunkey, knowing that William was more backward in his Greek than most of his class, sought to curry favour with the Prince by warning him that the morrow's examination was to be, let us say, upon a certain chapter of Xenophon. The boy William received this hint in silence, but early the next morning went down to the classroom and wrote upon the blackboard in big letters the information he had received, so that he might have no advantage over his fellows. This struck me when I heard it as a curious illustration of the boy's character. There seems to have been no excited indignation at the meanness of the tutor—but only the manifestation of a towering personal and family pride, which would not allow him to win a prize through profiting by knowledge withhold from the others.

During his three years at Cassel William was very democratic in his intercourse with the other boys. He may have been helped to this by the fact that he was one of the worst-dressed boys in the school—in accordance with an ancient family rule which makes the Hohenzollern children wear out their old clothes in a way that would astonish the average grocer's progeny. He was only an ordinary scholar so far as his studies went. At that time his brother Henry, who went to a different school, was conspicuously the brighter pupil of the two. Those who were at Cassel with the future Emperor have the idea that he was contented there, but he himself, upon reflection, is convinced that he did not like it. At all events, he gathered there a very intimate knowledge of the gymnasium system which, as will be seen later on, he now greatly disapproves.

At the age of eighteen William left Cassel and entered upon his university course at Bonn. Here his tutor, Hinzpeter, who had been his daily companion and mentor from childhood, parted company with him, and the young Prince passed into the hands of soldiers and men of the world. The change marks an important epoch in the formation of his character.

There is a photograph of him belonging to the earlier part of this Cassel period which depicts a refined, gentle, dreamy-faced German boy, with a soft, girlish chin, small arched lips with a suggestion of dimples at the corners, and fine meditative eyes. The forehead, though not broad, is of fair height and fulness. The dominant effect of the face is that of sweetness. Looking at it, one instinctively thinks "How fond that boy's parents must have been of him!" And they were fond in the extreme.

In the Crown Prince Frederic's diary, written while the German headquarters were at Versailles, are these words:—

"This is William's thirteenth birthday. May he grow up to be an able, honest, and upright man, a true German, prepared to continue without

prejudice what has now been begun! Heaven be praised; between him and us there is a simple, hearty, and natural relationship, which we shall strive to preserve, so that he may thus always look upon us as his best and truest friends. It is really an oppressive reflection when one realizes what hopes have already been placed on the head of this child, and how great is our responsibility to the nation for his education, which family considerations and questions of rank, and the whole Court life at Berlin and other things will tend to make so much more difficult."

The retirement of Dr. Hinzpeter from his charge was an event the significance of which recent occurrences have helped us to appreciate. When history is called upon to make her final summing up upon William's character and career, she will allot a very prominent place to the influence of this relatively unknown man. A curious romance of time's revenge hangs about Dr. Hinzpeter. He is a native of the Westphalian manufacturing town, Bielefeld, and was a poor young tutor at Darmstadt when he was recommended to the parents of William as one exceptionally fitted to take charge of their son. The man who gave this recommendation was the then Mr. Robert Morier, British Minister at Darmstadt. Nearly a quarter of a century later Sir Robert Morier was able to see his ancient and implacable enemy, Bismarck, tripped, thrown, and thrust out of power, and to sweeten the spectacle by reflecting that he owed this ideal vengeance to the work of the tutor he had befriended in the old Darmstadt days.

It is more than probable that the idea of sending the young Prince to the Cassel gymnasium originated with Dr. Hinzpeter. At all events, we know that he held advanced and even extreme views as to the necessity of emphasizing the popular side of the Hohenzollern tradition.

This Prussian family has always differed radically from its other German neighbours in professing to be solicitous for the poor people rather than for the nobility's privileges and claims. Sometimes this has sunk to be a profession merely; more often it has been an active guiding principle. The lives of the second and third Kings of Prussia are filled with the most astonishing details of vigilant, ceaseless intermeddling in the affairs of peasant farmers, artisans, and wage-earners generally, hearing complaints, spying out injustice, and roughly seeing wrongs righted. When Prussia grew too big to be thus paternally administered by a King poking about on his rounds with a rattan and a taker of notes, the tradition still survived. We find traces of it all along down to our times in the legislation of the Diet in the direction of what is called State Socialism.

Dr. Hinzpeter felt the full inspiration of this tradition. He longed to make it more a reality in the mind of his princely pupil than it had ever been before.

Thus it was that the lad was sent to Cassel, to sit on hard benches with the sons of simple citizens, and to get to know what the life of the people was like. Years afterwards this inspiration was to bear fruit.

But in 1877 the work of creating an ideally democratic and popular Hohenzollern was abruptly interrupted. Dr. Hinzpeter went back to Bielefeld, and young William entered the University of Bonn. The soft-faced, gentle-minded boy, still full of his mother's milk, his young mind sweetened and strengthened by the dreams of clemency, compassion, and earnest searchings after duty which he had imbibed from his teacher, suddenly found himself transplanted in new ground. The atmosphere was absolutely novel. Instead of being a boy among boys, he all at once found himself a prince amongst aristocratic toadies. In place of Hinzpeter, he had a military *aide* given him for principal companion, friend, and guide.

These next few years at the Rhenish university did not, we see now, wholly efface what Dr. Hinz-peter had done. But they obscured and buried his work, and reared upon it a superstructure of another sort—a different kind of William, redolent of royal pretensions and youthful self-conceit, delighting in the rattle and clank of spurs and swords and dreaming of battlefields.

Poor Hinzpeter, in his Bielefeld retreat, could have had but small satisfaction in learning of the growth of the new William. The parents at Potsdam, too, who had built such loving hopes upon the tender and gracious promise of boyhood—they could not have been happy either.

CHAPTER III.—UNDER CHANGED INFLUENCES AT BONN

The act of matriculation at Bonn meant to young William many things apart from the beginning of a university career. In fact, it was almost a sign of his emancipation from academic studies. He was a student among students in only a formal sense. The theory of a complete civic education was respected by his attendance at certain lectures, and by his perfunctory compliance with sundry university regulations. But, in reality, he now belonged to the army. He had attained his majority, like other Prussian princes, at the age of eighteen, and thereupon had been given his Second Lieutenant's commission in the First Foot Regiment of the Guards, where his father had been trained before him. The routine of his military service, and the exigencies of the martial education which now supplanted all else, kept him much more in Berlin than at Bonn.

Both at the Prussian capital and Rhenish university town he now wore his uniform, his sword, and his epaulets, and, chin well in air, sniffed his fill of the incense burned before him by the young men of the army. The glitter and colour of the parade ground, the peremptory discipline, the sense of power given by these superb wheeling lines and walls of bayonets and exact geometrical movements as of some mighty machine, fascinated his imagination. He threw himself into military work with feverish eagerness. Pacific Cassel, with its gymnasium and the kindly figure of the tutor, Hinzpeter, faded away into a remote memory of childhood.

Public events, meanwhile, had been working out a condition of affairs which gave a marked importance to this change in William's character. The German peoples, having got over the first rapt enthusiasm at beholding their ancient Frankish enemy rolled in the dust at their feet, and at finding themselves once more all together under an imperial German flag, began to devote attention to domestic politics. It was high time that they did so.

Prussia had roared as gently as any sucking dove the while the question was still one of enticing the smaller German States into the federated empire. But once the Emperor-King felt his footing secure upon the imperial throne, the old hungry Hohenzollern blood began stirring in his veins. His great Chancellor, Prince Bismarck, needed no prompting; every fibre of his bulky frame responded intuitively to this inborn Prussian instinct of aggrandisement. Together these two began putting the screws upon the minor States. "Solidifying the Empire" was what they called their work. The

Hohenzollerns were always notable "solidifiers," as their neighbours have had frequent occasion to observe tearfully during the last three centuries.

The humiliation and expulsion of Austria had been the pivot upon which the creation of the new Germany turned. In its most obvious aspect this had appeared to all men to be the triumph of a Protestant over a Catholic power. Later events had contributed to associate Prussia's ascendency with the religious issue. The great OEcumenical Council at Rome had been followed by a French declaration of war, which every good Lutheran confidently ascribed to the dictation of the Jesuits.

These things grouped themselves together in the public mind just as similar arguments did in England in the days of the Armada. To be a Catholic grew to seem synonymous with being a sympathizer with Austria and France. It is an old law of human action that if you persistently impute certain views to a man, and persecute him on account of them, the effect is to reconcile his mind to those views. The melancholy history of theologico-political quarrels is peculiarly filled with examples of this. The Catholics of Germany were in the main as loyal to the idea of imperial unity as their Protestant neighbours, and they had shed their blood quite as freely to establish it as a fact. Their bishops and priests had over and over again testified by deeds their independence of Rome in matters which affected them as Germans. But when they found Bismarck ceaselessly insisting that they were hostile to Prussia, it was natural enough that they should discover that they did dislike his kind of a Prussia, and that some of the least cautious among them should say so.

Prussia's answer—coming with the promptness of deliberate preparation— was the *Kulturkampf,* Into the miserable chaos which followed we need not go. Bishops were exiled or imprisoned; schools were broken up and Catholic professors chased from the universities; a thousand parishes were bereft of their priests; the whole empire was filled with angry suspicions, recriminations, and violence, hot-tempered roughness on one side, grim obstinacy of hate on the other—to the joy of all Germany's enemies outside and the confusion of all her friends.

Despotism begets lawlessness, and Bismarck and old William, busy with their priest hunt, suddenly discovered that out of this disorder had somehow sprouted a strange new thing called Socialism. They halted briefly to stamp this evil growth out—and lo! from an upper window of the beer house on Unter den Linden, called the Three Ravens, the Socialist Nobiling fired two charges of buckshot into the head and shoulders of the aged Emperor, riddling his helmet like a sieve and laying him on a sick bed for the ensuing six months.

As a consequence, the Crown Prince Frederic was installed as Regent from

June till December of 1878, and from this period dates young William's public attitude of antagonism to the policy of his parents.

For the present we need examine this only in its outer and political phases. It is too much, perhaps, to say that heretofore there had been no divisions inside the Hohenzollern family. The Crown Prince and his English wife had been in tacit opposition to the Kaiser-Chancellor *régime* for many years. But this opposition took on palpable form and substance during the Regency of 1878.

A new Pope—the present Leo XIII—had been elected only a few months before, and with him the Regent Frederic opened a personal correspondence, with a view to compromising the unhappy religious wrangles which were doing such injury to Germany. The letters written from Berlin were models of gentle firmness and wise statesmanship, and they laid a foundation of conciliatory understanding upon which Bismarck afterward gladly reared his superstructure of partial settlement when the time came for him to need and bargain for the Clerical vote in the Reichstag. But at the time their friendly tone gave grave offence to the Prussian Protestants, and was peculiarly repugnant to the Junker court circles of Berlin.

It is no pleasant task to picture to one's self the grief and chagrin with which the Regent and his wife must have noted that their elder son ranged himself among their foes. The change which had been wrought in him during the year in the regiment and at Bonn revealed itself now in open and unmistakable fashion. Prince William ostentatiously joined himself with those who criticised the Regent. He assiduously cultivated the friendship of the men who led hostile attacks upon his parents. He had his greatest pride in being known for a staunch supporter of Bismarck, a firm believer in divine right, Protestant supremacy, and all the other catchwords of the absolutist party. The praises which these reactionary people sang in his honour mounted like the fumes of spirits to his young brain. Instinctively he began posing as the Hope of the Monarchy—as the providential young prince, handsome, wise and strong, who was in good time to ascend the throne and gloriously undo all that the weak dreamer, his father, had done toward liberalizing the institutions of Prussia and Germany.

A lamentable and odious attitude this, truly! Yet, which of us was wholly wise at nineteen? And which of us, it may be added fairly, has encountered such magnificent and overpowering temptations to foolishness as these that beset young William?

Remember that all his associates, alike in his daily routine with his regiment or at the University and in his larger intercourse among the aristocratic social circles of Berlin, took only one view of this subject. At their head were Bismarck, the most powerful and impressive personality in Europe, and the aged Emperor, the one furiously inveighing against the manner in which the Protestant religion and political security were being endangered, the other deploring from his sick-bed the grievous inroads which were threatened upon the personal rights and prerogatives of the Hohenzollerns.

It is not strange that young William adopted the opinion of his grandfather and of Bismarck, chiming as it did with the new impulses of militarism that had risen so strongly within him, and being re-echoed, as it was, from the lips of all his friends.

But the event of this brief Regency which most clearly marked the chasm separating the Crown Prince from the Junker circles of his son's adoption, was the appointment of Dr. Friedberg to high office. And this is particularly worth studying, because its effects are still felt in German social and political life.

Dr. Friedberg was then a man of sixty-five, and one of the most distinguished jurists of Germany. He had adorned a responsible post in the Ministry of Justice for over twenty years, and had written numerous valuable works, those relating to his special subject of prison reform and the efficacy of criminal law in social improvement standing in the very front rank of literature of that kind. His promotion, however, had been hopelessly blocked by two considerations; he was professedly a Liberal in politics and a close friend of the Crown Prince and Princess, and, what was still worse, he was a Jew.

On the second day of his Regency, Frederic astounded and scandalized aristocratic Berlin by appointing Dr. Friedberg to the highest judicial-administrative post in the kingdom. To glance forward for a moment, it may be noted that when old Kaiser Wilhelm returned to active power in December, he refused to remove Friedberg, out of a feeling of loyalty to his son's actions as Regent. But he vented his wrath in another way by conspicuously neglecting to give Friedberg the Black Eagle after he had served nine years in the Ministry, though all his associates obtained the decoration upon only six years' service. This slight upon the Hebrew Minister explains the well-remembered action of Frederic, when he was on his journey home from San Remo to ascend the throne after his father's death:—as the Ministerial delegation met his train at Leipsic, and entered the carriage, he took the Black Eagle from his own neck and placed it about that of Friedberg.

This action of the emotional sick man, returning through the March snowstorm to play his brief part of phantom Kaiser, created much talk in Germany three years ago, and Friedberg, upon the strength of it, plumed himself greatly as the chief friend of the new monarch. He was the first Jew ever decorated by that exalted and exclusive Black Eagle—and during the short reign of ninety-nine days he held himself like the foremost man in the Empire.

It is a melancholy reflection that this mean-spirited old man, as soon as Frederic died, made haste to lend himself to the work of blackening his benefactor's memory. He had owed more to Frederic's friendship and loyalty than any other in Germany, and he requited the debt to the dead Kaiser with such base ingratitude that even Frederic's enemies were disgusted, and, under the pressure of general disfavour, he had soon to quit his post. But enough of Friedberg's unpleasant personality. Let us return to 1878.

The Regent's action in giving Prussia a Jewish Minister lent an enormous original impulse to the anti-Semitic movement in Berlin, which soon grew into a veritable *Judenhetze*. This Jewish question, while it ran its course of excitement in Germany, completely dwarfed the earlier clerical issue, just as it in turn has been submerged by the rising tide of Socialistic agitation. But though the anti-semitic party has ceased to exert any power at the polls the feeling back of it is still a potent factor in Berlin life.

In the new Berlin, of which I shall speak presently, the Jews occupy a more commanding and dominant position than they have ever had in any other important city since the fall of Jerusalem. For this the Germans have themselves largely to blame. The military bent of the ascendant Prussians has warped the whole Teutonic mind toward unduly glorifying the army. The prizes of German upper-class life are all of a military sort. Every nobleman's son, every bright boy in the wealthier citizens' stratum, aspires to the uniform. The tacit rule which excludes the Jews from positions in this epauletted aristocracy drives them into the other professions. They may not wear the sword: they revenge themselves by owning the vast bulk of the newspapers, by writing most of the books, by almost monopolizing law, medicine, banking, architecture, engineering, and the more intellectual branches of the civil service.

This preponderance of Hebrews in the liberal professions seems unnatural to the Tory German, who has vainly tried to break it down by political action and by social ostracism. These attempts in turn have thrown the Jews into opposition. Of the seven Israelites in the present Reichstag six are Socialist Democrats and one is a Freisinnige leader. Every paper in Germany owned or edited by a Jew is uncompromisingly Radical in its politics. This in turn further exasperates the German Tories and keeps alive the latent fires of hatred which bigots like Stocker from time to time fan into flame.

In finance, too, the German aristocrats find themselves getting more and more helplessly into Jewish hands. Their wonderful new city of Berlin not only acts as a sieve for the great wave of Hebrew migration steadily moving westward from Russia, but it is becoming the Jewish banking and money centre of Europe. The grain trade of Russia is concentrated in Berlin. To buy wheat from Odessa you apply to one of the three hundred Jewish middleman firms at Berlin. To borrow money in Europe you go with equal certainty to Berlin. The German nobleman was never very rich; he has of late years become distinctly poor—and all the mortgages which mar his sleep o' nights are locked in Jewish safes at Berlin.

To revenge himself the German aristocrat can only assume an added contempt for literature and the peaceful professions generally because they are Jewish; insist more strongly than ever that the army is the only place for German gentlemen because it is not Jewish, and dream of the time when a beneficent fate shall once more hand Jerusalem over to conquest and rapine.

This German nobleman, however, does not disdain in the meanwhile to lend himself to the spoliation of the loathed tribes when chance offers itself. There is a famous Jewish banker in Berlin, who, in his senile years, is weak enough to desire social position for his children. One of his sons, a stupid and debauched youngster, is permitted to associate with sundry fashionable German officers—just up to the point where he loses his money to them with sufficient regularity—and, of course, never gets an inch beyond that point.

A daughter of this old banker had an even more disastrous experience. She was an ugly girl, but with her enormous dower the ambitious parents were able to buy a titled husband in the person of a penniless German Baron. Delighted with this success, the banker settled upon the couple a handsome estate in Silesia, The Baron and his bride were provided with a special train to convey them to their future home, and in that very train the Baron installed his mistress, and with her a lawyer friend who had already arranged for the sale of the estate. The Jewish bride arrived in Silesia to find herself contemptuously deserted by her husband and robbed of her estate. She returned to Berlin, obtained a divorce, and as soon as might be was married again—this time to a diamond merchant of her own race.

As for the Baron who perpetrated this unspeakably brutal and callous outrage, I did not learn that he had lost caste among his friends by the exploit. Indeed, the story was told to me as a merry joke on the Jews.

Prince Bismarck, almost alone among the Junker group, did not associate himself with this anti-Semitic agitation. In the work which he was carrying forward Jewish bankers were extremely useful. Both in a visibly regular way, and by subterranean means, capitalists like Bleichroder played a most important part in his performance of the task of centralizing power at Berlin. Hence he always held aloof from the movement against the Jews, and on occasions made his dislike for it manifest.

Doubtless it was his counsel which restrained the impetuous young William from openly identifying himself with this bigoted and proscriptive demonstration. At all events, the youthful Prince avoided any overt sign of his sympathy with the anti-Jewish outcry, yet continued to find all his friends among the class which supported the *Judenhetze*. It seems a curious fact now that in those days he created the impression of a silent and reserved young man—almost taciturn. As to where his likes and dislikes lay, no uncertainty existed. He was heart and soul with the aristocratic Court party and against all the tendencies and theories of the small academic group attached to his father. He made this obvious enough by his choice of associations, but kept a dignified curb on his tongue.

In addition to his course of studies at Bonn and his practical labours with his regiment, the Prince devoted a set amount of time each week to instruction of a less common order. He had regular weekly appointments with two very distinguished professors—the Emperor William, who spoke on Kingcraft, and Chancellor Bismarck, whose theme was Statecraft. The former series of discourses was continued almost without intermission, even during the old Kaiser's period of retirement after Nobiling's attempt on his life. The Prince saw these eminent instructors regularly, but it did not enter into their scheme of education that he should profess to learn anything from his father.

Among the ideas which the impressionable young man imbibed from Bismarck there could be nothing calculated to increase his filial affection or respect. Bismarck had cherished a bitter dislike for the English Crown Princess, conceived even before her marriage, at a time when she represented to him only the girlish embodiment of an impolitic matrimonial alliance, and strengthened year by year after she came to Berlin to live. He did not scruple to charge to a conspiracy between her and the Empress Augusta all the political obstacles which from time to time blocked his path. He not only believed, but openly declared, that the Crown Princess was responsible for the whole Arnim episode; and it is an open secret that even the State papers emanating from the German Foreign Office during his Chancellorship contain the grossest and most insulting allusions to her. As for the Crown Prince, Bismarck was at no pains to conceal his contempt for one of whom he habitually thought as a henpecked husband.

Enough of this feeling about his parents must have filtered through into young William's mind, from his intercourse with the powerful Chancellor, to render any reassertion of parental influence impossible.

In the summer of 1880 the Emperor and his Chancellor decided that it was time for their pupil to marry, and they selected for his bride an amiable, robust and comely-faced German princess of the dispossessed Schleswig-Holstein family. I gain no information anywhere as to William's parents having been more than formally consulted in this matter—and no hint that William himself took any deep personal interest in the transaction. The marriage ceremony came in February of 1881, and William was now installed in a residence of his own—the pretty little Marble Palace at Potsdam. His daily life remained otherwise unaltered. He worked hard at his military and civil tasks, and continued to pose—not at all through mere levity of character, but inspired by a genuine, if misguided, sense of duty—as the darling of all reactionary elements in modern Germany.

CHAPTER IV.—THE TIDINGS OF FREDERIC'S DOOM

Six years of married and semi-independent life went by, and left Prince William of Prussia but little changed. He worked diligently up through the grades of military training and responsibility, fulfilling all the public duties of his position with exactness, but showing no inclination to create a separate *rôle* in the State for himself. The young men of the German upper and middle classes, alive with the new spirit of absolutism and lust for conquest with which boyish memories of 1870 imbued their minds, looked toward him and spoke of him as their leader that was to be when their generation should come into its own—but that seemed something an indefinite way ahead. He could afford to wait silently.

His summer home at Marmorpalais, charmingly situated on the shore of the Heiligen Sea at Potsdam, did not in any obvious sense become a political centre. The men who came to it were chiefly hard-working officers, and the talk of their scant leisure, over wine and cigars, was of military tasks, hunting experiences, and personal gossip rather than of graver matters. The library, which was William's workroom in these days, has most of its walls covered with racks arranged to hold maps, presumably for strategic studies and *Kriegspiel* work. The next most important piece of furniture in the room is a tall cabinet for cigars. The bookcase is much smaller.

When winter came Prince William and his family returned to their apartments in the Schloss at Berlin. Nurses clad in the picturesque Wendish dress of the Spreewald bore an increasing prominent part in this annual exodus from Potsdam—for almost every year brought its new male Hohenzollern.

Thus the early spring of 1887 found William, now past his twenty-eighth year, a major, commanding a battalion of Foot guards, the father of four handsome, sturdy boys, and two lives removed from the throne.

Then came, without warning, one of those terrible, world-changing moments wherein destiny reveals her face to the awed beholder—moments about which the imagination of the outside public lingers with curiosity forever unsatisfied. No one will ever tell what happens in that soul-trying instant of time, We shall never know, for example, just what William felt and thought one March day in 1887, when somebody—identity unknown to us as well—whispered in his ear that the Crown Prince, his father, had a cancer in the throat.

The world heard this sinister news some weeks later, and was so grieved at the intelligence that for over a year thereafter it fostered the hope of its falsity, and was even grateful to courtier physicians and interested flatterers who encouraged this hope. Civilization had elected Frederic to a place among its heroes, and clung despairingly to the belief that his life might, after all, be saved.

But in the inner family circle of the Hohenzollerns there was from the first no illusion on this point. The old Emperor and his Chancellor and the Prince William knew that the malady was cancerous. Their information came from Ems, whither Frederic went upon medical advice in the spring of 1887, to be treated for "a bad cold with bronchial complications." Later a strenuous and determined attempt was made to represent the disease as something else, and out of this grew one of the most painful and cruel domestic tragedies known to history. At this point it is enough to say that the Emperor and his grandson knew about the cancer before even rumours of it reached the general public, and that their belief in its fatal character remained unshaken throughout.

To comprehend fully and fairly what followed, it will be necessary to try to look at Frederic through the eyes of the Court party. The view of him which we of England and America take has been, beyond doubt, of great and lasting service to the human race—in much the same sense that the world has been benefited by the idealized purities and sweetnesses of the Arthurian legend. We are helped by our heroes in this practical, work-a-day, modern world as truly as were our pagan fathers who followed the sons of Woden. Every one of us is the richer and stronger for this image of Frederic the Noble which the English-speaking peoples have erected in their Valhalla.

But it is fair to reflect, on the other hand, that this fine, handsome, able, and good-hearted Prince could not have created for himself such hosts of hostile critics in his own country, could not have continually found himself year by year losing his hold upon even the minority of his fellow-countrymen, without reason. It is certain that in 1886—the year before his illness befell—he had come to a minimum of usefulness, influence, and popularity in the Empire. Deplore this as we may, it would be unintelligent to refuse to inquire into its causes.

Moreover, we are engaged upon the study of a living man, holding a great position, possibly destined to do great things. All our thoughts of this living man are instinctively coloured by prejudices based upon his relations with his father, who is dead. Justice to William demands that we shall strive fairly to get at the opinions and feelings which swayed him and his advisers in their attitude of antagonism to our hero, his father.

His critics say that Frederic was an actor. They do not insist upon his insincerity—in fact, for the most part credit him with honesty and candour—but regard him as the victim of hereditary histrionism. His mother, the late Empress Augusta, had always impressed Berliners in the same way—as playing in the *rôle* of an exiled Princess, with her little property Court accessories, her little tea-party circle of imitation French *littérateurs*, and her "Mrs. Haller" sighs and headshakings over the coarseness and cruelty of the big roaring world outside. And her grandfather was that play-actor gone mad, Czar Paul of Russia, who tore the passion so into tatters that his own sons rose and killed him.

Once given the key to this view of Frederic's character, a strange cloud of corroborative witnesses are at hand. Take one example. Most of the pictures of him drawn at the period of his greatest popularity—during and just after the Franco-German war—pourtray him with a long-bowled porcelain pipe in his hand. The artists in the field made much of this: every war correspondent wrote about it. The effect upon the public mind was that of a kindly, unostentatious, pipe-loving burgher—and so lasting was it that when, seventeen years later, he was attacked by cancer, many good people hastened to ascribe it to excessive smoking. I had this same notion, too, and therefore was vastly surprised, in Berlin, years after, when a General Staff officer told me that Frederic rather disliked tobacco. I instanced the familiar pictures of him with his pipe. The instant reply was: "Ah, yes, that was like him. He always carried a pipe about at headquarters to produce an impression of comradeship on the soldiers, although it often made him sick."

It was hard work to credit this theory—until it was confirmed by a passage in Sir Morell Mackenzie's book. In response to the physician's question, Frederic said the report of his being a great smoker was "quite untrue, and that for many years he had hardly smoked at all." He added that probably this report, coming from soldiers who had seen him sometimes solacing himself after a hard-fought battle with a pipe, had given him his "perfectly undeserved reputation" as a devotee of tobacco.*

* "The Fatal Illness of Frederic the Noble," p. 20.

But the most striking illustrations of this trait, which Germans suspected in Frederic, are given in Gustav Freytag's interesting book, "The Crown Prince and the Imperial Crown." It may be said in passing that even among Conservatives in Berlin there is a feeling that Freytag should not have published this book. No doubt it tells the truth, but then Freytag owed very much to the tender friendship and liking of Frederic, who conspicuously favoured him above other German writers, and wrote kindly things about him in his diary—and, if the truth had to be told, some other than Freytag should have told it. Coupled as it is in the public mind with Dr. Friedberg's desertion, heretofore spoken of, this behaviour of another of the dead Prince's friends is felt to help justify the low opinion of German gratitude held among scoffing neighbours. As a Berlin official said in comment to the writer: "When men like Friedberg and Freytag do these things to the memory of their dead patron, it is no wonder that foreigners call us Prussians a pack of wolves, ready always to leap upon and devour any comrade who is down."

Freytag was the foremost correspondent attached to Frederic's headquarters in 1870-71, and enjoyed the confidence of the Crown Prince in extraordinary measure. Thus he is able to give us a detailed picture of the man's moods and mental workings, day by day, during that eventful time. And this picture is a perfect panorama of varying phases of histrionism.

The Crown Prince was sedulously cultivating the popular impression of himself as a plain, hail-fellow-well-met, friendly Prince. But Freytag says:

"The traditional conception of rank and position dwelt ineradicably in his soul; when he had occasion to remember his own claims, he stood more vehemently on his dignity than others of his class.... Had destiny allowed him a real reign, this peculiarity would probably have shown itself in a manner unpleasantly surprising to his contemporaries." *

* "The Crown Prince and the German Imperial Crown," by Gustav Freytag, p. 27.

More important still is this remark on the following page: "The idea of the German Empire grew out of princely pride in his soul; it became an ardent wish, and I think he was the originator and motive power of this innovation."

The fact that it was Frederic who conceived the idea of the Empire first came to the world when Dr. Geffcken printed that famous portion of the Crown Prince's diary which led to prosecutions and infinite scandal. Freytag's subsequent publication surrounds the fact with most curious minutiae of detail.

As early as August 1st, before his Third Army had even crossed the Rhine, Frederic had broached the idea of an empire, with Prussia at its head. All through the campaign which followed his head was full of it. He busied his mind with questions of titles, precedence, &c., to grow out of the new creation. One afternoon—August 11th—he strolled on the hillside with Freytag for a talk. "He had put on his general's cloak so that it fell around his tall figure like a king's mantle, and had thrown around his neck the gold chain of the Hohenzollern order, which he was not wont to wear in the quiet of the camp—and paced elated along the village green. Filled with the importance which the emperor idea had for him, he evidently adapted his external appearance to the conversation." During this talk he asked what the new title of the King of Prussia should be, and the anti-imperialist Freytag suggested Duke of Germany. Then "the Crown Prince broke out with emphasis, his eyes flashing: 'No! he must be Emperor!'" * To create this empire Frederic was quite ready to forcibly coerce the Southern German States. Bismarck and William I., whom we think of as rough, hard, arbitrary men, shrank from even considering such a course. To the enthusiastic and slightly unreal Frederic it seemed the most natural thing in the world. The account in his diary of the long interview of Nov. 16, 1870, with Bismarck makes all this curiously clear. "What about the South Germans? Would you threaten them, then?" asks the Chancellor. "Yes, indeed!" answers our ideal constitutional Frederic, with a light heart. The interview was protracted and stormy, Bismarck ending it by resort to his accustomed trick of threatening to resign, a well-worn device which twenty years later was to be used just once too often.

* Freytag, p. 20.

In this same diary, under date of the following March (1871), Frederic writes: "I doubt whether the necessary uprightness exists for the free development of the Empire, and think that only a new epoch, which shall one day come to terms with me, will see that.... More especially I shall be the first Prince who has to appear before his people after having honourably declared for constitutional methods without any reserve."

One feels that these two passages from his own diary—the utterances of November and the reflections of March—show distinctly why the practical rulers, soldiers, and statesmen of Prussia distrusted Frederic. They saw him more eager and strenuous about grasping the imperial dignity than any one else—willing even to break treaties and force Bavaria, Saxony, and Würtemberg into the empire at the cannon's mouth, and then they heard him lamenting that until he came to the throne there would not be enough "uprightness" to insure The Empress Frederic "constitutional methods." Candidly, it is impossible to wonder at their failure to reconcile the two.

THE EMPRESS FREDERIC.

(From a photograph by Elliott & Fry, 55 Baker Street, London, W.)

An even more acute reason for this suspicion and dislike lay in Frederic's relations with the English Court. To begin with, there was a sensational and fantastic uxoriousness about his attitude toward his wife which could not command sympathy in Germany. Freytag tells of his lying on his camp bed watching the photographs of his wife and children on the table before him, with tears in his eyes, and rhapsodizing about his wife's qualities of heart and intellect to the newspaper correspondent, until Freytag promised to dedicate his next book to her. "He gave me a look of assent and lay back satisfied." This in itself would rather pall on the German taste.

Worse still, Frederic used to write long letters home to his wife every day— often the work of striking the camp would be delayed until these epistles could be finished—and then the Crown Princess at Berlin would as regularly send the purport of these to her royal relatives in England and thence it would be telegraphed to France. Bismarck always believed, or professed to believe, that there was concerted treachery in this business. No one else is likely to credit this assumption. But at all events the fact is that this embarrassing diffusion of news was discovered and complained of at the time, and charged against Frederic, and was the reason, as Bismarck bluntly declared during the discussion over the diary, why the Crown Prince was not trusted by his father or allowed to share state secrets.

As for the Empire itself, though the original idea of it was his, Frederic suffered the fate of many other inventors in having very little to do with it after it was put into working order. He presented a magnificently heroic figure on horseback in out-of-door spectacles, and his cultured tastes made the task of presiding over museums and learned societies congenial. But there his participation in public affairs ended.

The Empire he had dreamed of was of a wholly different sort from this prosaic, machine-like, departmental structure which Bismarck and Delbruck made. Frederic's vision had been of some splendid, picturesque, richly-decorated revival of the Holy Roman Empire. There are a number of delightful pages in Freytag's book giving the Crown Prince's romantic views on this point. * When the first Reichstag met in 1871, to acclaim the new Emperor in his own capital, Frederic introduced into the ceremony the ancient throne chair of the Saxon Emperors, which may now be seen in Henry's palace at Goslar, and which, having lain unknown for centuries in a Harz village, was discovered by being offered for sale by a peasant as old metal some seventy years ago.

* Fryetag, pp. 115-130.

Among practical Germans this attempt to link their new Empire with the discredited and disreputable old fabric, which had been too rotten for even the Hapsburgs to hold together, was extremely distasteful. Yet Frederic clung to this pseudo-mediævalism to the last. When he came to the throne as Kaiser his first proclamation spoke of "the re-established Empire." And those who were in Berlin at the time know how a whole day's delay was caused by the dissension over what title the new ruler should assume—the secret of which was that he desired to call himself Kaiser Friedrich IV, thus going back for imperial continuity to that Friedrich III who died while Martin Luther was a boy, and who is remembered only because he was the father of the great Max and was the original possessor of the Austrian under lip.

Freytag indeed says that to that first proclamation Frederic did affix a signature with an IV—the assumption being that Bismarck altered it.

The reader has been shown this less satisfying aspect of Frederic, as his associates saw him, because without understanding it the attitude of both his father and his son towards him would be flatly unintelligible. They did not believe that he would make a safe Emperor for Germany.

The old William all the same loved his son deeply, and manifested an almost extravagant delight at the creditable way in which he carried himself through the Bohemian and French campaigns. In the succeeding years of peace it is obvious enough that the venerable Kaiser grew despondent about his son's association with Radicals and their dreams—and it is equally clear that there were plenty of advisers at hand to confirm the old man in these gloomy doubts. Hence, though he cherished a sincere affection for "Unser Fritz" and his English wife, and would gladly have had them much about him, he could not help being of the party opposed to them—the party which lost no opportunity of exalting young William in his grandfather's eyes as the real hope of the Hohenzollerns. Thus there was a growing, though tacit, estrangement between the father and son.

When Frederic was stricken with disease, however, the kindly old father suffered keenly. There was great sweetness of nature in the tough martial frame of William I, and there is an abiding pathos in the picture we have of his last moments—the stout nonogenarian who fought death so valiantly even to his last breath that it seemed as if he could not die, rolling his white head on the pillow, and moaning piteously, "Poor Fritz! Poor Fritz!" with his rambling thoughts beyond the snow-clad Alps, where his son was also in the destroyer's grasp.

As for young William, his estrangement from his father, if less noted, had been more complete. He belonged openly to another party, and moreover smarted under the reproach of being unfilial, which the friends of his parents, largely of the writing and printing class, publicly levelled at him.

Placed in this position, the shock of the news that his father had an incurable disease must have come upon him with peculiar force. We can only dimly imagine to ourselves the great struggles fought out in his breast between grief for the father, who had really been an ideal parent, loving, gentle, solicitous, and tenderly proud, and concern for the Empire, which might be doomed to have a wasting invalid at its head for years. On the one side was the repellent thought that this father's death would mean his own swift advancement, for the grandfather could clearly live but little longer. On the other side, if his father's life was prolonged, it meant the elevation to the throne of a sick man, whose fitness for the crown of this armed and beleaguered nation would at all times have been doubtful, and who, in his enfeebled state, at the mercy of the radical agitators and adventurers about him, might jeopardize the fortunes of Empire and dynasty alike.

Torn between these conflicting views, it is not strange that William welcomed a middle course, suggested, I am authoritatively informed, by Frederic himself.

The Crown Prince returned to Berlin from Ems thoroughly frightened. He had no doubt whatever that he was suffering from cancer and expected to die within the year. Like all men of an expansive and impressionable temperament, he was subject to fits of profound melancholia—as Freytag puts it, "fond of indulging in gloomy thoughts and pessimistic humours;" so much so that he "sometimes cherished the idea of renouncing the throne, in case of its being vacant, and leaving the government to his son." * He had grown lethargic and dispirited through years of inaction and systematic exclusion from governmental labours and interests. He returned from Ems now, in this April of 1887, in a state of complete depression.

* Freytag, p. 78,

The evident affection and sympathy with which both his father and son received him, gave an added impulse to the despairing ideas which had conquered his mind since his sentence of death by cancer had been uttered.

In the course of a touching interview between the three Hohenzollerns, Frederic with tears in his eyes declared that he did not desire to reign, and that if by chance he survived his father he would waive his rights of succession in favour of his elder son. This declaration was within a brief space of time repeated in the presence of Prince Bismarck, and was by him reduced to writing. The paper was deposited among the official private archives of the Crown at Berlin, and presumably is still in existence there.

CHAPTER V.—THROUGH THE SHADOWS TO THE THRONE

The fact that the Crown Prince Frederic, despondent and unnerved in the presence of a mortal disease, had voluntarily pledged himself to renounce his rights of succession, was naturally not published to the world. Although it is beyond doubt that such a pledge was given, nothing more definite than a roundabout hint has to this day been printed in Germany upon the subject. There are no means of ascertaining the exact number of personages in high position to whom this intelligence was imparted at the time. As has been said, the Emperor, the Chancellor, and the young heir were parties to Frederic's original action. Certain indications exist that for a time the secret was kept locked in the breasts of these four men. Then Frederic confessed to his wife what he had done.

The strangest feature of this whole curious business is that Frederic should ever have taken this gravely important step, not only without his wife's knowledge, but against all her interests. Her influence over him was of such commanding completeness, and his devotion to her so dominated his whole career and character, that the thing can only be explained by laying stress upon his admitted tendency to melancholia and assuming that his shaken nerves collapsed under the emotional strain of meeting his father and son with sympathetic tears in their eyes.

With the moment when the wife first learned of this abdication the active drama begins. She did not for an instant dream of suffering the arrangement to be carried out—at least until every conceivable form of resistance had been exhausted. We can fancy this proud, energetic princess casting about anxiously here, there, everywhere, for means with which to fight the grimly-powerful combination against her husband's future and her own, and can well believe that in the darkest hour of the struggle which ensued this true daughter of the Fighting Guelphs never lost heart.

For friends it was hopeless to look anywhere in Germany. She had lived in Berlin and Potsdam for nearly thirty years, devoting her large talents and wide sympathies to the encouragement of literature, science, and the arts, to the inculcation of softening and merciful thoughts embodied in new hospitals, asylums, and charitable institutions, and the formation of orders of nurses; most earnestly of all, to the task of lifting the women of Germany up in the domestic and social scale, and making of them something higher than mere mothers of families and household drudges. Nobody thanked her for her pains, least of all the women she had striven to befriend. Her undoubted want of tact and reserve in commenting upon the foibles of her adopted countrymen kept her an alien in the German mind, in spite of everything she did to foster a kindlier attitude. The feelings of the country at large were passively hostile to her. The influential classes hated her vehemently.

That she should link together in her mind this widespread and assiduously-cultivated enmity to her, and this new and alarming conspiracy to keep her husband from the throne, was most natural. She leaped to the conclusion that it was all a plot, planned by her ancient and implacable foe, Bismarck. That her own son was in it made the thing more acutely painful, but only increased her determination to fight.

Instinctively she turned to her English home for help. Although nearly two centuries have passed since George I entered upon his English inheritance, and more than half a century has gone by since the last signs of British dominion were removed from Hanover, the dynastic family politics of Windsor and Balmoral remain almost exclusively German. In all the confused and embittered squabbles which have kept the royal and princely houses of Germany by the ears since the close of the Napoleonic wars, the interference of the British Guelph has been steadily pitted against the influence of the Prussian Hohenzollern. Hardly one of the changes which, taken altogether, have whittled the reigning families of Germany from thirty down to a shadowy score since 1820, has been made without the active meddling of English royalty on one side or the other—most generally on the losing side. Hence, while it was natural that the Crown Princess should remember in her time of sore trial that she was also Princess Royal in England, it was equally to be expected that Germany should prepare itself to resent this fresh case of British intermeddling.

The scheme of battle which the Crown Princess, in counsel with her insular relatives, decided upon was at once ingenious and bold. It could not, unfortunately, be gainsaid that her husband, Frederic, had formally pledged himself to relinquish the crown *if* he proved to be afflicted with a mortal disease. Very well; the war must be waged upon that "if".

A good many momentous letters had crossed the North Sea, heavily sealed and borne by trusted messengers, before the system of defence was disclosed by the first overt movement. On the 20th of May, 1887, Dr. Morell Mackenzie, the best known of London specialists in throat diseases, arrived in Berlin, and was immediately introduced to a conference of German physicians, heretofore in charge of the case, as a colleague who was to take henceforth the leading part. They told him that to the best of their belief they had to deal with a cancer, but were awaiting his diagnosis. On the following day, and a fortnight later, he performed operations upon the illustrious patient's throat to serve as the basis for a microscopical examination. With his forceps he drew out bits of flesh, which were sent to Prof. Virchow for scientific scrutiny. Upon examining these Prof. Virchow reported he discovered nothing to "excite the suspicion of wider and graver disease," * thus giving the most powerful support imaginable to Dr. Mackenzie's diagnosis of "a benign growth."

The German physicians allege that Dr. Mackenzie drew out pieces of the comparatively healthful right vocal cord. The London specialist denies this. Nothing could be further from the purpose of this work than to take sides upon any phase of the unhappy and undignified controversy which ensued. It is enough here to note the charge, as indicating the view which Prof. Gerhardt and his German colleagues took from the first of Mackenzie's mission in Berlin.

This double declaration against the theory of cancer having been obtained, the next step was to secure the removal of Frederic. The celebration of the Queen's jubilee afforded a most valuable occasion. He came to England on June 14th—and he never again stepped foot in Berlin until he returned as Kaiser the following year. Nearly three months were spent at Norwood, and in Scotland and the Isle of Wight. A brief stop in the Austrian Tyrol followed, and then the Crown Prince settled in his winter home at San Remo. On the day of his arrival there Mackenzie was telegraphed for, as very dangerous symptoms had presented themselves. He reached San Remo on November 5, 1887, and discovered so grave a situation that Prince William was immediately summoned from Berlin.

That the young Prince had been placed in a most trying position by the quarrel which now raged about his father's sick-room, need not be pointed out. The physicians who stood highest in Berlin, and who were backed by the liking and confidence of William's friends, were deeply indignant at having been superseded by two Englishmen like Mackenzie and Hovell. This national prejudice became easily confounded with partisan antagonisms. The Germans are not celebrated for calm, or for skill in conducting controversies with delicacy, and in this instance the worst side of everybody concerned was exhibited.

One recalls now with astonishment the boundless rancour and recklessness of accusation which characterized that bitter wrangle. Many good people of one party seriously believed that the German physicians wanted to gain access to Frederic in order to kill him. On the other hand, a great number insisted that Mackenzie was deceiving the public, and had subjected Frederic to the most terrible maimings and tortures in order to conceal from Germany the fact of the cancer. The basest motives were ascribed by either side to the other. The Court circle asked what they were doing, then, to the Crown Prince that they hid him away in Italy; the answering insinuation was that very good reasons existed for not allowing him to fall into the hands of the Berlin doctors, who were so openly devoted to his heir.

In a state of public mind where hints of assassination grow familiar to the ear, the mere charge of a lack of filial affection sounds very tame indeed.

That William deserved during this painful period the reproaches heaped upon him by the whole English-speaking world is by no means clear. Such fault as may be with fairness imputed to him, seems to have grown quite naturally out of the circumstances. He was on the side of the German physicians as against Mackenzie; but after all that has happened that can scarcely be regarded as a crime. He could not but range himself with those who resented the tone Dr. Mackenzie and his friends assumed toward what they called "the Court circles of Berlin."

When he reached San Remo in November, it was to note the death mark clearly stamped on his father's face; yet he heard the English *entourage* still talking about the possibility of the disease not being cancer. The German doctors had grievous stories to tell him about how they had been crowded out and put under the heel of the foreigner. Whether he would or not, he was made a party to the whole wretched wrangle which henceforth vexed the atmosphere of the Villa Zirio.

The outside world was subjecting this villa and its inhabitants to the most tirelessly inquisitive scrutiny. Newspaper correspondents engirdled San Remo with a cordon of espionage, through which filtered the gossip of servants and the stray babbling of tradespeople. Dr. Mackenzie—now become Sir Morell —confided his views of the case to journalists who desired them. The German physicians furtively promulgated stories of quite a different hue, through the medium of the German press. Thus it came about that, while Germany as a whole disliked deeply the manner in which Frederic's case was managed, the English-speaking peoples espoused the opposite view and condemned as cruel and unnatural the position occupied by the Germans, with young William at their head.

As the winter of 1887-8 went forward, it became apparent that the Kaiser's prolonged life had run its span. The question which would die first, old William or middle-aged Frederic, hung in a fluttering balance. Germany watched the uncertain development of this dual tragedy with bated breath, and all Christendom bent its attention upon Germany and her two dying Hohenzollerns.

March came, with its black skies and drifting snow wreaths and bitter winds blown a thousand miles across the Sclavonic sand plains, and laid the aged Kaiser upon his deathbed. Prince William, having alternated through the winter between Berlin and San Remo, was at the last in attendance upon his grandfather. The dying old man spoke to him as if he were the immediate heir. Upon him all the injunctions of state and family policy which the departing monarch wished to utter were directly laid. The story of those conferences will doubtless never be revealed in its entirety. But it is known that, if any notion had up to that time existed of keeping Frederic from the throne, it was now abandoned. William was counselled to loving patience and submission during the little reign which his father at best could have. Bismarck was pledged to remain in office upon any and all terms short of peremptory dismissal through this same brief period.

It was to William, too, that that last exhortation to be "considerate" with Russia was muttered by the dying man—that strange domestic legacy of the Hohenzollerns which hints at the murder of Charles XII, recalls the partition of Poland, the despair of Jena, and the triumph of Waterloo, and has yet in store we know not what still stranger things.

William I died on March 9, 1888. On the morning of the following day Frederic and his wife and daughters left San Remo in a special train and arrived at Berlin on the night of the 11th, having made the swiftest long journey known in the records of continental railways. The new Kaiser's proclamation—"To my People"—bears the date of March 12th, but it was really not issued until the next day.

During that period of delay, the Schloss at Charlottenburg, which had been hastily fitted up for the reception of the invalid, was the scene of protracted conferences between Frederic, his son William, and Bismarck. Hints are not lacking that these interviews had their stormy and unpleasant side, for Frederic had up to this time fairly maintained his general health, and could to a limited extent make use of his voice. But all that is visible to us of this is the fact that some sort of understanding was arrived at, by which Bismarck could remain in office and accept responsibility for the acts of the reign.

The story of those melancholy ninety-nine days need not detain us long. Young William himself, though standing now in the strong light of public scrutiny, on the steps of the throne, remained silent, and for the most part motionless. The world gossiped busily about his heartless conduct toward his mother, his callous behaviour in the presence of his father's terrible affliction, his sympathy with those who most fiercely abused the good Sir Morell Mackenzie. As there had been tales of his unfilial actions at San Remo, so now there were stories of his shameless haste to snatch the reins of power from his father's hands. So late as August, 1889, an anonymous writer alleged in "The New Review" that "the watchers by the sick bed in Charlottenburg were always in dread when 'Willie' visited his father lest he might brusquely demand the establishment of a Regency."

Next to no proof of these assertions can be discovered in Berlin. If there was talk of a Regency—as well there might be among those who knew of the existence of Frederic's offer to abdicate—it did not in any way come before the public. I know of no one qualified to speak who says that it ever came before even Frederic.

That a feeling of bitterness existed between William and his parents is not to be denied. All the events of the past year had contributed to intensify this feeling and to put them wider and wider apart. Even if the young man had been able to divest himself of the last emotion of self-sensitiveness, there would still have remained the dislike for the whole England-Mackenzie-San Remo episode which rankled in every conservative German mind. But neither the blood nor the training of princes helps them to put thoughts of self aside— and in William's case a long chain of circumstances bound him to a position which, though we may find it extremely unpleasant to the eye, seemed to him a simple matter of duty and of justice to himself and to Prussia.

The world gladly preserves and cherishes an idealized picture of the knightly Kaiser Frederic, facing certain death with intrepid calm, and labouring devotedly to turn what fleeting days might be left him to the advantage of liberalism in Germany. It is a beautiful and elevating picture, and we are all of us the richer for its possession.

But, in truth, Frederic practically accomplished but one reform during his reign, and that came in the very last week of his life and was bought at a heavy price. To the end he gave a surprisingly regular attention to the tasks of a ruler. Both at Charlottenburg and, later, at Potsdam, he forced himself, dying though he was, to daily devote two hours or more to audiences with ministers and officials, and an even greater space of time in his library to signing State papers and writing up his diary. But this labour was almost wholly upon routine matters.

Two incidents of the brief reign are remembered—the frustrated attempt to marry one of the Prussian Princesses to a Battenberg and the successful expulsion of Puttkamer from the Prussian Ministry of the Interior.

The Battenberg episode attracted much the greater share of public attention at the time, not only from the element of romance inherent in the subject, but because it seemed to be an obvious continuation of the Anglo-German feud which had been flashing its lightnings about Frederic's devoted head for a twelvemonth. Of the four Battenberg Princes—cousins of the Grand Duke of Hesse by a morganatic marriage, and hence, according to Prussian notions, not "born" at all—one had married a daughter, another a granddaughter of the Queen of England. This seemed to the German aristocracy a most remarkable thing, and excited a good deal of class feeling, but was not important so long as these upstart *protégés* of English eccentricity kept out of reach of German snubs.

A third Battenberg, Alexander, had made for himself a considerable name as Prince of Bulgaria: in fact, had done so well that the Germans felt like liking him in spite of his brothers. The way in which he had completely thrashed the Servians, moreover, reflected credit upon the training he had had in the German Army. In his sensational quarrel with the Czar, too, German opinion leaned to his side, and altogether there was a kindly feeling toward him. Perhaps if there had been no antecedent quarrel about English interference, even his matrimonial adoption into the Hohenzollern family might have been tolerated with good grace.

As it was, the announcement at the end of March that he was to be betrothed to the Princess Victoria, the second daughter of Frederic, provoked on the instant a furious uproar. The Junker class all over Germany protested indignantly. The "reptile" press promptly raised the cry that this was more of the alien work of the English Empress, who had been prompted by her English mother to put this fresh affront upon all true Germans. Prince Bismarck himself hastened to Berlin and sternly insisted upon the abandonment of the obnoxious idea. There was a fierce struggle before a result was reached, with hot feminine words and tears of rage on one side, with square-jawed, gruff-voiced obstinacy and much plain talk on the other. At last Bismarck overbore opposition and had his way. Prince William manifested almost effusive gratitude to the Chancellor for having dispelled this nightmare of a Battenberg brother-in-law.

The solicitude about this project seems to have been largely maternal. Sir Morell Mackenzie says of the popular excitement over the subject: "I cannot say that it produced much effect on the Emperor." As for the Princess Victoria, she has now for some time been the wife of Prince Adolph of Schaumburg-Lippe.

Although it did not attract a tithe of the attention given the Battenberg marriage sensation, the dismissal of Puttkamer was really an important act, the effects of which were lasting in Germany. This official had been Minister of the Interior since 1881—a thoroughgoing Bismarckian administrator, whose use of the great machinery of his office to coerce voters, intimidate opposition, and generally grease the wheels of despotic government, had become the terror and despair of Prussian Liberalism; To have thrown him out of office it was worth while to reign only ninety-nine days.

Ostensibly his retirement was a condition imposed by Frederic before he would sign the Reichstag's bill lengthening the Parliamentary term to five years. The Radicals had hoped he would veto it, and the overthrow of Puttkamer was offered as a solace to these wounded hopes. But in reality Puttkamer had been doomed from the outset of the new reign. He was conspicuous among those who spoke with contempt of Frederic, and in his ministerial announcement of the old Kaiser's death to the public, insolently neglected to say a word about his successor. Questioned about this later, he had the impertinence to say that he could not find out what title the new Kaiser would choose to assume.

Puttkamer's resignation was gazetted on June 11th, and that very evening Prince Bismarck gave a great dinner, at which the fallen Minister was the guest of honour. In one sense the insult was wasted, for out at Potsdam the invalid at whom it was levelled could no longer eat, and was obviously close to death. Indirectly, however, the affront made a mark upon the world's memory. We shall hear of Puttkamer again.

On the 1st day of June Frederic had been conveyed by boat to Potsdam, where he wished to spend his remaining weeks in the most familiar of his former homes, the New Palace, the name of which he changed to Friedrichskron. He was already a dying man. Two clever observers, who were on the little pier at Gleinicke, described to me the appearance of the Emperor when he was carried up out of the cabin to land. Said one: "He was crouched down, wretched, scared, and pallid, like a man going to execution." The other added: "Say rather like an enfeebled maniac in charge of his keepers."

Yet, broken and crushed as he was, he was Kaiser to the last. The announcement of Putt-kamer's downfall came on June 11th. Frederic died on June 15th.

It was in the late forenoon of that rainy, gray summer day that the black and white royal standard above the palace fell—signifying that the eighth King of Prussia was no more. A moment later orderlies were running hither and thither outside; the troops within the palace park hastily threw themselves into line, and detachments were at once marched to each of the gates to draw a cordon between Friedrichskron and all the world besides.

In an inner room in the great palace the elder son of the dead Kaiser, all at once become William II, German Emperor, King in Prussia, eighteen times a Duke, twice a Grand Duke, ten times a Count, fifteen times a Seigneur, and three times a Margrave—this young man, with fifty-four titles thus suddenly plumped down upon him, * seated himself to write proclamations to his Army and his Navy.

* With the possible exception of the Emperor of Austria,
William is the most betitled man in Europe. Beside being
German Emperor and King of Prussia, he is Margrave of
Brandenburg, and the two Lausitzes; Grand Duke of Lower
Rhineland and Posen; Duke of Silesia, Glatz, Saxony,
Westphalia, Engern, Pomerania, Luneburg, Holstein-Schleswig,
Magdeburg, Bremen, Geldern, Cleve, Juliers and Berg,
Crossen, Lauenburg, Mecklenburg, of the Wends and of the
Cassubes; Landgrave of Hesse and Thuringia; Prince of

Orange; Count-Prince of Henneburg; Count of the Mark, of
Ravensberg, of Hohenstein, of Lingen and Tecklenburg, of
Mansfeld, Sigmaringen, Veringen, and of Hohenzollern;
Burgrave of Nuremberg; Seigneur of Frankfurt, Rügen, East
Friesland, Paderborn, Pyrmont, Halber-stadt, Münster,
Minden, Osnabrück, Hildesheim, Verden, Kammin, Fulda, Nassau
and Moers.

CHAPTER VI.—UNDER THE SWAY OF THE BISMARCKS

During the three days between the death and burial of Frederic the world saw and heard nothing of his successor save these two proclamations to the Army and Navy. This in itself was sufficiently strange. It was like a slap in the face of nineteenth-century civilization that this young man, upon whom the vast task of ruling an empire rich in historical memories of peaceful progress had devolved, should take such a barbaric view of his position. In this country which gave birth to the art of printing, this Germany wherein Dürer and Cranach worked and Luther changed the moral history of mankind and Lessing cleared the way for that noble band of poets of whom Goethe stands first and Wagner is not last, it seemed nothing less than monstrous that a youth called to be Emperor should see only columns of troops and iron-clads.

The purport of these proclamations, shot forth from the printing press while the news of Frederic's death was still in the air, fitted well the precipitancy of their appearance. William delivered a long eulogy upon his grandfather, made only a passing allusion to his father, recited the warlike achievements and character of his remoter ancestors, and closed by saying: "Thus we belong to each other, I and the army; thus we were born for one another; and firmly and inseparably will we hold together, whether it is God's will to give us peace or storm."

Exultant militarism rang out from every line of these utterances. The world listened to this young man boasting about being a war lord, with feelings nicely graded upon a scale of distances. Those near by put hands on sword hilts; those further away laughed contemptuously; but all alike, far and near, felt that an evil day for Germany had dawned.

The funeral of old William at Berlin in March had been a spectacle memorable in the history of mankind—the climacteric demonstration of the pomp and circumstance of European monarchical systems. A simple military funeral, a trifle more ornate than that of a General of division, was given to his successor. The day, June 18th, was the anniversary of Waterloo.

It may have been due to thoughts upon what this day meant in Prussian history; more probably it reflected the chastened and softening influences of these three days' meditation in the palace of death; from whatever cause, William's address to the Prussian people, issued on the 18th, was a much more satisfactory performance. The tone of the drill sergeant was entirely lacking, and the words about his father, the departed Frederic, were full of filial sweetness. The closing paragraph fairly mirrors the whole proclamation:

"I have vowed to God that, after the example of my fathers, I will be a just and clement Prince to my people, that I will foster piety and the fear of God, and that I will protect the peace, promote the welfare of the country, be a helper of the poor and distressed, and a true guardian of the right." Pondering upon the marked difference between this address and the excited and vain-glorious harangue to the fighting men of Germany which heralded William's accession, it occurred to me to inquire whether or not Dr. Hinzpeter had in the interim made his appearance at Potsdam. No one could remember, but the point may be worth the attention of the future historian.

Studying all that has since happened in the variant lights of these proclamations of June 15th and June 18th, one sees a constant struggle between two Williams—between the gentle, dreamy-eyed, soft-faced boy of Cassel, and the vain, arrogant youth who learned to clank a sword at his heels and twist a baby moustache in Bonn. Such conflicts and clashings between two hostile inner selves have a part in the personal history of each of us. Only we are not out under the searching glare of illumination which beats upon a prince, and the records and results of these internal warrings are of interest to ourselves alone.

William, moreover, has one of those nervous, delicately-poised, highly-sensitized temperaments which responds readily and without reserve to the emotion of the moment. Increasing years seem to be strengthening his judgment, but they do not advance him out of the impressionable age. In the romantic idealism and mysticism of his mind, and in the histrionic bent of his impulses, he is a true son of his father, a genuine heir of the strange fantastic Ascanien strain, which meant greatness in Catharine II, madness in her son Paul, and whimsical staginess in his grand-daughter Augusta.

Like his father, too, his nature is peculiarly susceptible to the domination of a stronger and more deeply rooted personality. The wide difference between them arises from this very similitude. Frederic spent all his adult life under the influence of the broad-minded, cultured, and high-thinking English Princess, his wife. William, during these years now under notice, was in the grip of the Bismarcks.

The ascendency of this family, which attained its zenith in these first months of the young Kaiser's reign, is a unique thing in the history of Prussia. The Hohenzollerns have been hereditarily a stiff-backed race, much addicted to personal government, and not at all given to leaning on other people. From 1660 to 1860 you will search their records in vain for the name of a minister who was allowed to usurp functions not strictly his own. The first Frederic William was a good deal pulled about and managed by inferiors, it is true, but they did it only by making themselves seem more his inferiors than any others about him. No Wolsey or Richelieu or Metternich could thrive in the keen air of the Mark of Brandenburg, under the old kingly traditions of Prussia.

Bismarck rose upon the ruins of those traditions. In 1862 the Prussian Diet and Prussian society generally were in open revolt against the new king, William I. Constitutionalism and the spread of modern ideas had made the old absolutist system of the Hohenzollerns impossible; budgets were thrown out, constituencies were abetted in their mutiny by the nobles, and the newspaper press was fiercely hostile. The King, a frank, kindly, slow-minded old soldier, did not know what to do. The thought of surrendering his historic prerogatives under pressure, and the resource of sweeping Berlin's streets with grape-shot, were equally hateful to him. In his perplexity he summoned his Ambassador at Paris to Berlin, and begged him to undertake the defence of the monarchy against its enemies. He made this statesman, Otto von Bismarck, Minister of the King's House and of Foreign Affairs, and avowedly a Premier who had undertaken to rule Prussia without a Parliament.

It was the old story of the Saxons, being invited to defend the British homestead, and remaining to enjoy it themselves.

The lapse of a quarter of a century found this King magnified into an Emperor, enjoying the peaceful semblance of a reign over 48,000,000 of people, where before he had stormily failed to govern much less than half that number. He had grown into the foremost place among European sovereigns so easily and without friction, and was withal so honest and amiable an old gentleman, that it did not disturb him to note how much greater a man than himself his Minister had come to be.

The relations between William I and Bismarck were always frank, loyal, and extremely simple. They were fond of each other, mutually grateful for what each had helped the other to do and to be. It illumines one of the finest traits in the great Chancellor's character to realize that, during the last eighteen years of the old Kaiser's life.

Bismarck would never go to the opera or theatre for fear the popular reception given to him might wound the royal sensitiveness of his master.

Bismarck, having all power in his own hands, became possessed of that most human of passions, the desire to found a dynasty, and hand this authority down to his posterity. There was a certain amount of promising material in his older son Herbert—a robust, rough-natured, fairly-acute, and altogether industrious man—ten years older than the Prince William, now become

Kaiser. The strength of Prince Bismarck's hold upon the old William was only matched by the supremacy he had thus far managed to exert over the imperial grandson. He dreamed a vision of having Herbert as omnipotent in the Germany of the twentieth century as he had been in the last half of the nineteenth.

The story of his terrible disillusion belongs to a later stage. At the time with which we are dealing, and indeed for nearly a year after William's accession in June of 1888, the ascendency of the Bismarcks was complete. Men with fewer infirmities of temper and feminine capacities for personal grudges and jealousies might possibly have maintained that ascendency, or the semblance of it, for years. But a long lease of absolute power had developed the petty sides of their characters. During the brief reign of Frederic they had had to suffer certain slights and rebuffs at the hands of his Liberal friends who were temporarily brought to the front. To their swollen *amour propre* nothing else seemed so important now as to avenge these indignities. The new Kaiser they thought of as wholly their man, and they proceeded to use him as a rod for the backs of their enemies.

It remains a surprising thing that they were allowed to go so far in this evil direction before William revolted and called a halt. For what they did before a stop was put to their career it is impossible not to blame him as well as them. In truth, he began by being so wholly under their influence that even his own individual acts were coloured by their prejudices and hates.

If he had been momentarily softened by the pathetic conditions surrounding his father's funeral, his heart steeled itself again soon enough under the sway of the Bismarcks. He entered with gratuitous zest upon a course of demonstrative disrespect to his father's memory.

Frederic had been born in the spacious, rambling New Palace at Potsdam, and in adult life had made it his principal home. Here all his children save William were born, and here William himself spent his boyhood, as Mr. Bigelow has so pleasantly told us, * playing with his brother Henry in their attic nursery, or cruising in their little toy frigate on the neighbouring lakes. Here Frederic at the end came home to die, and in the last fortnight of his life formally decreed that the name of the New Palace should henceforth be Friedrichskron—or Frederic's Crown.

* New Review, August, 1889.

All who have seen the splendid edifice, embowered in the ancient royal forest parks, will recognize the poetic and historic fitness of the name. From its centre rises a dome, surmounted by three female figures supporting an enormous kingly crown. There was a time when Europe talked as much about this emblematic dome as we did a year or so ago about the Eiffel Tower, though for widely different reasons. It was not remarkable from any scientific point of view, but it embodied in visible bronze a colossal insult levelled by Frederic the Great at the three most powerful women in the world. When that tireless creature emerged from the Seven Years' War, he began busying himself by the construction of this palace. Everybody had supposed him to be ruined financially, but he had his father's secret hoards almost intact, and during the six years 1763-9 drew from them over £2,000,000 to complete this structure. With characteristic insolence he reared upon the dome, in the act of upholding his crown, three naked figures having the faces of Catherine of Russia, Maria Theresa of Austria, and Mme. Pompadour of France, each with her back turned toward her respective country. The irony was coarse, but perhaps it may be forgiven to a man who had so notably come through the prolonged life-and-death struggle forced upon him by these women.

At all events, it was an intelligent and proper thing to give the palace the name of Friedrichskron, and one would think that, even if the change had been less fitting than it was, the wish of the dying man about the house of his birth could not but command respect.

One of William's first acts was to order the discontinuance of the new name, and in his proclamation he ostentatiously reverted to the former usage of "New Palace."

To glance ahead for a moment, there came in September an even more painful illustration of the unfilial attitude to which William had hardened himself. The *Deutsche Rundschau* created a sudden sensation by printing the diary of Frederic, from July 11, 1870, to March 12th of the following year, covering the entire French campaign and all the negotiations leading up to the formation of the German Empire. Quotations have already been made in these pages showing that this diary demonstrated authoritatively the fallacy of Bismarck's claim to be the originator of the Empire. Frederic and the others had had, in fact, to drag him into a reluctant acceptance of the imperial idea. The shock of now all at once learning this was felt all over Germany. Every mind comprehended that the blow had been aimed straight at the Chancellor's head. Nobody seemed to see, least of all Bismarck, that the diary really gave the Chancellor a higher title than that of inventor of the Empire, and revealed him as a wise, far-seeing statesman, who would not submit to the fascination of the imperial scheme until he made sure that its realization would be of genuine benefit to all Germany. So far, indeed, was he from recognizing this that he allowed the publication to rob him of all control over his temper.

The edition of the *Rundschau* was at once confiscated, and on September 23rd Bismarck sent a "report" to the Emperor upon the diary. He set up the pretence of doubting its genuineness as a cloak for saying the most brutal

51

things about its dead author. The charge was openly made that Frederic could not be trusted with any State secrets owing to the fear of "indiscreet revelations to the English Court," and therefore "stood without the sphere of all business negotiations." Further, he asserted that the portions of the diary expressing willingness to force the Southern States into the Empire must be forgeries, because "such ideas are equally contemptible from the standpoint of honourable feeling and that of policy." In conclusion he pointed out that, even if the diary were genuine, Frederic in giving it for publication would be a traitor under Article XCII of the Penal Code.

Of the genuineness of the diary there was, of course, no question whatever in anybody's mind, least of all in Bismarck's or William's. Yet the young Kaiser permitted this gross attack by the Chancellor upon his father's honour and patriotism to be officially published, and gave his consent to a prosecution of those responsible for the appearance of the diary in the *Rundschau*.

The story of the prosecution is a familiar one. Dr. Geffcken was found to be the friend to whom Frederic had entrusted this portion of his diary, and he was arrested and thrown into prison, to be brought before the imperial tribunal at Leipsic. The ingrate Friedberg put his talents at the disposal of the Bismarcks to draw up the case against him. The houses of Geffcken and Baron von Roggenbach were ransacked, and a correspondence covering many years was seized and searched by Bismarck's emissaries. These letters were said to contain many compromising references to the Crown Princess, Princess Alice, Sir Robert Morier, and others whom Bismarck alleged to be in a conspiracy against him. This charge of being desirous of the Chancellor's downfall grew indeed to be the principal item in the attack upon Geffcken.

The indictment for high treason was at last, on January 2, 1889, brought before the Judges of the Supreme Court of Judicature at Leipsic, and they threw it out with ignominious swiftness. Geffcken himself, badly broken in health and mind, was released on the 4th. This was Bismarck's first public mishap under the new reign, and it attracted much surprised attention at the time, as showing both the Chancellor's lack of intelligent self-restraint in getting into a fury over a revelation which really redounded to his credit, and his ignorance of German law. The opening month of the year 1889, in which this happened, was invested with importance in another way, as we shall see in due course.

But for the time, returning now to the middle of 1888, William seemed to delight in exhibiting himself to the public eye as the man of the Bismarcks. One of his earliest acts was to make a special journey to Friedrichsruh to visit the Chancellor, and the most popular photograph of the year was that representing him standing on the lawn in front of this château, in company with Bismarck and the famous "Reichshund." In Berlin, too, people noted his custom of paying early morning calls at the house of Herbert Bismarck, and wondered how long this enthusiastic self-abasement would last.

While it did last, this influence of the Bismarcks was so powerful and all-pervasive that it is very difficult to follow the thread of the young Kaiser's own personality through the busy period of his first half-year's reign. One continually confronts this embarrassment of inability to separate what he himself wanted to do from what was suggested by these powers behind the throne. We know now that the Kaiser possesses a strongly-marked individuality and an unusually active and fertile mind. Doubtless these asserted themselves a great deal at even this early stage, but there is little or nothing to guide us in distinguishing their effects.

The truth seems to be that at this time, in these opening months of his reign, William's inclinations ran so wholly in Bismarckian channels that even what he himself initiated was in practice a part of the Bismarcks' work.

This is especially true of the young Kaiser's first important step in the field of international politics. He had been on the throne for less than four weeks when he started off to pay a State visit to the Czar of Russia. He had not been invited, and it was apparent enough in Russian Court circles that his hasty and impulsive descent upon their summer leisure was as unwelcome as it was surprising. He himself appears to have been swayed both by memories of his grandfather's injunction to friendliness toward Russia, and by Bismarck's desire to make a demonstration of unfriendliness to England.

This note of anti-English prejudice is dominant throughout all that immediately followed. During Frederic's brief tenure of power, in April of 1888, Queen Victoria had made a journey to Berlin, and had spent several days in the company of her dying son-in-law and afflicted daughter at the palace of Charlottenburg. Her coming was not at all grateful to the Junker class, and it was rendered highly unpopular among Berliners generally by a curiously tactless performance on the part of the Empress Frederic. To properly receive her royal mother it was necessary to refurnish and decorate a suite of rooms in the Charlottenburg Schloss, and orders were sent to London for all this new furniture, and for English workmen to make the needed alterations. As may be imagined, this slight upon the tradesmen and artizans of Berlin was deeply resented, and there was considerable ground for nervousness lest the Queen should have some manifestation of this dislike thrust upon her notice during her stay. Fortunately, this did not happen, but Prince William behaved so coldly toward his grandmother that her Majesty could have had no doubt as to the attitude of his friends.

Later on, after Frederic's death? came confused stories about the arbitrary and unjust way in which his widow had been treated, both personally and as regarded her property rights. These matters are all settled now, and were the subject of great exaggeration even then, but they created so much bad blood at the time that the Prince of Wales in the following autumn left Vienna upon a hastily improvised and wholly fictitious hunting tour, rather than remain and meet his nephew, Kaiser William, who was coming that way.

Nothing very notable occurred during the July journeys to Russia, Sweden, and Denmark, and the autumnal trip to Austria and Italy presented no incidents of importance save this sudden flight of the indignant Prince of Wales, and a distinctly unpleasant bungling of the visit to the Pope. This latter episode has become famous in the annals of Prussian brusqueness and incivility. The young Kaiser in his white cuirassier uniform and eagle-capped helmet bluntly told the venerable Pontiff that his dreams of regaining temporal power were all childish nonsense, and the still ruder Herbert Bismarck broke up the interview by forcing his way into the Pope's private apartments, dragging amiable young Prince Henry with him as a pretext for his boisterous insolence. This was thought to be a smart trick at the time, and Herbert and the German Ambassador openly chuckled over it.

William himself is said to have remarked to King Humbert after his return from the call upon Leo XIII: "I have destroyed his illusions." At least the Holy Father no longer indulged illusions as to what the German Emperor was like—but in his mild, tranquil manner confided to certain members of his intimate household the pious fear that William was a conceited and headstrong young man, whose reign would end in disaster.

These journeys did little more than confirm the world in sharing the Pope's unfavourable opinion of William. Both by his ostentatious visit to Russia before even his two allies of the triple compact had been greeted, and by his marked avoidance of England while visiting all the other maritime nations of the north, he was credited with desiring to offend the country of his mother's birth. That country returned his dislike with interest.

Finally, on the 1st day of January, 1889, he put the capstone upon this evil and unfilial reputation which he had been for a year building up in the minds of English-speaking people. Badly as the outside world thought of him by this time, it learned now with amazement that he had selected for special New Year's honours the ex-Minister Puttkamer. The one important act of Frederic's reign had been the dismissal of this man, to whom William now, with marks of peculiar distinction, gave the order of the Black Eagle.

A groan of despairing disgust rose from every part of the globe where people were watching German affairs. How could any good thing whatsoever be expected from such a son?

CHAPTER VII.—THE BEGINNINGS OF A BENEFICENT CHANGE

The opening month of 1889 was a momentous period in the history of the young Emperor. The decoration of Puttkamer, who stood in all eyes as a type of the late Kaiser's bitterest and most malignant foes, put the finishing touch to the demonstrative unfilial stage of William's career. Men had been brought by this deed to think as badly of him as they could—when lo! the whole situation suddenly changed. This crowning act of affront to his father's memory was also the last. From that very month it is a new William who presents himself for consideration.

It is not possible to put the finger upon any one special cause for the change in the Kaiser's views and feelings which from this time began to manifest itself. There were in truth many reasons working together to effect this alteration, at once so subtle and so swift.

In its essence the abrupt new departure was due to the awakened consciousness in William's mind that the Bismarcks had been making a fool of him. Royalty can bear any calamity better than this. The saying ascribed to Louis XVIII, "For the love of God, do not render me ridiculous!" puts into words the thought that has lain closest to every monarch's heart since kings have had a being. And it was in William's nature to regard himself and his position with exceptional seriousness.

It would be extremely interesting to follow the mental processes by which William all at once reached this realizing sense of his position, and saw how poor and contemptible a figure he had been made to cut in the eyes of the civilized world. As it is, we can only glance briefly at the more obvious of the causes which led to this welcome awakening.

First of all, the High Court of Leipsic, on January 4th, threw out the indictment which Bismarck had been so savagely pressing against Dr. Geffcken, for the treasonable publication of a part of the Emperor Frederic's diary. The official ransacking of all his correspondence, and that of his most intimate associates, had revealed nothing save additional proof that the late Princess Alice of Hesse, Sir Robert Morier, and Dr. Geffcken were close friends of Frederic and his wife—which, of course, everybody knew before, but which the Bismarckian journals had paraded afresh as a reason for new insults to the dead Kaiser's memory and to the widowed Empress Frederic. The prompt adverse decision of the court dealt a sharp blow to this scandalous abuse of power.

In addition, the Bismarcks were meanwhile conducting a fierce public campaign against Sir Robert Morier, the British Ambassador at St. Petersburg —or rather, through him, against the honour of the late Emperor. Their accusation, based upon some alleged verbal statement of Marshal Bazaine, made at a time when he was most hopelessly discredited and new in exile, was that Frederic had systematically revealed the secrets of the German Army plans to Morier, who had sent them to England to be wired across to France. When Sir Robert Morier produced Bazaine's written denial of the alleged utterances and sent it to Herbert Bismarck, with a polite request for a withdrawal of the odious charge, he received a letter of refusal, couched in grossly insulting terms. This controversy, culminating about the time of the collapse of the Geffcken prosecution, no doubt contributed much to the opening of William's eyes.

There were not wanting at Berlin clever people ready to take advantage of these foolish excesses of the arrogant and over-confident Bismarcks. Their arbitrary and despotic courses had offended many besides those who would naturally be opposed to them politically, and there now sprang up, as out of the earth, a singular combination of the most diverse political elements, united only in their hatred for the Bismarcks. In this incongruous alliance Radicals and Jew-baiters joined hands, and ultra-Conservatives stood side by side with the Empress Frederic's Liberal faction. The headquarters of this odd combination were at the residence of Alfred Count von Waldersee.

This powerful personage, who for years, as Quartermaster-General, was in training as Moltke's visible heir, and was until recently at the head of the greatest fighting machine the human race ever saw, is still but little known to the general public. This is because press popularity and interesting personal qualities and connections have nothing whatever to do with a man's promotion in the German Army. Heroic actions on the field advance him no more than does the advertising faculty in times of peace. He rises to each place because he is judged to be fittest for that particular post, and this judgment sternly sets aside all considerations not immediately concerned with the duties of that post.

Thus it happens that of Count von Waldersee, who is one of the most important military officers in the world, not much is known save that he is now grey and bald, and has for his wife a very astute and influential American lady.

Twenty-seven years ago an elderly prince of the Schleswig-Holstein family produced a temporary sensation by renouncing his ancestral rank, in order to marry a beautiful young Miss Lee, whom he had met at Paris. He was then just the age of the century—sixty-four—and the bride, who, with true American courage, states the year of her birth in the *Almanach de Gotha*, was twenty-six. Less than a year later the bridegroom, who had been given the title of Prince de Noër at the Austrian Court, died in Syria. Nine years afterwards—in 1874—his widow married Count Waldersee, and went to Berlin to live.

It happened, in 1881, that young Prince William of Prussia was wedded to a Schleswig-Holstein Princess, to whom the Countess Waldersee, by her first marriage, stood in the relation of great-aunt. Young William and Waldersee were already friends. This connection between their wives led to a closer intimacy, the results of which have been tremendous in Germany.

I have said that the home of the Waldersees now became the centre of the rising opposition to the Bismarcks. Count Waldersee himself represented the ancient Prussian nobles' traditions of an absolute monarchy and a Hohenzollern's unlimited kingly power—traditions which were all at war with this Bismarckian usurpation of authority. The Countess Waldersee, with the privilege of an American, was able to gather into association with this aristocratic conservatism many elements in German political life which, under any other roof than hers, would have been antagonistic. Here it was that the women's conclave was formed—the young Empress Victoria and her widowed mother-in-law, the Empress Frederic, joining hands with the Countess Waldersee—with the blessing of the aged Empress Augusta, who all her life long had hated Bismarck, resting upon their work.

Bismarck had been supreme for so many years, and had put so many of these feminine cabals under his feet in bygone days, that he failed to recognize the deadly peril which confronted him in this newly-unmasked battery. He proceeded to charge upon it with all his old recklessness of confidence, and with his accustomed weapons of newspaper insults, personal browbeatings and threats to resign. To his great bewilderment nothing gave way. He had come at last upon a force greater than himself. He maintained the struggle for over a year—scornfully at first, and later with a despairing tenacity as pitiful as it was undignified, until at last he was fairly cudgeled off the field.

This was the trick of it: Bismarck, in all his extended series of conquests over previous attacks by the women of the Court, had had the King at his back. He was supported by old William in his long campaign against the old Empress and the English Crown Princess. He had had the sanction of young William in his warfare upon the Empress Frederic. It had been with royal consent that he bore himself like the foremost man in Prussia, and he had allowed himself to forget the importance of this fact. The tables were completely turned upon him the instant these adroit and sagacious women whispered in young William's ear, "Why not be foremost man in Prussia yourself?"

The young Kaiser's thirtieth birthday came on January 27, 1889. We can put down to about that date his advance to an independent position in front of everybody else in his kingdom—including the Bismarcks. No single striking event marked the change; but the feeling that the change had come spread with strange swiftness throughout the length and breadth of Germany. The half-intuitive sense that Bismarck was done for ran like wildfire over the country. The Iron Chancellor for thirty years had done his best to reduce German manhood to the serf-like condition of the courtier, and it is proverbial that there is no other keenness of scent like that of courtiers for the fall of a favourite.

The open reconciliation between William and his mother belongs to a somewhat later period, but the spirit of it was already in the air. The terrible news of the death of Crown Prince Rudolph of Austria, which came on January 30th, is also to be taken into account as bearing upon this change at Berlin. The Austrian heir-apparent was only six months older than William, and of late years they had not been friends. Rudolph had been peculiarly intimate with the Prince of Wales and with the late Emperor Frederic, and had not concealed his sympathy with the English view of William's behaviour. His tragic ending now produced the most painful and softening effect upon the emotional young Kaiser. He could only be restrained from going *incognito* to the funeral at Vienna by the urgent pleas of the stricken Austrian Emperor, and he made obviously sincere expressions of grief to the friends of the Prince of Wales, which went far toward removing the ill-feelings between them.

As it became apparent that the young Kaiser had thrown off his Bismarckian leading-strings, and, after a miserable interlude of small personal persecutions and revenges, was at last coming to comprehend the vastness of his duties and responsibilities, the world began watching him with an interest of another sort.

It was not easy for outsiders to follow with much clearness the details of the fight which Bismarck was now making to retain his position and prestige. No one but a German politician could understand the excitement about the appointment of the National Liberal, von Bennigsen, to the Governorship of Hanover—an act, by the way, which definitely ranged the ultra-Tories against Bismarck—or apprehend the significance of Bismarck's fruitless attempts to secure the dismissal of Court Chaplain Stocker, who was too much a partisan of Waldersee's. The general public preferred rather to study the personality of the young Kaiser as revealed by his individual acts and utterances.

William's fondness for travelling had from the first attracted attention. It is not generally known that in order to gratify this taste he at the beginning of his reign decided to devote to it the money which would be saved by foregoing a coronation ceremony. This decision accorded with historic Prussian precedents. From the year 1701, when Prussia was raised to royal estate, and the first King was crowned with such memorable and costly pomp at Königsberg, no Hohenzollern had a coronation ceremony until William I put the crown upon his own head in October of 1861. Each of the intervening monarchs held instead what is called a *Hudligung*, or solemn homage from the assembled representatives of the estates of the realm—a curious ceremonial relic from feudal times which survived into the present century in its antique form as a public function in the Schloss Platz. William I's avowed reason for breaking over the rule was that during his predecessor's reign a Constitution had been promulgated in Prussia, and that this new-fangled innovation rendered it necessary to remind people anew of the powers and prerogatives of the monarch by visible signs of crown and sceptre.

Young William was so enthusiastic a follower of his grandfather that people assumed he would imitate him in this, all the more because his own tastes are toward display. Upon this theory there has been a great deal printed about a forthcoming coronation which never comes. Only last year an unusually impressive statement appeared to the effect that William, moved by meditating upon the historic splendours of the old Holy Roman Empire, intended to have himself crowned German Emperor in the famous mediaeval church of the ancient imperial city of Frankfort-on-the-Main. The idea is a beautiful one, but there is no fact at the back of it. According to William's present intention, he will not be crowned at all.

In the restless course of his travels during these first six months William had made numerous speeches, almost every one of which contained a sentence or two of enough significance to be reprinted everywhere. As a rule his utterances at foreign Courts were polite and amiable to a fault, while his speeches at home, made among cheering after-dinner audiences in various parts of Germany, were characterized by much violent extravagance of language. The most intemperate of these harangues were reserved for his State visits to the provincial divisions of Prussia. At the beginning of last year, on the occasion of a visit of this nature to Königsberg, capital of East Prussia, he was led by his enthusiasm into so fervid a strain of eloquence, and flourished the metaphorical sword so recklessly, that one of the Russian papers ironically congratulated the world upon the fact that Prussia only had thirteen provinces, and that the Kaiser had now exhausted the rhetorical possibilities of eleven of them.

The earliest and most interesting of these speeches was delivered at Frankfurt-am-Oder just two months after his accession. He referred of his own volition to the undoubtedly foolish talk that had been heard during his father's brief reign, of Frederic's alleged idea of giving back Alsace-Lorraine, an imputation which William characterized as shameful to his father's memory.

"There is upon this point but one mind," he went on amid loud hurrahs, "namely, that our eighteen army corps, and our 42,000,000 people should be left upon the field rather than that we should permit a solitary stone of what we have gained to be taken from us."

Equally characteristic, and perhaps even more important as a clue to the manner in which the young Kaiser's conceptions of his position shaped themselves, was his celebrated rebuke to the Burgomaster and municipal authorities of Berlin, which has for its date, October 28 1888. That we may the better comprehend this, it will be well to glance for a moment at the remarkable development of the new Berlin.

Twenty years ago—that is to say, when the Empire was founded—Berlin was of course much the largest city within the new German boundaries, but it was scarcely a capital in the sense that Paris, Vienna, or London is. Frankfurt-am-Main was the great banking centre of Germany; Hamburg was its commercial metropolis; Dresden, Hanover, Stuttgart, Wiesbaden, and even smaller towns were more esteemed as places of fashionable residence and resort. Berlin was big and powerful, and rich in manufactures, no doubt, but nobody thought of it as beautiful or attractive, and nobody wanted to live there who could maintain himself in pleasanter surroundings.

The change which has been wrought in all this since 1870 is only to be matched by the phenomenal growth of great cities in the American West. Europe has seen nothing like it before. Within these twenty years Berlin has grown like a veritable Chicago. And not only has it attracted to itself hundreds of thousands of new citizens, and spread itself out on the Brandenburg plain over new square miles of stately brick and mortar and asphalt, but it has sapped the pre-eminence of its more ancient rivals, each in its speciality. Berlin has so absorbed the monetary power of the Empire that Frankfort is now scarcely thought of as a banking centre at all, and even Amsterdam and Paris are dwarfed financially. In similar fashion, the German nobility and wealthy classes, instead of scattering their town homes among a dozen local centres of social life, swarm now all to Berlin, and bid so strenuously for available building sites that prices for land and houses and floor rents are higher there than anywhere else in Europe.

Obviously, it is the establishment of the imperial Court in Berlin which has done this, and both the strength and weakness of the imperial system are reflected in greatest perfection of form and colour in the social conditions of this mighty new metropolis.

The enormous concentration here of rich or pretentious young nobles in the various regiments of the Guard Corps; of the ablest and most influential soldiers of Germany in the General Staff and the central military offices; of the cleverest politicians and administrators in the various civic departments, and of the great aristocratic and monied classes who must live where the Court is settled and the Reichstag meets and the finance of Europe is controlled—all this makes Berlin a peculiarly responsive mirror of the ideas and methods of German government.

In turn Berlin has imposed its character with increasing force upon the whole German people. The dear old indolent, amiable, incapable, happy-go-lucky, waltz-loving Vienna used to be the type of what people had in mind when they spoke of the sentimental German. Berlin has made Vienna seem now as remote and non-German almost as Pesth itself, and instead has impressed its own strongly-marked individuality upon the new Empire— energetic, exact, harsh under slight provocation, methodical as the multiplication table, coldly just to law-abiding people, and a fire-and-steel terror to everybody else.

As might be naturally expected in this bustle of busy officials, of bankers and merchants burdened with a novel wealth, of the ceaseless rattle of bayonets and clatter of swords and spurs, art and literature are pretty well pushed to the wall. The vast new growth of Berlin and the rush toward it of German wealth, rank, and fashion, have drawn in their train a certain current of painters and writers, but nothing at all in proportion with the expansion in other lines of activity. Berlin's new supremacy has not affected Leipsic as the book centre of German-speaking people, or Munich and Düsseldorf as homes of art study.

These changes may come, too, in time, particularly if the young Emperor exerts himself to achieve such an end. Up to the present, he has been too busy even to think of such a thing. The exactions of his daily routine of labour are so great that he simply has no time for the softer and more intellectual side of life, even if the taste were there. He has found leisure to sit for several portraits since his accession, but that seems to have been the sum of his attention to art. As for literature, an observant official in Berlin assured me of his conviction that William had not had the time to read a single book since his accession.

Whatever may come in the future, it is undeniable that the author now cuts a poor figure in Berlin. The city's drift is toward material things—toward business, official rank, and martial perfection. Even the most prosperous and popular writers of books in Berlin strive to obtain some small post in the civil service in order to command social position. Among many instances of this brought to my notice one will serve as an illustration. Ernst von Wilderbruch is the most successful of contemporary Berlin playwrights, but on his card you will read that he is a Counsellor of Legation at the Foreign Office. This office yields him a salary equal to a twentieth part of his income from his plays, but it is of the greatest importance to him because it insures his rank. Here in England Edmund Gosse has an official place—just as in Boston Robert Grant holds a post in the municipal service. But can you fancy either of these gentlemen putting the fact on his card, or preferring to be known as an official rather than as a writer?

Even the splendid University of Berlin exerts a liberalizing influence rather through the public political attitude of its professors than by the diffusion of literary tastes among the community. This fact, together with the recollections which associate the late Emperor Frederic with bookish people, and the irritated consciousness that a very large proportion of Germany's present authors are Jews and Radicals, gives the contemptuous attitude of Berlin's aristocratic and military classes toward literature a decided political twist.

This is rendered the more marked by the overwhelming Radicalism of the city's electorate. The immense balloon-like rise of the value of land, and the tremendous race to erect buildings everywhere, brought to the city a great concourse of artizans and labourers from all parts of Germany. Competition gave them big wages, but it also incited the formation of powerful trades' unions, the best of which were in effect Radical clubs, and the worst of which became centres of Socialist agitation. Berlin has six members in the Reichstag, of which four are Radicals, or *Freisinnige*, and two are Social Democrats. One of the Radicals is Prof. Rudolph Virchow, and one of the Socialists is Paul Singer, a Jew. The municipal institutions of Berlin, so far as they depend upon the popular vote, are also in the hands of the Radicals.

So much for the new Berlin. On Oct. 28, 1888, William, who had just returned from his Italian visit, the last of his series of journeys for that year, received the Burgomaster and a delegation from the Town Council, who came to the Schloss to congratulate him upon his return. They presented an effusively loyal address, clearly intended as a peace-offering from the Radical city to the new sovereign, and announced the intention of erecting a great fountain in the Schloss-Platz to commemorate the event.

William received this polite expression with studied insolence. After ironically commenting upon the unexpectedness of such a demonstration, he brusquely told them to build more churches in Berlin and to choke off their

63

Radical editors, who, during his absence, had shamelessly discussed the most private affairs of his family. He had been particularly angered by their insistence upon drawing comparisons between himself and his late father, an affront which he would not longer tolerate. He was about to take up his residence in Berlin, and "considering the relations which existed between the municipal authorities of Berlin and this Radical section of the press," he concluded that his hearers could stop this editorial impudence if they liked. Their address was full of loyal professions; very well, let them put these into practice.

Having said this in his roughest manner, William turned on his heel and left the room without shaking hands with the Burgomaster or so much as nodding to his colleagues.

This happened four months or so before the change in the young Kaiser's views and attitude which has been dealt with above. It is not out of place here, however, because, although William was now swiftly and with steady progress to alter his opinions on most other public subjects, he has not even yet altogether outgrown the notion that editors ought to wear muzzles.

CHAPTER VIII.—A YEAR OF EXPERIMENTAL ABSOLUTISM

The young Emperor's dislike for the press was indeed a fruitful source of sensational incidents during the first year or two of his reign, and still is uneasily felt to contain the elements of possibly further disturbance. The fault of this attitude is by no means entirely on one side. Both the character of the Kaiser and the character of the German press are in large part what Bismarck has made them, and if their less admirable sides clash and grind into each other with painful friction from time to time, it is only what might be expected. During Bismarck's twenty-eight years of power in Prussia he so by turns debauched and coerced the press that the adjective "reptile" had to be invented by outsiders properly to describe its venomous cowardice. He openly and contemptuously prostituted it to serve his poorest and pettiest uses, so that it was not possible for any one to think of it with respect; yet, oddly enough, he always showed the keenest and most thin-skinned sensitiveness when its attacks or inuendoes were aimed at himself.

This whimsical susceptibility to affront in the printed word, no matter how mean or trivial the force back of it, is a trait which has often come near making Bismarck ridiculous, and it is not pleasant to note how largely William seems also to be possessed with it. He is as nervous about what the papers will say as a young *débutante* on the stage. Not only does he keep an anxious watch upon the talk of the German editors, but he ordains a vigilant scrutiny of the articles printed in foreign countries from the pens of correspondents stationed at Berlin. In this he is very German. Nobody in England, for example, ever dreams of caring about, or for the most part of even taking the trouble to learn, what is printed abroad about English personages or politics. The foreign correspondents in London are as free as the wind that blows. But matters were ordered very differently at the beginning of the present reign in Berlin, and to this day journalists pursue their calling there under a sense of espionage hardly to be imagined in Fleet Street. It is true that a change for the better is distinctly visible of late, but it will be the work of many years to eradicate the low views of German journalism which Bismarck instilled, alike, unfortunately, in the royal palaces and the editorial offices of Prussia.

One of the very first acts of William's reign was the expulsion from Berlin of two French journalists whose sympathetic accounts of his father's dismissal of Puttkamer had been distasteful to the royal eye. In the following

January the correspondents of the *Figaro* and *National* of Paris were similarly driven out. In March, 1889, simultaneously with the seizure of the Berlin *Volks-Zeitung* and the prosecution of the *Freisinnige Zeitung*, a new Penal Code was presented to the Reichstag which contained such arbitrary provisions for stamping out the remaining liberties of the press that even the Cologne *Gazette* denounced it as "putting a frightful weapon into the hands of the Government for suppressing freedom of speech and silencing opposition." This measure did not pass, but the odium of having introduced it remained.

Although in other respects William was already observed to be separating himself from his Chancellor, it is clear that he has a large share in this odium. All his utterances, both at this time and up to the present date, show how thoroughly he believes in editing the editors. This tendency was during the year 1889 to exhibit its comical side.

The special organ of the Waldersee party was the high-and-dry old Tory journal, the *Kreuz-Zeitung*. Early in the year this mouthpiece of the anti-Bismarck coalition was raided by the Chancellor, and both its offices and the house of its editor, Baron Hammerstein, ransacked for incriminating documents. The Kaiser is believed to have intervened to prevent more serious steps being taken. Later in the year, as the success of the Waldersee combination in weaning the Kaiser away from Bismarck grew more and more marked, the *Kreuz-Zeitung* foolishly gave voice to its elation, and attacked the "Cartel" coalition of parties which controlled the Reichstag. The Kaiser thereupon printed a personal *communique* in the official paper saying that he approved of the "Cartel" and was "unable to reconcile the means by which the *Kreuz-Zeitung* assailed it with respect for his own person." This warning proved insufficient, for in the following January Baron Hammerstein put up as a candidate for a vacancy at Bielefeld, and talked so openly about being the real nominee of the Kaiser that William caused to be inserted in all the papers a notice of his order that the *Kreuz-Zeitung* should not henceforth be taken at any of the royal palaces, or allowed in public reading-rooms. It may be imagined how the Liberal editors chuckled over this.

So recently as in May of last year, two months after the retirement of Bismarck, when the regular official deputation from the new Reichstag waited upon William, he pointed out to the Radical members that the *Freisinnige* press was criticizing the army estimates, which he and his generals had made as low as possible, and sharply warned them to see that a stop was put to such conduct on the part of their friends, the Radical editors. And only last December, in his remarkable speech to the Educational Conference, he lightly grouped journalists with the "hunger candidates" and others who formed an over-educated class "dangerous to society."

This inability to tolerate the expression of opinions different from his own is very Bismarckian.

The ex-Chancellor, in fact, has for years past acted and talked upon the theory that anybody who did not agree with him must of necessity be unpatriotic, and came at last to hurl the epithet of *Reichsfeind*—enemy of the Empire—every time any one disputed him on any point whatsoever.

William has roughly shorn away Bismarck's pretence to infallibility, but about the divine nature of his own claims he has no doubt. Some of his deliverances on questions of morals and ethics, in his capacity as a sort of helmeted Northern Pope, are calculated to bring a smile to the face of the Muse of History. His celebrated harangue to the Rector of the Berlin University, Professor Gebhardt, wherein he complained that, under the lead of democratic professors, the students were filled with destructive political doctrines, and concluded by gruffly saying, "Let your students go more to churches and less to beer cellars and fencing saloons"—was put down to his youth, for it dates from the close of 1888. It is interesting to note, from William's recent speech at Bonn, that he has decidedly altered his views on both beer-drinking and duelling among students. He began his reign, however, with ultra-puritanical notions on these as well as other subjects.

Long after this early deliverance his confidence in himself, so far from suffering abatement, had so magnified itself that he called the professors of another University together and lectured them upon the bad way in which they taught history. He had discovered, he said, that there was now much fondness for treating the French Revolution as a great political movement, not without its helpful and beneficent results. This pernicious notion must no longer be encouraged in German universities, but students should be taught to regard the whole thing as one vast and unmitigated crime against God and man.

In this dogmatic phase of his character William is much more like Frederic William I than like any of his nearer ancestors in the Hohenzollern line. These later monarchs, beginning with Frederic the Great and following his luminous example, were habitually chary about bothering themselves with their subjects' opinions. William at one time thought a good deal upon the fact that he was a successor of Frederic the Great, and by fits and starts set himself to imitate the earlier acts of that sovereign. His restless flying about from place to place, and, even more clearly, his edicts rebuking the army officers for gambling and for harshness to their men, were copied from that illustrious original. But in his attitude toward the mental and moral liberty of his subjects he goes back a generation to Frederic's father—and suggests to us also the reflection that he is a grandson of that highly self-confident gentleman whom

English-speaking people knew as the Prince Consort.

Frederic the Great had so little of this spirit in him that he made himself memorably unique among eighteenth-century sovereigns by allowing such freedom to the press that liberty sank into license, and the most scandalous and mendacious attacks upon his personal life were printed in and hawked about Berlin to the end of his days. As for his refusal to interfere in the alleged perversion of Protestant children by Catholic teachers, his comment on the margin of the ministerial complaint, "In this country every man must get to heaven in his own way," is justly cherished to this day as worth all his other writings put together.

William's spasms, so to speak, of imitative loyalty to the memories of his ancestors have been productive of many curious, not to say diverting, results. Their progressive consecutiveness is not always easy to make out, but they afford, as a whole, very interesting insights into the young man's temperament.

When tragic chance thrust him forward and upon the throne, his youthful imagination happened to be in some mysterious way under the spell of that most astounding of all his forefathers, Frederic William I. He spoke frequently with enthusiasm of the character of this rude, choleric barbarian, and even brought himself to believe that there was something fine in that strange creature's inability to speak any language but German. It was under the sway of this admiration for the second Prussian King that William, in January of 1889, had all the French cooks in his palaces discharged, and ordered that hereafter the royal bill of fare should be a *Speisekarte*, with the names of dishes in German, instead of the accustomed *menu* in French. It will not, however, have escaped notice that William is a changeable young man, and this ultra-Teutonic mood did not last very long. In the following autumn he had so far recovered from it that his visit to Constantinople was reported to have been marred by the Sultan's mistaken hospitality in giving him nothing but German champagnes to drink. It must be admitted, however, that scarcely the most robust prejudice could stand out long under such a test.

In the spring of 1890 there came the 150th anniversary of the accession of Frederic the Great, and with it a sudden shift in the young Kaiser's admiration. For a long time thereafter he made no speech without alluding to this most splendid figure in Prussian history, and quoting him as an example to be followed with reverential loyalty.

Then in December came the turn of still a third bygone Hohenzollern. It was on December 1, 1640, that the youth of twenty, who was later to be known as the Great Elector, entered upon the herculean task of saving hapless, bankrupt little Brandenburg from literal annihilation. William has told us that as a boy he scarcely learned anything at all about this illustrious ancestor of his. Apparently little had been done to make good this lack of information up to the time when, toward the close of 1890, he found that the Great Elector's 250th anniversary was near at hand, and felt that it ought to be celebrated. He began reading the history of that memorable reign, and was at once excitedly interested and impressed. There has always been a charming, if childish, *naivete* about the manner in which William frankly exposes his mental processes, and, having just heard of something for the first time which everybody else knows, brings it forward to public notice as if it were a fresh and most remarkable discovery. The effect produced upon him by his belated introduction to the life and works of the last Elector affords an apt illustration of this tendency. At the celebration William made a long speech in eulogy of his ancestor, which in every sentence seemed to take it for granted that heretofore no one had written or thought or known about the Great Elector. Since that time the young Emperor has rarely spoken in public, at least to a Prussian audience, without some reference to this distinguished predecessor— whereas we never hear now of either Frederic the Great or his savage father.

Doubtless the fervour with which William has adopted the Great Elector as his model ancestor is in large part due to the fact that the latter's first important act was the summary dismissal of his father's Prime Minister, Schwarzenberg. The parallel to be drawn between the disgrace of this powerful favourite and the fall of Bismarck is often faulty and nowhere exact, but it is evident that it impressed William's imagination greatly when he came upon it, and that he could not resist the temptation to suggest it to the world at large. In this same anniversary speech he said: "My stout ancestor had no one to lean upon."

The eminent statesman who had served his predecessor was revealed to have worked for his own personal ends, and the young sovereign was forced to mark out his own path unaided. The comparison was a cruel one, because the manner in which Schwarzenberg "worked for his own personal ends" was that of taking bribes to betray his royal master and his country. Yet the loose phrase could also describe Bismarck's hot-headed use of his vast governmental powers to crush his individual enemies, and in this sense every one felt that William was instituting a comparison.

But this embittered remark belongs to a much later period than has as yet come under our view, and marks an acute stage of the dramatic and momentous quarrel between Kaiser and Chancellor, of the dawning of which there were only vague anticipatory rumours in 1889.

CHAPTER IX.—A YEAR OF HELPFUL LESSONS

The first few months of 1889 present nothing of special note to the observer. There was perhaps a trifle more nervousness on the bourses during that early spring-time which, for some occult reason, is the chosen season of alarmist war rumours, than had been usual in the lifetime of the old Kaiser, but this signified no more than a vague uneasiness born of the sword-clanking reputation which had preceded William's accession to the throne. The surface of events at Berlin seemed smooth enough, although dissensions and jealousies were warring fiercely underneath. Everybody was talking about the tremendous battle going on between the Bismarcks and the Waldersees, but of public evidence of this conflict there was none, This very reticence shows that the Chancellor must thus early have become impressed with the menacing power of the combinations confronting him, for it was never his habit to be silent about quarrels in which he was confident of victory. He must have become truly alarmed when, on February 25th, he gave a great dinner, at which the Kaiser and Waldersee were the principal guests. So far from creating a false impression of cordiality, this banquet, with its incongruous people and its hollow gaiety, only strengthened the notion that Bismarck was toppling.

In May, however, two things happened which at the time much occupied the world's attention—the abortive Strasburg visit incident and the great miners' strike in Westphalia. These two episodes are particularly noteworthy in that they for the first time show us William confronted by something bigger than questions of personal politics and individual piques and prejudices. A dangerous international quarrel and a threatening domestic convulsion loomed up suddenly side by side before him—and the experience left him a wiser and more serious man.

To glance first at the incident which, creating the greater furor at the time, has left the slighter mark upon history—the King of Italy, with his son and his Premier, came, on May 21st, to visit William in Berlin, There were many reasons why the reception extended to him should have been, as indeed it was, of the most affectionate and enthusiastic character. The old Emperor William had grown to be considered at the Quirinal as Victor Emmanuel's best friend, and Prussia was proudly pleased to be thought of as the chief protector and sponsor of young United Italy. The more romantic Frederic had cultivated a highly sentimental intimacy, later on, with King Humbert and

Queen Marguerite, and had made all Rome a party to it by that celebrated spectacular appearance on the balcony of the Quirinal with the little Italian Crown Prince in his arms. Thus peculiarly emotional ties bound Humbert now to Frederic's son, and his coming to Berlin was hailed as the arrival of a warm personal friend even more than as the advent of a powerful ally.

It may have been from mere lightness of heart—conceivably there was a deeper motive—but at all events William proposed to this good friend that on his way home they should together visit Strasburg, and the amiable Humbert, a slow, patient, honest fellow, consented. The assertion has since been authoritatively made by Italian statesmen that the idea really originated with the adventurous Italian Premier, Crispi, and that Bismarck and William merely fell in with it. However that may it is fact that the visit was agreed upon, and that orders were despatched to Strasburg to make things ready for the royal party.

When the news of this intended trip became public, its effect was that of a shock of earthquake. During the twenty-four hours which elapsed before the frightened Crispi could issue a statement that the report of such a visit was a pure Bourse canard, Europe was sensibly nearer a war than at any time in the last fifteen years. The French press raised a clamorous and vibrant call to arms, and the politicians of Rome and Vienna kept the wires to Berlin hot with panic-stricken protests. What it all meant was, of course, that Europe has tacitly consented to regard the possession of Alsace-Lorraine as an open question, to be finally settled when France and Germany fight next time. Upon this understanding, no outside sovereign has formally sanctioned the annexation of 1871 by appearing in person within the disputed territory. King Humbert's violation of this point of international etiquette would have been a deliberate blow in the face of the French Republic. Luckily he had the courage to draw back when the lightnings began playing upon his path, and with diminishing storm mutterings the cloud passed away. Its net result had been to show the world William's foolhardiness in favouring such a wanton insult to France, and his humiliation in having publicly to abandon an advertised intention—and the spectacle was not reassuring.

The episode is chiefly interesting now because it seems to have been of great educational value to the young Emperor. It really marked out for him, in a striking object lesson, the grave international limitations by which his position is hemmed in. He has never since made another such false step. Indeed the solitary other cause of friction between France and Germany which has arisen during his reign proceeded from an action of a diametrically opposite nature—to wit, an attempt to conciliate instead of offend.

Of much more permanent importance in the history of William and of his

Empire was the great miners' strike in Westphalia, which may be said to have begun on the 1st of May. This tremendous upheaval of labour at one time involved the idleness of over 100,000 men—by no means all miners or all Westphalians. The shortened coal supply affected industries everywhere, and other trades struck because the spirit of mutiny was in the air. In many districts the military were called out to guard the pits' mouths, and sanguinary conflicts with the strikers ensued.

Evidently this big convulsion took William completely by surprise. Up to this time he had been deeply engrossed in the spectacular side of his position —the showy and laborious routine of an Emperor who is also a practical working soldier. Such thought as he had given to the great economic problems pressing for solution all about him, seems to have been of the most casual sort and cast wholly in the Bismarckian mould. What Bismarck's views on this subject were and are, is well known. He believes that over-education has filled the labouring classes of Germany with unnatural and unreasonable discontent, which is sedulously played upon by depraved Socialist agitators, and that the only way to deal with the trouble is to imprison or banish as many of these latter as possible, and crush out the disaffection by physical force wherever it manifests itself. He decorates this position with varying sophistical frills and furbelows from time to time, but in its essence that is what he thinks. And up to May of 1889 that is apparently what William thought, too.

The huge proportions of this sudden revolt of labour made William nervous, however, and in this excited state he was open to new impressions. The anti-Bismarck coalition saw their chance and swiftly utilized it. With all haste they summoned Dr. Hinzpeter from his home at Bielefeld, and persuaded William to confer with his old tutor upon this alarming industrial complication, with which it was clearly enough to be seen his other advisers did not know how to deal. No exact date is given for the interview which William had with Dr. Hinzpeter, but the day upon which it was held should be a memorable one in German history. For then dawned upon the mind of the young Kaiser that dream of Christian Socialism with the influence of which we must always thereafter count.

It is true that the angered and dispossessed ex-Chancellor declares now that William never was morally affected by the painful aspects of the labour question, and that he took the side of the workmen solely because he thought it would pay politically. But men who know the Kaiser equally well, and who have the added advantage of speaking dispassionately, say that the new humanitarian views which Dr. Hinzpeter now unfolded to him took deep hold upon his imagination, and made a lasting mark upon his character. Even if the weight of evidence were not on its side, one would like to believe this rather than the cynical theory propounded from Friedrichsruh.

William did not become a full-fledged economic philosopher all at once under this new influence.

There was a great deal of the rough absolutist in the little harangue he delivered to the three working-men delegates who, on May 14th, were admitted to his presence to lay the case of the strikers before him. He listened gravely to their recital of grievances, asked numerous questions, and seemed considerably impressed. When their spokesman had finished he said that he was anxiously watching the situation, had ordered a careful inquiry into all the facts, and would see that evenhanded justice was done. Then, in a sharper voice, he warned them to avoid like poison all Socialist agitators, and specially to see to it that there were no riots or attempts to prevent the non-strikers from working. If this warning was not heeded, he concluded, in high peremptory tones, he would send his troops "to batter and shoot them down in heaps."

It must be admitted that this sentiment does not touch the high-water mark of Christian Socialism, but the drift of the Kaiser's mind was obviously forward. Two days later he received a delegation of mine masters, and to them spoke rather bitterly of the perversity and greed of capitalists, and their selfish unwillingness to "make certain sacrifices in order to terminate this perilous and troublous state of things." On May 17th it was announced that Dr. Hinzpeter had been commissioned to travel through the disturbed districts and report to the Kaiser upon the origin and merits of the strike. This practically settled the matter. The masters as a whole made concessions, under which work was resumed. Those owners who displayed stubbornness were in one way or another made to feel the imperial displeasure, and soon the trouble was at an end. It is worthy of note that Germany has since that time been far less agitated by labour troubles than any of the states by which she is surrounded, and that upon the occasion of the recent May-day demonstrations German workmen were practically the only ones on the Continent who did not come into collision with the police.

But, after all, the vitally important thing was the reappearance of Dr. Hinzpeter, involving, as it did, the revival in the young Kaiser's daily thoughts and moods of the gentle and softening influences of those old school days at Cassel, before Bonn and the Bismarcks came to harden and pervert.

Upon the heels of the Strasburg incident followed another flurry in international politics, which for the moment seemed almost as menacing, and which hurried forward a highly significant step on the part of William.

The precipitate haste with which the young Kaiser had rushed off to visit St. Petersburg, almost before the public signs of mourning for his father had been removed in Berlin and Potsdam, had impressed everybody as curious. Nearly a year had now elapsed, and the failure of the Czar to say anything about returning the visit was growing to seem odder still. It was, of course no secret that the Czar did not like William. No two men could present greater points of difference, physically and mentally. The autocrat of all the Russias is a huge, lumbering, slow, and tenacious man, growing somewhat fat with increasing years, hating all forms of regular exercise, and cherishing a veritable horror of noisy, overzealous, and bustling people. Every smart public servant in Russia is governed by the knowledge that his imperial master has a peculiar aversion to all forms of bother, and values his officials precisely in proportion as they make short and infrequent reports, free from all accounts of unpleasant things, and, still more important, from all meddlesome suggestions of reform. When a Russian diplomat was asked, a year ago, what the Czar's personal attitude toward William was, he answered expressively by shrugging his shoulders and putting his fingers in his ears.

But now the Czar, from passively affronting William by not returning his visit, summoned the energy for a direct provocation. A palace luncheon was given in St. Petersburg, celebrating the betrothal of a Montenegrin Princess to a Russian Grand Duke, and the Czar, standing and in a loud, clear voice, drank to Prince Nikolo of Montenegro as "the only sincere and faithful friend Russia had" among European sovereigns. That there might be no doubt about this, the Czar had the words printed next day in the *Official Messenger*.

Germany was not slow to comprehend the meaning of this remarkable speech. But to make it still clearer the Czarowitch, three weeks later, paid a formal visit to Stuttgart to attend some Court festivities, and passed through Berlin both going and coming—though the Breslau-Dresden route would have been more direct—apparently for no other purpose than to insult the Kaiser by stopping for an hour each time inside the railway station, as if there were no such people as the Hohenzollerns to so much as leave a card upon. As a capstone to this insolence, the Russian officers of his suite refused to drink the toast to the German Empire at the Stuttgart banquet, and, when a dispute arose, left the room in a body.

The immediate effect of this was to remove the last vestige of reserve existing between William and his English relatives. He at once sent word that, if convenient, he would visit his grandmother, the Queen, at the beginning of August. An assurance of hearty welcome was as promptly returned.

This decision marked another stage in the decline of Bismarck's power. We have seen how he had been gradually pushed aside in the management of German internal affairs. Now the Kaiser was to break through the dearest traditions of Bismarck's foreign policy—the cultivation of Russian amiability at whatever cost of dignity, and the contemptuous snubbing of England. With a fatal inability to distinguish between the promptings of passion and the dictates of true policy, the Chancellor had been led into a position where he could maintain himself only if every one of the elements and chances combined to play his game for him, and keep William at daggers-drawn with all things English. The miracle did not happen. As we have seen, even the Czar took it into his head to interfere to the damage of Bismarck's plans.

So the perplexed and baffled old Chancellor, noting with new rage and mortification how power was slipping from his hands, yet helpless to do other than fight doggedly to hold what yet remained, stopped behind in Berlin, the while Kaiser William steamed at the head of his splendid new squadron into Portsmouth Harbour, and the very sea shook with the thunderous cannon roar of his welcome. The world had never before seen such a show of fighting ships as was gathered before Cowes to greet him. There was one other thing which may be assumed to have been unique in human chronicles. William, in the exuberance of his delight at his really splendid reception, and at being created a British Admiral, issued a solemn imperial order making his grandmother a Colonel of Dragoons.

The English did well to surround the young Kaiser's visit with all imaginable pomp and display of overwhelming naval force, for it meant very much more both to them and to him than any one is likely to have imagined at the time. The splendour of the material spectacle, and the sentimental interest attaching to the fact that this young man coming to greet his grandmother was the first German Emperor to set foot on English soil since the days of the Crusaders, were much-dwelt upon in the press. To us who have been striving to trace the inner workings of the influences shaping the young man's character, the event has a nearer significance. It meant that William—having for years been estranged from the liberalizing English impulses and feelings of his boyish education; having since his majority exulted in the false notion that to be truly German involved hatred of all things English—had come to see his mistake.

It is not possible to exaggerate the importance of this visit, and of the causes leading up to it, upon William's mind. The Hohenzollerns, until within our own times the comparatively needy Princes of a poor country, have always been greatly impressed by the superior wealth and luxurious civilization of the English. The famous Double-Marriage project of Frederic William I's days was clung to in Berlin through years of British snubs and rebuffs because thrifty Prussian eyes saw these islands through a golden mist. To the imagination of German royalty, English Princesses appear in the guise of fairies, not invariably beautiful, perhaps, but each bearing the purse of Fortunatus. This view of the English colours the thoughts of more lowly-born Germans. When Freytag * seeks to explain the late Kaiser Frederic's complete and almost worshipping subjection to his wife, he says: "She had come to him from superior surroundings."

* "The Crown Prince and the German Imperial Crown," p. 49.

William had tried hard, in his ultra-German days, to despise English wealth along with English political ideas. The theory of a Spartan severity, governing expenditure and all other conditions of daily life, was the keynote of his Teutonic period. But when he became Kaiser he had yielded to the temptation of getting the Reichstag to augment his annual civil list by 3,500,000 marks. That in itself considerably modified his austere hatred of luxury. Now, as the guest of the richest nation in the-world, he was able to feel himself a relative, and wholly at home. The English conquest of William was complete.

No hint of unfilial conduct had been heard, now, for a long time, nor was henceforth to be heard. William had by this time become fully reconciled to his mother, and in the following month, September of 1889, he purchased for and presented to her the Villa Reiss, a delightful summer *chateau* in the Taunus Mountains.

Thereafter a strong sympathy with England has manifested itself in all his actions. The Czar did at last, in the most frosty, formal manner, pay a brief visit to Berlin, and William the following year returned the courtesy by attending the Russian manoeuvres, but this has not at all affected his open preference for English friendship. He always spoke German with an English accent—which now is more marked than ever.

He has a bewildering variety of uniforms, but the one which affords him the greatest pride is the dress of the British Admiral. He wears it whenever the least excuse offers. Upon his journey to Athens in October of 1889, to attend the wedding of his sister and the Greek Crown Prince, he was so much affected by his new English naval title that when he steamed into the classic Ægean Sea on his imperial yacht he flew the British Admiral's flag from her top. A British fleet was also there to participate in the ceremonies, and William took his new position so seriously, and had such delight in descending suddenly upon the squadron at unexpected and unreasonable hours, and routing everybody out for parade and inspection, that the British officers themselves revolted and preferred an informal complaint to the British Minister. "This thing is played out," they said. "If he would merely wear the uniform and let it end with that, we shouldn't mind. But we didn't make him Admiral to worry the lives out of us in this fashion."

CHAPTER X.—THE FALL OF THE BISMARCKS

We have come now to a time when the effects of this reasserted English influence began to be apparent throughout Germany. Since his successful tour through the Westphalian strike district, Dr. Hinzpeter had been visibly growing in men's eyes as the new power behind the throne. Another friend of William's, Count William Douglas, began also to attract attention. This nobleman, ten years older than the Kaiser, and a capable writer and speaker as well as soldier is a descendant of one of the numerous Scotch cadets of aristocratic families who carried their swords into Continental service when the Stuarts were driven from the British throne. Both in appearance and temperament no one could be more wholly German than Count Douglas is, but his intimacy with William only became marked after the English visit.

Immediately upon his return from England, William delivered a speech at Münster in which he eulogized Hinzpeter as a representative Westphalian, whose splendid principles he had imbibed in his boyhood. During the ensuing autumn and winter the presence of Dr. Hinzpeter at the palace became so much a matter of comment that some of Bismarck's "reptile" papers began to complain that if the Westphalian was to exert such power he ought to take office so that he could be openly discussed.

Similar attacks were made by the Chancellor's organs upon Count Douglas, who had written a very complimentary pamphlet about the young Kaiser shortly after his accession, and who now, as an Independent Conservative, was thought to reflect the Kaiser's own political preferences. Public opinion bracketed Hinzpeter and Douglas together as the active forces at the head of the Waldersee coalition, and we shall see that William himself treated them as such when the time for action came.

New men had gradually supplanted old ones in many important official posts. The gentlest of soft hints had long since (in August of 1888) been borne in by a little bird to the aged Count von Moltke, and he, on the instant, with the perfect dignity and pure gentility of his nature, had responded with a request to be permitted to retire from active labour. His letter, with its quaintly pathetic explanation that "I am no longer able to mount a horse." was answered with effusion by William, who visited him personally at his residence, and made him President of the National Defence Commission, *vice* the Emperor Frederic, deceased. Later events rendered it natural to contrast the loyal behaviour of the great soldier with the mutinous and perverse conduct of the statesman whose name is popularly linked with his, and during the last year of his life Moltke existed in a veritable apotheosis of demonstrative imperial affection, which indeed followed his coffin to the grave with such symbols of royal favour as no commoner's bier had ever before borne in Germany.

Somewhat later the Minister of Marine, General von Caprivi, received a delicate intimation that the Kaiser thought a soldier was out of place in charge of the navy, and he also promptly but gracefully resigned, and accepted the command of an army corps instead with cheerful obedience. It is a great gift to know when and how to get out, and Caprivi did it so amiably and intelligently that the Kaiser made a mental note of him as a good man to rely upon when the time should come.

General Bronsart von Schellendorf similarly resigned the War Ministry. He was a descendant of one of the large colony of Huguenot families which took refuge in Berlin after the revocation of the Edict of Nantes—and it was a strange freak of Fate's irony which, in 1871, sent him as Colonel out from the German headquarters before Sedan to convey a demand for surrender to the French Emperor. Curiously enough he was succeeded now as Minister of War by another descendant of these exiled French Protestants, General von Verdy du Vernois, the ablest military writer of his generation, a notably clever organizer and a deservedly popular man.

Neither von Verdy nor Waldersee, who succeeded to Moltke's proud position as Chief of the General Staff, remained long in their new posts. The world had nothing but vague surmises as to the causes of their retirement, and, noting that they still retain the friendly regard of their sovereign, did not dally long with these. Here again the contrast forces itself upon public attention, for these two good soldiers and able administrators neither sought interviews with travelling correspondents in which to vent their grievances, nor inspired spiteful attacks in provincial newspapers against their young chief. They went loyally out of office, as they had entered it, and kept their silence.

Thus throughout the public service, civil and military alike, these changes went forward—the greybeards who had helped to create the Empire on the field or in the council-room, one by one stepping down and out to make room for the new generation—but Bismarck, though becoming more and more isolated, clung resolutely to his place. It was no secret to him that the Kaiser's principal advisers and friends were keen to throw him out of the Chancellorship; it must have long been apparent to him that the Kaiser was accustoming his mind to thoughts of a Berlin without Bismarck. But the Iron Chancellor had neither the simple dignity of Moltke nor the shrewd suavity of Caprivi. He would not leave until he had been violently thrust forth, and even then he would stand on the doorstep and shout.

The opponents of Bismarck had long been gathering their forces for a grand attack. Their difficulty had been the unwillingness of the Kaiser definitely to give his assent to the overthrow of the great man. Often, in moments of impatience at the autocratic airs assumed by Bismarck and his son, William had seemed on the point of turning down his thumb as a signal for slaughter. But there always would come a realization of how mighty a figure in German history Bismarck truly was—and perhaps, too, some modified reassertion of the tremendous personal influence with which for years the Chancellor had magnetized him. Almost to the end the young man had recurring spasms of subjection to this old ideal of his youth. Even while he was sporting his British ensign in Greek waters, and showing to the whole world how completely the breach between him and English royalty had been healed, he salved his conscience, as it were, by addressing enthusiastic and affectionate despatches to Bismarck from every new stopping-place on those classic shores.

But now, in January of 1890, the long-looked-for opportunity came. The natural term of the Reichstag elected in 1887—the last one chosen for only three years' service—was on the point of expiration. The anti-Socialist penal laws would lapse in September of 1890 unless renewed either by this dying Reichstag or, without delay, by its successor. Prince Bismarck was, of course, committed to their prompt and emphatic renewal. His enemies—another term for William's new friends—had secretly been preparing for the defeat of these laws in the Reichstag, and now, in the middle of the month, found that they had secured an absolute majority. They conveyed this fact to the Kaiser, with the obvious corollary that the time had arrived for him to take the popular lead in his Empire, and make an issue on this question with his Chancellor. William saw the point, and reluctantly took the decisive step.

Space permits only the most cursory glance at this parliamentary battlefield, whereon Bismarck had waged so many rough Berserker fights, and which now was to see his complete annihilation.

The Reichstag at Berlin is by no means powerful in the sense that Parliament is in London or Congress in Washington. It is a convention of spectacled professors, country nobles, and professional men desirous of advertisement or the pretence of employment, with a sprinkling of smart financiers and professional politicians who have personal ends to serve. They play at legislation—some seriously, others not—but as a rule what they do and say makes next to no difference whatever. They have not even the power of initiating legislation. That function belongs to the Bundes-rath or Federal Council, which means the Prussian Ministry, which in turn meant Bismarck.

His historic conception of law-making was to combine by bribes and threats a sufficient number of the fragmentary parties to constitute a majority, and to use this to pass his measures as far as it would go. Then he would swing around, create a different majority out of other groups, and carry forward another line of legislation. In turn he had been at the head of every important political faction and the enemy of each, and if he was unable to get his way through one combination always managed sooner or later to obtain it by a new shaking-up of the dice.

Parliamentary institutions were not always at this low estate in Prussia. Three hundred years ago the Brandenburg Diet was a strong and influential body, which stoutly held the purse-strings and gave the law to sovereigns. The Hohenzollerns broke it down, first by establishing and fostering *Stände*, or small local diets, to dispute its power and jurisdiction, and then, in 1652, by the Great Elector boldly putting his mailed heel on it as a nuisance. It still lingered on in a formal, colourless, ineffective fashion until in the time of Frederic William I, when it was contemptuously kicked out of sight. That stalwart despot explained this parting kick by saying: "I am establishing the King's sovereignty like a rock of bronze;" and, whatever its composition, there the rock stood indubitably in all men's sight for much more than a century, with neither parliaments to shake its foundations nor powerful ministers to crumble away its sides.

Bismarck had made it a condition of his acceptance of office in 1862 that he would govern Prussia without a Parliament. When the fortune of war and the federation of the states enlarged the scope of his responsibilities to the limits of the new Empire, he proceeded upon the same autocratic lines. There was a greater necessity, it is true, of pretending to defer to the parliamentary idea, but he never dissembled his disgust at this necessity. He bullied the leaders of the opposition factions with such open coarseness, imputing evil and dishonest motives, introducing details of personal life which his spies had gathered, and using all the great powers at his command to insult and injure, that a large proportion of the educated and refined gentlemen of Germany, who should have been its natural political leaders, either declined to enter the Reichstag at all, or withdrew, disheartened and humiliated, after a brief term of service. All this reflected, and brought down in embodied form into our own times, the traditional attitude of the Hohenzollerns toward the poor thing called a Parliament.

It was therefore very much of an anachronism to find, in the year of grace 1890, a Prussian King invoking the aid of a Parliament to help him encompass the overthrow of his Prime Minister.

The situation on January 20th, briefly stated, was this: The Reichstag, consisting of 397 members, had been governed by Bismarck's "Cartel" combination of 94 National Liberals, 78 Conservatives, and 37 Imperialists, a clear majority of 21. The efforts of the Waldersee party, however, had honeycombed this majority with disaffection, and the National Liberals had been induced to agree that they would not vote for a renewal of the clause giving the Government power to expel obnoxious citizens. On the other hand, the Conservatives promised not to vote for the renewal of the anti-Socialist law at all unless it contained the expulsion clause. Thus, of course, the measure was bound to fall between two stools. This apparent clashing of cross purposes might have been stopped in ten minutes if it had proceeded spontaneously from the two factions themselves. But everybody knew that it had been carefully arranged from above, and that the leader of each party had had an interview with the Kaiser. This affectation of irreconcilable views on the expulsion clause, therefore, deceived no one—least of all Prince Bismarck. He ostentatiously remained at Friedrichsruh until the very last day of the Reichstag; then, indeed, he arrived in Berlin, but did not deign to show himself at either the Chamber or the Schloss.

The National Liberals voted down the expulsion clause on January 23rd. Then the Conservatives, two days later, joined the Clerical, *Freisinnige*, and Socialist Parties in throwing out the whole measure. Thereupon the dissolution of the Reichstag was immediately announced, and the members proceeded to the Schloss to receive their formal dismissal from the Kaiser. William spoke somewhat more nervously than usual, but was extremely cordial in his manner. He praised the labours of the Reichstag, dwelt upon his desires to improve the condition of the working classes, and said never a word about the defeated Socialist laws. Everybody felt that the imperial reticence and the absence of Bismarck portended big events.

Next week came the first overt movement in the struggle which all Germany now realized that Bismarck was waging for political life itself. He resigned his minor post as Prussian Minister of Commerce, and the place was promptly filled by the appointment of Baron Berlepsch. This selection was felt to be symbolical—because Berlepsch had been Governor of the Rhineland during the strikes, and had managed to preserve order without recourse to violence, and to gain the liking of the working men. To make the meaning of this promotion more clear, the Governor of Westphalia, who had rushed to declare his province in a state of siege when the strike broke out, and had called in soldiers to overawe the miners, was now curtly dismissed from office.

All this signified that the Hinzpeter propaganda of Christian Socialism had at last definitely captured the young Kaiser. Once enlisted, he threw himself with characteristic vehemence of energy into the movement. Events now crowded on each other's heels.

On February 4th William issued his famous brace of rescripts to Bismarck and to the Minister of Commerce, reciting the woes and perils of German industrial classes, and ordaining negotiations with certain European States for a Labour Conference, "with a view to coming to an understanding about the possibility of complying with the needs and desires of labourers, as manifested by them during the strikes of the last few years and otherwise."

"I am resolved," wrote the Emperor, "to lend my hand toward bettering the condition of German working men as far as my solicitude for their welfare is reconcilable with the necessity of enabling German industry to retain its power of competing in the world's market, and thus securing its own existence and that of its labourers. The dwindling of our native industries through any such loss of their foreign-markets would deprive not only the masters, but the men, of their bread.... The difficulties in the way of improving our working men's condition have their origin in the stress of international competition, and are only to be surmounted, or lessened, by international agreement between those countries which dominate the world's market." Hence, he had decided upon summoning an International Labour Conference.

On the evening of the day on which William thus astonished Germany and Europe, he was the principal guest at a dinner given by Bismarck in his palatial residence in the Wilhelmstrasse, and it was noted that he took special pleasure in talking with Dr. Miquel, Chief Burgomaster of Frankfort, to whom he spoke with zeal and at length upon his desire to promote the welfare and protect the natural rights of the labouring classes. Court gossip was swift to mark Miquel as a coming man, and to draw deductions of its own from the story that Bismarck had, even as the host of an emperor, seemed preoccupied and depressed.

A fortnight of unexampled uncertainty, of contradictory guesses and paradoxical rumours, now kept Berlin, and all Germany for that matter, in anxious suspense. That Bismarck had been confronted with a crisis was evident enough. Day after day he was seen to be holding prolonged conferences with the young Emperor, and the wildest surmises as to the character of these interviews obtained currency. There were stories of stormy scenes, of excited imperial dictation and angry ministerial resistance, which had no value whatever as contributions to the sum of popular information, but which were everywhere eagerly discussed. The weight of Berlin opinion inclined toward the theory that Bismarck would in the end submit. He had never in his life shown any disposition to make sacrifices for political consistency, and it was assumed that, once his personal objections were overcome, he would not at all mind adapting his political position to the new order of things. This view was, of course, based upon the idea that the Kaiser really desired to retain Bismarck in office; the loosest German imagination did not conceive the actual truth: to wit, that the Chancellor's retirement had been decided upon, and was the one end at which all these mystifying moves and counter-moves aimed.

The preparations for the Conference went on, meanwhile. A new Council of State for Prussia was founded, to have charge of the general social and fiscal reforms contemplated. The public noted that chief among the names gazetted were those of Dr. Hinzpeter and Count Douglas, and these were given such associates as Herr Krupp, of Essen; Prince Pless, a great Silesian mine-owner; Baron von Stumm, another large employer; and Baron von Hune, a leading Catholic and important landed proprietor. These were new strong names, altogether out of the old Bismarckian official rut, and their significance was emphasized by the Emperor's selection of Dr. Miquel as reporter of the Council. People recognized that events were being shaped at last from the royal palace instead of the Chancellery.

In the very middle of this period of political suspense came the elections for the new Reichstag. Never before had Germany seen such a lamb-like and sweet-tempered electoral campaign. Three years before Bismarck had literally moved heaven and earth to wrest a majority from the ballot-boxes, for he had induced the Vatican to formally recommend his nominees to Catholic voters, and had gone far beyond the bounds of diplomatic safety in his famous "*sturm und drang*" speech, threatening nothing less than war if a hostile Reichstag should be elected. But this time he preserved an obstinate and ominous silence. Nothing could tempt him to say a word in favour of any candidate.

Under the double influence of the Kaiser's enthusiastic new Socialism and the Chancellor's grim seclusion, the German electorate knocked the old "Cartel" parties into splinters. The polling results amazed everybody. Of the "Cartel" factions, the National Liberals fell from 94 to 39, the Conservatives from 78 to 66, and the Imperialists from 37 to 20. On the other hand, the *Freisinnigen* rose from 35 to 80, and the Socialists from 11 to 37. Equally interesting was the fact that for the first time the German imperial idea had made an impression on the Alsacian mind, and from sending a solid delegation of 15 dissentients, the two conquered provinces now elected 5 who accepted the situation.

Allusion has heretofore been made to Bismarck's recent declaration that the Kaiser took up the whole Social-reform policy solely as a political dodge. If we could accept this theory, it would be of distinct interest to know what

William thought of his bargain, after the returns were all in. The stupendous triumph of the dreaded Socialists and hated *Freisinnigen* must have indeed been a bitter mouthful to the proud young Hohenzollern. But he swallowed it manfully, and the results have been the reverse of harmful. No parliamentary session of the year, anywhere in the world, was more businesslike, dignified, and patriotic than that of the new Reichstag at Berlin.

But at the outset this political earthquake threw William into a great state of excitement. One might almost say that the electrical disturbances which ushered in the convulsion affected the young man's mind, for he did perhaps his most eccentric action on election day. While the voters of Berlin were going to the polls at noon, on this 20th of February, the Kaiser suddenly "alarmed" the entire garrison of the capital, and sent the whole surprised force, cavalry, artillery, baggage trains and foot, rattling and scurrying through the streets of the capital at their utmost speed. It turned out to be nothing more serious than an abrupt freak of the Kaiser to utilize the fine weather for a drill on the Tempelhof. At least that was the explanation given: but the spectacle produced a sinister impression at the time, and there are still those who believe it to have been intended to influence and overawe the voters.

No doubt consciousness of the gravity of the quarrel with Bismarck, which the Kaiser and his new friends saw now must come swiftly to a point, contributed with the unexpected election results to temporarily unsettle William's nerves. For a week or so, during this momentous period, there were actual fears lest his mental balance should break down under the strain. Fortunately the excited tension relaxed itself in good time, and there has since been no recurrence of the symptoms which then caused genuine alarm.

It was at the culmination of this unsettled period that William made his celebrated speech to the Brandenburg Diet. The occasion was the session dinner, March 5th, and those present noted that the Kaiser's manner was unwontedly *distrait* and abstracted. His words curiously reflected his mood— half poetic, half pugilistic. He began by a tender reference to the way in which the Brandenburgers had through evil and joyous days alike stood at the back of the Hohenzollerns. With a gloomy sigh he added: "It is in the hour of need that one comes to know his true friends." After an abrupt reference to a joke which had recently been made about him as the *reisende*, or Travelling, Kaiser, and a pedagogic injunction to his hearers to by all means travel as much in foreign lands as they could, he drifted into a lofty and beautiful description of the spiritualizing effects his recent sea voyages had had upon him. Standing alone on the great deck at night, he said, communing with the vast starry firmament, he had been able to look beyond politics and to realize the magnitude and tremendous responsibilities of the position he held. He had returned with a new and more exalted resolve to rule mercifully and well under God's providence, and to benefit all his people. Then there came a sudden anti-climax to this graceful and captivating rhetoric. "All who will assist me in my great task," he called out, throwing a lion's glance over the tables, "I shall heartily welcome; but those who attempt to oppose me I will dash to pieces!"

The reporters were so frightened at these menacing words that they toned them down in their accounts of the speech; but the Kaiser with his own hand restored the original expression in the report of the official *Reichsanzeiger*. Naturally the phrase created a painful sensation throughout Germany. Everybody leaped to the conclusion that the threat was levelled at the Socialist and Radical leaders in particular, and the new Reichstag in general. But within a fortnight the astonished world learned that it was Bismarck who was to be dashed to pieces.

The time has not yet arrived for a detailed account of the circumstances surrounding Bismarck's actual fall. We have been able to trace clearly enough the progression of causes and changes which led up to that fall. Of the event itself a great deal has been printed, but extremely little is known. The reason for this is simple. The Kaiser and his present friends are possessed with the rigid Prussian military sense of the duty of absolute silence about official secrets. Prince Bismarck has insisted vehemently upon the necessity of this quality in other people, yet has not always distinguished himself by respecting its demands. In his surprising latter-day garrulity, it is easy to believe that he would tell the story about which the others preserve so strict a reticence, if it were not that the story involves his own cruel personal humiliation.

Throughout the trying crisis William never lost sight of the proud and historic reputation of the man with whom he had to deal, or of the great personal reverence and affection which he, as a young King, owed to this giant among European statesmen, this most illustrious of the servants of his dynasty, this true creator of the new German Empire. Every step of the Emperor during the whole affair is marked with delicate courtesy and the most painstaking anxiety to avoid giving the doomed Chancellor unnecessary pain. Although it was entirely settled in the more intimate palace counsels at the end of 1889 that the Prince was to be retired from office, William sent him the following New Year's greeting, than which nothing could be more cordial or kindly:

"In view of the impending change from one year to another, I send you, dear Prince, my heartiest and warmest congratulations. I look back on the expiring year, in which it was vouchsafed to us not only to preserve to our dear Fatherland external peace, but also to strengthen the pledges of its maintenance, with sincere gratitude to God. It is to me also a matter for deep satisfaction that, with the trusty aid of the Reichstag, we have secured the law establishing old age and indigence assurance, and thus taken a considerable forward step toward the realization of that solicitude for the welfare of the working classes which I have so wholly at heart. I know well how large a share of this success is due to your self-sacrificing and creative energy, and I pray God that He may for many more years grant me the benefit of your approved and trusted counsel in my difficult and responsible post as ruler.

"Wilhelm.

"Berlin, Dec. 31,1889. "

A few days later came the death of the venerable Empress Augusta, and William wrote again to Bismarck at Friedrichsruh, affectionately enjoining him not to endanger his health by trying to make the winter journey to Berlin for the funeral.

This friendly attitude was, to the Kaiser's mind, entirely compatible with the decision that a new Chancellor was needed to carry on the enlightened programme of the new reign. But Bismarck stubbornly refused to recognize this. When his obstinacy made peremptory measures necessary, he had even the bad taste to instance these recent amiable messages as proofs of the duplicity with which he had been treated.

The best authenticated story in Berlin, of all the legion grown up about this historic episode, is to the effect that one afternoon, in the course of an interview between Kaiser and Chancellor on the approaching Labour Conference, Bismarck was incautious enough to use the old familiar threat of resignation with which he had been wont to terrify and subdue the first Kaiser. Young William said nothing, but two or three hours later an imperial *aide-de-camp* appeared at the Foreign Office in Wilhelmstrasse with the statement that he had come for that resignation. Bismarck, flushed and shaken, sent an evasive reply. The *aide-de-camp* came again, with a reiterated demand. Bismarck stammered out that he had not had the time to write it as yet, but that he would himself wait upon the Emperor with it the next day. He made this visit to the Schloss, prepared to urge with all the powers at his command, in the stress of a personal appeal, that the demand be reconsidered. But at the palace he was met with that equivalent for the housemaid's transparent "Not at home" which is used in the halls of kings; and on his return to Wilhelmstrasse he found the inexorable *aide-de-camp* once more waiting for the resignation. Then only, in bitter mortification and wrath, did Bismarck write out his own official death-warrant, which a few days later was to be followed by his son Herbert's resignation.

The widely circulated report that, in his extremity, the Chancellor appealed for aid to the Empress Frederic, seems to be apocryphal. It is certain, however, that he did, during the twenty-four hours in which that stolidly-waiting *aide-de-camp* darkened his life, make strenuous efforts in other almost equally unlikely and hostile quarters to save himself. They availed nothing save to reveal in some dim fashion to his racked and despairing mind how deeply and implacably he was hated by the officials and magnates all about him. But to the general public, astonished and bewildered at this sudden necessity to imagine a Germany without Bismarck, the glamour about his name was still dazzling. When it came their turn to act, they made the fallen Chancellor's departure from Berlin a great popular demonstration. It is well that they did so. With all his faults, Bismarck was *the* chief German of his generation, and the spectacle of cold-blooded desertion which the official and journalistic classes of Berlin presented in their attitude toward him upon the instant of his tumble, offended human nature. Nothing could be more true than that he himself was responsible for this attitude. It was the only possible harvest to be expected from his sowing. He had done his best to make all preferment and power in Germany depend upon callous treachery and the calculation of self-interest. He had contemptuously thrust ideals and generous aspirations out of the domain of practical politics. He had systematically accustomed the German mind to the rule of force and cunning, to the savage crushing of political opponents, and the shameless use of slander and scandal as political weapons. That this official mind of his own moulding, inured to sacrificial horrors, familiar with the spectacle of statesmen destroyed and eminent politicians flung headlong from the "rock of bronze," should have viewed his own prodigious downward crash without pity, was not at all unnatural. But for the credit of Germany with the outside world it is fortunate that the Berliners, as a whole, responded to the pathetic side of the episode.

William's emotional nature was peculiarly stirred by the separation, when it finally came. The *Reichsanzeiger* of March 20th—two days after the final act in the comedy of the unresigned resignation—contained the imperial message granting Prince Bismarck permission to retire. The phraseology of the document was excessively eulogistic of the passing statesman, and no hint of differing opinions was allowed to appear. Bismarck was created Duke of Lauenburg, and given the rank of a Field Marshal.

More eloquent by far, however, than any rhetorical professions of grief in his public proclamations, were the Emperor's statements to personal friends of the distress he suffered at seeing Bismarck depart. The ordeal was rendered none the less painful by the fact that it had been foreseen for months, or by the consideration that it was really unavoidable. On the 22nd William wrote to an intimate, in response to a message of sympathy:

"Many thanks for your kindly letter. I have, indeed, gone through bitter experiences, and have passed many painful hours. My heart is as sorrowful as if I had again lost my grandfather. But it is so ordered for me by God, and it must be borne, even if I should sink under the burden. The post of officer of the watch on the Ship of State has devolved upon me. Her course remains the same. So now full steam ahead!"

CHAPTER XI—A YEAR WITHOUT BISMARCK

The first and most obvious thing to be said of the twelvemonth during which the Ship of State has sailed with no Bismarck at the helm, is that the course has been one of novel smoothness. Since the foundation of the Empire Germany has not known such another tranquil and comfortable period. Nothing has arisen calculated to make men regret the ex-Chancellor's retirement. Almost every month has contributed some new warrant for the now practically unanimous sense of satisfaction in his being out of office. When astounded Germany first grasped the fact of his downfall, even those whose hatred of him was most implacable could not dissemble their nervousness lest Germany should be the sufferer in some way by it. He had so persistently kept before the mind of the nation that they were surrounded by vindictive armed enemies; he had year after year so industriously beaten the war drum and predicted the speedy breaking of the storm-clouds if his own way were denied him; he had so accustomed everybody to the idea that he was personally responsible for the continued existence from day to day of the German Empire, the peace of Europe, and almost every other desirable thing, that the mere thought of what would happen now he was actually gone dazed and terrified the public mind.

But lo! nothing whatever happened. The world continued its placid sweep through space without the sign of an interruption. The spring sun rose in the marshes of the Vistula and set behind the fir-clad ridges of the Vosges, just the same as ever. When Germany recovered her breath after the shock, it was to discover that respiration was an easier matter than it had formerly been. It was really a weight which had been lifted from the national breast. The sensation gradually took form as one of great relief, akin to that of filling the lungs to their utmost with the cool morning air after a night of confinement, unrest, and a tainted atmosphere. It is too much to say that apprehension fled at once; the anxious habit of mind still exists in Germany, and, indeed, must continue to exist so long as France and Russia stand on the map where they do. But a very short space of time served to make clear that Germany was in adroit and capable hands, and that the old-time notion of the impossibility of supporting national life without Bismarck had been the most childish of chimeras. Then little by little the new civility, freedom, and absence of friction which began to mark Parliamentary debates and official administration, attracted notice. The spectacle of a Chancellor who actually assumed the patriotism and personal honour of his political opponents in the Reichstag, who spoke to them like reasonable beings, and who said their views and criticisms would always receive his-respectful consideration, was not lost upon the German brain. People found themselves, before long, actively liking the new *régime*.

In reaching this attitude they were greatly helped by Bismarck's own behaviour, after he retired to Friedrichsruh. It does not fall within the purpose of this work to dwell upon the unhappy way in which, during the year, this statesman who was so great has laboured to belittle himself in the eyes of the world. Allusion to it is made here only to append the note that the Kaiser, under extreme provocation, has steadfastly declined to sanction the slightest movement toward reprisals. Although Bismarck has permitted himself to affront authority much more openly and seriously than Count Harry von Arnim ever did, his threats, his revelations, and his incitements to schism have all been treated with serene indifference. And so, too, we may pass them by, and push on to greater matters.

On May 6th the new Reichstag was opened by a speech from the throne, almost exclusively reflecting the Emperor's absorption in schemes of social reform and progress, and the new Chancellor, Caprivi, laid before Parliament a Trades Law Amendment Act, as a first attempt at embodying these schemes. After a year of deliberation this measure has just been passed, and, unless the Federal Council interposes some wholly unlooked-for obstacles, will come into effect on April 1, 1892. By this law Sunday labour is absolutely forbidden in all industries, save a selected few connected with entertainment and travelling, and the integrity of the great Church festival holidays is also secured. The Federal Council is given the power to supervise and control the maximum hours of labour in such trades as endanger the health of workmen by overwork. Both journeymen and apprentices are to be able to bring suit against their employers for wrongful dismissal. Female labour is forbidden at night, and is given at all times a maximum of eleven hours. Careful restrictions are also placed upon juvenile labour, and after April of 1894 children under the age of thirteen are not to be employed at all in factories. These reforms, which practically embody the recommendations of the Labour Conference, do little more than bring Germany abreast of England and America. A more extended programme of social reform is promised when the Reichstag meets again next November.

But it is not on specific achievements that the tremendous popularity which William has won for himself during the past year is founded. We are by no means within view of the end of the game, but it is already apparent that his greatest strength lies in the certainty and sureness of touch with which he appeals to the inborn German liking for lofty and noble visions of actions. The possibility—probability if you like—that these visions will never get themselves materialized, is not so important as it seems. Socialism in

Germany is far more a matter of imagination than of fact. Mr. Baring-Gould quotes an observer of the election phenomena of 1878, to show that "decorous people, dressed in an unexceptionable manner, and even to some extent wearing kid-gloves," went to the polls as Socialists then. This has been still more true of later elections. The element of imaginative men who had themselves little or nothing to complain of, but who dreamed of a vague Social Democracy as an idealized refuge from the harsh, dry bureaucracy and brutal militarism of Bismarck's government, played a large and larger part in each successive augmentation of the Socialists' voting strength. For want of a better word we may say that William is a dreamer too. In place of their amorphous Utopia, he throws upon the canvas before the Socialists the splendid fantasy of a beneficent absolutism which shall be also a democracy, in which everybody shall be good to everybody else, and all shall sleep soundly every night, rocked in the consciousness that their Kaiser is looking out for them, to see justice done in every corner, and happiness the law of the land.

It is all fantastic, no doubt, but it *is* generous and elevated and inspiring. Granted the premises of government by dreams, it is a much better dream than any which flames in the weak brains of the miners at Fourmies or in the dwarfed skulls of the Berlin slums. And the Germany which, under the impulse of a chivalrous and ardent young leader, finds itself thrilled now by this apocalyptic picture of ideals realized, and of government by the best that is in men instead of the worst, is certainly a much pleasanter subject for contemplation than that recent Germany which, under Bismarck, sneered at every spiritualizing ambition or thought, and roughly thrust its visionaries into prison or exile.

The chronological record of what remained of 1890 is meagre enough. Caprivi's first quarter in office was rendered brilliant by the bargain which gave Heligoland to Germany, and discussion over this notable piece of fortune was prolonged until the idleness of the summer solstice withdrew men's minds from politics. William made visits to Scandinavia, first of all, and then to the south shore of England, to Russia, and to Austria. In November the excitement over Dr. Koch's alleged specific for tuberculosis was promptly reflected by the Emperor's interest. He gave personal audience to the eminent microscopist, saying that he felt it his duty to buy the wonderful invention and confer the benefit of it freely upon not only his own people but the world at large. A fortnight later he bestowed upon Dr. Koch the order of the Red Eagle of the first class—a novel innovation upon the rule that there must be regular progression in the inferior degrees of the order.

In the same month William accepted the resignation of Court Chaplain

Stoecker, and met Dr. Windhorst in conversation for the first time. The two events are bracketed thus because they have an interesting bearing upon the altered state of the religious question in Germany.

The *Kulturkampf* had already, as we have seen, dwindled greatly under the parliamentary necessities of Bismarck's last years in power. But there had been no reconciliation, and the unjust old quarrel still drew a malignant gash of division through the political and social relations of the German people. Anti-Semitism in the same way lingered on, powerless for much overt mischief, but serving to keep alive the miserable race dissensions which have wrought such harm in Germany, and lending the apparent sanction of the Court to Berlin's, social ostracism of the Jews. William's broadening perceptions grasped now the necessity of putting an end to both these survivals of intolerance. The blatant Stoecker was given the hint to resign and an enlightened clergyman was installed in his place. At a Parliamentary dinner, given by Caprivi on November 25th, to which, according to the new order of things, the leaders in opposition were invited quite as freely as supporters of the Ministry, the Emperor met Dr. Windhorst, the venerable chief of the Ultramontane party. All present noted the exceptional courtesy and attention which William paid to "the Pearl of Meppen," and construed it to signify that the days of anti-Catholic bias were dead and gone. This judgment has been so far justified by events that, when Dr. Windhorst died in the succeeding March, it was said of him that of all his aims he left only the readmission of the Jesuits unaccomplished.

William's speeches during the year marked a distinct advance in the art of oratory, and gave fewer evidences of loose and random thinking after he rose to his feet than were offered by his earlier harangues. At the swearing-in of the recruits for the Berlin garrison, on November 20th, he delivered a curiously theological address, saying that though the situation abroad was peaceful enough, the soldiers must bear their share with other honest Germans in combating an internal foe, who was only to be overcome by the aid of Christianity. No one could be a good soldier without being a good Christian, and therefore the recruits who took an oath of allegiance to their earthly master, should even more resolve to be true to their heavenly Lord and Saviour.

Ten days later William made a speech of a notably different sort in front of the statue of the Great Elector, the 250th anniversary of whose accession to the throne of Brandenburg fell upon the 1st of December. Reference has heretofore been made to the powerful effect produced upon the young man's mind by reading the story of this ancestor, in preparation for this speech. There was nothing at all in it about loyalty to celestial sovereignties, but it bristled with fervent eulogies of the fighting Hohenzollerns, and was filled with military similes and phraseology. It contained as well the veiled comparison between Schwarzenberg and Bismarck which has been spoken of elsewhere.

Within the week the Kaiser delivered another speech, much longer than the other, and of vastly closer human interest. It had evidently been thought out with great care, and may unquestionably be described as the most important public deliverance of his reign. When he ascended the throne no one on earth would have hazarded the guess that, at the expiration of three years, William's principal speech would remain one upon the subject of middle education!

The occasion was a special conference convened by him to discuss educational reform in Prussia, and the gathering included not only the most distinguished professors and specialists within the kingdom, but representative men from various other German states. A list of the members would present to the reader the names of half the living Germans who are illustrious in literature and the sciences. The session was opened by the Emperor as presiding officer at Berlin, on December 4th.

It was wholly characteristic of the young man that, having tabled a series of inquiries upon the subject, he should start off with a comprehensive and sustained attack upon the whole *gymnasium*, or higher public school, system of the country. The Conference, having been summoned to examine the possibility of any further improvement upon this system, heard with astonishment its imperial chairman open the proceedings by roundly assailing everything connected with, and typical of, the entire institution.

The importance of the speech can best be grasped by keeping in mind the unique reputation which the Prussian school system has for years enjoyed in the eyes of the world. Its praises have been the burden of whole libraries of books. The amazing succession of victories on the fields of 1870-71 which rendered the Franco-Prussian War so pitifully one-sided a conflict, have been over and over again ascribed to the superior education of the German *gymnasia* even more than to the needle-gun—and this too by French writers among the rest. The Germans are justifiably proud of their wonderful army, but it is probable that a year ago they had an even loftier pride in their schools. The teachers are in themselves an army, and have traditionally exerted an influence, and commanded a measure of public deference, which the pedagogues of other lands know nothing about. It required, therefore, an abnormal degree of moral courage for even an Emperor to stand up in cold blood and make an attack upon the sacred institution of the *gymnasium*. It is even more remarkable that what the young man had to say was so fresh and strong and nervously to the point, that it carried conviction to the minds of a great majority of the scholastic greybeards who heard it.

He began by saying that the *gymnasia* (answering roughly to the Latin schools of England and the grammar-schools or academies of America) had in their time done good service, but no longer answered the requirements of the nation or the necessities of the time. They produced crammed minds, not virile men; wasting on musty Latin and general classical lore the time which should be devoted to inculcating a knowledge of German language and history—knowledge which was of infinitely more value to a German than all the chronicles of an alien antiquity combined. Had these schools done anything to combat the follies and chimeras of Social Democracy? Alas! the answer must be something worse than a negative—and tell not alone of an urgent duty left undone, but of evil wrought on the other side. He himself had sat on the various forms of a *gymnasium* at Cassel—a very fair sample of that whole class of schools—and he therefore knew all about their ways and methods, and the sooner these were mended the better it would be for every one.

It was undoubtedly true, William went on to admit, that in 1864, 1866, and 1870 the Prussian teachers' work showed to advantage. They had in those past years done a good deal to inculcate, and thus help to fruition, the idea of national unity—and it was safe to say that during that period every one who completed his *gymnasium* course went away after the final examination convinced that the German Empire should be reestablished, and crowned by the restoration of Alsace-Lorraine. But with 1871 this practical process of education came abruptly to an end, although as a matter of fact there was more than ever a need of teaching young Germans the importance of preserving their Empire and its political system intact. The consequence was that certain malignant forces had grown up and developed to a threatening degree, and for this the schools were clearly to blame.

Since 1870, he proceeded, there had been in German education a veritable reign of the philologists. They had been sitting there enthroned in the *gymnasia*, devoting all their attention to stuffing their pupils' skulls with mere book-learning, without even a thought of striving to form their characters aright, or training them for the real needs and trials of practical life. This evil had gone so far that it could go no farther. He knew that it was the custom to describe him as a fanatical foe to the *gymnasium* system. This was not true; only he had an open eye for its defects as well as its merits—of which, unfortunately, there seemed a heavy preponderance of the former.

Chief among these defects, to his mind, was a preposterous partiality for the classics. He submitted to his hearers, as patriots no less than professors, that the basis of this public school education should be German, and the aim kept always in view should be to turn out young Germans, not young Greeks and Romans. There must be an end to this folly. They must courageously break away from the mediaeval and monkish habit of mumbling over much Latin and some Greek, and take to the German language as the basis of their teaching. This remark applied also to history. Thoroughness in German history, both authenticated and legendary, and in its geographical and ethnological connections, should be first of all insisted upon. It was only when, they were wholly familiar with the ins and outs of their own house that they could afford the time to moon about in a museum.

"When I was at school at Cassel," said William, "the Great Elector, for instance, was to me only a nebulous personage. As for the Seven Years' War, it lay outside my region of study altogether, and for me history ended with the French Revolution at the close of the last century. The Liberation Wars, all-important as they are for the young German, were not even mentioned, and it was only, thank God! by means of supplementary and most valuable lectures from my private tutor, Dr. Hinzpeter, whom I rejoice now to see before me, that I got to know anything at all about modern history. How is it that so many of our young Germans are seduced from the path of political virtue? How is it that we have so many muddleheaded would-be world-improvers amongst us?

"How is it that we all the time hear so much nagging at our own government and so much praise of every other government under the sun? The answer is very easy. It is due to the simple ignorance of all these professional reformers and renovators as to the genesis of modern Germany. They were not taught, the boys of to-day are not taught, to comprehend at all the transition period between the French Revolution and our own time, by the light of which alone can our present questions be understood!"

"Not only would the *gymnasia* have to mend their methods," he continued, both as to matter taught and the method of teaching it, but they must also reduce the time burden under which they now crush their pupils. It was cruel and inhuman to compel boys to work so hard at their books that they had no leisure for healthful recreation, and the necessary physical training and development of the body. If he himself, while at Cassel, had not had special opportunities for riding to and fro, and looking about him a little, he would never have got to know at all what the outside world was like. It was this barbarous one-sided and eternal cramming which had already made the nation suffer from a plethora of learned and so-called educated people, the number of whom was now more than the people themselves could bear, or the Empire either. So true it was what Bismarck had once said about all this "proletariat of pass-men"—this army of what were called hunger candidates, and of journalists who were also for the most part unsuccessful graduates of the *gymnasia*, was here on their hands, forming a class truly dangerous to society!

The speech contained a great many practical and even technical references to bad ventilation, the curse of near-sightedness, and other details which need no mention here, but which indicated deep interest in, and a very comprehensive grasp of, the entire subject. At the close of the Conference, on December 17th, he made another address, from which we may cull a paragraph as a peroration to this whole curious imperial deliverance upon education. After an apology for having in his previous remarks neglected any reference to religion—upon which his profound belief that his duty as King was to foster religious sentiments and a Christian spirit was as clearly visible to the German people as the noonday light itself—he struck this true *fin de siécle* note as the key to his attitude on the entire subject:

"We find ourselves now, after marking step so long, upon the order of a general forward movement into the new century. My ancestors, with their fingers upon the pulse of time, have ever kept an alert and intelligent lookout upon the promises and threats of the future, and thus have throughout been able to maintain themselves at the head of whatever movement they resolved to embrace and direct. I believe that I have mastered the aims and impulses of this new spirit which thrills the expiring century. As on the question of social reform, so in this grave matter of the teaching of our young, I have decided to lead, rather than oppose, the working out of these new and progressive tendencies. The maxim of my family, 'To every one his due,' has for its true meaning 'To each what is properly his,' which is a very different thing from 'The same to all.' Thus interpreted the motto governs our position here, and the decisions we have arrived at. Hitherto our course in education has been from Thermopylae, by Cannæ, up to Rossbach and Vionville. It is my desire to lead the youth of Germany from the starting-point of Sedan and Gravelotte, by Leuthen and Rossbach, back to Mantinea and Thermopylae, which I hold to be the more excellent way."

The effect of this pronouncement upon the German public was electrical. For years there had been growing up in the popular mind a notion that something was wrong with the *gymnasium*, but no one had had the courage to define, much less proclaim, what the real trouble was. Parents had seen their sons condemned to thirty hours per week in the *gymnasium* (involving an even greater study time outside), and vaguely marvelled that of these thirty hours ten should be given to Latin and six to Greek, whereas mathematics claimed only four, geography and history combined got only three, German and French had but two each, natural science fluctuated between two and one, and English did not appear at all. * But though there was everywhere a nebulous suspicion and dislike of the system, it enjoyed the sacred immunity from attack of a fetich. So wonderful a thing was it held to be, in all printed and spoken speech, that people hardly dared harbour their own skeptical thoughts about it. But when the young Kaiser bluntly announced his conviction that it was all stupid and vicious and harmful, and pledged himself with boldness to sweep away the classical rubbish and put practical modern education in its place, the parents of Germany, to use Herr von Bunsen's phrase, were simply enchanted.

*See the interesting tabular statement in S. Baring-Gould's
 "Germany Past and Present," p. 181. London, 1881.

During the five months which have elapsed no miracle has been wrought; the character of the *gymnasia* has not been changed by magic. But it is perfectly understood by everybody that the Kaiser intends having his own way, and being as good as his word. Important steps have already been taken to enforce his views upon the system—notably by a change in the Ministry of Instruction.

Dr. Gustav von Gossler had held the portfolio for ten years, and was so entrenched in the liking of the great body of professors and teachers that he assumed his position to be perfectly secure. When, in the summer of 1889, the young Emperor despatched to him a long memorandum on the reforms necessary in the higher schools of Prussia, he received it submissively, even sympathetically, put it in a pigeon-hole, and went on in the same old dry-as-dust classical rut. William said nothing more, but eighteen months later, when he summoned the Educational Conference, he simultaneously published the text of the memorandum of the previous year. Even then Gossler seems to have suspected no danger, and made an official speech at the opening of the session full of amiable and confident commonplaces. On the following New Year's Day, however—January 1st, of the present year—a peremptory warning came to him in the form of a gift from the palace. It was a handsomely framed photograph of William II, and above the dashing signature were written the significant words, "*Sic volo, sic jubeo.*" It is not strange that shortly thereafter the retirement of von Gossler was announced.

His successor, Count Zedlitz-Trutschler, although beginning his career in the army, long ago revealed abilities which suggested his being drafted off into civil work. He has sat in the Reichstag as a Free Conservative, has been Governor of Silesia, and is both an excellent speaker and a man of great tact and resource. Among the reforms which he has already seen his way to enforce is one by which the students of the *gymnasia* report the number of hours out of school in which they are compelled to study to keep up with their lessons—these reports serving as a basis for the monthly rearrangement of tasks in such a way as to leave enough time for recreation. The study of German and other modern tongues has also largely displaced the classical curriculum in the three lower classes of the *gymnasia*. Count Zedlitz is the Minister, moreover, having to deal with ecclesiastical affairs, and his sympathies are all upon the side of toleration and of a good understanding with the Vatican.

On this same New Year's Day William sent a photograph also to the venerable Postmaster-General, Herr von Stephan, bearing a written legend not less characteristic than the other. It ran thus: "Intercommunication is the sign under which the world stands at the close of the present century. The barriers separating nations are thereby overthrown, and new relations established between them." Upon the sentiment thus expressed much of great importance to Germany and to Europe depends.

Brief as has been the career of the present German Empire among nations, its history already covers one very remarkable and complete *volte face* on economic subjects, and the beginnings of what promises to be a second and almost as sweeping change. Up to 1876, with Delbrück as President of the Chancellery and Camphausen as Minister of Finance, Germany stood for as liberal a spirit of international trade relations as at least any other nation on the Continent. But in that year Bismarck, by a combination of the various Conservative factions which leaned toward high tariffs, inaugurated a Protectionist policy which forced these Ministers out and ranged the German Empire definitely on the other side of the economic wall. To the end of Bismarck's rule, Germany steadily drifted away from Free Trade and toward the ideals of Russia, Thibet, and the Republican party in the United States. But even before Bismarck's fall it became apparent that the young Emperor took broader views on this subject than his Chancellor, and during the past year several important steps have been taken toward bringing Germany forward once more into line with modern conceptions of emancipated trade. A liberal Treaty of Commerce has been signed with Austro-Hungary—the precursor, it is believed, of others with countries now committed to stupid and injurious tariff wars, while at home no secret is made of the ministerial intention to in time reduce duties on cereals, lumber, and other necessaries, and generally pursue a tariff reform policy. The Reichstag has during the year passed a bill which, beginning in August of 1892, spreads over five years the extinction of the sugar bounties, another great bulwark of the rich protectionist ring. An attack upon the spirit bounties is expected next, while the Upper House of the Prussian Diet has just passed the new Graded Income Tax Bill which is to pave the way to a return from tariff to direct taxation.

The inspiring source of these reforms is Dr. Miquel, whose rise to imperial favour during the labour crisis has been noted, and who succeeded von Scholz as Minister of Finance in June of 1890. He furnishes still another illustration of the debt which German public life owes to the absorption, two centuries ago, of that leaven of Huguenot blood to which reference has heretofore been made—and which has long played in Prussia as disproportionately important a part as the remaining Protestant strain has in the politics of France. Herr Miquel looks like a Frenchman, and his manner, at once polished, genial, and grave, is that of a statesman reared on the Seine rather than the Vecht.

In one sense he is scarcely a new man, since he sat in the Prussian Parliament before the days of the Empire, and was years ago regarded as dividing with Bennigsen the leadership of the National Liberal party. He is in his sixty-third year, and might long since have been a Minister had he not felt it incompatible with his self-respect to take a portfolio under Bismarck's whimsical and arrogant mastership. In this present period of uncertainty in German politics, filled as it is with warring rumours of impending reconciliations and hints of even more deeply embittered quarrels, prophecy is forbidden, but no one on either side attempts a forecast of the future which does not assign to Miquel a predominant part.

His administrative abilities are of a very high order, and he combines with them much breadth of vision and great personal authority. The reliance placed upon him by the Emperor has been a subject of comment, almost from the first meeting of the two men, and German public opinion gives him no rival in influence over the imperial mind. It was at the dinner-table of this Minister last February that William is said to have replied to a long argument by Baron Kardorff in favour of bimetallism: "Personally I am a gold man, and for the rest I leave everything to Miquel."

With the impending retirement of von Maybach, Minister of Public Works and Railways, von Boetticher will be the only remaining Minister of eleven who held portfolios when William I died in March, 1888. It seems probable that the present year will outlive even this exception. The change in governmental spirit and methods of which Berlin is more and more conscious, is not wholly a matter of new men. The weight of militarism is being lifted. Generals no longer play the part they did in purely civil affairs. Count Waldersee's retirement from his great post as Chief of the General Staff is popularly ascribed to his having attempted to interfere with the amount and distribution of the military budget. Five years ago such an interference would have seemed to everybody the most natural thing in the world. The Emperor, too, grows less fond of obtruding the martial side of his training and temperament. From a beginning in which he seemed to think that Germany existed principally for the purpose of supporting an army, he has grown to see the true proportion of things and to give military matters hardly more than their legitimate share of his attention. The death of Moltke has removed the last great soldier who could speak authoritatively for the army in the Reichstag. In that sense at least he has left no heir.

In the more troubled domain of foreign affairs, the year without Bismarck has been marked by fewer visible changes. We are well along into "a year without Crispi," also, but the Triple Alliance, if less demonstrative in its professions of mutual affection and pride than formerly, seems no whit diminished in substantial unity. At the moment, peace appears to be as secure as it has been during any year since 1880—which is another way of saying that the weight of force and determination is still on the side of the Triple Alliance.

There has been during the twelvemonth only one sensational incident to mar the polite, business-like relations which Caprivi maintains with the nations of the earth. The unfortunate incidents attending the visit in February of the Empress Frederic to Paris, are too fresh in the public memory to call for recapitulation here. It seems fair to say that it is not easy to imagine so pacific and sensible an ending to such a stormy episode having been arrived at in the days of Bismarck. The young Kaiser, whom Europe thought of as a firebrand when he ascended the throne, kept his temper, or at least prevented its making a mark upon the policy of his government, in a striking manner. He had just gone out of his way to conciliate French feeling by writing a graceful message of condolence upon the death of Meissonier. The foolish insults to his mother, with which this act of courtesy was answered by the Parisian rabble, failed to provoke any retort in kind. Indeed, when it was represented to him that the increased rigour of passport regulations in Alsace-Lorraine was being construed as a reprisal, he issued orders to modify this rigour.

With this exhibition of judicious restraint, which rises to the full measure of the vast responsibilities and anxious necessities of his position, our chronological record of William's three-years' reign may be fittingly brought to a close. The added narrative which is held in store for us by the future may be tempestuous and discoloured by fire and blood; far better, it may be a gentle story of increasing wisdom, of good deeds done and peace made a natural state instead of an emergency in the minds of men. But whichever betides, we have seen enough to feel that it will be the chronicle of a real man, active, self-centred, eager to achieve and resolute to act, of high temper and great ambitions, and who has been given such a chance by the fates to help or hurt his fellow-mortals as perhaps no other young man ever had.

In a concluding chapter some notice may properly be taken of the personal attributes of William, and of his daily walk and talk as a human being as well as a Kaiser.

CHAPTER XII.—PERSONAL CHARACTERISTICS

I n the matter of personal appearance there are two quite distinct and different Williams. Those who see the young German Emperor on a State occasion think of him as almost a tall man, with a stern, thoughtful face and the most distinguished bearing of any sovereign in Europe. He holds himself with arrow-like straightness, bears his uniform or robes with proud grace, and draws his features into a kind of mask of imperial dignity and reserved wisdom and strength very impressive to the beholder. It is with what may be called this official countenance of William's that the general public is chiefly familiar, for he assumes it in front of the photographer's camera, just as he does on parade, at formal gatherings, and even in his carriage when he drives through the streets.

There is nothing to cavil at in this. One of the most important functions of an Emperor must surely be to look like an Emperor.

But in private life, when the absence of ceremonial and the presence of none but friends permit him to unbend, we see quite another William. He does not now give, the impression of being a tall man, and his face wears a softened and kindly expression prone to break into an extremely sweet and winning smile. When this smiling mood is upon him he looks curiously like his uncle, the Duke of Connaught, although at other times the resemblance is not apparent. As a boy he was very white-skinned, with pale flaxen hair. Years of military outdoor life burned his face to a tawny brown, through which of late an unhealthy pallor, the product of overwork and sleeplessness, at times shows itself. His hair is of average darkness, but his small and habitually curled moustache is of a light yellowish colour.

An observer who studied him closely during a whole day when he visited Russia three years ago describes him at the first morning review of troops as carrying himself almost pompously erect, and wearing a countenance of such gloomy severity that everybody was afraid to approach him, so that the officers who saw him for the first time jokingly whispered to one another that a new William the Taciturn had come into being. But in the afternoon, when the Czarina presided over a little garden party, limited almost to the circle of royalty, William appeared in a straw hat and jaunty holiday costume, smoked cigarettes continuously, and laughed and chatted with everybody as gaily and affably as any little bank bookkeeper snatching an unaccustomed day in the country.

The dominant feature of his make-up is a restless and tireless physical energy. In this he is perhaps more English than German. The insular tendency of his out-of-door tastes is very marked. Probably there is no gentleman on the Continent who keeps a keener or more interested watch upon the details of English sport, year by year, than William does. Oxford will not soon forget his characteristic telegram to Max Müller, recently, congratulating the University crew upon their victory in the annual race, and every British yachtsman looks forward to this season's regatta at Cowes with added interest, from the fact that the Emperor intends personally competing with his newly-purchased yacht.

William rides like an Englishman—which is another way of saying that he cuts a better figure in the saddle than most of the other Hohenzollerns, notoriously bad horsemen as a rule, have done. He has all the British passion for the sea and matters maritime. In his speech to the officers of the English fleet at Athens he said that his interest in their navy dated from the earliest days of his boyhood, when he played about Portsmouth dockyard and gained impressions of the vastness and splendour of British shipping which had vividly coloured his imagination for all time. No other German ruler has ever given so much thought to naval matters, and it is his openly-expressed ambition to give the Empire during his reign a fighting fleet which shall rank among the great navies of the world. During the debates in the Reichstag last March on the excessive naval estimates, he sent to the chairman of that special budget committee a copy of an old painting representing the fleet of the Great Elector, with footnotes in his own imperial hand giving the names and armaments of the various vessels, and bearing the inscription: "To Herr von Koscielski, in remembrance of his manly advocacy of my navy, from his grateful Emperor and King."

WILLIAM II. IN HUNTING COSTUME.
(From a photograph by Selle & Kuntze, Potsdam.)

William's love of exercise for its own sake is truly English. He fences admirably, is a skilful boatman, swims and bowls well and with zest, and delights in mountain climbing. No other Prussian Prince has ever been so fond of shooting. Hohenzollern notions of this particular sport have for generations been a matter for derision among Englishmen. Even Carlyle, who will hardly be described as a sportsman, was alive to the grotesque features of the *Parforce Fagd*, that curious institution in the Potsdam Green Forest which owes its origin to Frederic William I. The *Saugarten* is still there, and young boars, bred in captivity and bereft of their tusks at a tender age, are still released from their pens when the first frosts of autumn fall, and after a start of a few minutes are chased by mounted and gaily caparisoned parties of huntsmen—for all the world like the tame lion hunts of the Sardanapalian decadence pictured for us by the Assyrian palace friezes. But William has never shown much admiration for this pet diversion of the Potsdam officers. His own tastes are for the most laborious and difficult forms of woodland sport, and he is an exceptionally good shot.

What renders all this the more remarkable is the fact that his left arm is practically paralyzed. He has trained himself to hold the rein with it when he rides, but that is the sum of its usefulness. This defect dates from the occasion of his birth, and is ascribed to the ignorance or ineptitude of a physician. The arm is four inches shorter than its fellow, and has a malformed hand with only rudimentary fingers. The arm is so wholly limp that William has to lift its hand to even place it on the hilt of his sword with his right hand. It is in this posture, or else in the breast of his coat, that he customarily carries it when out of the saddle. All his photographs show it thus disposed of. At the table he has a combined knife and fork, which slide into each other. He uses this with much dexterity, first to cut up his meat and then to eat it, all of course with one hand.

To have become a skilled marksman under such a weighty disadvantage indicates great patience and determination. William uses a very light English gun, having abandoned in despair the attempt to get any made to his liking in Germany, and carries it on his shoulder with the stock behind him. At the proper moment he brings the weapon forward by a movement of his right arm, with incredible swiftness and deadly accuracy of aim.

Of much graver importance, of course, is the internal inflammation of the ear, formerly complicated at times with an acute earache, with which he has now been afflicted for a number of years. Just what the affection is no one has yet been able to determine. It grows worse in cold and wet weather, and that is about all that is known of it. The physicians disagree as to its character. William himself, though occasionally suffering grievously from it, has never been alarmed about it, and really believes it to be a local ailment. Its existence naturally enough suffices to create a certain uneasiness in the minds of his friends, and of Germans generally, and serves as the fruitful source of alarming rumours by which, from time to time, the virtue of Continental bourses is systematically assailed. But no responsible professional man seems to regard it as necessarily dangerous. This year, although the Emperor's appearance shows evident signs of the wear and strain of his great burdens upon his strength and spirits, this particular affection is said to be less troublesome than usual.

Undoubtedly, however, this annoying and wearying burden of the flesh has a great deal to do with William's disposition towards nervous excitability and restlessness. A man with the earache cannot be expected to hold calm mastery over all his moods. It is a reasonable assumption, too, that to this affliction is in some measure due his phenomenal and unseasonable physical activity. Sometimes it happens that he is unable to sleep at all, and he habitually keeps notebooks and pencils within reach of his bedside, upon which to work until the demon of insomnia is exorcised. Upon occasion, for distraction, he routs out the garrison of Berlin, or some regiment of it, before daybreak. In any case he rises at five.

Both at home and when abroad the amount of labour he gets through in a day is almost without parallel. It is a commonplace experience for him to do four hours' work in his Berlin study in the early morning; then take a train to Potsdam and spend the remainder of the forenoon in reviewing troops; then trot back in the saddle with his staff over the distance of eighteen miles; devote the afternoon to the transaction of business with his Ministers and officials; receive and return the calls of two or three visiting royal personages; then dine somewhere where a speech must be made, and get back to the palace for more work before bedtime.

In Constantinople and the scarcely less Oriental Athens they still recall his energetic daily routine with bewildered astonishment. He was up long before the drowsy muezzins from the minarets summon the faithful at the hour of prayer—rattling indefatigably about to see all the sights, reviewing the Sultan's troops, inspecting all the chief military establishments, War Ministry, military school, artillery barracks, and what not besides, asking questions of everybody who had anything to tell, peering into every nook and cranny with an insatiable curiosity, working through it all upon notes of instruction and reference to be forwarded to Berlin every evening, and then sitting up until all the others were yawning with sleep.

Of course he could not bear the strain of this constant activity if he were not endowed with two great gifts—prodigious physical vitality and imagination. Mere strength alone, mated with dulness of mind, would be broken down and destroyed by the wear and tear of such a life. William is, physically and mentally, the heir of the best things which European royalty has to offer. He inherits the bodily force and resolution of the Hohenzollerns, the *savoir faire* and comeliness of the Guelphs, the intellectual acuteness and philosophical tastes of the Coburgs, and the romantic mediaeval Ascanien strain which Catherine II took to Russia and her granddaughter brought back again to Weimar—a leaven half divine half daemonic, which swings between genius and madness. The product of these marriages might be expected to be what he is—by far the most striking personality in the whole gallery of contemporary kings.

What other dynasty in Western Europe does not envy William his six handsome, sturdy, and superbly healthy little sons? Seeing them with their shining, bright-eyed faces and ordinary well-worn clothes, one cannot but reflect upon the contrast afforded at Vienna, where the great rival house of Hapsburg is dying miserably out in pallid epileptics and vicious dullards.

These six fine boys, the oldest of whom is now in his tenth year, are reared in the Spartan traditions of the Hohenzollerns. Winter and summer they are up at six o'clock and into their cold tubs with merciless punctuality. As a rule they breakfast with their father half an hour later, and throughout the meal he talks with them alone. They salute him on entering, and again on leaving, in military fashion; even at this tender age a considerable portion of their education is upon martial subjects. The Emperor, in his recent speech at Bonn, indicated an intention of having the Crown Prince eventually matriculate there, but for the present, as soon as the lads outgrow their private tutors it is understood that they are to go to the great cadet school at Lichterfelde, just outside Berlin. Evidently the *gymnasium* has no part in the plans for their education.

The predominance of the military idea, which envelops even these little baby princes, is indeed the keynote to every phase of their father's character. He is first of all a soldier. He lives a plain and simple life; the service and routine of his palaces are those of an officer's mess. He is a heavy eater, with a preference for homely dishes; he smokes great numbers of light Dutch cigars which cost about three halfpence each. He addresses all persons whom he meets in an official capacity in the terse form and curt, sharp tone of a drill sergeant. Although in private conversation with friends his voice is soft and pleasant, all his public speeches are declaimed in a harsh and rattling voice, with abruptly ended sentences. His relations with other Germans, from the kings down to the peasants, are, in short, those of a commanding officer on the parade ground. This attitude does not suggest tact, or lend itself to roundabout' methods. The bluntly-expressed rescripts to the officers of the army which William from time to time has issued, complaining about the harsh personal treatment of the men, denouncing gambling and extravagant living, and so on, might easily have provoked a spirit of discontent in a country less wholly ruled by the idea of military discipline.

Naturally enough, his innate liking for display and scenic effects is strongly coloured by militarism. He cannot see too many uniforms about him, and he literally inundates Berlin with martial pageants. One might suppose that the effect of this would be to satiate the Berliners, but they maintain a most vigorous and unabated interest in seeing the troops march by, and throng the sidewalks every time as if the spectacle had all the excitement of novelty.

In almost every other country the personal tastes or whims of the sovereign, if he be at all a man of the world, leave a certain mark upon the every-day dress of the people about him. The Prince of Wales, for example, during the quarter century in which he has assumed the social work of his mother's reign, has made a good many changes in the fashions of men's clothes— changes which have been respected in Melbourne and Washington and

Toronto as well as in London. But hardly anybody in Germany has ever seen the adult William in citizen's clothes—and positively no one ever thinks of him save as in uniform.

As William is a soldier in manners and habits, so his conceptions of government and of domestic statecraft are largely those which might be expected in a chief of staff. He addresses his people always as their commander-in-chief. The starting-point of his resolve to get rid of Bismarck and bring in new men like Miquel and Caprivi, was his discovery that the Chancellor and the various political parties and factions which he alternately bullied and cajoled were really so many impediments standing between him and his subjects. The Hohenzollern desired to speak directly to the people, as a general to his army, and he has swept aside whatever stood in the way. Such a posture does not, at first sight, seem to promise much for progress and enlightened development, but it must be remembered that universal service in the army has had the effect of familiarizing all other Germans with this same point of view, so that really sovereign and subjects get on much better together than in many countries nominally more free.

The difficulties of government in Germany are almost wholly social and economic. The Prussian artizan, perforce, spends seven years at school and three years in the army before he seriously takes up his trade and sets to working for himself. He marries early and has a swarm of children, and the necessity of toiling to support all these in an overcrowded and underpaid labour market grinds upon his temper. He has, to begin with, a racial tendency to think highly of himself and to criticize other people; he is afforded only too much justification for his rooted dislike of aristocrats, employers, and rich people generally, who in Germany are much less generous and considerate than in some other countries. Thus he is peculiarly open to the arguments and allurements of the social democratic propaganda.

The Kaiser's idea is to meet and counteract this by appealing to the workman's military recollections and pride. It is difficult for outsiders to realize the potency of this appeal. Americans and Englishmen see the scores of thousands of young Germans who expatriate themselves to escape military service, and assume, therefore, that it must be a hateful thing. To those who look forward to it this may be true. But to the poor German artizan who looks backward upon it this term of service in the army is apt to seem the pleasantest period of his life. By comparison with the hardships of his later independent struggle for existence, he comes to regard this time when he was fed and clothed and instructed and lodged, and wore a uniform, with affectionate regret.

William, with what seems a sound instinct, lays great stress upon keeping alive and strengthening this army spirit. His wish is so to extend a semi-military organization throughout the social structure that every German may continue to feel that he belongs to the army. To this end he encourages the founding in each village of a *Landwehrbezirksverein*, or military club, where veterans and reservists are invited to come and read the papers over their beer and pipes, take charge of anniversary celebrations, promote local shooting festivals, and keep Social Democrats at a healthful distance. This plan is reported to be working well in small places, but it has not been thus far of much service in cities and factory centres, and in Mainz the attempt has just been abandoned owing to the discovery that all the members had become Social Democrats. But it is important to notice that since William has actively interested himself in the condition of these lower social strata, and sharply rated employers and army officers for harsh treatment of their men, the tone of the Socialists in the Reichstag toward him has been quite as civil as that of the other members.

For a young man descended from such phenomenally thrifty people as the Hohenzollerns and Wettins have always been, William has remarkably lavish, not to say prodigal, notions about money. He was left a very rich man by his father's death, and a complaisant Reichstag shortly thereafter largely increased the amount of his civil list, but for all that prudent Germans shake their heads over the immense schemes of expenditure to which he is already committed. The outlay upon the renovation of the Old Schloss in Berlin, entered upon in the first months of his reign, startled these good souls, but that turned out to be a mere drop in the bucket. The whole park arrangements at Potsdam are to be altered, and the unsightly old Dom—or cathedral—facing the Lustgarten in Berlin, has been torn down to make room for a magnificent ecclesiastical edifice worthy of the German capital. This means a heavy bill of expense, and Berliners hear with mingled emotions that their Royal Opera House is also to come down, to be supplanted by a wonderful new structure rivalling in dimensions and cost the Grand Opera House in Paris.

This last plan reflects the most marked artistic sense discoverable in William. He is passionately fond of the theatre, and has enlightened views about its popular usefulness. In decorating the tragedian, Ludwig Barnay, he has put on record an act by a Prussian King which not even his grandfather, the old Kaiser, enamoured of all things connected with the stage as he was, could be brought to contemplate. He delighted in the company of players to the end of his days, but he always frowned when the possibility of stars and ribbons was hinted at. William's action, therefore, deserves special notice. It must be admitted that his attitude toward the drama is dictatorial to a degree —very like that which a general might be assumed to occupy toward a band of mummers allowed inside the camp to amuse the soldiers; but the German drama is framed to resist a great deal of pressure to the square inch, and is indeed rather the better for it. Very comical are the stories told in Berlin of the way in which William personally superintended the rehearsals of Wildenbruch's "The New Lord" last winter, criticizing and instructing the actors, and rearranging the distribution of the cast to suit his notions of their several capabilities. The fact that the drama had for its principal incident the Great Elector's dismissal of his father's Minister, Schwarzenberg, doubtless accounted for much of the Emperor's personal solicitude as to its proper presentation. But it is not in William's nature to refrain from meddling and dictating about anything, no matter how trivial, in which his interest is aroused.

The young Kaiser was never what is called a bookish man, and, as has been said before, the tremendous pressure of his daily work now leaves him no time whatever for reading. But he still manages to secure a certain amount of leisure for association with intimate friends, and among these are a number of highly-cultured men. He gets from them what others are obliged to seek in books. His inclinations seem to develop steadily in the direction of respect for intellectual people and products. It is a part of the phenomenon of belated growth which we have traced from his thirtieth birthday; mentally and spiritually cramped up to that time by the despotic influence of the small Bismarckian clique, he had still the strength and ability to expand his mind and character with splendid swiftness when finally the bonds were thrown off. One of the pleasantest features of the Labour Conference gathering in Berlin was the kindly and appreciative way in which William gave his chief attention to the venerable Jules Simon, talked with him intelligently about his works, and presented him with what of all possible gifts he would most prize—some of the manuscript French writings of Frederic the Great. It is more than likely that a twelvemonth before William did not know anything at all about either Jules Simon or his books.

His special liking for the scholarly King of Sweden, and his annual choice of the sombre solitudes of the Norwegian coast for his summer season of entire rest, are very interesting evidences of this progressive mental elevation. William has a natural tendency to deference and a display of youthful humility toward able men much older than himself, as all who have seen him in the company of his grandfather, Moltke, Windhorst, or Bismarck must have noted, but his attraction toward the learned and gentle Scandinavian monarch is hardly to be put down to that score. Most other princes of William's age, or even much older, devote as little time to King Oscar as politeness will permit, and for choice prefer to spend their holidays at Homburg or Monte Carlo.

No gambling Casino or mere frivolous watering-place so much as knows William by sight. He detests the whole spirit of these princely resorts. He drinks with tolerable freedom at dinner, and is neither a prig nor a prude. But he is distinctly a moral man. People who are close to him aver that he is sincerely religious, and that by no means in a latitudinarian sense. So far as his actions have thrown light on this subject they have indicated a spirit of theological tolerance. In the fourth month of his reign, when the Senior Council of the Evangelical Lutheran Church sought to overturn the election of the heterodox Professor Harnack to the chair of Church History and Dogma at Berlin, William emphatically tossed aside their protest and confirmed the selection of the University. At about the same time he delivered a public rebuke to certain enthusiasts who sought to commit him to an approval of Jew-baiting, and since then, as we have seen, Dr. Stocker has gone for good. Last winter the Emperor gave a most interesting and characteristic proof of this broad-minded spirit. Two earnestly religious young Germans named Haase and May, belonging to a sect called the New Church, the basis of which is non-resistance, refused on moral grounds to do military service. Their persistence naturally brought them into collision with the courts, and they were sentenced to six weeks' imprisonment. William heard of the case, and, while it would not do to remit the punishment, he issued directions that their stay in prison should be made as comfortable as possible. Upon their release he personally gave the money to pay their passage to America, whither they sailed with the intention of becoming missionaries.

When William ascended the German throne, under such unpleasant and prejudicial conditions, the world thought of him as an ill-conditioned and wildly-reckless young swashbuckler, whose head would speedily be turned by the intoxicating sense of power, and who would make haste to plunge Europe into war.

Three years of authority have worked such a change in him—or, perhaps better, have brought to the top so many strong and admirable qualities in him which had been dwarfed and obscured by adverse circumstances—that the world has insensibly come to alter its opinion of his character. We think of him no longer as a firebrand. He preserves enough of the eccentricities of a nervous and impetuous individuality, it is true, to still impart to public scrutiny of his words and deeds an element of apprehension. One still instinctively reads the reports of his speeches with an eye cast ahead for wild or thoughtless utterances—and only too often, as in the case of the "salamander" remarks to the Borussian Students' Corps at Bonn the other day, finds what was anticipated. But even in this matter of an over-hasty and unrestrained tongue three years have wrought an important improvement, and in almost all other respects he is unquestionably a better man and a better ruler than the world took it for granted he would be. Doubtless as time goes on we shall come to regard him in a still more altered light.

At present what can be fairly said is that he stands out with clearness from among European sovereigns as a living and genuine personality—a young man of imagination, of great activity and executive ability, taking gravely serious views of his duties and responsibilities, keenly anxious to do what he believes to be right, and increasingly disposed to look to wise and elevated sources of judgment for suggestions as to what is right.

THE END.

Lightning Source UK Ltd.
Milton Keynes UK
UKHW010654300720
367419UK00002B/522

9 783752 351699